CW01020644

The Materna

Why do women want to have children? How does one 'learn' to be a mother? Does having babies have anything to do with sex?

At a time when mothers are bombarded by prescriptive and contradicting advice on how to behave with their children, *The Maternal Lineage* highlights various psychological aspects of the mothering experience.

International contributors provide clinical examples of frequent and challenging situations that have received scarce attention in psychoanalysis, such as issues of neglect and psychical abuse. The transgenerational repetition from mother to daughter of distressing mothering patterns is evident throughout the book, and may seem inevitable. However, clinical examples and theoretical research indicate that, when the support of partner and friends is not enough, the cycle can be brought to an end if the mother receives psychoanalytic-informed professional help.

The Maternal Lineage is divided into four parts, covering:

- An Introduction including a review of the literature focusing on the mother–daughter relationship
- Pregnancy and very early issues
- Subfertility and its effects on a woman's psyche
- The psychological aspects of major mothering problems: miscarriages, post-natal depression, adolescent motherhood.

This timely book will be of value to psychoanalysts, psychotherapists and health professionals – obstetricians, psychiatrists, midwives and social workers.

Paola Mariotti is a fellow of the British Psychoanalytical Society. She is a psychoanalyst in private practice. She was supervisor of a Unit in an NHS Hospital working with patients suffering from Borderline Personality Disorder and has lectured and published on sexuality, reproductive issues and maternity extensively.

Contributors: Edna Adelson, Rosemary Balsam, Tessa Baradon, Dana Birksted-Breen, Selma Fraiberg, Erna Furman, Hendrika Halberstadt-Freud, Alessandra Lemma, Marianne Leuzinger-Bohleber, Paola Mariotti, Rozsika Parker, Dinora Pines, Joan Raphael-Leff, Estela Welldon, Donald Woods Winnicott, Sharon Zalusky Blum.

THE NEW LIBRARY OF PSYCHOANALYSIS
General Editor: Alessandra Lemma

The New Library of Psychoanalysis was launched in 1987 in association with the Institute of Psychoanalysis, London. It took over from the International Psychoanalytical Library which published many of the early translations of the works of Freud and the writings of most of the leading British and Continental psychoanalysts.

The purpose of the New Library of Psychoanalysis is to facilitate a greater and more widespread appreciation of psychoanalysis and to provide a forum for increasing mutual understanding between psychoanalysts and those working in other disciplines such as the social sciences, medicine, philosophy, history, linguistics, literature and the arts. It aims to represent different trends both in British psychoanalysis and in psychoanalysis generally. The New Library of Psychoanalysis is well placed to make available to the English-speaking world psychoanalytic writings from other European countries and to increase the interchange of ideas between British and American psycho-analysts. Through the *Teaching Series*, the New Library of Psychoanalysis now also publishes books that provide comprehensive, yet accessible, overviews of selected subject areas aimed at those studying psychoanalysis and related fields such as the social sciences, philosophy, literature and the arts.

The Institute, together with the British Psychoanalytical Society, runs a low-fee psychoanalytic clinic, organizes lectures and scientific events concerned with psychoanalysis and publishes the *International Journal of Psychoanalysis*. It runs a training course in psychoanalysis which leads to membership of the International Psychoanalytical Association – the body which preserves interna-tionally agreed standards of training, of professional entry, and of professional ethics and practice for psychoanalysis as initiated and developed by Sigmund Freud. Distinguished members of the Institute have included Michael Balint, Wilfred Bion, Ronald Fairbairn, Anna Freud, Ernest Jones, Melanie Klein, John Rickman and Donald Winnicott.

Previous general editors have included David Tuckett, who played a very active role in the establishment of the New Library. He was followed as general editor by Elizabeth Bott Spillius, who was in turn followed by Susan Budd and then by Dana Birksted-Breen.

Current Members of the Advisory Board include Liz Allison, Giovanna di Ceglie, Rosemary Davies and Richard Rusbridger.

Previous Members of the Advisory Board include Christopher Bollas, Ronald Britton, Catalina Bronstein, Donald Campbell, Sara Flanders, Stephen Grosz, John Keene, Eglé Laufer, Alessandra Lemma, Juliet Mitchell, Michael Parsons, Rosine Jozef Perelberg, Mary Target and David Taylor.

ALSO IN THIS SERIES

TITLES IN THE NEW LIBRARY OF PSYCHOANALYSIS TEACHING SERIES

The Maternal Lineage

Identification, Desire, and Transgenerational Issues

Edited by Paola Mariotti

Routledge
Taylor & Francis Group
LONDON AND NEW YORK

First published 2012
by Routledge
27 Church Road, Hove, East Sussex BN3 2FA

Simultaneously published in the USA and Canada
by Routledge
711 Third Avenue, New York NY 10017

Routledge is an imprint of the Taylor & Francis Group, an Informa business

British Library Cataloguing in Publication Data
A catalogue record for this book is available from the British Library

Library of Congress Cataloging in Publication Data

The maternal lineage : identification, desire, and transgenerational issues /
edited by Paola Mariotti.
   p. cm. — (The new library of psychoanalysis)
  ISBN 978–0–415–68164–3 (hardback) — ISBN 978–0–415–68165–0 (pbk)
1. Motherhood—Psychological aspects. 2. Pregnancy—Psychological aspects
3. Mother and child—Psychological aspects. I. Mariotti, Paola.
  HQ759.M37326 2012
  155.6'46324—dc23

                                                2011028978

ISBN: 978–0–415–68164–3 (hbk)
ISBN: 978–0–415–68165–0 (pbk)

Typeset in Bembo by RefineCatch Limited, Bungay, Suffolk
Cover design by Sandra Heath; cover image: Rijksmuseum Amsterdam
(colour altered)

To my daughters and stepdaughters
and,
when all is said and done,
to my mother

Contents

Contents

Contributors

Edna Adelson has cooperated closely with Selma Fraiberg in the Child Development Project, University of Michigan Medical Center, where she worked as Research Psychologist.

Rosemary Balsam MD, from Belfast, N. Ireland, is Associate Clinical Professor of Psychiatry in the Yale Medical School and Staff Psychiatrist at the Dept of Student Health. She is a training and supervising analyst at the Western New England Institute for Psychoanalysis in New Haven, CT. Her special interest is in female development, and she has published a book on this subject, *Women's Bodies in Psychoanalysis* (2009). She is on the editorial boards of *Psychoanalytic Quarterly* and *American Imago* and is a Book Review section co-editor (with her husband Paul Schwaber) for the *Journal of the American Psychoanalytic Association*.

Tessa Baradon came from the field of public health to child psychoanalysis and psychotherapy. She has been responsible for the development and provision of psychotherapy services for parents and infants in the National Health Service and the Anna Freud Centre, where she leads on the Infancy and Early Years Programme. She is a practising child therapist and supervisor and writes and lectures on child and parent infant psychotherapy. Her most recent publication is *Relational Trauma in Infancy: Psychoanalytic, Attachment and Neuropsychological Contributions to Parent-Infant Psychotherapy* (Routledge, 2009).

Dana Birksted-Breen PhD is a training and supervising psychoanalyst of the British Psychoanalytical Society working in private practice. Her publications include *The Gender Conundrum* (Routledge, 1993). She recently collaborated on *Reading French Psychoanalysis* (Rougledge, 2010). She was the General Editor of The New Library of Psychoanalysis series of books from 2000 to 2010. She is currently joint Editor-in-Chief of the *International Journal of Psychoanalysis.*

Selma Fraiberg (1918–1981) was a leading figure in the field of infant mental health. She trained originally as a social worker and then as a psychoanalyst in Detroit. She worked with and wrote about infants with congenital blindness. Her book *The Magic Years* (1959) discusses the child's development in the first five years. A collection of her papers, *Selected Writings*, was published in 1982. She integrated her approach as social worker with her impressive psychoanalytic skills, applying psychoanalytic understanding to socially deprived situations. She and her co-workers developed a treatment model that is still relevant today.

Erna Furman (1926–2002) was an Austrian-born American child psychoanalyst, psychologist and teacher. She came to London in her late teens and trained at the Hampstead Clinic with Anna Freud. She emigrated to the United States in the 1950s. She worked at the Hannah Perkins Centre for Child Development and published several papers and books concerning the relationship between children and parents, and mothering issues. She was an influential teacher and in 1999 she was made an honorary member of the American Psychoanalytic Association in recognition of her outstanding contributions to the field.

Hendrika Halberstadt-Freud is a Training Analyst and Member of the Dutch Psychoanalytic Society. She is a Child and Adult Psychoanalyst. In English she has published *Freud, Proust, Perversion and Love* (1991) and *Electra vs. Oedipus. The Drama of the Mother–Daughter Relationship* (Routledge, 2010).

Alessandra Lemma is a clinical psychologist and psychoanalyst. She is a Visiting Professor in the Psychoanalysis Unit at University College London, and Visiting Professor of Psychological Therapies at Essex University. She is the Director of the Psychological

Therapies Development Unit at the Tavistock and Portman NHS Foundation Trust where she also works as a clinician in the Adolescent Department. She is a Fellow of the British Psychoanalytical Society and General Editor of The New Library of Psychoanalysis. She has written and edited books on a wide range of psychological and psychoanalytic issues.

Marianne Leuzinger-Bohleber is a Training Analyst of the German Psychoanalytic Association. She has written numerous papers on neuropsychoanalysis and on research in psychoanalysis and on the impact of prenatal diagnostics on women considering a pregnancy.

Paola Mariotti is a Fellow of the British Psychoanalytical Society. She has lectured and published on the theme of sexuality and maternity.

Rozsika Parker (1945–2010) has written extensively on various subjects from feminism, to art history. She was interested in the vicissitudes of women's lives and she wrote on the subject of embroidery (*The Subversive Stitch: Embroidery and the Making of the Feminine*, 1983) and gardening (*The Anxious Gardener*, 2006). With Griselda Pollock she wrote on women and art (*Old Mistresses: Women, Art and Ideology*, 1981). She trained as a psychotherapist, and her book *Torn in Two – The Experience of Maternal Ambivalence* (1995) is an in-depth study of conflictual situations in mothering.

Dinora Pines (1918–2002) was born in what is now Poland from Russian parents; the family moved to London when she was still a child. In 1945 she took a medical degree. In 1965 she completed her training as a psychoanalyst, later becoming a Training Analyst of the British Society of Psychoanalysis. She is best known for her work on the survivors of the Holocaust and for her book *A Woman's Unconscious Use of Her Body* (1993), in which she collected most of her papers. She was one of the first psychoanalysts who approached analytically problems relating to women's life cycle.

Joan Raphael-Leff, Psychoanalyst (Fellow of the British Psychoanalytical Society) and Social Psychologist, is Leader of UCL/Anna Freud Centre Academic Faculty for Psychoanalytic Research. She was previously Head of University College

London's MSc in Psychoanalytic Developmental Psychology, and Professor of Psychoanalysis at the Centre for Psychoanalytic Studies, University of Essex. In 1998 she co-founded COWAP, the International Psychoanalytical's Association's Committee on Women and Psychoanalysis, and was its first international Chair. She specialised in reproductive and early parenting issues, with 100 single-author publications and eight books, including *Psychological Processes of Childbearing: Pregnancy – The Inside Story* (1991). Currently she leads a national project at the Anna Freud Centre for practitioners working with teenage parents and is Consultant to perinatal projects in many different countries.

Estela V. Welldon is the Founder and Honorary Elected President for Life of the International Association for Forensic Psychotherapy. She is an Honorary Consultant Psychiatrist in Psychotherapy at Tavistock Portman NHS Clinics. In 1997 she was awarded by Oxford Brookes University a DSc Honorary Doctorate of Science degree for her contributions to the field of forensic psychotherapy. She is the author of *Mother, Madonna, Whore: The Idealization and Denigration of Motherhood* (1988); *Sadomasochism* (2002) translated into many languages; *Playing with Dynamite: A Personal Approach to the Psychoanalytic Understanding of Perversions, Violence, and Criminality* (2011); and main editor of *A Practical Guide to Forensic Psychotherapy* (1997). She lectures worldwide and is on the teaching staff of several Universities. She works privately as a psychoanalytical psychotherapist.

Donald Woods Winnicott (1896–1971) trained and worked as a pediatrician and a psychoanalyst. His experience before, during, and after the Second World War treating disturbed children and their mothers led him to develop his most original theories. Many of his writings are still considered of prime importance worldwide. His contribution to psychoanalysis is recognized as a major influence and has shaped the development of psychoanalytic theory and technique.

Sharon Zalusky Blum is a member of the American Psychoanalytic Association, and works in private practice in Los Angeles. She has written about issues concerning the psychoanalytic setting, and about mothering.

Acknowledgements

I would like to thank Dana Birksted-Breen, at the time Editor of The New Library of Psychoanalysis, for offering me the opportunity to edit a book on this subject and for being an encouraging presence in the initial stages. I hope it will contribute to the ongoing (and long overdue) evaluation and reflection on the importance of maternality in the lives of women.

My thanks also to the present Editor, Alessandra Lemma, for her invaluable feedback and suggestions, and for having given such helpful and positive support. I am also immensely grateful to my friends for their encouragement and interest in this project, and to Susannah Taffler for her comments on early drafts of my Introduction.

I would like to mention the psychoanalysts who have contributed to this book. Some papers are classics, and their authors are long dead. But many are very much alive, and what a pleasure it has been to meet, in person or via email, so many intelligent, creative, interesting women. Rozsika Parker who died just before I had completed the book, was one such woman, both creative and kind, impressive and unaffected.

Finally, I wish to thank my husband David, my daughters and stepdaughters, who have put up in good humour with the very long gestation of this book.

Permissions

The editor and publishers are grateful to the following for their permission to reproduce from copyright material as follows:

Chapter 1, 'Primary Maternal Preoccupation' by D. W. Winnicott, is reproduced by permission of Paterson Marsh Ltd on behalf of The Winnicott Trust.

Chapter 4, 'The Pregnant Mother and the Body Image of the Daughter' by R. H. Balsam, is reproduced by permission of the *Journal of the American Psychoanalytic Association*, 44S: 401–427.

Chapter 5, 'On Motherhood' by E. Furman, is reproduced by permission of the *Journal of the American Psychoanalytic Association*, 44S: 429–447.

Chapter 6, 'The Medea Fantasy' by M. Leuzinger-Bohleber, is reproduced by permission of the *International Journal of Psycho-Analysis*, 82: 323–345.

Chapter 7, 'The Baby-Makers' by Joan Raphael-Leff, is reproduced by permission of the author and the *British Journal of Psychotherapy*, 8 (3): 266–277.

Chapter 8, 'Infertility in the Age of Technology' by S. Zalusky-Blum, is reproduced by permission of the *Journal of the American Psychoanalytic Association*, volume 48, pp. 1541–1562.

Chapter 9, 'Pregnancy, Miscarriage and Abortion' by D. Pines, is reproduced by permission of the *International Journal of Psycho-Analysis*, 71: 301–307.

Chapter 10, 'Postpartum Depression and Symbiotic Illusion' by H. Halberstadt-Freud, is based on a paper published in *Psychoanalytic Psychology*, 10: 407–423.

Chapter 11, 'Keeping Envy in Mind' is reproduced by permission of Karnac Books Ltd.

Chapter 12, 'What is Genuine Maternal Love' by T. Baradon, is reproduced by permission of the *Psychoanalytic Study of the Child*, 60: 47–73. © Yale University Press.

Chapter 13, 'Infant-Parent Psychotherapy on Behalf of a Child in a Critical Nutritional State' by S. Fraiberg and E. Adelson, is reproduced by permission of the *Psychoanalytic Study of the Child*, 31: 461–491. © Yale University Press.

Chapter 14, 'Bodies across Generations and Cycles of Abuse' by E. Welldon, is based upon a paper originally given in Italian at a conference in Italy.

General Introduction

Paola Mariotti

> A mother's love for the infant she suckles and cares for
> is something far more profound than her later affection
> for the growing child. It is in the nature of a completely
> satisfying love-relation, which not only fulfils every
> mental wish but also every physical need.
>
> S. Freud, 1910, *Leonardo Da Vinci and
> a Memory of his Childhood*

Why would a woman want children? And how and when does the wish for a child begin? What does it mean to a woman to 'become a mother'? Maternity is an experience of body and of mind in equal measure, consciously experienced but also resting on unconscious beliefs, expectations and anxieties. Life events can greatly influence it, but, as we shall see, it is rooted in early infancy, in the first exchanges with the mother interwoven with the early Oedipal vicissitudes.

Clinical papers in psychoanalysis refer almost invariably to the patient's mother who often occupies a prominent place. The mother who is being discussed is the *mother brought by the patient into the consulting room* and this figure can be seen at two levels. First, she is the image that inhabits the patient's psychic life, and the analyst directs her interpretative work to this level. Gradually, however, the patient becomes able to think about his mother as a person with a specific complex personality, who has had an impact on his growth and development. She acquires depth and so does the patient's relationship with her. Some snippets of her history, some vignettes from

1

the past emerge, indicating some aspects of her life that the patient cannot at first integrate. For example, the mother who loved home-made cakes with abandon: 'disgusting', said the patient; or the mother who, when her infant had a cold, put him in his pram and walked for hours in a snow blizzard to get to the doctor – eventually the child developed pneumonia: wasn't his mother wonderful, asks the son. The capacity for pleasure is introduced in the analysis by the first patient, whereas a self-sacrificing murderousness is hinted at by the second patient. These are reflections of the patients' inner life, but they also signal the existence of an external reality that they will, sooner or later, have to learn to accept.

However, the actual experience of being a mother is not often described and explored in the psychoanalytic literature, notwith-standing its importance in women's psychic life. A woman may be unsure of her desire for a baby, another may want a child very much but not be able to conceive. When pregnant a mother-to-be may be overwhelmed by the irruption in her mind of tremendous feelings of love for her baby, or by fears and anxieties, or by rejection and hatred of her child, and more often, consciously and unconsciously, by all these conflicting feelings. With her first child, she has to accept the loss of some of her expectations and plans, and be disappointed for not being a perfect mother with a perfect child.

These issues have fallen below the radar of psychoanalytic atten-tion until recently. Winnicott, for instance, describing the mother's state of mind in the perinatal period, which he called 'primary maternal preoccupation', was able to describe with extreme sensi-tivity her attunement with her newborn baby, but the effect of this attunement – which 'would be an illness were it not for the fact of the pregnancy' (1956: 61) – on the mother's mind was hardly mentioned. Klein (1961) depicted the wealth of primitive phantasies in the young child's mind, regarding the mother's mind and body, and Bion (1962) posited the importance of the mother as a 'container' of her child's projection.

Other experiences more or less closely connected to maternality – abortion, miscarriage, postnatal disturbances, menarche, menstru-ation and menopause – have not registered their importance in the psychoanalytic literature, in spite of being, for women, very frequent or even universal events. A change of perspective is needed – and it has been taking place – where the maternal experience is in the foreground, with all its complexity.

The papers collected in this book explore, from a psychoanalytic point of view, how a woman arrives at wanting (or not wanting) to have children: how psychic factors rooted in her early experiences foster or hinder her mothering desires and choices throughout her life. These contributions are based on the clinical work done with patients on the issue of maternality, and they focus mainly on the early stages of procreation that present a woman with complex challenges and opportunities.

Maternality is a concept that has been used in psychoanalytic writings[1] to designate the quality of the actual experience of having children, and also the thoughts and the unconscious phantasies associated with carrying a symbolic maternal function in a wider sense. This is often characterised by the wish and capacity to nurture and support one's own and others' personal creativity, at a personal, social or cultural level. In this book I am using the term in the sense attributed to it by the *OED*, that is, to refer to 'the quality or condition of being maternal'.

We can gain much understanding from an exploration of when things do not go well – for example, when there are difficulties in conceiving or when the relationship between mother and child is highly problematic. These situations, if approached in a psychoanalytic treatment, reveal processes that are by no means unique to troubled or disturbed people – they are phantasies and anxieties that to some extent are common to all, and when known and worked through they may become a source of strength and creativity.

This Introduction is intended to provide a background to the papers I have selected for inclusion. Three aspects, in my view, are particularly relevant to the issues discussed throughout the book, namely: (a) the meaning and desire to be a mother start in the bodily and affective exchanges between an infant and her[2] mother; (b) the psychic manifestations of maternality are organised around issues of identification with a maternal image, highlighting a transgenerational aspect, which links a woman to her mother, and to her mother's mother – to her own child, and to her child's children;[3] and finally (c) that maternality is also the expression of a profound and multilayered wish structured within the Oedipal configuration: in the space between mother and baby the father may be hidden, sometimes himself a 'dark continent' in the background – and yet inescapably present. These three strands are, of course, interconnected, and hence their separation is somewhat artificial, but it provides some help in navigating the vast and complex field relating to motherhood.

The body

I would like to start by thinking about the importance of the body in the early relationship between mother and infant. I am proposing that it is through the early bodily contacts that a mother communicates to her daughter the first messages that will gradually be organised within the area of maternality. She conveys her pleasure in her baby, while her daughter's response revives in the mother memories that are not less present for being unremembered. In her daughter's body a mother finds the same potential which she herself had in her own mother's arms and a glimpse of her long-past experience (Raphael-Leff 1993). Anxiety and fears are part of their interaction, and they strengthen the bond. The (mostly unconscious) communication between a mother and her infant conveys, encrypted in the manifest content, what the object of desire should be and what is to be perceived as threat or transgression. From the beginning the child engages at all levels with those messages, in her so-called tantrums as a young child, her rebellion as an adolescent, and her emotional and intellectual turmoil as a woman.

Bodily contact between the mother and her newborn are shaped by and inseparable from their emotional relationship. Studies of the early mother–infant exchanges carried out in the framework of attachment theory have provided evidence of the ongoing complex interaction taking place at a nearly imperceptible level:

> In sustained mutual gaze transactions, the mother's facial expression stimulates and amplifies positive affects in the infant. The child's internal pleasurable state is communicated back to the mother, and in this interactive system of reciprocal stimulation both members of the dyad enter into a symbiotic state of heightened positive affect.
>
> (Schore 1994: 71)

Attachment theorists, as well as relational and intersubjective psychoanalysts, have stressed the importance of the relationship with the caregiver in the individual's development:

> The self is a social self to begin with. The research . . . indicates that, from infancy, innately given brain processes support social reciprocity and the development of 'we-ness'.
>
> (Emde 2009: 556)

Visual and auditory expressions are immediately inscribed by the mother in a context of emotional meaning:

> Back-and-forth imitations and reciprocal interactions with significant caring others lead to and sustain a developing world of shared meaning (Condon and Sander, 1974; Meltzoff and Moore, 1977).
>
> (Emde 2009: 559)

Moreover, in neurobiology the concepts of mirror neurons and 'embodied simulation' may lead to an understanding of how the mother–infant empathic contact is rooted in the brain (for a discussion of this subject see Ammaniti and Trentini 2009).

From a different psychoanalytic point of view, Anzieu (1989) has proposed that the contact through the skin is also an important aspect of the mother–infant bond. Anzieu suggests that beside other functions the skin 'is a site and a primary means of communicating with others', and 'an "inscribing surface" for the marks left by those others' (p. 40). The skin maintains the quality of an erotogenic zone throughout life. In part through the skin, the baby's whole body experiences the pleasure or the anxiety of being physically held by her mother. Anzieu speculates that a phantasy is created of a 'common skin', an interface between the child and his mother: 'a unique screen which comes to resonate with the sensations, emotions, mental images and vital rhythms of the two' (1989: 63).

These early bodily communications to the young child are never directly available to consciousness, but as we shall see they contribute to shape the structure of his or her personality.

The erotic side of maternality

The erotic element in a mother's ministrations to her infant is sometimes overlooked. It is perhaps part of that 'dark continent' about which Freud felt not enough was known, a facet of the 'secret' between mother and child (Cournut-Janin 1998, which we will discuss later), and it constitutes an essential aspect of their bond. Freud maintained that the mother 'regards [her child] with feelings that are derived from her own sexual life' (1905: 223) and that in so doing '[s]he is only fulfilling her task in teaching the child to love'

(1905: 223). Maternal erotism and sexuality contribute to structuring the child's gender identity and to the early foundation of her maternality.

The concept of primary homosexuality, introduced by Evelyne Kestemberg (1984) to designate an aspect of the relationship between the young infant and the mother, is relevant to this discussion. The attachment between mother and infant is seen as sexual but not necessarily gendered, so that also in the case of a boy infant we talk of primary homosexual desire of his mother (Denis 1982; Shaeffer 2006). Kestemberg described primary homosexuality as 'the first loving exchanges between a subject and his/her mother through a series of bodily contacts involving the entire body, especially the skin, the gaze, the voice' (Kestemberg 1984: 255–256). These exchanges involve both members of this couple and, if all goes well, produce pleasure in both. The infant is stimulated by the washing and caring of her or his body, by looking and by being looked at, by the sound of mother's voice, and the child's pleasure resonates with the mother's. The baby's oral pleasure in feeding has a correspondence in the mother, not only due to her identification with the satisfied infant and to her narcissistic gratification in feeding her child, but also to erotic enjoyment of her own orality and of her milk-producing breast. It is important to clarify that in primary homosexuality adult genitality is involved in a very limited way, mostly unconsciously. If the genital excitement in the caregiver is in the foreground, we may surmise that her experience is substantially alien to her child, and in this case it generates a repetitively traumatising situation for the infant.

Laplanche (1987, 1997) has suggested that the mother's unconscious communications regarding sexuality from the beginning orientate the newborn's sensations and his proto-sexuality. She gives him an 'enigmatic' sexual message, in this way seducing the infant into the world of sexuality. The message, or 'sign', is 'enigmatic' because it comes from the adult to the young child, who cannot decipher it fully. This message will become an essential aspect of the child's unconscious and constitutes the presence of the Other within the individual, creating a powerful dynamic tension at the heart of a person's identity. The sexual message is communicated through the bodily contacts shared between the adult, usually the mother, and the child, and also by exposing the baby in the course of family life to direct or indirect allusions to parental sexuality. A young child may witness the primal scene in its actuality and, just as importantly, he is inevitably exposed to its unconscious representations intimated by the parents. This enigmatic message is therefore impregnated with the deepest elemental signals from mother to infant about sex, gender, and making babies.

Multiple identifications with both parents leading to homosexual and bisexual dynamics, which have the function of *structuring* the child's sexual and psychic life, have also been stressed in the literature (e.g. David 1973; Kestemberg 1984; McDougall 1995). Moreover, if the child later becomes a mother, she is able to offer her own child a relationship and possibly an identification with her own paternal figure. Equally, a child who later becomes a father and who has been able to internalise a maternal image, will be able to provide his child not only with a paternal identification, but also with a maternal one. Both parents offer unconscious communications about genders and, crucially, about the erotic and sexual relationship between the genders, providing their child with sustaining or undermining images that may support or prevent different and original manifestations of the child's psychic life.

Whatever the mother is teaching her child with those early communications 'which are derived from her own sexual life' (Freud 1905), whatever is contained in the 'enigmatic message', remains profoundly unconscious, and only its derivatives may emerge in analysis. But reconstructions and memories of later events help to reveal some of the meanings that are transmitted between mother and child relating to sexuality and procreation and to their intimate connection.

The concepts of primary homosexuality and 'enigmatic message' subsume a sexual communication and mutual acknowledgement of the infant and of the mother as sexual beings capable of experiencing and of generating sexual desire and pleasure in each other. In this sense, maternality has an intrinsically erotic quality.

Maternality and gender identity

The young child gradually integrates her experiences of her body within the dynamic relationship with her mother and this becomes an important aspect of her sense of herself as a woman – her core gender identity.

However, gender identity is not a monolithic acquisition. It implicitly accepts shifts and contradictions resulting from the multiple identifications with the parental figures. In the United States psychoanalysts informed by feminist ideas have contributed to this discussion. Harris (2000) describes 'the complex phenomenon' of gender as 'a softly assembled system'. Referring to chaos theory she concludes that:

> Gender development, recast in the terms of chaos theory as a 'soft assembly,' puts on an equal plane of possibility negative and positive oedipal identifications, active and passive sexual aims, and multiple and complex characterizations of parental objects and self-objects.
>
> (p. 246)

Benjamin is interested in the process and significance of the daughter's identification with the father and its contribution to her gender identity. She describes (1991) the daughter's identification with the father as 'an important basis of the love of the other: it is not so much the opposite of object love as an important precursor and ongoing constituent of it' (1991: 277). She goes on to discuss the child's wish to be her 'father's son', besides being his daughter. The complexity of gender is seen not only as inevitable but also as a source of creativity and rich inner life, resonating with McDougall's (1995) remarks on creativity and sexuality: 'creative acts can be conceptualised as a fusion of the masculine and feminine elements in the psychic structure' (1995: 113).

Yet there are limits to the fluidity of one's gender identification, and the limits reside in one particular bodily function – reproduction, and particularly conception. For conception to take place, two specifically different cells are required – the body presents a reality that gives rise to immense potential for symbolisation and transformation, but it is not exhausted by it. Maternality is the highly symbolic transformation of the body's raw processes, which are perceived, enriched or misunderstood though the lenses of one's personal experiences. There is, however, a non–symbolic 'leftover' in the body that is approached in the actual childbearing process, and perhaps even there it can be experienced only fleetingly.

The observation of her own body and of other women's plays an important role in the child's recognition of her self as female. Erikson

(1968) proposed the concept of 'inner space' as contributing to female gender identity, with a direct reference to the female genitals and to maternity. He noted:

> The female child . . . is disposed to observe evidence in older girls and women and in female animals of the fact that an inner space – with productive as well as dangerous potentials – does exist. Here one thinks not only of pregnancy and childbirth, but also of lactation and all the richly convex parts of the female anatomy which suggests fullness, warmth, and generosity.
> (Erikson 1968: 267)

Birksted-Breen in Chapter 2 illustrates clinically the relevance of the concept of inner and outer space in pregnancy.

The importance in the girl's development of observing the specifically feminine body is underlined by Balsam (2003) who has discussed the pregnant shape, which she sees on a par with the phallus as a representation of fertility and potency. In Chapter 4 Balsam describes the significance to the young child of the mother's body pregnant with a younger sibling – if not the mother, the child will meet other relatives and friends whose body is mysteriously changing shape. This has a particular significance for the young girl, who is developing a gender identity that includes awareness of her actual and potential body. I surmise that women's concern for the shape of their body and the comparison with other women's body may be a continuation of childhood curiosity. What amounted almost to an obsession with a slim waist in the nineteenth century or a flat abdomen in modern days may suggest, in part, a kind of reaction formation to the wish for its opposite – for a full, rounded belly.

At puberty changes take place gradually in the girl's hormonal functioning and in the shape of her body. However, menarche occurs suddenly, and usually without recognisable warning signs. It is worth noticing that very little has been written in psychoanalysis about menstruation – yet menarche is a focal life event, often remembered by patients as somewhat traumatic. Perhaps menarche is intrinsically shocking, a kind of normal trauma of life, as it suddenly propels the child into adulthood. She has no choice but to take charge of her sexuality and of the possibility of conceiving a child – a responsibility she will have to carry, alone or sharing it with her partner, all through her fertile years. From puberty onward the girl's concern with procreation – with creation and loss – is repeated each month, ignored as such for the most part, and yet present in her recurrently bleeding womb.

Sexuality and maternality

The connection between a woman's sexuality and her maternality has been the object of much debate. Freud (1937) postulated a direct link between the girl's envy of the penis – which he saw as the bedrock in the psychoanalysis of a woman and fundamental to her sexuality – and her desire to have a child. I shall briefly mention some authors whose views are relevant to a discussion of a woman's experience of herself as a maternal and sexual being.

The primacy of reproductive feelings in women was claimed by Helene Deutsch. In her treatise, *The Psychology of Women* (1945), she made a clear distinction between sexuality and motherliness, which in optimal circumstances are both present in women – and yet 'in woman, the sexual act is a pleasure prize that is appended to her service to the species' (p. 77), and again 'for woman coitus is above all an act of fecundation, the beginning of the reproductive function, which ends with the birth of the child' (p. 91). Sexual feelings as such are linked primarily to the clitoris, while the vagina is 'for reproduction' (p. 80), even though the latter organ also acquires in due time a sexual resonance. For a woman sexuality is in the service of reproduction; Deutsch is very subtle in recognising in the clinical vignettes she presents her patients' motherliness and wish for a child, even when this is hidden by a sexual, apparently non-maternal, behaviour.

Issues surrounding the link between maternity and sexuality were not in the forefront of psychoanalytic writings until the 1970s. There are, however, important exceptions. Bálint (1949) saw 'the relation between mother and child [as being] built upon the interdependence of the reciprocal instinctual aims' (p. 256). Judith Kestenberg (1956) suggested that the early diffused vaginal sensations and excitation are projected by the little girl on to her dolls, to whom she lavishes her cares, compensating for the lack of a visible and well-defined sexual organ. Benedek (1959, 1960), as we shall see later, stressed the relevance of parenthood throughout the parents' life.

The question of maternal feelings and female sexuality has been taken up directly by Braunschweig and Fain (1975). They suggested that a woman's sexuality maintains a parallel position to her maternality. They introduced the concept of the 'censorship of the lover' (*la censure de l'amante*) to describe how at night the woman who is a mother becomes the lover (of the father). Her adult sexual life, resulting in her temporary absence from the child's life, is subject to a process of 'censorship' in the child. Fain (1971) believes that there is no possibility of integration between the woman as lover and the woman as mother: 'The mother and the woman will always remain implacable enemies' (p. 345). More recently Guignard (2006) described maternality and sexuality as pertaining to two different levels, or 'spheres', which however are not 'enemies' of each other: she describes a *primary maternal sphere* and a *primary feminine sphere*. The former refers to the development, common to but different in the two genders, of a 'mental space' – an initial maternal interaction, based mainly on projective identification. In its wake, the primary feminine sphere is 'a part of mental space that is organised in terms of the primary triangulation of object relations and identifications' (2006: 99). It includes the primary feminine phase described by Melanie Klein (1932), in which the identification with the maternal/feminine object takes place. Guignard suggests that this 'identification with the mother's feminine desire significantly increases the infant's capacity to introject' (2006: 99). According to Guignard, these two spheres persist in a woman's life and cannot be truly integrated – on the contrary, their cathexis 'functions quite naturally in a switch-over or flip-flop fashion, and is marked by feelings of guilt' (2006: 104). She underlines the importance of the frontier, the border between maternal and feminine, a 'boundary' which 'borders on incest with the mother figure' (p. 105).

This 'frontier' allows the parents themselves and the surrounding adults to welcome the newborn while keeping the parental sexuality in abeyance, perhaps 'censored' to use Braunschweig and Fain's (1975) concept (which, however, they use to refer specifically to the mother's sexuality). The child too maintains in his or her mind the frontier, and children are often extremely reluctant to admit that their parents may have a sexual life. However, if the frontier between sexuality and maternity is too rigid, perhaps defensively so, the individual may not be able to reconcile the two images in themselves or in their partner: a partner will be seen either as a caring parent to one's children, or as an exciting lover, the two images never to be found together in one person.

The distinction between sexuality and reproduction has historically been easier for men. With the availability of contraception it has become possible for women also to have a full heterosexual life without ongoing concern about procreation. It is an open question whether this is true at the level of the deepest meaning of a satisfying sexual intercourse, or whether at that level Guignard's 'boundary' is constantly in danger of coming undone. The girl's identification with the maternal image has to be kept separate from, but coexistent with, her identification with the mother as sexual woman. As we shall see later, for the boundary to hold, the Oedipal structure has to be firmly in place in the parents' psyche.

The vicissitudes of identification

We have looked very briefly at the early development of maternality from the point of view of bodily sensations, which begin to be transformed into psychic elements in the context of the dyadic relationship with the mother. I would now like to discuss further this relationship, which not only involves an intense closeness between mother and infant but also includes a gradual possibility of separation and autonomy. It is in this context that a process of identification develops which, in turn, strongly influences the shaping of maternality. I will also look at the identification with an idealised maternal figure and link it to a host of problems deriving from it, and suggest a distinction between imitative identification with an idealised parental *object* and identification with a parental *function*. Of course, the parental image internalised by the young child is based on whatever she can perceive of her mother (and father) which is more or less modified, charged, and coloured with her own sensations or feelings.

Symbiosis and relatedness

The capacity of a young infant to experience himself or herself as an individual separate from mother has long been debated in psycho-

12

analysis. The little girl's internalisation of a maternal figure starts at a time when the infant is utterly dependent on the mother, a state described by Margaret Mahler (Mahler *et al.* 1975) as 'symbiosis'. She sees symbiosis as 'a metaphor' (p. 44) to describe 'a state of indifferentiation, of fusion with mother, in which the "I" is not yet differentiated from the "not-I".' If all goes well, this is followed by the process of separation–individuation. Other authors do not agree with Mahler's theories of development. Daniel Stern (1985), for example, states that '[i]nfants begin to experience a sense of an emergent self from birth. . . . There is no confusion between self and other in the beginning or at any point during infancy' (p. 10). Winnicott (1975) seems to concord when he writes that birth 'is a temporary phase of reaction and therefore of loss of identity' (p. 183) implying that something that can be called identity is already present in utero. Yet, he states that '*there is not such a thing as a baby*', explaining that 'the unit is not the individual, the unit is an environment–individual set-up. The centre of gravity of the being does not start off in the individual. It is in the total set-up' (1952: 99).[4] For Winnicott, in his paper 'Primary Maternal Preoccupation' (Chapter 1 this volume), the relationship between the two members of the dyad is not symmetrical, but has a correspondence in both – the mother too at some level is not quite separate and autonomous from her baby, certainly not during pregnancy and to an extent not for some time after birth.

Even before conception a mother may harbour fantasies about her child; she may imagine a 'fantasy child' (Deutsch 1933; Raphael-Leff 1993; Lax 2003), endowed at times with the most desirable qualities and at other times with the most fearsome attributes. A woman needs to let go of her fantasy child to give her real baby the sense of being a separate individual with his own personality.

Birksted-Breen describes in Chapter 2 the fears and phantasies of a pregnant patient. Elaboration of those phantasies, at a conscious and unconscious level, is an essential aspect of pregnancy, and takes place, for instance, in the vivid and intense dreams which are so frequent in expecting mothers. It is a necessary psychic work enabling the mother to carry and welcome her child as a part of herself and at the same time as a separate person – a unique and momentous experience which requires great emotional resources. Not surprisingly, pregnant women can be extremely concerned about the state of the foetus, if the image of a damaged and damaging child becomes confused with the sense of themselves as inadequate or dangerous mother figures.

While consciously a woman is perfectly capable of acknowledging her newborn as a person in his own right, unconsciously she is also experiencing him as carrying aspects of herself and of her psychic life which she regards as being highly desirable or, on the contrary, abhorrent to her (Pines 1993). Mahler's concept of 'metaphor' to describe her theory of symbiosis between mother and infant is useful in this context. A state of fusion exists as an aspiration in the adult – perhaps a phantasy – which is *almost* reached in particular circumstances, such as being in love (Freud 1930),[5] sexual intercourse, contemplation of a work of art (Magherini 1989), or of natural beauty. We are reminded also of Freud's oceanic feeling, the 'feeling of indissoluble bond, of being one with the external world as a whole' (Freud 1930: 63). These states seem to resonate with the early experience between the mother and her newborn – when they are entranced by and in love with each other.

The mother's state of mind is crucial in helping the young child to reinforce or indeed to find the sense of herself or himself as an autonomous individual. But if she experiences her child as an extension of herself, she may contribute to a state of boundary confusion in her offspring.

While the child is in the process of finding her autonomy, working through issues of identification and separation, the mother too is revisiting those same issues, in relation to her child, and to her own mother. If all goes well, the child will internalise from her an experience of boundaries that are protective and foster a boundaried self, but are 'porous' enough to allow communication with others. This is a transgenerational process, as the issue of symbiosis (lack of boundaries) and relatedness (requiring flexible boundaries) which is negotiated between mother and infant reaches back to the mother's relationship to her own mother, and to the future generations, as it will be internalised by the child (see also the three generations model of Blos 2003). It will present itself as an unconscious model for the daughter's experience with her own babies.

As indicated above, the mother's own sense of boundaried self is not clearly defined during the pregnancy and in the first weeks of her infant's life. The unique state of mind of a woman in the perinatal period is described as 'primary maternal preoccupation' in a seminal paper by Winnicott (1956, reprinted in this volume). He points out that this particular state of mind is essential to enable the mother to respond with intimate understanding to her baby's needs. He stresses the importance of the mother's identification with her infant in allowing her to protect him from – external or internal – impinging experiences.

Within this context of necessarily fluid boundaries both mother and baby have to delineate their own individuality. The mother's sense of a reasonably well balanced narcissistic investment in herself and her life are essential to enable her to foster her child's autonomy. Fain (1971) suggests that the sexual relationship between the parents allows the child much needed moments of solitude, which make it possible and necessary for him to develop a capacity to fantasise.

The mother on her part needs to be able to use her imagination at the level of transitional processes (Winnicott 1951) in order to relate to her baby as part of herself, *'created'* by her, invested with all the narcissistic attention that can be reserved to one's body–mind, and also to see the child as *'found'*, to be discovered in his or her intrinsic, unknown individuality. Without access to this aspect of transitionality, a mother may be stuck in a symbiotic fusion with her child, dominated by unyielding projective identification. This leads her to seeing the child as part of herself, with desired or feared characteristics of her own and not belonging to the child. The real individual child goes unrecognised, and is therefore neglected. Here the mother who needs a container for her own unbearable psychic contents may use and experience her child as a repository for her feelings – of anger or vulnerability or even competence and success. Excessive and chaotic projections weaken the sense of individuality in both mother and child, with a resulting pathological symbiosis between the two, which may alternate with the mother rejecting the child as she tries to get away from what she has projected on him. Projection into the infant of her own neediness may lead the mother to feeling profoundly envious of whatever care the child receives and to see him in a competitive fashion as the one who takes away the attention and the pleasure she feels entitled to – as described by Lemma in her chapter on maternal envy.

Welldon (1980) and Motz (2005) have shown that mothers who abuse their children have often little awareness of them being auton-omous human beings – what they see in the child is an unbearable reminder of their own pain and rage, which has to be silenced at all

15

costs. The child is being denied acknowledgement as an individual, indeed he may be actively rejected, while at the same time she or he is offered, or rather she or he is coerced into, a merging relationship, which may seductively promise omnipotent control over the mother and avoidance of loss. Moreover, a fusional bond is experienced as the only possible contact with the caregiver, often in the absence of a sustaining relationship with the father.

In these cases the girl child is in danger of contracting her maternality within the confines of symbiotic mothering. When she becomes a mother, she may be unable to allow her children's autonomous individual existence, and she may unconsciously strive to reproduce with them the paradigmatic image of motherhood she has inherited from her mother. To this aim all her energies will be unconsciously devoted – to fashion a child as dependent on her as she is on the child.

The difficulties of separation encountered by mothers in less tragic circumstances are well described by Furman (1982) in her aptly titled paper 'Mothers Have to Be There to Be Left', and in her contribution published in this book ('On Motherhood, Chapter 5'). Furman proposes that sometimes a mother may have unconscious difficulties of her own with separation. She may be overprotective of her child, effectively curtailing his chances to have his own experiences away from her. In some cases a mother may seem to encourage her child's autonomy, but in fact she may set up a situation where the child has to carry feelings linked to separation that she finds unbearable. Pappenheim and Sweeney (1952) give a convincing example of a mother who, wishing to go back to work, was apparently desperate to introduce her son to a nursery. Yet she was constantly triggering anxiety and fear in her son with her reproaches, and denied him autonomy by giving him instructions and taking over his activities. As a result, the child would panic if separated from her.

A mother may also actively reject her child, but this does not lead to his independence or autonomy – on the contrary, it may encourage a rigid and unyielding identification with her. There is a very thin line between allowing independence and communicating rejection, just as there is between emotional closeness and lack of proper boundaries.

A gradual and age-appropriate separation and autonomy is helped by the capacity, in the child and in the mother, of finding areas of interest and activities in one's own life from which the other is absent. The child fantasises in her cot, plays with her body, listens to the sounds she makes; the mother enjoys her sexual life, her thinking life . . . Sometimes the wish to be left alone becomes annoyance, even anger, at the requests of the other person. The child will learn from the mother how to handle contrasting feelings of love and hatred; the mother has to rely on her capacity to accept that she hates the child she loves so much. Her capacity to handle her negative feelings toward her child involves the acceptance that she is not a perfect mother.

The concept of ambivalence is discussed by Parker (1995) in depth in her book *Torn in Two*, and taken up in this volume with a paper on 'Shame and Maternal Ambivalence' (Chapter 3), and is very relevant to the process of separation. The ambivalence of a mother toward her child is instrumental in fostering and prompting a gradual development from the close intimacy of early childhood to the more autonomous relatedness of later years, with greater space for independence in both members of the dyad. In some circumstances, however, ambivalence becomes *unmanageable*, for instance, because of excessive guilt or shame, and the consequences range from difficult to catastrophic. Parker points out that ambivalence is not an accidental and undesirable aspect of mothering, but it is an essential element, source of guilt and self-recriminations, and yet an indispensable support to the creation and maintenance of flexible boundaries. In tussling with her ambivalence toward her child, a mother communicates to her (or him) how to engage in what Klein describes as the depressive position, in which the other person is recognised as the one, whole object to whom loving and hateful feelings are directed. (Problematic ambivalence will be further discussed in the introduction to Part One of the book.)

The Great Mother

If a mother experiences ambivalence as dangerous and shameful, and her child's growing autonomy as an unbearable loss, she may unconsciously set in motion defensive measures of which idealisation is particularly relevant to the development of maternality.

The image of an idealised and omnipotent object is hard to relinquish. 'The Great Mother' (Neumann 1955) is a figure that appears

17

as symbol of fertility among the first artefacts in human prehistory. The image of a woman who finds her complete realisation as a mother totally and exclusively devoted to her children, ignored when things go well, exalted when she is available to fulfil whatever need is required, is a fantasy that women as much as men carry inside. It is a dangerous image of motherhood.

The image of the perfect mother is rooted in very early experiences of dependency on a mother who is seen by her baby as all-powerful. With the start of her pregnancy a woman is cast in the position, once occupied by her own mother, of someone who is expected to provide life and sustenance, and without whom life is not conceivable. The line between her realistic life-giving capacity and being the omnipotent provider of all that's good is sometimes blurred, and the revelation of her human failures may seem to herself, to her offspring and even to observers, to be an unforgivable disappointment or a cruel rebuff. But '[b]eing in the *locus* of omnipotence doesn't mean that she is omnipotent' (Leisse de Lustgarten 2006: 194), and she has to imaginatively and creatively fill the gap between the sometimes unconscious phantasy she has herself, which her baby will experience in her, and the huge but realistically limited goodness she can actually provide.

Idealisation is a seductive phantasy. Idealisation of the maternal figure starts in very early infancy. The negotiation of that image, I would argue, is a lifelong process which takes place every time intense feelings are evoked, of love or hatred. When a woman has a child, she *becomes* that image. Depending on how she has been able to negotiate it, she will be able to balance it with a narcissistically satisfactory state of mind, with appropriately flexible boundaries. Otherwise, a childhood internalisation of an idealised image of her mother may leave a woman in later years prisoner of a tyrannical maternal figure; in those conditions she limits her responses to her child to what is seen as the 'right' or the 'best' thing to do, irrespective of the child's needs.

If a woman feels that she has to conform to an ideal, she has little hope of succeeding. Birksted-Breen (1974) has shown that women who had an idealised image of their mothers were more likely to have problems with their first child, while women who talked about their mothers in more realistic terms reported an easier relationship with their baby. The internalisation of an unattainable ideal mother leaves the new mother with a sense of her own inadequacy and saps strength and self-confidence from her contact with her baby. It can be a central element in postnatal depressive reactions (Mills 1997). Baradon in Chapter 12 describes a mother whose idea of 'selfless' maternal love left her prey to guilt and shame at her incapacity to deliver it to her baby. A mother who expects perfection from herself will feel disappointed and humiliated when she realises that her feelings and behaviour toward her child are in fact rather mixed – for her, ambivalence may be what Parker describes in her chapter as an 'unmanageable' condition.

The maternal function

Idealisation fosters a symbiotic attachment to a perfect object, which may be located outside, in the actual mother, or may be an internal image to whom a woman feels she is succeeding, or more often failing, to measure up to. It hinders or precludes identification as described by Freud (1924), who saw identification as a transformation of object cathexis: 'The object-cathexes are given up and replaced by identifications' (p. 176). This concept of identification implies the capacity to bear the loss of the (omnipotently controlled) object and the internalisation of (more or less specific but limited) aspects of it. It requires a burgeoning capacity to distinguish the symbolised from the symbol and to *abstract the function from the object*. In the identification process one's sense of self is enriched, its shape modified, perhaps threatened, but its boundaries are maintained. If we think of fusion on the other hand, we describe a situation where there is failure to experience subjective boundaries. A concrete, or near-concrete, sensorial contact with the object is sought,[6] which fosters a sort of 'negative hallucination', not noticed as such but conspicuous in its effects, blanking out the existence of one's individual boundaries.

The question of symbiotic fusion versus identification with a maternal image is particularly important in the development of maternality. I have found it useful to make a distinction between *maternal (or mothering) function* and *motherhood* (Mariotti 1997). The mothering function refers to the symbolic level and it is an essential component of maternality. Childless women can hold a creative maternal function, placing themselves within a symbolic creative couple, whereupon mothers of many children can experience significant difficulties in relation to their own capacity to be, and to feel, authentically creative.

The capacity to renounce the illusion of omnipotence is a crucial factor. Paradoxically, actual mothering can be based on a firm belief of what could be called 'virgin birth' (Deutsch 1933), or parthenogenic birth (Mitchell 2000), or Kristeva's (1989) 'virgin mother', a process from which the other, in particular the husband/father is excluded and regarded as somewhat irrelevant.[7] This may be fostered by medical techniques that assist fecundation and pregnancy and can be seen as taking the place of the father. Faure-Pragier (1997) drawing on her extensive work with subfertile patients, maintains that in several cases the link with the mother had not allowed for the father's presence: the maternal relationship was psychically all absorbing and the young woman had little space where she may develop her creativity, physically and mentally. Following from the devaluation of her father, a woman may devalue her partner and this supports her sense of her own power – the disappointment, recrimination and bitterness in having such an apparently useless partner increase in contrast to the sense of her own effectiveness. If the girl identifies with such a maternal object she will devalue her husband as she felt her father was devalued.

The capacity to hold a maternal function requires that the woman accepts that her creativity depends and resides within a creative couple, where the presence of her partner is consciously, but especially unconsciously, acknowledged and valued.

Identifying with mother's creative *maternal function*, the child implicitly recognises that she is not the same as her mother but that in her own way she can carry through the same function. It requires awareness of differences, of need for internal work, of possibility of failure, acceptance of the need of the other, and gratefulness for help. It involves the capacity to mourn the loss of the union with the maternal object and with the concrete person of the mother. Boys and men too can and do internalise a maternal capacity – not in imitation of or competition with their mother or partner, but as an individual creative capacity.

If the mourning of the lost object is not possible – because of too much ambivalence – the child's identification may be based purely on imitation (Gaddini 1969). Aggressive feelings against the mother are not fully acknowledged. Halberstadt-Freud's patient (see

Chapter 10) suffered from postnatal depression, but the recognition in her analysis of her anger at her mother, until then completely hidden, allowed her to disentangle from their symbiotic relationship. If the separation does not take place, all spontaneous creativity may be stifled in favour of a more or less successful imitative behaviour (Mariotti 1997). When she becomes a mother, the woman may try to impose the same or a similar pattern on her child (especially, but not only, her female child), and the process is repeated through generations.

In the more malignant cases the daughter's imitative identification with her mother is a variation of what Anna Freud (1936) described as identification with the aggressor. Welldon, in Chapter 14 in this volume, 'Bodies across Generations and Cycles of Abuse,' shows how a woman who as a child was the victim of abusive and cruel behaviour may become a mother who exposes her children to similar experiences. In milder forms, imitation is one in a range of factors constituting a more imaginative identification with the maternal image. For instance, Balsam (2000) has shown how a new mother, who was critical of her mother's obsessive traits, ended up repeating unconsciously with her infant in the consulting room a subtly obsessional behaviour. Balsam also suggested that some Russian dolls in a dream came to imaginatively represent the daughter, the patient and the mother/analyst, in a combination of introjection and projection.

A particular aspect of identification with the maternal image takes place when through her children a woman in some way repeats her own childhood experiences with her own siblings. There are many variations on the theme of siblings, according to the object of the mother's identifications – her own mother, the child who is in the same position as she herself was in her original family, her children as her siblings, etc. It may happen that one of the children stands, more or less unconsciously, for oneself, and another as one's sibling, and they are treated accordingly (Abarbanel 1993). These issues are present in the analysis of women who are (becoming) mothers. Sibling rivalry often figures directly in their analysis, in terms of who has more children, whose children are more beloved by the grandparents, and so on. Abarbanel illustrates the importance of the siblings' experience by reporting her observations of two mothers and their children. In both cases, the women's identification with their maternal figure was expressed through the relationship with

21

their own two children, one of which represented herself, and the other her sister.

The fit between mother and baby

I will make a digression here to introduce the concept of *fit* between a mother and her child, which I believe may help to dispel the tendency toward blaming one member of the dyad for whatever problems are encountered in their relationship. By 'fit' I intend the way that the mother's and infant's expectations and responses meet and interact. In my view this is often critical in generating in the infant the experience of mother as a good-enough object or on the contrary as a dangerous, 'alien',[8] 'bad' object. If the 'fit' is poor the baby, who is in position of extreme dependency and vulnerability, may try to adapt to mother's pattern of relationship. Depending on the child's resources and on mother's flexibility the adaptive behaviour may be experienced as autonomous and creative, or alien and false.

In clinical practice considerations on the importance of the fit are very much part of the analyst's implicit models – if the patient's problems are seen as deriving from a defective upbringing, or if on the contrary seem to reside exclusively within the patient's inner life, the issue of fit is not relevant. Often, however, in the course of an analysis different emphasis is given to the patient's elaboration of what they perceive as their external reality and to the exploration of what is seen as pertaining to one's own innermost psyche. The concept of fit has a place here shifting the analytic work away from blame and guilt and maintaining the process open and not fixed.

Winnicott's 'good-enough' mother is a mother who is experienced as such by one specific child, a mother who is able to meet and satisfy that child's needs and whose inevitably frustrating behaviour is manageable and age-appropriate to him or her. But if the child's needs are too urgent, his capacity to bear frustration limited, his sensitivity to internal stimulation very high, his mother's failure to satisfy him immediately and completely are experienced by the child as unbearable disasters against which extreme defensive measures have to be put in place early and drastically, creating a situation where mother and child feel hopelessly out of contact with each other. The interaction takes place in a unique relationship between an individual woman and a specific baby – neither of them are amorphous entities but they are active, responsive, peculiarly sensitive creatures who contribute and respond to each other in ways which are special and exclusive to their relationship. Writing about the experience of parenthood Benedek (1959) states:

> Each child in a different way and in a different measure stirs up through his own phasic development the corresponding unconscious developmental conflict of the parent. The parent meets in each child in a particular way the projections of his own conflicts.
>
> (p. 415)

Stern (1985) has stressed the importance of the infant communication to the mother in shaping the relationship between the two, and this has been supported by extensive research (Beebe 2005) which has shown that:

> Although the mother has the greater capacity and range of resources, the infant is a very active participant in this exchange, bringing remarkable capacities to seek and avoid engagement (Beebe and Lachmann, 2002; Beebe and Stern, 1977; Stern, 1971, 1985; Tronick, 1989). This emphasis on the contribution of both partners to the organization of the exchange avoids the temptation to locate the source of difficulty in only one partner or the other, for example, in maternal intrusiveness or in infant temperament difficulty.
>
> (pp. 10–11)

A quiet infant may be welcomed with joy by a self-contained mother who appreciates some space between herself and her child, but the same baby could be a source of frustration and anxiety to a woman who wishes for a closer contact with her child. By converse, a very physical mother provides pleasure and stimulation to a lively child, but may be experienced as intrusive by a quiet one. Given that the relationship is in any case so close and important for both mother and baby, if the fit is poor and things don't go well the situation can deteriorate very fast. The infant becomes unhappy, anxious, may be clinging and demanding, or withdrawn – the mother feels anxious and she may respond with denial or withdrawal, rage or fear, generating in each other an ever worsening climate of anxiety and unhappiness. The baby has little choice but to take in mother's response to his message. If mother offers a total denial that there are difficulties, the baby will get the message that problems are unacceptable as they seem to have no place in mother's mental universe. If mother is overanxious the message will be along the line that problems are impossible to deal with and indeed a source of unbearable fear. As we are talking about very young children their internal reaction to the environment is of course not verbal.

Bowlby (1969) has suggested that the child internalises, or learns, a blueprint for how to process internal states, described as 'internal working models'. There are of course multiple models in the mind of the same person, each coloured with important affective values. The more they are rooted in the unconscious, the more they may be contradictory. It would seem that the term 'identification' may be seen to include deeply seated inner models[9] of how to deal with mental contents – such as affects. The model may be represented by the possibility of establishing meaningful contact with an internal (and also external) good object, in order to hold and transform difficult emotions, or the use of denial or recourse to physical action to get rid of unpleasant mental contents. Such models have been internalised within the infant's psyche in the very early relationship with mother as part of his or her sense of self, using whatever mental processes are present and available to a baby, gradually confirmed or modified or rejected in the course of childhood and later life.[10]

The qualities of the mother–child relationship provide a powerful model of relationship, sometimes repeated in the choice of partner, when, as Freud remarked, the husband can become 'the inheritor of [a woman's] relationship with her mother' (1931: 231). However, the child and the mother are not passive receptacles of each other's projections, even though in some cases a child may have very limited opportunities to transform the models of relationship she is being presented with in her infancy.

The 'wish for a baby' and the Oedipal situation

The 'wish for a child' cannot be understood without consideration of the Oedipal situation, finally evolving into what may, or may not, become in the adult woman the wish to have a child and to take care of her, or him.

The 'wish for a child' is not as straightforward as it might appear. Pines (1982) maintains that 'there is a marked distinction between the wish to become pregnant and the wish to bring a live child into the world and become a mother' (p. 97). She suggests that a woman may use a pregnancy to prove that she is separated from mother. Welldon (in Chapter 14) points out that for some women it is a way to reassure themselves that there is something good in their body.

If a woman's relationship with her mother has a strong imitative component, her aim and her underlying fantasy of pregnancy may have little to do with caring for a child – what she wants is to adapt herself to the image of her mother that she has internalised (Mariotti 1997). On the other hand, if there are strong issues of rivalry she may want many children, more than her mother had. Or she may unconsciously want to go back to an early, perhaps imaginary, relationship with her mother – she may then identify with her baby, to the point of appearing exceptionally sensitive to his messages, but have great difficulties in allowing him to grow out of dependent babyhood. In all these situations the woman's wish for a baby is coloured with her own needs and unresolved issues. This is brought to the fore in the case of repeated terminations of pregnancy, when a woman who apparently does not wish to have children becomes repeatedly pregnant (Pines 1982). Perhaps more tragically, Welldon's patients are desperately keen to be mothers, but end up effectively rejecting their 'real' child – a child with needs and demands that a too conflicted mother cannot fulfil or accept.

Adolescent girls may feel a strong desire to have a child, and sometimes if they become pregnant without having planned it they may be delighted. Maternity at this stage may be a project destined to fail, if the teenager hopes to find in the infant a source of self-confidence and love she is missing in her relationships (Pines 1988, 1993; Fraiberg and Adelson 1987, reprinted in this volume, Chapter 13). If she has not succeeded in separating from her mother, a young woman may feel unconsciously driven to repeat what her mother has done, and become a mother herself. On the other hand, a pregnancy may give her a sense that she, not her mother, is in control of her body, and this, she hopes, would prove her independence. Lemma (Chapter 11) shows how the infant can be seen by a very young mother as a rival to her own needy self, or as an envied depriving maternal image, which is both hateful and hated.

Welldon and Fraiberg stress that the wish for a child can be part of a phantasy quite detached from considering the child's needs and also the parents' real need of support from each other. Sometimes the father has left his partner and their child – he is then present as an abandoning, cruel or useless image. Or he may be ineffectual, or violent, or simply too young. The mother is unsupported and unable to recreate, in herself and for her baby, a valid parental couple. Fraiberg and Adelson (Chapter 13) describe the terrible state one such girl found herself in, having to provide for her baby when she felt very depleted, with her young partner equally helpless and lost. Even in these cases the Oedipal father/partner is not truly absent – but he is being sidelined, or actively excluded, if the young mother's needs of and psychic involvement with her own mother are too great.

The father and the space of the third

We have seen how intense, and intensely sexual, is the early loving relationship between the infant and her mother. Gradually the girl shifts her primitive sexual feelings from her mother, whose desire the girl senses she is not well equipped to satisfy, to her father. The conditions that bring about this shift have been debated ever since Freud (1925) asked the question: 'How does it happen that girls abandon [the original object] and instead take their father as their object?' (1925: 251). In his paper on 'Female Sexuality' (1931) Freud is very concerned with the first part of the question. He recognises that 'the pre-Oedipus phase gains an importance which we have not attributed to it hitherto' (p. 226). He suggests several reasons to explain 'the mechanisms that are at work in her turning away from the mother who was an object so intensely and exclusively loved. . . . First and foremost we may mention jealousy of other people, of brothers and sisters, rivals, among whom the father too has a place' (p. 231).

But Freud soon introduces what for him is the crucial 'bedrock' of female psychology: the envy of the penis. Finding herself deprived of this organ and, according to Freud, unable to recognise her vagina as a sexual organ, the little girl is devastated by her own 'deficiency'.

At that point, 'femaleness, and with it, of course, her mother – suffers a great depreciation in her eyes' (p. 233). He concludes that 'there emerges, as the girl's strongest motive for turning away from her, the reproach that her mother did not give her a proper penis'. It is interesting that he follows this argument with 'a second reproach', from the little girl to her mother: it 'is that her mother did not give her enough milk, did not suckle her long enough' (p. 234). Had Freud taken more seriously than he did this 'second reproach', he might have concluded that the girl's 'depreciation' of her mother's femaleness may have relatively little to do with the penis and be instead expression of love, attachment, envy, hatred, loss, need for autonomy. This view had already been expressed by Melanie Klein in 1928, when she stated: 'I regard the deprivation of the breast as the most fundamental cause of the turning to the father' (p. 193).

However, in his 1925 paper, on 'Some Psychical Consequences of the Anatomical Distinction between the Sexes', Freud had concluded that the reason why the girl turns to the father is that she 'gives up her wish for a penis and puts in place of it a wish for a child: and *with that purpose in view* [in italics in the text] she takes her father as a love object'. He returned to the issue of feminine sexuality many times, but he never seemed to have modified this opinion.

Freud's theories on the subject of female sexuality have been widely debated. His view proposes as normative for the girl the overvaluation of the male sexual organ, and a dismissal, and at first total ignorance, of her own genitals. This dismissal extends to motherhood, which becomes a substitute for what is really desirable – to have a penis. Many psychoanalysts would recognise that there are cases where a woman's narcissistic needs, and sometimes her penis envy, are a motivating force in wanting a child, but nowadays few would consider Freud's theory as normative for all women. I will not enter into a critical discussion of Freud's views, as this has been done extensively ever since he published his theories (see, for instance, Horney 1926, 1933; Jones 1927; Klein 1928; Chasseguet-Smirgel 1976; Chiland 1980). Freud's critics maintain that the infant girl is more aware of her body and of her many erotic zones, including the vagina, than she is of an organ that she does not possess. Her penis envy, when present, is seen not as 'the bedrock' of her psychosexual life but as one element in a complex set of dynamics.

Melanie Klein (1932) asserts that 'in every case it is the woman's attitude to her introjected objects, especially her father's penis, which will determine her attitude to her husband and child' (p. 230). Depending on the intensity of the woman's sadistic attacks against the introjected paternal penis and against her own parental couple, the infant can represent a restored good penis, or a hostile presence. However, Klein is in no doubt that '[t]he girl's attitude to the introjected penis is strongly influenced by her attitude to her mother's breast. The first objects that she introjects are her 'good' mother and her 'bad' one, as represented by the breast' (p. 206). A good internal object will help the girl to mitigate her envious and sadistic attacks against a 'bad' penis and to repair the damage she is afraid she has done to her inner world. In due time, her children represent that capacity to repair and bring to life the introjected objects.

Freud's starting point, in the terms he expressed it, was not correct: the girl does not 'abandon' her original object. Her relationship with her mother, which can be described as the introjection of Klein's 'good breast', supports (or it may hinder) the girl's subsequent development. Moreover, McDougall (1995) maintains that the early erotic charge of their relationship is limited, sublimated, and repressed, but it does not disappear – in fact it enriches a woman's heterosexual and emotional life. The bond between mother and daughter, including and beyond the erotic aspect, remains active – it is not static, but undergoes continuous imaginative reworkings in a woman's mind, from childhood, through adolescence, childbearing years, menopause and old age.

Ogden (1987) proposes an interesting view on the girl's presumed 'change of object' and her subsequent Oedipal development. He suggests that before falling in love with her father, the little girl is in love with the 'father in mother'. When mother is still the primary source and recipient of affectionate feelings, the little girl recognises in her a paternal object, that is, the aspect of mother identified with her own father – (i.e. mother's Oedipal father). If all goes well, according to Ogden, the little girl will enjoy her love affair with the 'father in mother', helped and supported by her mother, who is able to bring to (unconscious) life that aspect of herself. At this point the little girl feels strong enough to take the momentous step of turning towards her father and offer her love to him. Her mother remains the 'environmental' mother offering potential for various flexible identifications (identifications in terms of functions) – and also becomes the object-mother but as such she is no longer the only object of love. Indeed, having given the child her blessing for her relationship with father, mother can be considered a rival alternatively admired and feared or despised and dismissed.

Summing up the girl's Oedipal development, we have seen that to an extent she loses her mother as object of lifelong erotic desire; at the same time she does maintain the identification with her, anchored to the reality of the body. Her love for her father is accentuated by the identification with her mother whose sexual attachment to father and his to her excludes the child. If the mother is raising her child alone, she conveys her feelings toward the image of a partner that she carries in her mind (Mariotti 1997). This situation introduces, or heightens, rivalrous feelings toward the mother and also toward the paternal figure. However, through her identification the girl has a glimpse of what lies in her future – issues around her sexuality, relationships and maternity.

From the beginning, in the dyadic relationship between mother and infant the presence is evoked of the third – who is part of the infant's world, and is connected to mother in ways that can be represented in the infant' fantasies as powerfully life-giving, exciting, dangerous or seductive. Lacan (1958) theorised that the Law of the Father separates the mother from the infant, and introduces the child to what Lacan describes as the Symbolic world of language, society and culture. This allows the subject a measure of freedom from the infinitely captivating Imaginary which constitutes the original bond with the mother.

The symbolic space of play allows the young child to be no longer (only) her mother's child but, in her identification with the maternal figure, she has become her own child's mother. The little girl needs to be potentially ready to relinquish her exclusive position as daughter in order to integrate her identity as potential mother. This she does in her play with dolls, which offers her a space where she will not be asked 'Are you a mother? Are you a daughter?' In the transitional space of play (Winnicott 1951) she can elaborate very many interesting questions – where do babies come from, and where am I situated in the context of this question? Am I the same as my mother or can I dare be different? If I grow up, how am I going to deal with my baby self? If she is able to play, she has an opportunity to begin to question, unconsciously, her mother's messages about gender and maternal identification, and she can find a space to elaborate her own views on what she wants or expects for herself.

The Oedipal father here plays an essential role. He offers the little girl the opportunity to both identify with and differentiate from mother. His acknowledgement and acceptance of his daughter's sexual identity confirms the statement already received from mother, to which it adds some colour, making it an object of excitement and delight – to be a girl is not anatomical destiny but a gender issue. At the same time the father must have a clear inner sense of the difference between child's sexuality and adult sexuality, in his relationship to his daughter and to his partner – in other words, he must have internalised a clear Oedipal structure of his own. His recognition helps the child to maintain a sense of her own individual boundaries within which difference from and identity with mother can be elaborated. Klein suggested that boys go through an early phase of identification with mother, the 'feminine complex' (Klein 1928), and Greenson (1968) describes a process of disidentification from the mother required in the boy. However, this disidentification can accommodate a feminine/maternal element which, I would say, is essential in allowing a man to express aspects of himself associated with femininity and/or maternality. Both parents convey to their children their unconscious image of a parental couple – the father's unconscious evaluation of his own femininity and its relation to his male identity may complement the maternal image, enrich it, or undermine it. When the mother has great difficulty in mothering her daughter, the father may come to represent a very positive source of internalisation of a caring and fundamentally maternal image, without necessarily losing his paternal position.

It is interesting to notice how often, in the papers discussing problems in motherhood, the young mother's father appears as a weak and ineffectual man, or else as an absent figure. This confirms the role of a potent father figure in the development of healthy maternality. Parker's patient only mentions her father as a disappointing figure, and Pines's patients have fathers who are 'retiring', 'passive', or dead. However, in some cases the father in the course of the analysis turns out to be quite supportive. We may surmise that the Oedipal father, brought by the patient to her sessions, is bound to be unsatisfactory because he has of course let down his daughter at the non-symbolic level of maternity. The daughter has not been allowed to replace the mother and carry the father's children, as she had wished in her early passionate Oedipal phantasies. (In those abusive cases where a blurring of the child's and of the adult sexuality has taken place in the father's mind, the genuinely helpful paternal figure is, at best, dangerously confused or else completely non-existent.) A degree of disappointment may therefore, in some cases, be the residue of the incomplete work of symbolisation and accept-ance of reality linked to the Oedipal situation.

Transmission of the Oedipal structure

Freud's description of the Oedipus complex related to the child's experience with his two heterosexual parents. Since then psycho-analysts have returned to this theoretical lynchpin proposing alternative, modified, or opposing points of view of the Oedipal predicament. In recent years, the Oedipal theory and the concept of the 'third' or third position has been developed in very different, fruitful and clinically relevant ways (see, for instance, Britton 1989; Benjamin 2004; Green 2005 among others). I will limit myself briefly to mentioning the issues raised by some writers who have stressed in their formulation the link between the child's Oedipus complex and the development of maternality

Aulagnier (2001), and Cournut-Janin (1998) underline the importance of the mother's own Oedipal background for the devel-opment of the child's Oedipal process. This shows once again how parenthood is a multigenerational concern, where unconscious communication is the key of the parent's behaviour toward their offspring.

Piera Aulagnier was a French-trained psychoanalyst whose thought was influenced by Lacan. She suggests that children of both sexes desire first of all to have a baby with their own mother. It is not unusual for a toddler whose mother is pregnant, to refer lovingly to the soon-to-be-born baby as 'our baby', while looking happily to his or her mother. The prohibition of this wish – mainly expressed and operated by the Law of the Father, with the Mother's essential support – requires successive modifications of the wish, which thus becomes a wish to have a child from father, and later, when the little girl has become a woman, she desires to have a child from someone who is not her father but who would 'possess his qualities' (Aulagnier

2001: 49). The woman's desire for a baby is therefore charged with the original wish and with its prohibition. When her actual child is born it cannot represent the fulfilment of the original wish (to have a baby from the mother, or the father). To fully comply with the Oedipal prohibition, the wish 'is deferred to a future time: one wishes a child on the child who has just been born' (p. 80). A further transformation, to remove even more the Oedipal origin of the wish could lead one to the formulation 'one wishes a desire to have a child onto the child' (p. 81). 'In this way the child inherits a wish that proves that he is not himself the fulfilment of the one that was hoped for. This wish dethrones him from the title of Oedipal object. [. . .] It pre-announces that it is forbidden to occupy a place that must remain vacant on the stage of the real' (p. 81).

The complexity of Aulagnier's language is not only an expression of her own idiosyncratic originality – it also derives from the multi-layered situation she is attempting to describe. The satisfaction of desire is maintained but deferred and displaced, the prohibition is obeyed, but only just. If one of the parents treats a child as 'the special one', as someone perhaps more clever or more sensitive than their partner, the Oedipal prohibition is shaken in the child's mind. The distinction between one's partner and one's child may become somewhat blurred – at the same time the child may perceive an invitation to enter into an intergenerational relationship with the parent, portrayed as preferable (for the parent) to being part of the parental couple.

If all goes well, Aulagnier's model implies that the child internalises and identifies with mother's *maternal function*, expressed as *a desire for a child*, as opposed to the introjection of the *mother*, which involves the concrete recreation of a mother-and-infant couple.

Cournut-Janin's (1998) reflections on the girl's Oedipal development start from her consideration of the female body in the relationship between the girl child and her mother. She distinguishes 'femininity' from 'the feminine'. Femininity is 'what the woman displays – attractive in her finery, make-up, everything that makes her beautiful . . . and deflects the gaze from the genital organs' (p. 624). Her genitals are hidden and must remain so, in order not to provoke the father's castration fear – and, in my view, his incestuous desire. The mother's own incorporative Oedipal desires, projected on her baby daughter, prompt her to give her daughter an 'implicit message', forbidding her to enjoy or to 'risk destroying' her father's sexual organs, and at the same time imposing the repression of the vagina and the displacement of the daughter's attractiveness on to her whole body – provided her inner genitals are kept secret.

A very different take on the triangular situation is suggested by Kulish and Holtzman (1998), who use the myth of Persephone to illustrate the experience of the mother when the daughter enters into a relationship with the father/lover. In the myth Demeter is dejected and heartbroken when her daughter, Persephone, is kidnapped by Hades, the Lord of Death. In her unhappiness she stops everything from growing on the earth, until the gods intervene and Persephone is allowed to live with her mother for six months each year. The myth's meanings are multilayered. It depicts a situation where the father is excluded and his procreative position denied, and the union between mother and daughter does not allow for a creative and fruitful separation. The parental couple is absent from the myth, and the mother is devastated without her daughter – fertility returns to the world only when mother and daughter are together, away from the male figure. Kulish and Holtzman highlight the importance of the mother–daughter connection, where the paternal figure is in abeyance but, in the myth, not absent and indeed it is a very powerful presence. His image as the Lord of Death suggests that with marriage and motherhood a young woman becomes aware of the passing of time, of life's transformations and eventually of death.

Aulagnier (2001) and Cournut-Janin (1998), underlining the transgenerational aspect of the Oedipus structure, point to how problematic situations can be passed on to the following generation if the mother (and the father) have not internalised the Oedipal situation. The Oedipal complex is not seen only in terms of content – you shall not have sexual relations with the parent of the other sex – but in terms of structure. The child must accept the difference between generations, and she must accept that a parental couple is necessary to generate children (Chasseguet-Smirgel 1976). The capacity to internalise this and to work it though symbolically will be necessary when she herself becomes a mother. I would suggest that the myth of Persephone can also be seen in terms of the danger of the sexual drive when the mother is excluded – the father/husband who ravishes the daughter and in so doing brings her into the realm of death represents a catastrophic conclusion of Oedipal phantasies from which the child can be rescued only by the mother's intervention. But the mother, who is aware of the horror, needs the gods, perhaps representing a 'good' paternal figure, to bring order and fertility.

Oedipal conflicts

Problematic Oedipal issues in the development of maternality are put in relief by Halberstadt-Freud (Chapter 10) and by Leuzinger-Bohleber (Chapter 6). Halberstadt-Freud describes a pathologically symbiotic mother–daughter relationship, going back perhaps to two generations. The father had been relegated to the position of 'a tyrant', even though he had offered a chance of identification with a masculine image which allowed some degree of separation from the mother. However, a more helpful and lively relationship with him could develop only when the patient became able to own her anger at her mother, leading to a better sense of her autonomy and enabling her to enjoy the positive sides of the relationship with her somewhat problematic father.

In Chapter 6 on the Medea fantasy, Leuzinger-Bohleber describes the Oedipal female phantasy of an unfaithful partner, who is the children's father but betrays the mother. Deceived and abandoned by her husband, in the Medea myth the woman's passions have no limits. She murders her rival and her own children – her rival out of hatred and jealousy, her children to hurt their father. Her children have lost their individuality and their humanity; they are seen as a part of herself, which she will not allow her husband to enjoy. A woman harbouring such unconscious images of the Oedipal couple and of sexual passion will perceive sexual dependency on a man as most dangerous – Leuzinger-Bohleber argues that this constellation may lead her to frigidity and contribute to conception difficulties.

Oedipal issues often figure strongly in the analysis of subfertile women, including when the father is presented as absent – his absence maintained by the exclusive relationship between mother and daughter while anger and pain at the loss of him are covered by barely expressed contempt. Sometimes the Oedipal situation can be recreated with the medical staff involved in the procedures of reproductive technology. For example, the staff may be experienced as benevolent parental figures sanctioning the woman's wish to have a child and providing reassurance that the child to be conceived is not the Oedipal child, perhaps giving permission to the woman to leave her own mother and enter into a fertile couple with her own husband. These unconscious phantasies may have a direct effect on the woman's ability to conceive, or at least they may contribute to it, while in other cases they may be of interest as the way the patient experiences *après coup* her sterility or its resolution investing it with deep personal meanings. This is particularly important as new technologies are evolved apparently proposing alternative ways to make babies. It may seem that the parental couple can once and for all be disposed of – with in vitro fertilisation fathers are no longer necessary, with surrogacy the maternal womb is not required.

A woman undergoing these procedures inevitably invests them with personal scenarios, in which her difficulty to conceive plays its part. When these phantasies are expressed, or acted, in the consulting room, the analyst is in danger of being drawn into omnipotent or persecutory phantasies shared with her patient. Zalusky-Blum describes in Chapter 8 the risks of falling into a protective or, on the contrary, a critical stance, and the vigilance and personal work required of the analyst to acknowledge one's emotional bias and allow the patient to work through and reach her own decisions. The analyst needs to keep in mind the third – represented by the analytic process, which creates a space where the analytic couple can reflect and develop their fertile work. (Reproductive technology and subfertility will be discussed further in the introduction to Part Two of this book.)

Adolescence and beyond

The papers collected in this book refer mostly to the perinatal period. If the development of maternality starts in the arms of one's own mother, it certainly does not end there. Parenthood itself contributes to the individual's growth, as described by Benedek (1959) in her well-known paper 'Parenthood as a Developmental Phase – A Contribution to the Libido Theory.' She showed how the important developmental stages in the child correspond to (the possibility of) further integration for the parents: 'in each "critical period" the child revives in the parent his related developmental conflicts. This brings about either pathologic manifestations in the parent, or by resolution of the conflict it achieves a new level of integration in the parent' (1959: 397). And later:

> The conflicts which were incorporated in the superego when the parent was a child are 'worked over' through the experiences of parenthood; this accounts for a new phase of maturation in the parent, but the opposite may also be true. Unsuccessful experience of the parent with unsuccessful children undermines the parent's self-esteem and enhances the strictness of his superego and thus renders it pathogenic for the parent as well as for the child. Incorporated into the psychic system of the parent, the child may mitigate or intensify the strictness of the parent's superego.
>
> (1959: 415)

Holmes (2000), reporting on her work with groups of pregnant and new mothers, states that 'by identifying with mother enough to get pregnant, a woman can finally in childbirth achieve true individuation and psychic separation from mother' (p. 112).

In this Introduction I have focused my attention on how maternality begins and on the internal, psychic challenges that have to be faced around the time of conception and early maternity by the mother and by her baby. These issues re-emerge later, throughout a woman's lifetime. Much more can be said – although little is to be found in the psychoanalytic literature – about the experience of having adult children, about the menopause, and about grandmothering, but these subjects are not within the scope of this collection. I shall limit myself to indicating here some aspects relevant to our topic of early maternality.

As I mentioned earlier, when the girl enters puberty the menarche brings to the fore the real possibility of making babies, and from then on every month she will be reminded of it, sometimes hardly noticing it, sometimes with relief, and sometimes with sadness. As she becomes an adolescent early issues of identification and separation are revisited and the young woman has to find a way forward in the middle of psychological and hormonal storms. Her gender identity becomes better defined. Signs of her maternal disposition are sometimes hidden but not absent.

There are opportunities to work on and resolve early difficulties, or on the contrary these may become more deeply ingrained. The struggle to develop further independence from her parents and to find her ground as a self-reliant adult requires capacity to bear anger and hatred of the parents, and enough narcissistic self-confidence to trust that life is possible on one's own terms, within one's boundaries. As part of her struggle for independence, the young person also needs to integrate her love for her parents and to elaborate the identification between her own and her mother's gender-related and maternal aspects. Her relationship with her parents changes and she may begin to enjoy a different kind of mutual recognition and closeness to her parents.

The mother's capacity to allow her daughter to become 'her own person' will help the girl in her development. A mother may be very upset and confused when she sees her daughter behaving in ways which she regards as highly inappropriate – but perhaps the daughter is carrying out mother's repressed fantasies and desires, or on the contrary, she is fighting to distance herself from her mother against her own regressive wish to remain for ever exclusively close to her.

Together with concern for her daughter's development the mother experiences the difficulties of separation and loss as she sees her child, once so dependent on her, become more self-reliant and dependent on her peer group. When the girl is involved in a relationship with close friends, both parents may feel excluded, in the position of the 'third', spectators to something exciting in which they themselves have no part.

The relationship with one's own maternal image continues through life, felt as a presence in oneself which can be nurturing or undermining – and sometimes both. Having children can strengthen that image; if all goes well it can lead to a greater understanding and closeness to one's mother. But if motherhood has increased conflicts and inner depletion, a mother may feel particularly unhappy about her circumstances when the daughter appears to have a whole life of possibilities in front of her. The envy that Melanie Klein (1957) has often described in the infant for the mother who can give life, can be rekindled, in the opposite direction, and the mother may feel, more or less consciously, intense envy of her daughter. This of course affects their relationship and may increase the young woman's apprehension about her burgeoning sexuality.

The positive aspects of maternality continue after a woman's childbearing age; when being a mother has been a mostly difficult and painful experience psychoanalytic work can address these issues in later life with a realistic degree of success. The older mother during and after menopause may also be able to find and take pleasure in aspects of herself that had been kept in abeyance while motherhood was a more or less full-time activity. However, this recovery brings the awareness that much is lost, and much will be left undone. Going through this work of mourning can lead a woman to a stronger narcissistic investment in herself and to the capacity to enjoy the new developments in her life.

Finally, a woman's inborn tendencies, her life experiences, and society's influences all play a central part in shaping the experience of maternality. The transmission of the traditional messages about motherhood has now been significantly challenged, but not completely disrupted, in particular by two interrelated social factors – women's position in society and the availability of contraception. From the late twentieth century, daughters have had far greater opportunities to choose whether or not to have children than their mothers had in the past, enabling them to have a family as result of choice and not as an inevitable consequence of having a sexual life. However, social changes are always filtered through the individual's psychic life, and it is on the latter that this book is focused.

Notes

1 The first time the word maternality is used extensively in a psychoanalytic paper is in 1968 by Judith Kestenberg: 'H. Deutsch emphasized the complementary roles of maternality and sexuality and felt that much of feminine genitality was spent in reproductive functioning' (p. 459). It has been used more recently in many discussions about motherhood and mothering issues.

2 I shall use both the feminine and masculine pronouns. It should be clear from the context whether the gender is relevant or not.

3 The transgenerational transmission of mothering models recognised in the analytic session is supported by a large number of studies on attachment theory (see, for instance, Main *et al.* 1985; Hesse and Main 1999), which have given empirical validation to the understanding gained from psychoanalytic clinical practice, showing that the model

of relationship relating to mother and child is carried over by the child when she becomes an adult with her own children.

4 From *Through Paediatrics to Psycho-Analysis* (p. 99): 'What then precedes the first object relationship? For my own part I have had a long struggle with this problem. It started when I found myself saying in this Society (about ten years ago) and I said it rather excitedly and with heat: "*There is no such a thing as a baby.*" I was alarmed to hear myself utter these words and tried to justify myself by pointing out that if you show me a baby you certainly show me also someone caring for the baby, or at least a pram with someone's eyes and ears glued to it. One sees a "nursing couple".'

5 'Against all the evidence of his senses, a man who is in love declares that "I" and "you" are one, and is prepared to behave as if it were a fact' (Freud 1930: 66).

6 An extreme example of how a child may be pathologically fixated at a sensorial level is given in the descriptions of autistic functioning by Frances Tustin (1986).

7 'Hysterics, and the hysterical in all of us, use partners only as audiences to their parthenogenetic creations – but somehow these audiences are never good enough, nor these cloned babies satisfy' (Mitchell 2000: 344).

8 The 'alien self' is how Fonagy and colleagues (2003) describe what the child experiences in herself (or himself) if she internalises a mother felt to be intrusive and unable to recognise and to respond to her baby's communication.

9 These inner models have also been conceptualised as 'procedural memory' (see, for instance, Fonagy 1999).

10 Recently the concept of internal working models has been criticised as being 'rigid' and not taking into account the affective experience it describes (Fonagy and Target 2007). However, it remains a good metaphor to describe the child's internalisation of specific ways of relating.

References

Abarbanel, J. (1983) 'The revival of the sibling experience during the mother's second pregnancy'. *Psychoanal. St. Child*, 38: 353–379.

Ammaniti, M. and Trentini, C. (2009) 'How new knowledge about parenting reveals the neurobiological implications of intersubjectivity: a conceptual synthesis of recent research. *Psychoanal. Dial.*, 19: 537–555.

Anzieu, D. (1989) *The Skin Ego*. New Haven, CT: Yale University Press.

Aulagnier, P. (2001) *The Violence of Interpretation*. London and New York: Routledge.

Bálint, A. (1949) 'Love for the mother and mother-love'. *Int. J. Psycho-Anal.*, 30: 251–259.

Balsam, R. H. (2000) 'The mother within the mother'. *Psychoanal Q.*, 69: 465–492.

Balsam, R. H. (2003) 'The vanished pregnant body in psychoanalytic female developmental theory. *J. Amer. Psychoanal. Assn.*, 51: 1153–1179.

Beebe, B. (2005) 'Mother–infant research informs mother–infant treatment'. *Psychoanal. St. Child*, 60: 7–46.

Beebe, B. and Lachmann, F. (2002) *Infant Research and Adult Treatment: Co-constructing Interactions*. Hillsdale, NJ: Analytic Press.

Beebe, B. and Stern, D. (1977) 'Engagement-disengagement and early object experiences', in N. Freedman and S. Grand (eds) *Communicative Structures and Psychic Structures*. New York: Plenum Press.

Benedek, T. (1959) 'Parenthood as a developmental phase – a contribution to the libido theory', *J. Amer. Psychoanal. Assn.*, 7: 389–417.

Benedek, T. (1960) 'The organization of the reproductive drive'. *Int. J. Psycho-Anal.*, 41: 1–15.

Benjamin, J. (1991) 'Father and daughter: identification with difference – a contribution to gender heterodoxy'. *Psychoanal. Dial.*, 1: 277–299.

Benjamin, J. (2004) 'Beyond doer and done to: an intersubjective view of thirdness'. *Psychoanal Q.*, 73: 5–46.

Bion, W. R. (1962) 'A theory of thinking'. *Int. J. Psycho-Anal.*, 43: 306–310. Also in *Second Thoughts*, 1967, pp. 110–119. London: William Heinemann Medical Books.

Birksted-Breen, D. (1974) *The Birth of a First Child*. London: Tavistock Publications.

Blos, P. (2003) 'The maternal experience: a contribution from clinical work', in D. Mendell and P. Turrini (eds) *The Inner World of the Mother*. Madison, CT: Psychosocial Press.

Bowlby, J. (1969) *Attachment and Loss: Volume 1: Attachment*. London: Hogarth Press and Institute of Psycho-Analysis.

Braunschweig, D. and Fain, M. (1975) *La Nuit, le Jour*. Paris: PUF Collection Fil Rouge.

Britton, R. (1989) 'The missing link: parental sexuality in the Oedipus complex', in J. Steiner (ed.) *The Oedipus Complex Today*. London: Karnac.

Chasseguet-Smirgel, J. (1976) 'Freud and female sexuality – the consideration of some blind spots in the exploration of the 'dark continent'. *Int. J. Psycho-Anal.*, 57: 275–286.

Chiland, C. (1980) 'Clinical practice, theory and their relationship in regard to female sexuality'. *Int. J. Psycho-Anal.*, 61: 359–365.

Condon, W. S. and Sander, L. W. (1974) 'Neonate movement is synchronized with adult speech: interactional participation and language acquisition'. *Science*, 183: 99–101.

Cournut-Janin, M. (1998) 'The feminine and femininity', in D. Birksted-Breen, S. Flanders and A. Gibeault (eds), *Reading French Psychoanalysis*. London and New York: Routledge, 2010.

David, C. (1973) 'English translation', in D. Birksted-Breen, S. Flanders and A. Gibeault (eds), *Reading French Psychoanalysis*. London and New York: Routledge, 2010.

Denis P. (1982) 'Homosexualité primaire, base de contradiction'. *Revue Française de Psychanalyse*, 46, 1, XLVI: 35–42. English translation 'Primary homosexuality, a foundation of contradictions', in D. Birksted-Breen, S. Flanders and A. Gibeault (eds) *Reading French Psychoanalysis*. London and New York: Routledge, 2010.

Deutsch, H. (1933) 'Motherhood and sexuality'. *Psychoanal Q.*, 2: 476–488.

Deutsch, H. (1945) *The Psychology of Women*. New York: Grune and Stratton.

Emde, R. N. (2009) 'From ego to "we-go": neurobiology and questions for psychoanalysis: commentary on papers by Trevarthen, Gallese, and Ammaniti and Trentini'. *Psychoanal. Dial.*, 19: 556–564.

Erikson, E. (1968) *Identity, Youth and Crisis*. London: Faber and Faber.

Fain, M. (1971) 'Prelude à la vie fantasmatique'. *Revue Francaise de Psychanalyse*, 5; English translation 'The prelude to fantasmatic life', in D. Birksted-Breen, S. Flanders and A. Gibeault (eds) *Reading French Psychoanalysis*. London and New York: Routledge, 2010.

Faure-Pragier, S. (1997) *Les bébés de l'inconscient. Le psychanalyste face aux stérilités féminines aujourd'hui*. Paris: PUF.

Fonagy, P. (1999) 'Memory and therapeutic action'. *Int. J. Psycho-Anal.*, 80: 215–223.

Fonagy, P. and Target, M. (2007) 'The rooting of the mind in the body: new links between attachment theory and psychoanalytic thought'. *J. Amer. Psychoanal. Assn.*, 55: 411–456.

Fonagy, P., Target, M., Gergely, G., Allen, J. G. and Bateman, A. W. (2003) 'The developmental roots of borderline personality disorder in early attachment relationships'. *Psychoanal. Inq.*, 23: 412–459.

Fraiberg, S. (1987) 'The adolescent mother and her infant', in L. Fraiberg (ed.) *Selected Writings of Selma Fraiberg*. Columbus, OH: Ohio State University Press.

Freud, A. (1936) *The Ego and the Mechanisms of Defence*. London: Hogarth Press.

Freud, S. (1905) 'Three essays on the theory of sexuality'. *S.E.* 7: 125–244.

Freud, S. (1910) 'Leonardo da Vinci and a memory of his childhood'. *S.E.* 11: 59–137.

Freud, S. (1912) 'On the universal tendency to debasement in the sphere of love'. *S.E.* 11: 177–190.

Freud, S. (1924) 'The dissolution of the Oedipus complex'. *S.E.* 19: 171–180.

Freud, S. (1925) 'Some psychical consequences of the anatomical distinction between the sexes'. *S.E.* 19: 241–258.

Freud, S. (1930) 'Civilization and its discontents'. *S.E.* 21: 64–145.

Freud, S. (1931) 'Female sexuality'. *S.E.* 21: 221–243.

Freud, S. (1937) 'Analysis terminable and interminable'. *S.E.* 23: 209–254.

Furman, E. (1982) 'Mothers have to be there to be left'. *Psychoanal. St. Child*, 37: 15–28.

Gaddini, E. (1969) 'On imitation'. *Int. J. Psycho-Anal.*, 50: 475–484.

Green, A. (2005) 'On thirdness'. In A. Green *Psychoanalysis: A Paradigm for Clinical Thinking*. London: Free Association Books.

Greenson, R. R. (1968) 'Dis-identifying from mother: its special importance for the boy'. *Int. J. Psycho-Anal.*, 49: 370–374.

Guignard, F. (2006) 'Maternity and femininity: sharing and splitting in the mother–daughter relationship', in A. M. Alizade (ed.) *Motherhood in the Twenty-first Century*. London: Karnac.

Harris, A. (2000) 'Gender as a soft assembly: tomboys' stories'. *Studies in Gender and Sexuality*, 1: 223–250.

Hesse, E. and Main, M. (1999) 'Second-generation effects of unresolved trauma in nonmaltreating parents'. *Psychoanal. Inq.*, 19: 481–540.

Holmes, L. (2000) 'The object within: childbirth as a developmental milestone'. *Mod. Psychoanal.*, 25: 109–134.

Horney, K. (1926) 'The flight from womanhood'. *Int. J. Psycho-Anal.*, 7: 324–339. Also in *Feminine Psychology*. New York: Norton, 1967.

Horney, K. (1933) 'The denial of the vagina'. *Int. J. Psycho-Anal.*, 14: 57–70. Also in *Feminine Psychology*. New York: Norton, 1967.

Jones, E. (1927) 'The early development of female sexuality'. *Int. J. Psycho-Anal.*, 7: 459–472.

Kestemberg, E. (1984) ' "Astrid" ou homosexualité, identité, adolescence. Quelques propositions hypothétiques'. *Cahiers du Centre de Psychanalyse et de Psychothérapie*, 8: 10. Also in *Adolescence a vif*. Paris: Presses Universitaires de France, 1999.

Kestenberg, J. S. (1956) 'On the development of maternal feelings in early childhood – observations and reflections'. *Psychoanal. St. Child*, 11: 257–291.

Kestenberg, J. S. (1968) 'Outside and inside, male and female'. *J. Amer. Psychoanal. Ass.*, 16: 457–520.

Klein, M. (1928) 'Early stages of the Oedipus conflict'. *Int. J. Psycho-Anal.*, 9. Also in *Love, Guilt and Reparation*. London: Hogarth Press.

Klein, M. (1932) *The Psycho-analysis of Children*. London: Hogarth Press.

Klein, M. (1961) *Narrative of a Child Analysis*. London: Hogarth Press.

Klein, M. (1975) 'Envy and gratitude', in *The Writings of Melanie Klein, Vol. 3: Envy and Gratitude and Other Works* (pp. 176–235). London: Hogarth Press, 1975. First published as *Envy and Gratitude: A Study of Unconscious Sources*. London: Tavistock Press, 1957.

Kristeva, J. (1989) *Black Sun*. New York: Columbia University Press.

Kulish, N. and Holtzman, D. (1998) 'Persephone, the loss of virginity and the female Oedipal complex'. *Int. J. Psycho-Anal.*, 79: 57–71.

Lacan, J. (1958) 'On a question preliminary to any possible treatment of psychosis', in J. Lacan *Ecrits: A Selection*, trans. A. Sheridan. New York: Norton, 1977.

Laplanche, J. (1987) *New Foundations for Psychoanalysis*, trans. D. Macey. Oxford: Blackwell, 1989.

Laplanche, J. (1997) 'The theory of seduction and the problem of the other'. *Int. J. Psycho-Anal.*, 78: 653–666.

Lax, R. F. (1995) 'Freud's views and the changing perspective on femaleness and femininity'. *Psychoanal. Psychol.*, 12: 393–406.

Lax, R. F. (2003) 'Motherhood is an ebb and flow – it lasts a lifetime: the vicissitudes of mother's interaction with her "fantasy child" ', in D. Mendell and P. Turrini (eds) *The Inner World of the Mother*. Madison, CT: Psychosocial Press.

Leisse de Lustgarten, A. (2006) 'The impossible being of the mother', in A. M. Alizade, (ed.) *Motherhood in the Twenty-first Century*. London: Karnac.

McDougall, J. (1995) *The Many Faces of Eros*. London: Free Association Books.

Magherini, G. (1989) *La sindrome di Standhal*. Firenze: Ponte Alle Grazie.

Mahler, M. S., Pine, F. and Bergman, A. (1975) *The Psychological Birth of the Human Infant*. New York: Basic Books.

Main, M., Kaplan, N. and Cassidy, J. (1985) 'Security in infancy, childhood and adulthood: a move to the level of representation', in I. Bretherton and E. Waters (eds) *Growing Points of Attachment Theory and Research*. Chicago: University of Chicago Press.

Mariotti, P. (1993) 'The analyst's pregnancy: the patient, the analyst, and the space of the unknown'. *Int. J. Psycho-Anal.*, 74: 151–164.

Mariotti, P. (1997) 'Creativity and fertility – the one-parent phantasy', in J. Raphael-Leff and R. J. Perelberg (eds) *Female Experience: Three Generations of British Women*. London and New York: Routledge.

Meltzoff, A. N. and Moore, M. K. (1977) 'Imitation of facial and manual gestures by human neonates'. *Science*, 198: 75–78.

Mills, M. (1997) ' "The waters under the earth": understanding maternal depression', in J. Raphael-Leff and R. J. Perelberg (eds) *Female Experience: Three Generations of British Women*. London and New York: Routledge.

Mitchell, J. (2000) *Mad Men and Medusas*. London: Penguin.

Motz, A. (2005) *The Psychology of Female Violence*. London and New York: Routledge.

Neumann, E. (1955) *The Great Mother*. Princeton, NJ: Princeton University Press.

Ogden, T. (1987) 'The transitional oedipal relationship in female development'. *Int. J. Psycho-Anal.*, 68: 485–498.

43

Pappenheim, E. and Sweeney, M. (1952) 'Separation anxiety in mother and child'. *Psychoanal. St. Child*, 7: 95–114.

Parker, R. (1995) *Torn in Two: The Experience of Maternal Ambivalence*. London: Virago Press.

Pines, D. (1982) 'The relevance of early psychic development to pregnancy and abortion'. *Int. J. Psycho-Anal.*, 63: 311–319. Also in D. Pines *A Woman's Unconscious Use of her Body*. London: Virago Press, 1993.

Pines, D. (1988) 'Adolescent pregnancy and motherhood: a psychoanalytical perspective'. *Psychoanal. Inq.*, 8: 234–251. Also in D. Pines *A Woman's Unconscious Use of her Body*. London: Virago Press, 1993.

Pines, D. (1993) *A Woman's Unconscious Use of her Body*. London: Virago Press.

Raphael-Leff, J. (1991) *Psychological Processes of Childbearing*. London: Chapman and Hall.

Raphael-Leff, J. (1993) *Pregnancy – The Inside Story*. London: Sheldon Press.

Raphael-Leff, J. (2003) *Parent–Infant Psychodynamics*. London: Whurr.

Schore, A. N. (1994) *Affect Regulation and the Origin of the Self: The Neurobiology of Emotional Development*. Mahwah, NJ: Lawrence Erlbaum Associates Inc.

Shaeffer, J. (2006) www.spp.asso.fr/main/ConferencesEnLigne/Items/39. htm.

Stern, D. N. (1971) 'A microanalysis of the mother–infant interaction'. *J. Amer. Acad. Child Psychiat.*, 10: 501–507.

Stern, D. N. (1985) *The Interpersonal World of the Infant: A View from Psychoanalysis and Developmental Psychology*. London: Karnac.

Tronick, E. (1989) 'Emotions and emotional communication in infants'. *Am. Psychol.*, 44, 2: 112–119.

Tustin, F. (1986) *Autistic Barriers in Neurotic Patients*, London: Karnac.

Welldon, E. (1980) *Mother, Madonna, Whore: The Idealization and Denigration of Motherhood*. New York: Free Association Books.

Winnicott, D. W. (1949) 'Birth memories, birth trauma, and anxiety', in D. W. Winnicott *Through Paediatrics to Psycho-Analysis*. London: Hogarth Press and the Institute of Psycho-Analysis, 1975.

Winnicott, D. W. (1951) 'Transitional objects and transitional phenomena', in D. W. Winnicott *Through Paediatrics to Psychoanalysis*. London: Hogarth Press and the Institute of Psycho-Analysis, 1975.

Winnicott, D. W. (1952) 'Anxiety associated with insecurity', in D. W. Winnicott *Through Paediatrics to Psychoanalysis*. London: Hogarth Press and the Institute of Psycho-Analysis, 1975.

Winnicott, D. W. (1956) 'Primary maternal preoccupation', in D. W. Winnicott *Through Paediatrics to Psychoanalysis*. London: Hogarth Press and the Institute of Psycho-Analysis, 1975.

Winnicott, D. W. (1960) 'The theory of the parent–infant relationship, in D. W. Winnicott *The Maturational Process and the Facilitating Environment*. London: Hogarth Press and the Institute of Psycho-Analysis, 1976.

PART ONE

Mothering in body and mind

Paola Mariotti

Approaching the various aspects of maternality explored in the first part of this book requires some considerations of female development in its specificity. As we have seen, Freud (1933) did not seem confident and satisfied with his own conclusions, which he described as 'certainly incomplete and fragmentary' (p. 135). However, some of his followers in the first half of the twentieth century had no hesitation in postulating a connection between female development, masochism and passivity:

> In the reproductive functions proper – menstruation, defloration, pregnancy and parturition – woman is biologically doomed to suffer. Nature seems to have no hesitation in administering to her strong doses of pain, and she can do nothing but submit passively to the regimen prescribed.
>
> (Bonaparte 1935: 326–327)

Helene Deutsch (1945), in her two-volume *The Psychology of Women*, embraced Freud's theories: the importance of penis envy in the little girl's early development, masochism as a major element in women's erotic pleasure, the role of passivity all concord with Freud's views. But in the section on motherhood, especially in her clinical material, a more nuanced understanding emerges – for instance, the desire for a child is not seen as a replacement for the penis. In Deutsch

45

a woman comes into her own with motherhood, and to mother-hood her sexuality is submitted.

In discussing the early development of maternal feelings in the little girl, Judith Kestenberg (1956) proposed a sophisticated connection between the young child's discovery of undefined vaginal (and genital) sensations, and her desire for a baby (or attachment to a doll). She suggested that early undischarged and confusing vaginal excitations were the basic source of the girl's wish for a child:

> The most powerful source of the girl's maternal interest, however, is the projection of the vaginal sensations upon the baby, and the equation of the inside of the body with the baby. . . . The baby doll which can be carried around everywhere and can be held close to the body during sleep, substitutes for the lack of organ entity and organ constancy inherent in early vaginal tensions.
>
> (Kestenberg 1956: 462)

Benedek studied women's sexuality and reproductive cycle, including infertility (Benedek *et al.* 1953) and the menopause (Benedek 1950), from the point of view of drive theory, aiming also to support her psychoanalytic observations with the findings of biology (Benedek 1960). In 'Parenthood as a Developmental Phase' (Benedek 1959), as I shall show later, she discussed the effect on the parents' psychic life of having and raising children.

In the 1960s the interest in sociological aspects of gender influenced the thinking of American psychoanalysts such as Dinnerstein (1976) and Chodorow (1978), while preparing the ground for the extensive work of gender studies theorists who have been active in recent decades. Various interrelated social factors have contributed to the interest in female development which has taken place in the last 30 or 40 years. The feminist movement, the availability of contraception, the improvement in quality of life with the extension of education for girls, have allowed women to bring to the fore issues of specific interest to the female gender, in psychoanalysis as in other areas. It is important to notice that these studies reveal aspects of women's life – such as the mother–daughter relationship – that until recently had not registered their importance in psychoanalysis.[1] There have been numerous North American contributions to the study of maternality from psychoanalysts sensitive to the work of gender theorists, often within the framework of intersubjective and relational psychoanalysis (see, for instance, Benjamin's work). It is beyond the scope of this book to do justice to these contributions.

In France close attention to Freud's theories of sexuality led to several important studies of maternal sexuality (Braunschweig and Fain 1975; Laplanche 1997; Cournut-Janin 1998), while the concept of primary homosexuality (Denis 1982; Kestemberg 1984) designated the early mother and infant erotic experience and contributed to a clarification of the structuring function of sexuality on the young person's psychic life. In the British Society, Dinora Pines (1982) and Joan Raphael-Leff (1991, 2001, 2003) have been pioneers in exploring psychoanalytically events specifically relevant to the reproductive life of women.

Winnicott was perhaps the first to focus on a woman's state of mind in the perinatal period, with his classic paper on 'Primary Maternal Preoccupation', written in 1958 and reprinted here (Chapter 1). He understood this state of 'preoccupation' to be specific to the experience of being a mother, and that it 'would be an illness were it not for the fact of the pregnancy'. The young mother experiences a 'heightened sensitivity', which is essential to enable her to provide her child with the responsiveness she or he needs, so that the infant can experience recovery from the state of extreme dependency and fear of annihilation that threatens him, and can 'go on being'. Winnicott stresses that the baby is unable to acknowledge mother's responsiveness: he writes that '[w]hat the mother does well is not in any way apprehended by the infant at this stage' (p. 64 this volume). What the mother intuitively recognises in her child is that with her cares he begins 'to exist, to have experience, to build a personal ego' (p. 64). From the very beginning the mother does not get a direct, narcissistically pleasing, acknowledgement from the baby of what she provides for him. Such acknowledgement requires the capacity to recognise his own 'absolute dependency', and this recognition, according to Winnicott, 'is something which belongs to *extreme sophistication* and to a stage not always reached by adults' (italics in the text, p. 64). It follows that the mother needs to have access to inner resources, to a nurturing and narcissistically reassuring 'mother within', if she is to trust confidently the loving mutuality of the relationship with her child.

In his writings, Winnicott has often described a good-enough mother as 'ordinarily devoted', which may suggest that maternality is an 'ordinary' quality of women. In 'Primary Maternal Preoccupation' he shows how extraordinary a mother's devotion actually is, and the kind of demands it puts on a woman's psychological resources.

It is interesting that Winnicott did not explore the effect of this particular state of mind on the mother herself. He indicated that, if all goes well, a woman on the whole will enjoy the experience. However, he was aware of the depth of maternal ambivalence – in 'Hate in the Counter-Transference' (1949) he writes:

> A mother has to be able to tolerate hating her baby without doing anything about it. She cannot express it to him. If, for fear of what she may do, she cannot hate appropriately when hurt by her child she must fall back on masochism, and I think it is this that gives rise to the false theory of a natural masochism in women. The most remarkable thing about a mother is her ability to be hurt so much by her baby and to hate so much without paying the child out, and her ability to wait for rewards that may or may not come at a later date. Perhaps she is helped by some of the nursery rhymes she sings, which her baby enjoys but fortunately does not understand?
>
> (p. 74)

And in 'The Theory of the Parent–Infant Relationship' (1960) he observes that 'after conception . . . the woman begins to alter in her orientation, and to be concerned with the changes that are taking place within her' (p. 53).

I would argue that the words 'ordinarily devoted mother', or 'good-enough mother' draw a veil on the real woman's experience. Indeed, they take it for granted, just as the infant naturally does. The question of the dynamics of this 'alteration', or of the effects on the mother's psyche of hating her beloved child, are central to the development of the mother–child relationship and to her own experience of maternality. The intensity of feelings for her child may surprise and overwhelm her, and while she may welcome the infant gradually settling inside her mind and overshadowing other concerns in her life, sooner or later her erotic and affectionate interest in the father, and her love and dedication to her family and external work, will reassert themselves. She may find that to some extent her personality has changed, that she has different priorities, a different sense of time, and that much has been gained, but something has been lost. The 'ordinarily devoted' mother is a woman who is able to accept and to

48

work through all these momentous changes, and when she cannot do it, she is able to accept and work through her limitations and failures.

Psychoanalysis in the perinatal period

A patient's pregnancy and early motherhood offer particular challenges in psychoanalysis. Some analysts see pregnancy as an obstacle to treatment, others as an opportunity to explore phantasies which would not otherwise be available. After the baby's birth some analysts accept his or her presence in the consulting room for several weeks, and others prefer to resume the analysis when arrangements can be made for the mother to attend alone. While of course one tries to analyse consistently the patient's responses to her condition, it is likely that the analyst's experiences and beliefs play a part in whatever arrangement is decided upon and, subtly, in their interpretative stance. Schematically, we can think of two opposite situations: in one case the analyst feels quite maternal toward her patient and more or less consciously she inclines toward a supportive approach. This is in fact advocated by Daniel Stern (1995) in the context of what he describes as the 'motherhood constellation', a state of mind of adaptation to pregnancy and nursing, which centres on 'the mother's discourse with her own mother, especially with her own mother–as–mother–to–her–as–a–child; her discourse with herself, especially with herself-as-mother; and her discourse with her baby' (p. 172). He emphasises the importance of a benevolent older female figure, representing the young mother's mother – that, if the mother is in analysis, can be represented by the analyst. One can see Stern's 'good grandmother' as fostering positive, narcissistically healthy unconscious processes in the new mother, providing a benign and supportive super-ego figure much needed in her new challenging tasks. At the opposite end of the spectrum, the analyst becomes concerned about her patient's mothering and its negative effect on the patient's child – the analyst may then unwittingly set up a persecutory atmosphere which repeats in the consulting room the sado–masochistic relationship the young mother has allegedly created with her child.

Aiming at maintaining a consistent analysis of the patient's material, Dana Birksted-Breen (Chapter 2) illustrates the complex work that can be done in treatment, and the positive results for the patient and for her child. It includes acknowledgement of the patient's love and competence as a mother and a robust investigation of her most aggressive phantasies and fears. She shows that analysis can acquire considerable depth during pregnancy. She writes about the 'work of worrying', that is the capacity to elaborate anxiety and repeatedly transform it, without attempting to eliminate it altogether, a work that can be facilitated in treatment and that tends to be avoided when there is excessive idealisation. The shadows of archaic phantasies are reawakened in pregnancy, a time during which a woman can work through, consciously and unconsciously, those old ghosts carrying the fear of death and the hope of life. How those phantasies can and need to be elaborated in psychoanalysis is the main thread of the paper. The pregnant patient's inward focus is respected by the analyst, while her defensiveness and narcissistic withdrawal can be interpreted, and the patient is allowed to experience her fears of the analyst's attacks and envy – a challenge not only for the patient but also for the analyst. Birksted–Breen conveys the importance of investigating the patient's negative feelings, her aggressive phantasies and fears in order to strengthen her capacity to hold them in mind and not be persecuted and threatened by them.

The advantages and limitations of psychoanalysis in the perinatal period have also been discussed by Rosemary Balsam. She has written extensively on issues of motherhood and female gender identification and is contributing significantly to the present debate around gender issues which is alive particularly in American psychoanalytic circles (Balsam 2010). She has shown (2000) how the perinatal patient is able to bring to the sessions feelings and images of her own mother and of her child that at other times may not be so vividly present, or perhaps may even be 'forgotten'. In the consulting room, the analyst is able to observe her patient repeating with her infant, subtly and unconsciously, a mitigated version of what she had been complaining was her mother's behaviour toward her. This exemplifies vividly how the repetition and transmission of modes of relating can be present but almost imperceptible, the mother being totally unaware of the nuances of her behaviour.

Psychoanalysis and the pregnant body

If we turn our attention to the child and to what she may internalise from the mother, we know from analytic work with children that they are indeed curious about the mother's body and its functioning, and that they have 'theories' to explain what is happening inside it. Freud was in no doubt about childhood sexual curiosity. Not only did he theorise that the child believes her mother has a penis, but he also presented us with Little Hans (1909) trying to find out how things really stand and asking pertinent questions to his pregnant mother. And it is well known that Melanie Klein (see, for instance, 1928) gave great importance in the child's development to his or her phantasies about the mother's body and about what goes on inside it.

Adult patients bring to analysis, often within the transference, memories from childhood that point to awareness of one's body development and to curiosity about the maternal body. Balsam (2003) proposes that the pregnant body as the 'premier icon of the mature female body' has been erased from psychoanalytic writings. In Chapter 4, this volume, she observes that 'this symbol of fertile maternity is a major conscious and social focus of attention for adults and children of both sexes', yet it is neglected in psychoanalysis. She focuses on her patients' communication regarding the body, in particular the pregnant body, and their memories of their mothers' pregnancy. She stresses the power of that image on the young female child who closely observes physical changes in her mother and their connections with mother's changes of mood and their significance. The extreme attention, easily observable, with which a young child looks at and touches her (or his) mother's body may give the little girl a positive indication of her future, or may contribute to a sense of distressing envious inferiority. The child makes a comparison between her own and her mother's body, a comparison that she may repeat all her life in her close observation of her body and other women's.

A different aspect of the mother–child bodily connection, seen now from the mother's point of view, is described by Erna Furman, who discusses the issues at stake in the process of separation between mother and child. In the first part of Chapter 5 in this book, 'On Motherhood', she focuses on the maternal bodily feelings in the traumatic aftermath of an infant's death. She points out the importance of understanding such death as a *bodily felt* loss for the mother, a loss which can become integrated psychologically only very gradually. This paper touches on and develops some of the main themes of her writing and working life. Furman was an eminent American psychoanalyst who wrote extensively on normal and pathological child development and parenting, on parental bereavement, and on the issue of separation between mothers and children. One of her best-known papers (1982) is entitled '*Mothers Have to Be There to Be Left*', on the theme of leaving and being left. The issue of separation and loss is picked up in the paper published in the present book. After writing about the traumatic loss due to a young child's death, she discusses healthy separation. She shows that in order for the mother to be able to separate from her child, she needs to be able to work on her own issues about separation. The importance of the mother's allowing her child to find her or his own way cannot be overestimated. It involves for the mother an ongoing sense of loss of the relationship with the younger child in whose life the mother held such an important place. However, in the mother's mind the relationship with the child continues even during the turmoil surrounding the child's search for autonomy, that often comes to a head in adolescence. This allows the daughter to find in due time her way to a relationship with her mother which takes into account her own development, and perhaps her mother's, a transformed relationship from that of childhood, but still very strong and valuable to both (Shrier *et al.* 2004). Mother and child have to come to terms with contrasting feelings for each other, and accept limitations in each other and ambivalent feelings in themselves.

Ambivalence

Maternal ambivalence towards the baby is invariably apparent from the start. Before and after birth the intermingling of love and hate directed at internal images is reflected and persists in the affects of the mother for her child. The capacity to deal with positive and negative feelings about motherhood, and therefore to accept her own ambivalence even toward a much loved infant, enables a woman to have realistic expectations on her capacity as a mother and on her child's development. In one of the first studies showing how the mother's psychological preparedness is correlated to her relationship with the newborn, Birksted-Breen (1974) followed a cohort of women during their pregnancy and early motherhood. She observes that those mothers who were most idealising of motherhood and of their own mothers did not fare better than the most insecure and anxious ones.

In her book *Torn in Two* (1995) and in Chapter 3 of this book, Rozsika Parker has explored psychoanalytic writings dealing with the importance of ambivalence. She discusses Klein's depressive position and suggests that we may want to place 'the mother as having to negotiate entry into a maternal depressive position. . . . Then we can see that the mother's achievement of ambivalence can promote a sense of concern and responsibility towards, and differentiation of self from, the baby' (Parker 1995: 17). She also notices the reluctance to fully value ambivalence, to take on board how universal and profound it is, and also how necessary it is in allowing the mother to reclaim her life, and the child his. The importance of maternal ambivalence and the capacity to handle and integrate aggressive feelings has been discussed by Winnicott (1949), quoted earlier, and by other authors, and recently underlined by Hoffman (2003), supported by his observations of mothers and toddlers. Feder (1980) has argued that ambivalence may be present even before conception – pre-conceptive ambivalence – maintaining that the parents' attitude and motivations to have a baby will be, often unconsciously, communicated to the child and affect his or her sense of their place in the world: 'the parents' ambivalence as external objects determine the child's psychological and characterological destiny, eventually sensed, incorporated, repeated, and perpetuated by the hurt child, now turned parent, throughout generations' (p. 163). However, Feder seems to see parental ambivalence only as a potential problem for the child, while Parker sees also its positive potential and I would argue that even pre-conceptive ambivalence, within limits, can be helpful: it may be an aspect of the parents' concern about having a baby, and help them to commit themselves responsibly to their role.

And yet, maternal ambivalence is rather a taboo subject. A mother's love is meant to be 'unconditional' – but what is usually meant by unconditional love is not that it survives in all conditions – which it often does – but that it should *ignore* all conditions including the mother's own emotional response to her child's behaviour. When the idealisation of a maternal figure prevails, the discovery of harbouring negative, angry, hateful feelings toward one's child may come as a shock, and provoke guilt and shame in the mother.

The impact of shame is described and discussed by Parker in her chapter. She reminds us that shame hides – the shameful person tries to cover up her shame and whatever she is ashamed of. To feel one is a 'bad mother' is shameful – women may feel shamed in front of their own children, and also ashamed of them. Shame can be projected on the child – and children tend to be very sensitive to shame – and the child may carry that sense about herself and/or about her mother, and re-experience it when she has children, to whom she will pass it on. As we shall see when thinking about situations which are going wrong, shame and guilt together can render unmanageable problems of ambivalence and insecurity. The opportunity to share one's experiences of mothering with other mothers is often welcome, and can be extremely helpful in diminishing shame and guilt. A woman though may be too ashamed to reveal her feelings to others and in that case seeking help is not seen as an option. As a consequence a mother, after having suffered tremendously in her childhood, may end up treating her children as she herself was treated by her own mother.

Siblings

The significance of siblings in one's psychic life has been somewhat understated, at least in British psychoanalysis, in spite of the frequency with which siblings figure in clinical material. Freud pointed out how children are interested in the arrival of siblings:

> It is not by theoretical interests but by practical ones that activities of research are set going in children. The threat to the bases of a child's existence offered by the discovery or the suspicion of the arrival of a new baby and the fear that he may, as a result of it, cease to be cared for and loved, make him thoughtful and clear-sighted.
>
> (1905 – this paragraph was added in 1925: 194)

Fraiberg (1987), here writing about adolescent mothers, makes a direct connection between the relationship with one's siblings in childhood, and the mother's feelings for her infant:

> Jealousy toward the baby, competition with the baby, anger toward the baby, and the feeling of being robbed of something precious by the baby were recurring themes which we could trace back in treatment to a sibling who had been a rival in childhood.
>
> (p. 171)

Recently, the relevance of siblings in the person's psychic life has been addressed by Appelbaum (1988), and more extensively by Mitchell (2003), Coles (2003), Lewin and Sharp (2009). The death of a sibling, especially in childhood, has an impact that can become evident when one becomes a parent (Ainslie and Solyom 1986; Klyman 1986). Blum (1978) shows that the birth of a younger brother with a mild congenital defect played a part in the postnatal difficulties his sister experienced in later life. A particular aspect of the transmission of mothering models is discussed in a paper by Abarbanel (1983) on siblings' relationship and pregnancies. She observed two mothers in the perinatal period, who both had siblings, and she describes how their relationship to their existing child – in both cases a daughter – repeated important aspects of their relationship with their own sister.

A mother may use her children to distance herself from her own childhood experiences by casting her offspring in the painful situation she had encountered herself, unconsciously using her power to do to them what she feels was done to her. But to have children also offers an opportunity to repair the hurts one has received or caused and to rediscover in one's offspring the intimacy and fun of being children together.

Note

1   A comprehensive review of the psychoanalytic literature centred on the mother–daughter relationship can be found in *Adult Mother– Daughter Relationships: A Review of the Theoretical and Research Literature* (Shrier *et al.* 2004).

References

Abarbanel, J. (1983) 'The revival of the sibling experience during the mother's second pregnancy'. *Psychoanal. St. Child*, 38: 353–379.

Ainslie, R. C. and Solyom, A. E. (1986) 'The replacement of the fantasied oedipal child: a disruptive effect of sibling loss on the mother–infant relationship'. *Psychoanal. Psychol.*, 3: 257–268.

Appelbaum, A. H. (1988) 'Psychoanalysis during pregnancy: the effect of sibling constellation'. *Psychoanal. Inq.*, 8: 177–195.

Balsam, R. H. (2000) 'The mother within the mother'. *Psychoanal. Q.*, 69: 465–492.

Balsam, R. H. (2003) 'The vanished pregnant body in psychoanalytic female developmental theory'. *J. Amer. Psychoanal. Assn.*, 51: 1153–1179.

Balsam, R. H. (2010) *Women's Bodies in Psychoanalysis*. London and New York: Routledge.

Benedek, T. (1950) 'Climacterium: a developmental phase'. *Psychoanal. Q.*, 19: 1–27.

Benedek, T. (1959) 'Parenthood as a developmental phase – A contribution to the libido theory'. *J. Amer. Psychoanal. Assn.*, 7: 389–417.

Benedek, T. (1960) 'The organization of the reproductive drive'. *Int. J. Psycho-Anal.*, 41: 1–15.

Benedek, T., Ham, G. C., Robbins, F. P. and Rubenstein, B. B. (1953) 'Some emotional factors in infertility'. *Psychosom. Med.*, 15: 485–498.

Birksted-Breen, D. (1974) *The Birth of a First Child*. London: Tavistock Publications.

Birksted-Breen, D. (1981) *Talking with Mothers*. London: Jill Norman.

Blum, H. P. (1978) 'Reconstruction in a case of postpartum depression'. *Psychoanal. St. Child*, 33: 335–362.

Bonaparte, M. (1935) 'Passivity, masochism and femininity'. *Int. J. Psycho-Anal.*, 16: 325–333.

Braunschweig, D. and Fain, M. (1975), *La Nuit, le Jour*. Paris: PUF.

Chodorow, N. (1978) *The Reproduction of Mothering: Psychoanalysis and the Sociology of Gender*. Berkeley and Los Angeles: University of California Press.

Coles, P. (2003) *The Importance of Sibling Relationships in Psychoanalysis*. London: Karnac.

Cournut-Janin, M. (1998) 'The feminine and femininity', in D. Birksted-Breen, S. Flanders and A. Gibeault (eds) *Reading French Psychoanalysis*. London and New York: Routledge, 2010.

Denis, P. (1982) 'Homosexualité primaire, base de contradiction'. *Revue française de psychanalyse*, 46, 1, XLVI: 35–42. English translation 'Primary homosexuality, a foundation of contradictions', in D. Birksted-Breen, S. Flanders and A. Gibeault (eds) *Reading French Psychoanalysis*. London and New York: Routledge, 2010.

Deutsch, H. (1945) *The Psychology of Women*. New York: Grune and Stratton.

Dinnerstein, D. (1976) *The Mermaid and the Minotaur: Sexual Arrangements and Human Malaise*. New York: Harper Colophon Books.

Feder, L. (1980) 'Preconceptive ambivalence and external reality'. *Int. J. Psycho-Anal.*, 61: 161–178.

Fraiberg, S. (1987) 'The adolescent mother and her infant', in L. Fraiberg (ed.) *Selected Writings of Selma Fraiberg*. Columbus, OH: Ohio State University Press.

Freud, S. (1909) 'Analysis of a phobia in a five-year-old boy'. *S.E.* 10: 3–149.

Freud, S. (1933) 'New introductory lectures on psycho-analysis'. *S.E.* 22: 1–182.

Furman, E. (1982) 'Mothers have to be there to be left'. *Psychoanal. St. Child*, 37: 15–28.

Hoffman, L. (2003) 'Mothers' ambivalence with their babies and toddlers'. *J. Amer. Psychoanal. Assn.*, 51: 1219–1240.

Kestemberg, E. (1984) ' "Astrid" ou homosexualité, identité, adolescence. Quelques propositions hypothétiques'. *Cahiers du Centre de Psychanalyse et de Psychothérapie*, 8: 10. Also in *Adolescence a vif*. Paris: Presses Universitaires de France, 1999.

Kestenberg, J. S. (1956) 'On the development of maternal feelings in early childhood – observations and reflections'. *Psychoanal. St. Child*, 11: 257–291.

Klein, M. (1928) 'Early stages of the oedipus conflict'. *Int. J. Psycho-Anal.*, 9. Also in *Love, Guilt and Reparation*. London: Hogarth Press.

Klyman, C. M. (1986) 'Pregnancy as a reaction to early childhood sibling loss'. *J. Amer. Acad. Psychoanal.*, 14: 323–335.

Laplanche, J. (1997) 'The theory of seduction and the problem of the other'. *Int. J. Psycho-Anal.*, 78: 653–666.

Lewin, V. and Sharp, B. (2009) *Siblings in Development*. London: Karnac.

Mitchell, J. (2003) *Siblings*. New York: Polity Press.

Parker, R. (1995) *Torn in Two: The Experience of Maternal Ambivalence*. London: Virago Press.

Pines, D. (1982) 'The relevance of early psychic development to pregnancy and abortion'. *Int. J. Psycho-Anal.*, 63: 311–319. Also in *A Woman's Unconscious Use of Her Body*. London: Virago Press, 1993.

Raphael-Leff, J. (1991) *Psychological Processes of Childbearing*. London: Chapman and Hall.

Raphael-Leff, J. (2001) *Pregnancy – The Inside Story*. London: Karnac.

Raphael-Leff, J. (2003) *Parent–Infant Psychodynamics – Wild Things, Mirrors and Ghosts*. London: Whurr.

Shrier, D. K., Tompsett, M. and Shrier, L. A. (2004) 'Adult mother–daughter relationships: a review of the theoretical and research literature'. *J. Amer. Acad. Psychoanal.*, 32: 91–115.

Stern, D. (1995) *The Motherhood Constellation*. New York: Basic Books.

Winnicott, D. W. (1949) 'Hate in the counter-transference'. *Int. J. Psycho-Anal.*, 30: 69–74.

Winnicott, D. W. (1958) 'Primary maternal preoccupation', in D. W. Winnicott *Collected Papers: Through Paediatrics to Psycho-analysis*. London: Tavistock.

Winnicott, D. W. (1960) 'The theory of the parent–infant relationship'. *Int. J. Psycho-Anal.* 41: 585–595.

Primary maternal preoccupation

D. W. Winnicott

This contribution is stimulated by the discussion published in the *Psychoanalytic Study of the Child*, Volume IX, under the heading: 'Problems of Infantile Neurosis'. The various contributions from Miss Freud in this discussion add up to an important statement of present-day psycho-analytic theory as it relates to the very early stages of infantile life, and of the establishment of personality.

I wish to develop the theme of the very early infant–mother relationship, a theme that is of maximal importance at the beginning, and that only gradually takes second place to that of the infant as an independent being.

It is necessary for me first to support what Miss Freud says under the heading 'Current Misconceptions'. 'Disappointments and frustrations are inseparable from the mother–child relationship . . . To put the blame for the infantile neurosis on the mother's shortcomings in the oral phase is no more than a facile and misleading generalization. Analysis has to probe further and deeper in its search for the causation of neurosis.' In these words Miss Freud expresses a view held by psycho-analysts generally.

In spite of this we may gain much by taking the mother's position into account. There is such a thing as an environment that is not good enough, and which distorts infant development, just as there can be a good enough environment, one that enables the infant to reach, at each stage, the appropriate innate satisfactions and anxieties and conflicts.

Miss Freud has reminded us that we may think of pregenital patterning in terms of two people joined to achieve what for brevity's sake one might call 'homeostatic equilibrium' (Mahler, 1954). The same thing is referred to under the term 'symbiotic relationship'. It is often stated that the mother of an infant becomes biologically conditioned for her job of special orientation to the needs of her child. In more ordinary language there is found to be an identification – conscious but also deeply unconscious – which the mother makes with her infant.

I think that these various concepts need joining together and the study of the mother needs to be rescued from the purely biological. The term symbiosis takes us no further than to compare the relationship of the mother and the infant with other examples in animal and plant life – physical interdependence. The words homeostatic equilibrium again avoid some of the fine points which appear before our eyes if we look at this relationship with the care it deserves.

We are concerned with the very great *psychological* differences between, on the one hand, the mother's identification with the infant and, on the other, the infant's dependence on the mother; the latter does not involve identification, identification being a complex state of affairs inapplicable to the early stages of infancy.

Miss Freud shows that we have gone far beyond that awkward stage in psycho-analytic theory in which we spoke as if life started for the infant with the oral instinctual experience. We are now engaged in the study of early development and of the early self which, if development has gone far enough, can be strengthened instead of disrupted by id experiences.

Miss Freud says, developing the theme of Freud's term 'anaclitic': 'the relationship to the mother, although the first to another human being, is not the infant's first relationship to the environment. What precedes it is an earlier phase in which not the object world but the body needs and their satisfaction or frustration play the decisive part.'

Incidentally I feel that the introduction of the word 'need' instead of 'desire' has been very important in our theorizing, but I wish Miss Freud had not used the words 'satisfaction' and 'frustration' here; a need is either met or not met, and the effect is not the same as that of satisfaction and frustration of id impulse.

I can bring Greenacre's reference (1954) to what she names the 'lulling' type of rhythmic pleasures. Here we find an example of need that is met or not met, but it would be a distortion to say that the infant who is not lulled reacts as to a frustration. Certainly there is not anger so much as some kind of distortion of development at an early phase.

Be that as it may, a further study of the function of the mother *at the earliest phase* seems to me to be overdue, and I wish to gather together the various hints and put forward a proposition for discussion.

Maternal preoccupation

It is my thesis that in the earliest phase we are dealing with a very special state of the mother, a psychological condition which deserves a name, such as *Primary Maternal Preoccupation*. I suggest that sufficient tribute has not yet been paid in our literature, or perhaps anywhere, to a very special psychiatric condition of the mother, of which I would say the following things:

> It gradually develops and becomes a state of heightened sensitivity during, and especially towards the end of, the pregnancy.
>
> It lasts for a few weeks after the birth of the child.
>
> It is not easily remembered by mothers once they have recovered from it.
>
> I would go further and say that the memory mothers have of this state tends to become repressed.

This organized state (that would be an illness were it not for the fact of the pregnancy) could be compared with a withdrawn state, or a dissociated state, or a fugue, or even with a disturbance at a deeper level such as a schizoid episode in which some aspect of the personality takes over temporarily. I would like to find a good name for this condition and to put it forward as something to be taken into account in all references to the earliest phase of infant life. I do not believe that it is possible to understand the functioning of the mother at the very beginning of the infant's life without seeing that she must be able to reach this state of heightened sensitivity, almost an illness, and to recover from it. (I bring in the word 'illness' because a woman must be healthy in order both to develop this state and to recover from it as the infant releases her. If the infant should die, the mother's state suddenly shows up as illness. The mother takes this risk.)

I have implied this in the term 'devoted' in the words 'ordinary devoted mother' (Winnicott, 1949). There are certainly many women who are good mothers in every other way and who are capable of a rich and fruitful life but who are not able to achieve this 'normal illness' which enables them to adapt delicately and sensitively to the infant's needs at the very beginning; or they achieve it with one child but not with another. Such women are not able to become preoccupied with their own infant to the exclusion of other interests, in the way that is normal and temporary. It may be supposed that there is a 'flight to sanity' in some of these people. Some of them certainly have very big alternative concerns which they do not readily abandon or they may not be able to allow this abandonment until they have had their first babies. When a woman has a strong male identification she finds this part of her mothering function most difficult to achieve, and repressed penis envy leaves but little room for primary maternal preoccupation.

In practice the result is that such women, having produced a child, but having missed the boat at the earliest stage, are faced with the task of making up for what has been missed. They have a long period in which they must closely adapt to their growing child's needs, and it is not certain that they can succeed in mending the early distortion. Instead of taking for granted the good effect of an early and temporary preoccupation they are caught up in the child's need for therapy, that is to say, for a prolonged period of adaptation to need, or spoiling. They do therapy instead of being parents.

The same phenomenon is referred to by Kanner (1943), Loretta Bender (1947) and others who have attempted to describe the type of mother who is liable to produce an 'autistic child' (Creak, 1951; Mahler, 1954).

It is possible to make a comparison here between the mother's task in making up for her past incapacity and that of society attempting (sometimes successfully) to bring round a deprived child from an antisocial state towards a social identification. This work of the mother (or of society) proves a great strain because it does not come naturally. The task in hand properly belongs to an earlier date, in this case to the time when the infant was only beginning to exist as an individual.

If this thesis of the normal mother's special state and her recovery from it be acceptable, then we can examine more closely the infant's corresponding state.

The infant has

A constitution.
Innate developmental tendencies ('conflict-free area in ego').
Motility and sensitivity.
Instincts, themselves involved in the developmental tendency,
    with changing zone-dominance.

The mother who develops this state that I have called 'primary maternal preoccupation' provides a setting for the infant's constitution to begin to make itself evident, for the developmental tendencies to start to unfold, and for the infant to experience spontaneous movement and become the owner of the sensations that are appropriate to this early phase of life. The instinctual life need not be referred to here because what I am discussing begins before the establishment of instinct patterns.

I have tried to describe this in my own language, saying that if the mother provides a good enough adaptation to need, the infant's own line of life is disturbed very little by reactions to impingement. (Naturally, it is the *reactions* to impingement that count, not the impingements themselves.) Maternal failures produce phases of reaction to impingement and these reactions interrupt the 'going on being' of the infant. An excess of this reacting produces not frustration but a *threat of annihilation*. This in my view is a very real primitive anxiety, long antedating any anxiety that includes the word death in its description.

In other words, the basis for ego establishment is the sufficiency of 'going on being', uncut by reactions to impingement. A sufficiency of 'going on being' is only possible at the beginning if the mother is in this state that (I suggest) is a very real thing when the healthy mother is near the end of her pregnancy, and over a period of a few weeks following the baby's birth.

Only if a mother is sensitized in the way I am describing can she feel herself into her infant's place, and so meet the infant's needs. These are at first body-needs, and they gradually becomes ego-needs as a psychology emerges out of the imaginative elaboration of physical experience.

There comes into existence an ego-relatedness between mother and baby, from which the mother recovers, and out of which the infant may eventually build the idea of a person in the mother. From this angle the recognition of the mother as a person comes in a positive way, normally, and not out of the experience of the mother as the symbol of frustration. The mother's failure to adapt in the earliest phase does not produce anything but an annihilation of the infant's self.

What the mother does well is not in any way apprehended by the infant at this stage. This is a fact according to my thesis. Her failures are not felt as maternal failures, but they act as threats to personal self-existence.

In the language of these considerations, the early building up of the ego is therefore silent. The first ego organization comes from the experience of threats of annihilation and from which, repeatedly, there is *recovery*. Out of such experiences confidence in recovery begins to be something which leads to an ego and to an ego capacity for coping with frustration.

It will, I hope, be felt that this thesis contributes to the subject of the infant's recognition of the mother as a frustrating mother. This is true later on but not at this very early stage. At the beginning the failing mother is not apprehended as such. Indeed a recognition of absolute dependence on the mother and of her capacity for primary maternal preoccupation, or whatever it is called, is something which belongs to *extreme sophistication*, and to a stage not always reached by adults. The general failure of recognition of absolute dependence at the start contributes to the fear of WOMAN that is the lot of both men and women (Winnicott, 1950, 1957a).

We can now say why we think the baby's mother is the most suitable person for the care of that baby; it is she who can reach this special state of primary maternal preoccupation without being ill. But an adoptive mother, or any woman who can be ill in the sense of 'primary maternal preoccupation', may be in a position to adapt well enough, on account of having some capacity for identification with the baby.

According to this thesis a good enough environmental provision in the earliest phase enables the infant to begin to exist, to have experience, to build a personal ego, to ride instincts, and to meet with all the difficulties inherent in life. All this feels real to the infant who becomes able to have a self that can eventually even afford to sacrifice spontaneity, even to die.

On the other hand, without the initial good-enough environmental provision, this self that can afford to die never develops. The feeling of real is absent and if there is not too much chaos the ultimate feeling is of futility. The inherent difficulties of life cannot be reached, let alone the satisfactions. If there is not chaos, there appears a false self that hides the true self, that complies with demands, that reacts to stimuli, that rids itself of instinctual experiences by having them, but that is only playing for time.

It will be seen that, by this thesis, constitutional factors are more likely to show up in the normal, where the environment in the first phase has been adaptive. By contrast, when there has been failure at this first phase, the infant is caught up in primitive defence mechanisms (false self, etc.) which belong to the threat of annihilation, and constitutional elements tend to become over-ridden (unless physically manifest).

It is necessary here to leave undeveloped the theme of the infant's introjection of illness patterns of the mother, though this subject is of great importance in consideration of the environmental factor in the next stages, after the first stage of absolute dependence.

In reconstructing the early development of an infant there is no point at all in talking of instincts, except on a basis of ego development.

There is a watershed:

Ego maturity – instinctual experiences strengthen ego.
Ego immaturity – instinctual experiences disrupt ego.

Ego here implies a summation of experience. The individual self starts a summation of resting experience, spontaneous motility, and sensation, return from activity to rest, and the gradual establishment of a capacity to wait for recovery from annihilations; annihilations that result from reactions to environmental impingement. For this reason the individual needs to start in the specialized environment to which I have here referred under the heading: Primary Maternal Preoccupation.

References

Bender, L. (1947) 'Childhood schizophrenia'. *Am. J. Orthopsychiat.*, XVII.

Creak, M. (1951) 'Psychoses in childhood'. *J. Ment. Sci.*, XCVII.

Freud, A. (1954) 'Problems of infantile neurosis – a discussion'. *Psychoanal. St. Child*, 9: 16–71.

Greenacre, P. (1954) 'Problems of infantile neurosis – a discussion'. *Psychoanal. St. Child*, 9: 16–71.

Kanner, L. (1943) 'Autistic disturbances of affective contact'. *The Nervous Child II.*

Mahler, M. S. (1954) 'Problems of infantile neurosis – a discussion'. *Psychoanal. St. Child*, 9: 16–71.

Winnicott, D. W. (1949) 'The ordinary devoted mother and her baby', in *The Child and the Family*. London: Tavistock, 1957, pp. 3–78.

Winnicott, D. W. (1950) 'Some thoughts on the meaning of the word democracy'. *Human Relations*. III, No. 2, June 1950.

Winnicott, D. W. (1957a) *The Child and the Family*. London: Tavistock Publications; New York: Basic Books (p. 141).

2

Peaceful islands and dangerous jungles

Pregnancy: opportunity or impediment. A psychoanalyst's view

Dana Birksted-Breen

One comes across two diametrically opposed opinions. One asserts categorically that pregnancy is a time when it is not possible to work psychoanalytically with a woman, and the other asserts equally assuredly that pregnancy is a time of particular availability for psychoanalytic work. The proponents of the former view tend not to write papers about the subject but it comes up in informal conversation about psychoanalytic patients. Goldberger (1991) even notes that she has heard the opinion that analysis should be interrupted during a patient's pregnancy (p. 208). She, herself, however writes that 'pregnancy is not a contradiction for analysis but, on the contrary, can facilitate analytic progress' (1991: 207).

It is those who believe that pregnancy is a helpful time for psychoanalytic work, who write papers on the subject (for instance, Kestenberg 1976; Lester and Notman 1986; Pines 1990; Ablon 1994; Raphael-Leff 2000, 2001), usually because they have a special interest in the subject but they do not necessarily focus on transference issues. So, for instance, reviewing the work of Lester and Notman (1986) on pregnancy, Goldberger notes that 'unfortunately, they did not specifically mention whether they thought the pregnancies interfered with or enhanced the analytic work'. The great paucity of papers on the subject of psychoanalysis during pregnancy is in itself noteworthy, considering that it happens not infrequently and often poses technical problems in terms of practical obstacles after the birth of the baby.

The contradiction between the opinions is intriguing and my attempt to see what this might mean will be the guiding thread of the chapter. I will argue that pregnancy is a time of increased anxiety offering the possibility of a reorganizing of defences and internal object relationships but that whether this takes place will depend on the individual woman and the analytic pair, and that it is the change in cathexes and how it affects the analytic pair which will determine this.

One of the characteristics of pregnancy is its very delimited time span; it has a beginning, if a bit nebulous, but especially a defined end. And this end is spectacular both in the event which marks the finale and also insofar as its end marks the start of a whole new life – a new life in the form of a baby and a new life for the woman, especially if it is a first pregnancy. Pregnancy is a time for reassessment of the past and for thoughts about the future, a time for thinking about one's place in the natural cycle of life and death.

The very defined time span with its inevitability can feel entrapping to some women. Pregnancy proceeds without respite. There is no going back and no slowing down. The inevitable progression towards childbirth can bring feelings of helplessness, claustrophobia and loss of control. Dreams of wild animals (Faraday 1972) suggest fears that uncontrollable and untamed primitive instincts are taking over. A woman has to accept powerful bodily processes and be able to give in to them. Anxiety about loss of control may contribute to the frequent problems in childbirth itself and preparation classes aim to make her feel more in control of the childbirth.

The inevitable progression towards birth is also a reminder of the inevitable progression towards death, and of time as a 'fact of life' (Money-Kyrle 1968) which cannot be avoided. For those women who want the pregnancy state more than they want a baby (Pines 1993), it is also an inevitable progression towards loss, and this will contribute to a difficult postpartum for them. For some women the decision to get pregnant is made in order to gain reassurance that they have an intact and fertile body and there is no idea of a real baby. Changes to the body can be disturbing when the body had been the main seat of preoccupation.

Anxieties become concretized around practical preparations: getting the baby's room ready, moving to a more suitable home, sorting out baby care arrangements, all representing a concern for a psychological reorganization.

> Belinda, an artist in her late twenties, had a number of very preoccupying worries when she was pregnant with her first child: she feared a miscarriage, an ectopic pregnancy or a stillbirth; she imagined the baby 'slipping out' of her womb. This not only directly connected with her own mother having had a miscarriage when she was two and a stillbirth before her birth but also reflected a feeling that she too had 'slipped' from her mother's mind much of the time and had been 'ectopic', not properly implanted there. She often described her mother's way of dealing with the stillbirth and the miscarriage by throwing herself into her career while leaving Belinda and her sister to their own devices, unsupervised, so that they repeatedly had fairly serious accidents. What the real life mother was like is not so much the issue, what mattered was that in the course of our work, it became apparent that her 'internal' mother was one who wanted to abort or kill her children. This unconscious belief generated the other unconscious belief that she herself could murder her children; this was fuelled by the unconscious belief that she was responsible for the death of the stillborn baby whose place she came to occupy (her name was the same as the one given to the stillborn baby). This lead to constant panic and compulsive protective actions. The conscious derivatives of all this were her fear that she could not hold her baby properly in her womb and keep her baby safely there until he or she was ready to be born.
>
> Belinda also panicked about getting the baby out. A dream about cutting open a baby's head lead to exploring her hatred of babies and the memory of how, as a child, she used to attack her favourite teddy bear with scissors. This in turn lead to an understanding of an unconscious idea that the birth canal would be like scissors which would attack the baby. Becoming conscious of this relieved her anxiety and Belinda was able to have an easy and straightforward childbirth.

Ambivalence around love and hate are central to all relationships and how this is negotiated and the balance between the two will affect the course of pregnancy and the relationship to the child. The fears common to pregnancy and to the upbringing of a child centre around this basic conflict, and as with all feelings, these will be less troublesome and lead to less dangerous consequences when they can be acknowledged. This is where the psychoanalyst can help, but there is also a great reluctance on the part of the psychoanalyst to put the negative thoughts about the baby and an image of a murderous mother into words, such is the power of magical thinking at this time. The fear that words and deeds are equivalent can besiege the psychoanalyst as well as the patient, when both get drawn by primitive modes of thinking easily elicited by this situation which evokes early life and fragility, and this can lead to a collusion of silence; the phantasy is that the analyst is the dangerous murderous mother, envious or simply not sufficiently containing. If this predominates over an experience of an analyst as a containing mother, this may lead to withdrawal and the inaccessibility to psychoanalysis at this time referred to earlier. Marianne Leuzinger-Bohleber (in Chapter 6) speaks of the taboo in regard to female destructiveness in which intense wounds and humiliations culminate in boundless despair, rage, hate and revenge – extending even to the killing of one's own children.

Unconscious projections of such split-off, taboo impulses of female destructiveness in psychoanalyses can give rise to difficult and often almost unbearable countertransference reactions in us analysts, 'making it hard for us accurately to perceive and recognise this dimension of the "dark continent" of femininity in our female analysands' (p. 170). In her work with women suffering from psychogenic sterility she refers to the Medea myth as told by Euripides in which Medea murdered her children. She describes how the analysis of these women's fear of murdering their infant has been a major factor in enabling her patients to get pregnant. The sterility had been a protection from their own unconscious destructive impulses which were aroused in an intimate relationship and were in danger of being directed at the offspring of this relationship in a wish for revenge. Without psychological help, in fact, it can happen that women who have become pregnant following physical infertility treatment request a termination once they fall pregnant (Christie and Pawson 1985).

Leuzinger-Bohleber further suggests that a Medea complex may be an ubiquitous unconscious fantasy of femininity, because it is based on infantile sexual fantasies in which the female body is experienced as a source of uncontrollable libidinal and aggressive impulses, with oral and anal destructive features. She concludes that 'a reflexive dialogue with *the shadow side of one's maternality* appears to be one of the prerequisites for an appropriate capacity for mothering (including the holding function, containing etc.), and for deriving mature narcissistic and libidinal satisfaction from it' (p. 171, italics mine).

The universal experience of being excluded from one's own mother's mind, which is linked in particular to the Oedipal triangular situation of exclusion from the parental relationship, also threatens the relationship of the new mother to herself and to her baby. How a woman is able to deal with the inevitable coexistence of feelings of love and hate aroused at this time, and the balance between these, will determine much of the course of the pregnancy and after.[1] These feelings contribute to the well-known symptoms of pregnancy such as cravings, disgust, vomiting, etc. For the psychoanalyst whose patient is becoming a mother and becomes preoccupied with herself and her body, splitting the transference between the analyst and the unborn baby, it can also be a testing time in which the analyst can feel excluded, with the danger of either enacting some rivalrous feelings or, on the contrary, becoming over-solicitous.

Inner space and pregnancy

Spatial references abound in pregnancy and characterize this time when the balance switches from outside 'people' to inside 'person', the baby but also herself, and the two are not always distinct. This is relevant to the question of availability or unavailability to the psychoanalyst, that is, how narcissistically turned inwards on herself is the pregnant woman.

In dreams, spatial references concern the woman's own bodily changes and the fact that what is inside takes on new significance, but also are used to express the configuration of her feelings. Inside and outside take on importance as two delineated spaces each taking on specific meaning. The phobias of certain foods, for instance, which have to be kept *outside* the body, the craving for other foods which have to be put *inside* the body, express the geometry of the spaces in which good and bad are carefully delineated and kept apart.

In fact each woman's experience could be depicted in terms of how she conceives of herself in terms of 'inside' and 'outside' and the sort of boundary which separates the two. For instance, does she think of herself and the baby as both 'inside' and needing to be kept safe from a dangerous outside world? Or is the baby the intruder and invader getting inside her as a dangerous representative of the outside world? Does the baby, from belonging to the outside world become a part of her, or on the contrary from being part of her separates out

71

as if by parthenogenesis? Is the baby good and herself bad or is she good and the baby bad? Or maybe she and the baby are good and the outside world bad, or vice versa. The question also arises as to the nature of the boundary between what is conceived of as *outside* and what is conceived of as *inside*.

Is the boundary like a fortress behind which the woman protects herself – with her baby, or against her baby? Or is the boundary more like a porous surface or like a curtain that is easily opened or shut? The various permutations and the nature of the boundary will obviously depend on a woman's own history, the meaning she attributes to this particular baby, and her usual way of dealing with conflict, anxiety and her own unconscious thoughts.

One can follow changes in the personal topography in the dreams of pregnancy. I took the title of this chapter from one of Belinda's dreams. She dreamt of a *'peaceful island inside the dangerous jungle; the natives had taken the white children and put them safely in underground trenches'*. This woman, who had not planned her pregnancy, now wanted to keep her womb, the island of the dream, as a very safe place, and the baby under the protection of the 'natural', 'primitive' part of herself (represented by the natives), and away from the intellectual, educated part of herself that wanted to have a mind and not a body and a baby, that part of her that could think of having an abortion, and combined with the teeth and poison of the jungle. She believed that her mother, who lived in a country which has a jungle, thought she wasn't mature enough to have a baby and that she should prioritize her studies. Her mother's own history of babies who don't survive added to this picture that the baby was in danger and needed protection.

If I have given this image as the title of my chapter, it is also as a reference to the question I addressed as my starting point, whether women become more or less available for psychoanalytic help during pregnancy. *What is the boundary, how rigid is it, what is the degree of 'paranoia', the fear of attack and the fear of being envied which restricts contact and makes a woman withdraw, what is the degree of fear of her own unconscious thoughts, of her own feelings? And where is the psychoanalyst placed in this topography? Is the psychoanalyst felt to be the persecutor or on the contrary the ally against internal attack?*

The peaceful island in the dangerous jungle I see as the retreat away from the intensity of feelings that threaten to take over, unpredictably, uncontrollably, savagely. The tendency to withdraw which is marked in pregnancy is a withdrawal from that jungle into safety, and when the analyst and her interpretations are associated with the teeth and poison of the jungle, her work can seem impossible. In that case, the peaceful island is one where a barrier has been erected for protection, a place away from hatred and envy. Particularly feared by the woman is the envy of others of her pregnant state. Especially so when she feels herself in a state of self-satisfaction, like the cat who has eaten the cream; she is the complete, replete satisfied mother with her precious possession deep inside her. There is also the envy of the baby enveloped and constantly nourished, sometimes her own envy. This will be coloured by how she has dealt with her envy of her own mother and how she dealt with her mother's subsequent pregnancies. Unconscious envy always causes more trouble than conscious envy, which is how the psychoanalyst can help. Irrespective of what the actual woman's own mother is like, an envious internal mother can cause anxieties and even risk provoking miscarriage.

The peaceful island may also be a place of narcissistic withdrawal. The woman is faced during pregnancy with an increased neediness due to a regressive identification with the baby inside her. Women will react differently depending on their own habitual psychic make-up. Some women easily welcome help from the psychoanalyst while others are threatened by their increased dependency. The peaceful island as narcissistic withdrawal is a reference to the woman who deals with the threat of neediness by withdrawing into herself and feeling she needs no one, or that the outside world, and the analyst's interpretations will harm, or at least be useless. In this case the analytic work may seem to stagnate and it is this sort of situation which leads to the view that it is not possible to work psychoanalytically with pregnant women.

This state of mind is different from the often observed self-absorption which accompanies pregnancy when the inside world and the inside of the body become the focus of interest; this is reflected in references in dreams to gardens inside houses, inner courtyards, cloisters. This self-absorption I understand as reflecting the shift of attention which is part of the normal work of pregnancy and often includes rethinking the past, and getting interested in ancestry and lineage, preparing for a new person. This state of self-absorption signals an increased relationship to the internal mother, a sort of internal conversation with her rather than an escape from her, and this can be fruitful to the analysis.

This distinction connects with the distinction I make between two attitudes to pregnancy which I call the 'hurdle approach' and the developmental approach (Breen 1975) — attitudes found in women but also attitudes found in the literature on pregnancy. The hurdle approach is the widely held belief that pregnancy is like an illness, that a woman will for a time-limited period act and feel odd and that after the birth of the baby she will get back to her old self again. On the contrary, I would argue in line with a developmental approach that the birth of a baby, as any major life event, offers an opportunity for a woman to work through internal conflicts and relationships, to modify her perception of herself and others and integrate this new experience, so that she will *not* be the same after the birth of the baby as before. Psychic life proceeds by resignification, and certain key times in a person's life — adolescence, early adulthood, parenthood, mid-life — are such times which require major reconfigurations. Some moments in the life of a person necessitate change if they are to be lived and not just survived. With a first pregnancy, the internal object relationships need modification, in particular the relationship of identification and differentiation from the woman's own mother. Some women express this concretely by getting very preoccupied with transforming the spatial organization of their house, which stands for the internal map where rooms, and roles get rearranged. In fact I would say 'the house' representing a woman's inner space and internal world cannot be 'ready' until after the birth as the early months after the birth are the time of greatest change.

Some women feel ill during pregnancy and wish for a return to normality along the hurdle model — this illness represents the tremendous upheaval, physical but also psychological, which is taking place. These women want to simply evacuate the uncomfortable, confusing feelings, to vomit it out, mentally or physically. They are unable to integrate the experience and to change with it, but they are in danger of running into serious difficulties in pregnancy and childbirth, and more especially postnatally.

Idealization and the 'work of worrying'

The birth of a baby *does* require change and the acceptance of time passing. Paradoxically, the very delimited and short time span of pregnancy brings up a new perception of the span of life. It brings a sense of the generations, of birth and death, of the new mother's place in the life cycle. Birth and death are closely connected in the unconscious. Sometimes it is the terminal illness of a parent which unconsciously leads to a conception, a birth replacing a death (almost like the idea of reincarnation in some cultures). This new perspective, and I am of course in particular referring to a first pregnancy, reorganizes a woman's perceptions of herself and her past and her relationship to significant others. This is the work which needs to be done, *has* to be done. When it can't be done, trouble lies ahead.

A woman with a fragile sense of her own identity feels very threatened by this because change for her threatens the continuity of self. Such a woman desperately holds on to the notion of pregnancy as illness from which, like flu, she feels she can eventually recover and be the same person as before. These are the women who are more at risk.

> Belinda had a fragile sense of her own identity and because of this she erected a strong boundary which often made it difficult to make contact with her. She wanted to be the perfect mother, and only rarely was it possible to discuss the full range of her feelings and fantasies in relation to the pregnancy and the baby. She was angry with her own mother for the inadequate care she felt she had received, the 'ectopic' place I described earlier, and wanted to be unlike her, to be perfect. She wanted to be completely ready for the birth of her baby, displaced her anxieties on to the house, and insisted that she and her husband move house to a different part of town during her pregnancy. In fact, studies record moving house as one of the stress factors in pregnancy.

A certain amount of anxiety is appropriate before such a major life event and life change. Worrying is an expression of psychic work, of the work of preparation and those women who show *no signs at all* of anxiety can also be at risk. In research I carried out with 60 first-time mothers (Breen 1975) an important finding was that the women who later showed a positive adjustment to the birth of their child were able to express more anxieties in late pregnancy. To be more precise, the difficulties occurred at the two extremes, those who expressed no anxiety and those who were overwhelmed with anxiety.

The fact that it is important to be able to experience and express some anxiety gives an indication of the complex processes at work, in particular of the importance of psychological preparation – what is called 'working through' anxiety and conflicts which will enable a woman to cope with the upheaval of childbirth and the relationship with her new infant. In fact this is true of other potentially traumatic events. A research study in America (Janis *et al.* 1969) with patients who required surgery[2], also found that moderate worry before a surgical operation was linked with a better postoperative adjustment. The patients who did not worry at all beforehand appeared to be much less able to cope with the stresses of surgery than those who had been moderately worried. He found that while the high worry group who also had difficulty adjusting postoperatively had long-term neurotic problems with a chronic sense of vulnerability, the only difference between the patients who did not worry at all and the ones who worried moderately was the amount of information received before the operation. He suggests that if no authoritative warning communications are given and if other circumstances are such that fear is not aroused beforehand, the normal person will lack the motivation to build up effective inner preparation and will thus have relatively low tolerance for stress when the crisis is actually at hand. Janis suggests the concept of the 'work of worrying' to emphasize the value of anticipatory fear. He writes:

> Sometimes an endangered person remains quite unworried and then finds himself unexpectedly confronted with actual danger stimuli. This is evidently what happens to many surgical patients who are given no explicit warning information that induces them to face up to what is in store for them. They anticipate little or no pain or suffering until the severe stresses of the postoperative period are encountered. Then they are unable to reassure themselves and no longer trust the authorities whose protection they had expected. The patient's failure to worry about the operation in advance seems to set the stage for intense feelings of helplessness as well as resentment toward the members of staff who, until the moment of crisis, had been counted on to take good care of them, just as good parents would do.
>
> (Janis *et al.* 1969: 101)

Janis goes on to say that there is failure to carry out the work of worrying when the person is accustomed to suppressing anticipatory fear by means of denial, over-optimism and by avoiding warnings that would stimulate the work of worrying, or when the stressful event is so sudden that it cannot be prepared for, or if adequate prior warning is not given or false reassurances offered.

I think this is very important in the case of childbirth, which often includes medical and surgical procedures. I have been very struck by how some women (and some men too) seem to remain traumatized for years by a childbirth experience. Usually what they mention is the unexpected side of a procedure. It is the fact that it was unexpected which felt traumatic rather than the procedure itself. The birth, a very complex psychosomatic event deeply influenced by how a woman feels about her body, about her instinctual drives, about her ability to deal with separation, is also significant in that it is a time when the woman needs to rely on parental figures in the shape of doctors and nurses and be able to let herself be helped. The unexpected shock arouses anger in the new mother, and she can feel disappointed in the figures around her who are thought to have let her down, harbouring resentment for years towards the partner, for instance, for not being more helpful or for putting her through the trauma. Or she can blame the baby for this. Alternatively she might blame herself and her body for not conforming to the perfect birth.

Both personality and preparation come into play. The lack of anxiety and of the 'work of worrying' in pregnancy is often accompanied by an idealization of the doctors and the hospital who they believe can make everything perfect. The flip side will kick in when there is a problem. These are women who split their views of people into ideal and denigrated, and accordingly expect themselves to be an ideal parent to their newborn child. They do not anticipate any problems and are shocked to be faced with a normal demanding baby and not a picture-book baby, or with a husband who is struggling with his own mixed feelings at this time.

> Belinda's wish to be completely ready for the birth was a sort of 'once and for all' idea. Not so much 'hurdle' as fairy-tale 'happy ever after' notion. This of course does not parallel life and the powerful and often painful and difficult emotions which will be evoked by a newborn baby and for years to come by family life. Belinda felt hugely disappointed in her husband for not coming fast enough when her waters broke and later for not being sufficiently happy about the baby. The wish to be the perfect mother, unlike the mothering she herself received, is a very common experience but one which, if not modified, is a danger signal. The discrepancy between how

77

a woman thinks she ought to be feeling and how she is feeling, in itself, can lead to guilt and depression. In a case I supervised this issue was central for Annabel who had sought ideal states for mind (through such things as religious ecstasy and drug use) throughout her life to get away from psychic pain. This had diminished during her analysis but she was pulled back in that direction during pregnancy, believing that she needed to reach a state of perfection free of all bad feelings.

Throughout her pregnancy Belinda had spoken with much hatred of both her parents and their failings: her father always on business trips abroad and disinterested in her and her sister, her mother only preoccupied with her career. She struggled with her resentment at the demands she thought her analyst made on her, while at the same time the baby had to be protected from any bad thoughts. As she neared the end of her pregnancy and I started hearing her speak more positively of her mother and of her analyst and to talk about a valued great uncle, but also for the first time to be able to voice some anger with the baby for taking her life away and of the associated fear that the baby would be born damaged, I thought to myself: Thank goodness for the nine months of pregnancy, and that possibility of repair of the internal relationships and the relationship to the analyst in a way which could be less split and allow for ambivalence.

In the research project mentioned above (Breen 1975), I found that the women who experienced most difficulties at some point in the childbearing process had a very idealized picture of what they felt a mother should be like. This picture was often the opposite to the bad mothering they believed they had received. After the birth, they felt themselves to be at odds with this ideal but they found it hard to admit directly to imperfection. They got stuck with this negative experience of motherhood – the need for perfection and the shame at not matching up.

On the contrary the women who were able to deal well with the experience of having a baby, sometimes had during pregnancy an equally idealized picture of what they thought a mother should be like. However, they were able to modify their picture of the good mother to a more realistic one after the birth of the baby so that it became possible for them to live up to this picture and feel positively about themselves. In the group of women who experienced difficulties with having a baby, a good mother tended to be described with words like 'loving, patient, unselfish, never losing her temper', whereas in the group of women who coped well, the good mother was described as needing these qualities: 'diligence, hard work, reliability, liking to be at home with children'. In other words in this second group they felt a mother needed more ordinary and practical qualities, as opposed to the other group who were making a judgement of themselves as good or bad, loving or hateful people.

An important point is that there was no difference between the groups when I tested them in the third or fourth month of pregnancy and again at the end of their pregnancy (ten weeks before the due date) and the difference between the two groups appeared only at the third test postnatally so it seems that it was probably only once they were faced with the reality of a baby that some of the mothers could readjust their own ideas about motherhood. These mothers may have hoped to make everything perfect, better than in their own life but this was based on a wishful thought rather than an entrenched split and could be easily modified when faced with the reality of a fragile infant whose needs are not always easily understood and met.

In my view if one can work with the pregnant woman with the negative as well as the positive transference (which means picking up on split off bad and dangerous objects projected into the outside world), one can hope to bring greater integration. If one encourages the split and becomes the purely good mother, there is a risk of leaving her with a bad internal mother, and more chance of a melancholic attack on the self postnatally. Depression is of course frequent after the birth, even when it does not take on pathological proportions.

Pregnancy is a time when a woman feels she ought to be happy and in fact she is having to face a number of losses: loss of her previous life, loss of the baby inside, loss of the self as ideal mother, loss of the baby as ideal baby. With the birth of the actual baby, a woman has to give up the fantasy of what kind of mother she will be and now feels she is being put to the test. Those early weeks are a very trying time and often not helped by the level of anxiety which can be generated not just in the mother herself but in the helpers. It seems that the whole system of professionals gets taken over with the mental state of the newborn infant, enacting the multiple splitting of the paranoid-schizoid world of the infant. The anxiety about the very real fragility of the infant and the terror of death often inhibits the capacity to reflect, and busy anxious activity gets set in motion, by health visitors, doctors, friends and family. This can make the new mother more anxious, she feels easily criticized for what she is doing and loses confidence in herself.

Often breastfeeding, which is imagined to be straightforward but in fact needs an un-anxious environment to enable the two partners to get used to each other, becomes the focus of ambivalence and anxiety. The consequence is that it may get undermined by even those helpers who consciously encourage it, because bottle feeding is so much easier to monitor and measure and thus is reassuring. The psychoanalyst's work at this time involves containing the deep anxieties surrounding these issues of life and death around the real fragility of the infant. If the analyst can contain the anxieties without getting too anxious herself and drawn into knowing what is best, she can help the woman to find her own resources and capacities to mother her baby and gain the confidence to make judgements and find solutions. This is a role some partners are also able to take if they are not trying to be the better mother or else withdraw into hurt exclusion. The latter can be exacerbated by women who think they want help from their husband but are in fact envious of anything he can offer and want to be the only one who can be satisfying to her infant so that in effect the partner is pushed out.[3]

Psychoanalysis and pregnancy

To come back to my original question: why is there a contradiction in how people view the possibility of working psychoanalytically with pregnant women as I described at the beginning of the chapter? The idea that pregnant women are unavailable to psychoanalytic work has to do largely with how women become very preoccupied with themselves and the baby and the transference issues can sometimes seem to them irrelevant or intrusive. They can withdraw into a state of great preoccupation with their body in which anxiety reduces an ability for symbolic thinking. They can become difficult to contact in the way that psychosomatic patients are difficult to contact. This narcissistic withdrawal can be intermittent or quite ingrained. The analyst has to tolerate the feelings this provokes.

The professionals' attitudes vary according to their own issues. Everybody has experienced childbirth as a baby and everybody has had a mother. The pregnant woman may arouse in the analyst profound feelings connected with separation and exclusion from the primal unity, feelings connected with hatred and jealousy of the mother who can have other babies and other preoccupations, envy of the mother who can create and feed a baby and of the baby whose needs are met and satisfied. The analyst's capacity to hold and privately reflect on her own feelings creates a space in the analytic work where the patient can elaborate her fears of those same feelings being present in herself, such as her own envy of the baby who is being cared for, and in other people close to her.

Another aspect of the difficulty is that there is a reluctance by both analyst and patient to tackle the more negative issues at this time, around envy and hatred in the analytic relationship, a reluctance which is there as I suggested earlier in both analyst and patient because of deep-seated primitive magical beliefs that feelings can kill unborn babies. Similar issues are there when it is the psychoanalyst who is pregnant, but this is beyond the scope of this chapter.

Conflicts of love and hate and issues around jealousy in the three-person Oedipal situation are at the fore at the time of pregnancy, but it is in this area that psychoanalytic work can be at its most difficult. In order to help a woman with this, the analyst has to be prepared to explore the more negative feelings in the transference, by which I mean the negative feelings about the analyst who comes to represent the bad mother and the envious mother, alongside the analyst as good mother. The woman wants the bad mother to be located somewhere else, sometimes in her actual mother, or in another female relative or acquaintance, in order to preserve the analyst as wholly good. But in that way she avoids bringing together love and hate.

Interestingly, some of the fears are so deep that it can also be difficult for women analysts not to want to be that good mother who will protect her pregnant patient from danger, and wish to create an idealized situation and new experience for her patient. The magical beliefs that bad thoughts and feelings harm the baby are often shared consciously or unconsciously by analyst and patient. This partly rests on an identification with the mother or with the baby. It may also be a defence against the deeply seated envy of the prenatal state. When the psychoanalyst is a man, the fear of envy may take a meaning in relation to the differences between the sexes, and male psychoanalysts have to work on different sets of feelings of their own.

When this is possible, and when a good birth and healthy baby can reassure a woman of her loving self, that her internal objects are undamaged and that she hasn't been prey to an envious and retaliating mother, it will be a crucial developmental stage in her life. The psychological work which takes place during pregnancy is not necessarily conscious, although it is well known that during pregnancy there is a tendency for women to become more intro- spective as I described above.

Those who point to the increased availability of women during pregnancy are referring to the fact that unconscious phantasies often become conscious or appear with little disguise in dreams (Ablon 1994) and symptoms, and thus offer an opportunity for integration, hence the potential for psychological growth. It is the ready availability of these phantasies, the sense that some repression seems to lift during pregnancy, which brings the view that pregnancy is a good time to work psychoanalytically with women. It also offers the opportunity to work on the fantasies and projections on to the baby of disowned parts of the self and to elaborate mournings so that the child's otherness can be recognized (Manzano *et al.* 1999; Scariati 2009).

The difference of opinion is sometimes a question of how 'working psychoanalytically' is understood. Those who understand this as being primarily situated in the analysis of the transference can find pregnant women unavailable due to the increase in narcissistic defences and the attempt to create a peaceful 'treasure' island from which the analyst is excluded in some cases, while those who are primarily focused on the woman's feelings about her family, her body, the new baby and the fantasies about them, can find this time fruitful.

The whole of pregnancy is characterized by the conflict between destruction and preservation of the baby, not only in the woman herself but also in people around her. The rituals surrounding child- birth and pregnancy such as the practice of giving birth away from home in straightforward cases (Lomas 1966) or of unnecessary medical and surgical procedures, relates to this unconscious conflict. The baby has to be protected at all costs from danger, while some- times exposing mother and baby to more danger through the proce- dures. The danger gets located either in 'Nature', one can't leave it to natural processes, or in the mother herself who is thought to be an obstacle to the birth – she needs to be made unconscious.

The woman's relationship and feelings about her own mother are central in this. I believe that with women at risk this needs to be worked on in the transference to the analyst as mother in order to try and help the woman be less fearful of her hate and to bring together love and hate. There is a reluctance to tackle this during pregnancy but I believe that the analyst will be helpful if she or he is able to take up all the feelings and not collude with the splitting off of the hatred into other figures. Otherwise the danger is that the analyst is idealized and that after the birth when the woman herself finds she is not the ideal mother to her baby, she may experience herself as the split-off bad mother and attack herself. This we see in postnatal depression.

During pregnancy the transference becomes more complex because there is also a transference to the unborn baby, and a three-person situation is created in the consulting room, in which the analyst has to tolerate being the excluded party at times or for lengthy periods. Envious and rivalrous feelings in the analyst have to be tolerated. It can become expressed in terms of the woman's 'work of pregnancy' versus the analyst's 'work of analysis'. If this opposition is created it can in itself become a fruitful line of work, touching as it does on issues of autonomy, separateness, jealousy, exclusion, and envy. Issues of dependency also come to the fore at this time and may make some women more available and others more cut off, depending on how they deal with their needs. It is those women who are not able to accept their needs and become more rejecting of help when their needs are in fact increased, as well as those who deny any worries, who give a sense that analysis is not possible at this time. For all these reasons, the countertransference can be tested at these times and it would be true to say that a development needs to be possible for the patient and analyst pair.

For women in analysis and sometimes too for their analyst, the pull is to want to retreat to a peaceful island, undisturbed by the wild animals of hatred, jealousy and envy, by feelings of hurt, pride, or neglect, or to decide that analysis is not possible. If this can be tolerated and seen as an opportunity to explore the living of a complex transference and countertransference situation around a three-person situation which is literally brought to life in the room, this work can become an opportunity.

Notes

1   In this chapter I am primarily dealing with normal ambivalence and not situations where there is an excess of hatred or cruelty due to early life circumstances or inherited factors.
2   Janis, I. L., Mahl, G. F., Kagan, J. and Holt, R. R. (1969) *Personality: Dynamics, Development and Assessment* (pp. 95–105). New York: Harcourt, Brace and World.

3   This paper is specifically about working psychoanalytically with pregnant women; working with women in the postnatal period and after
would require another paper. The postnatal period brings in the issue of
'primary maternal preoccupation' (Winnicott), and of the place of the
psychoanalyst in the new configuration. It also brings in technical issues.

References

Ablon, S. L. (1994) 'The usefulness of dreams during pregnancy'. *Int.
J. Psycho-Anal.*, 75: 291–299.
Breen, D. (1975) *The Birth of a First Child*. London: Tavistock Publications.
Christie, G. L. and Pawson, M. (1985) 'Some thoughts about psycho–analytical
aspects of infertility'. Paper given at The Institute of Psychoanalysis,
Mansfield House, New Cavendish Street, London, 25 September.
Faraday, A. (1972) *Dream Power*. London: Pan.
Goldberger, M. (1991) 'Pregnancy during analysis – help or hindrance?'
Psychoanal. Q., 60: 207–226.
Janis, L. L., Mahl, G. F., Kagan, J. and Holt, R. R. (1969) *Personality: Dynamics,
Development and Assessment*. New York: Harcourt, Brace and World.
Kestenberg, J. S. (1976) 'Regression and reintegration in pregnancy'. *J. Am.
Psychoanal. Assoc.*, 24: 213–250.
Lester, E. P. and Notman, M. (1986) 'Pregnancy, developmental crisis and object
relations: psychoanalytic considerations'. *Int. J. Psycho-Anal.* 67: 357–366.
Leuzinger-Bohleber, M. (2001) 'The "Medea fantasy": an unconscious
determinant of psychogenic sterility'. *Int. J. Psycho-Anal.*, 82: 323.
Lomas, P. (1966) 'Ritualistic elements in the management of childbirth'.
Br. J. Med. Psychol., 39: 207–213.
Manzano, J., Espasa, F. P. and Zilkha, N. (1999) 'The narcissistic scenarios of
parenthood'. *Int. J. Psycho-Anal.*, 80: 465–476.
Money-Kyrle, R. E. (1968) 'Cognitive development'. *Int. J. Psycho-Anal.*, 49:
691–698.
Pines, D. (1990) 'Pregnancy, miscarriage and abortion. A psychoanalytic
perspective'. *Int. J. Psycho-Anal.* 71: 301–307.
Pines, D. (1993) *A Woman's Unconscious Use of Her Body: A Psychoanalytic
Perspective*. London: Virago Press.
Raphael-Leff, J. (2000) ' "Climbing the walls": puerperal disturbance and
perinatal therapy', in J. Raphael-Leff (ed.) *Spilt Milk: Perinatal Loss and
Breakdown*. London and New York: Routledge.
Raphael-Leff, J. (2001) *The Inside Story*. London: Karnac.
Scariati, G. (2009) 'Alienating identifications and the psychoanalytic process'.
Int. J. Psycho-Anal., 90: 1025–1038.

Shame and maternal ambivalence

Rozsika Parker

'It was only the other day when I read Freud for the first time that I discovered that this violently disturbing conflict between love and hate is a common feeling and called ambivalence,' wrote Virginia Woolf (1941). Her words indicate a crucial feature of ambivalence. There is both the 'violently disturbing' experience itself and the distress engendered by detecting the affect and the owning – or disowning – of the conflict. Woolf's words indicate a measure of relief that she is not alone in suffering ambivalence; it's 'a common feeling' with a name. There is something inimical about ambivalence and to none more so than to mothers.

In my work on maternal ambivalence I have, nevertheless, claimed a creative role for manageable maternal ambivalence, suggesting that it is in the very anguish of maternal ambivalence that fruitfulness for mothers and children can reside (Parker 1995). The crucial issue is how a mother manages the anxiety that ambivalence provokes. Here I shall begin by mapping the specificities of maternal ambivalence and then, following a case history, explore the role of shame in rendering ambivalence unmanageable.

Freud (1915) himself betrays a certain ambivalence towards ambivalence. In 1915 he wrote of the creative potential of ambivalence, observing that 'it is indeed foreign to our intelligence as well as to our feelings to couple love and hate: but Nature, by making use of this pair of opposites, contrives to keep love ever vigilant and fresh, so as to guard against the hate which lurks behind it' (p. 299). Despite this passionate acknowledgement of the inevitability and positive purpose of ambivalence, by 1931 his negative conclusion was that ambivalence was an 'archaic inheritance' to be grown out of: 'Normal adults do undoubtedly succeed in separating those two attitudes from each other, and do not find themselves obliged to hate their love-objects' (p. 235).

Perhaps the best-known text on maternal ambivalence is D. W. Winnicott's (1949) 'Hate in the Countertransference', but he dwells primarily on the developmental importance for the baby of maternal ambivalence and says little on the role of ambivalence in what I have termed maternal development (Parker 1995). He sees maternal hatred as facilitating a baby's capacity for hatred while, where the mother is concerned, he suggests that without the ability to hate appropriately she is constrained to fall back on masochism. I have argued that maternal ambivalence, despite – even because of – the distress it can engender in mothers, may have a transformative and positive impact on mothers and, hence, on the work they have to do.

For Melanie Klein the notion of ambivalence became central in that she considered that the capacity to 'hold' ambivalence signified the infant's shift from paranoid schizoid to depressive position functioning. Because psychoanalysis has, perhaps inevitably, viewed the mother from the child's position, whether current or recollected, concrete or symbolic, maternal ambivalence is primarily read from the point of view of the dangers and advantages to the child. I shall first, very briefly, sketch in the main lines of Klein's theory of infantile development, and then reverse it to gain an understanding of maternal subjectivity and an image of maternal development.

During the second quarter of the first year, the child begins to experience the mother as a whole person, in contrast to the previous state in which the mother is phantasised as split into part objects, specifically into a persecuting and an ideal maternal image. This mode of organising experience separates the endangering and the nurturing aspects of the mother, and of life itself. Splitting safeguards the infant's need to love and its need to hate. With growing integration the infant begins to experience the mother as a whole object who can safely be loved as a whole person. The depressive position involves the gradual recognition of the fact that the loved and hated mother are one and the same. With the dawning of ambivalence the (m)other is seen as a loved person who might be lost and driven away by hatred. Though reparation can be attempted, harm is nevertheless felt to have been done. Therefore with the depressive position comes a sense of responsibility, an awareness of there having been a relational history, a differentiation of self from others, and a capacity for symbol formation, in that concrete modes of understanding are superseded by a 'psychological capacity'. But equally associated with the achievement of the recognition of ambivalence are loss, sorrow and separation.

Following this schematic account of Klein's thinking, I want, as mentioned above, to ask what would happen if we were to reverse the schema, placing the mother as having to negotiate entry into a maternal depressive position. Then we can see that the awareness of her coexisting love and hate for the baby can promote a sense of concern and responsibility towards, and differentiation of self from, the baby. Maternal ambivalence signifies a mother's capacity to know herself and to tolerate traits in herself that she may consider less than admirable – and to hold a more complete image of her baby. Accordingly, idealisation and/or denigration of self, and by extension her baby, diminish. There is a letting go of phantasies of omnipotence and perfectability, and the abandonment of represen-tations of mother and child as a united, mutually fulfilled and fulfilling couple. But the sense of loss and sorrow that accompanies maternal ambivalence is unavoidable. Acknowledging that she hates where she loves is acutely painful for a mother. The parallel is with the loss that Klein's baby undergoes when it gives up the image of the all–perfect, all–loving mother.

According to W. R. Bion, in addition to the conflict between love and hate, there is a crucial clash in the mind between knowl-edge and the desire to understand and the aversion to knowing and understanding. Where motherhood is concerned, I think that the conflict between love and hate can actually spur a mother on to struggle to understand and know her child. In other words, the suffering of ambivalence can promote thought – and the capacity to think about her child is arguably one of the most important aspects of mothering.

Klein emphasises that ambivalence is not a static condition, and this has huge importance in relation to maternal ambivalence. The specific experiences of mothering inevitably produce fluctuation of feeling and varying degrees of splitting of love and hate within ambivalence. Crucially, ambivalence is a dynamic experience of conflict felt by a mother at different times in a child's development and varying between her different children. The polarity of love/hate remains constant but the relationship between the two changes.

Where the developing child is concerned, the changes are brought about by increasing rapprochement of love and hate that Klein (1940) describes as:

> The all-important process of bringing together more closely the various aspects of objects (external, internal; 'good' and 'bad'; loved and hated) and thus for hatred to become actually mitigated by love – which means a decrease in ambivalence.
>
> (p. 349)

Klein's phrase 'a decrease in ambivalence' is somewhat confusing. From a developmental standpoint her theory suggests that ambivalence is an achievement, yet here she seems to be depicting ambivalence as a problem to be decreased. To minimise confusion, where mothers are concerned, I have avoided referring to ambivalence as increased or decreased; instead I speak of manageable and unmanageable ambivalence. The conflicts generated by ambivalence are potentially creative yet there is a continuum from manageable to unmanageable ambivalence. Manageable ambivalence stimulates concern for the child and a greater trust in love. When ambivalence becomes unmanageable, paranoid schizoid processes come into play with associated defences. Employing excessive splitting and projection she experiences herself as the good, persecuted mother, while the baby or child is seen as primarily bad, utterly persecuting and the justifiable object of hatred. For some women, sometimes, the conflict evoked by motherhood becomes unthinkable. The child may be shut out of mind to the extent that she neither feels nor fears being a bad mother, nor experiences emotional concern for the child. Ambivalence denied cannot provide a spur to thought.

Given that ambivalence creates a spectrum of mothering from creative to destructive possibilities, the crucial issue is what maintains the affect at a manageable level and what provokes unmanageable maternal ambivalence. As I commented above, of central importance is how a mother manages the anxiety provoked by ambivalence.

Writing in 1995 I identified unbearable guilt as the major factor rendering ambivalence unmanageable. Since then, clinical experience has alerted me to the significance of shame in magnifying the anxiety and fear mobilised by ambivalence. Clifford Yorke (2008) writes that 'guilt brings material into analysis while shame keeps it out' (p. 37). Despite my belief in the constructive potential of maternal ambivalence I found myself at times over-identifying with my patients' shame and resisting offering interpretations of ambivalence to mothers in my practice, whilst my patients denied its very existence. Shame powerfully institutes concealment. Both my patients and I myself metaphorically hid our faces.

Sylvia and Eve

Sylvia's presenting problem was panic attacks. I saw her for psychoanalytic psychotherapy over six years at frequencies varying between once and three times a week. Names, circumstances and details of the work have been changed to protect confidentiality. Sylvia was in her mid-thirties, married with three children, two girls and a boy. She was one of four siblings. Her parents had separated acrimoniously when she was three years old. She was married to a man whose work kept him away from home for long periods. Her panic attacks both expressed and denied the depth of the pain and shame generated by her relationship with her oldest daughter, Eve. So powerful was her shame that we had been working together for more than a year before she began to acknowledge it. In retrospect her behaviour should have alerted me to how shame-prone she was. The fundamental experience of psychotherapy – encountering the unconscious – entails surprise, incongruity, discrepancy and helplessness that are all profoundly painful for the shame-prone (Mollon 2002). The eye of the other, embodied by the psychotherapist, is assumed to be critical and all-powerful. Sylvia's defence against shame was to be a model patient, always arriving on time, letting me know how much she valued me, and eagerly anticipating my interpretations. All attempts to interpret negative transference were strenuously denied, while in the countertransference I felt there to be an unbridgeable distance between us. A sense of numbness or deadness can be a response to severe shame (Fonagy *et al.* 2002).

Eve, Sylvia's daughter, had just reached puberty. She, so to speak, forced her way into her mother's therapy with wildly disruptive behaviour to the point of running away from home. Initially, Sylvia experienced me as a mocking, humiliating figure as she and Eve ricocheted from one crisis to another. And, indeed, I found it a struggle not to incarnate the shaming other. Working with parents and children, it is all too easy to identify with one and not the other. I found it difficult to maintain a third position, tending to identify either with Sylvia or Eve – which inevitably promoted judgment not understanding.

The objective sense of self, which dominates in shame experience, entails feeling judged and defined from without. Hence the analysis of shame requires great care, tact and patience. The need of the patients to hide behind layers of silence, evasion and omission has to be respected for an extended time (Nathanson 1987). After a prolonged period of stalled analysis, it was Sylvia herself who moved us out of the shame impasse. Unconsciously she began to use me to gain a subjective sense of self in relation to her daughter, diminishing the shame of feeling a failure as a mother and maximising pride (the obverse of shame) by describing the girl's beauty to me. If both of us together could 'observe' Eve, Sylvia's sense of herself as her daughter's object, with the attendant shame, lessened. Moreover, in persuading me of her daughter's beauty Sylvia accessed her love for the child, mitigating hatred. It was a beginning.

Sylvia told me that she had enjoyed pregnancy. It had endowed her with a sense of potency and purpose. While for some women the uncontrollable bodily changes of pregnancy, with associations of, for example, sexuality or of obesity, can be shaming, Sylvia was proud to be pregnant. The affects associated with pride – joy, plenitude, a sense of success – persisted up until the birth of her daughter. Hence she was entirely unprepared for the shame that assailed her when Eve was born. As the midwife placed the baby in her arms she experienced the baby giving her look which seemed to say, 'Is this the best you can do?'

In part, the projection of a harsh, critical voice into the baby was due to Sylvia's difficulty in assuming the new identity of mother. There was a sense in which Sylvia identified herself as Mistress rather than Wife and Mother. Her self-presentation was almost stereotypically glamorous. She had been able to maintain an idealised image of femininity throughout the pregnancy as well as nurturing idealised expectations of motherhood. The reality of mothering rendered her imaginings of motherhood totally incongruous and she filled with self-doubt and disgust. She told me:

I could have coped with a doll. I was good at all the changing, feeding and bathing. What I couldn't cope with was the emotional side. That Eve

90

was a person – that frightened me – that was horrible. I was frightened that she would be horrible to me. And I think I was frightened that I would be horrible to her. When she looked at me I felt constantly challenged. She was so clever and quick, and like Mummy, she went on and on. And just as I wanted to scream at Mummy to stop, so I wanted to put a pillow over Eve's head.

Mothering is multigenerational. For most women images of their own mothers dominate the experience of mothering as a reproving presence or cautionary tale – making them feel that they were either reproducing the mother they hate or letting down the mother they loved. Above all their 'mother' – meaning the primary internal object – admonishes them for their ambivalence. This was certainly the case with Sylvia.

It seemed from Sylvia's account that her mother had employed idealisation of herself as a mother, and of her children, in response to divorce in a social context where divorce was considered shameful. When Sylvia began psychotherapy she maintained the idealisation while unconsciously holding a very different representation of her mother. 'She gave us all four such very beautiful names,' she repeatedly told me. In the transference I was initially idealised by Sylvia while in the countertransference I experienced the full force of the denied negativity. As the work evolved, Sylvia slowly became able to own her criticisms of her mother. Nevertheless, in her mothering, she repeated her own mother's employment of idealisation as a defence against shame and ambivalence. She struggled to be entirely loving, and to be as giving as she now felt her own mother had been withholding and attacking. She was determined to provide her children with all the care and opportunities she thought had been denied her. She believed that if she tried hard enough she ought to be able to entirely fulfil her children's needs as well as protecting them and giving them direction in their lives. Her expectations of herself as a mother – the extremes of self-abnegation and love that she wanted to offer – meant that her children's ordinary insatiability felt like a ravenous hunger that she was bound, but unable, to answer. When Eve breastfed, she felt as if the baby was about to devour the entire breast. Defending against the fantasised consequences of her aggression and maintaining an ideal of unconditional love, she became a tirelessly loving mother, mobilising masochism as a defence, and manifesting a false self in relation to the children. To a large extent the care she bestowed on her children was a counterfeit reparation, and they sensed it.

All her life Sylvia had maintained a pattern of loving others 'despite' their behaviour towards her. This was evident, as mentioned above, in the transference/countertransference dynamics in which she played the part of the good appreciative patient while I felt curiously blank or short changed. She had loved her father despite feeling deeply let down by him. She loved her brother despite his violence. She told me, 'I have a need to love, it's inside me.' Eve, however, was kicking through the defence. In tears Sylvia would exclaim, 'I never expected to have a child who would fight my love.' Unconsciously, however, it was precisely what she did expect. The shame of the frustrated desire to give unconditional love had deep roots. As a child she had felt forever in danger of being shamed. Graphically illustrating her fear of parental projections, she told me, 'I could only tell my mother I loved her when her back was turned.'

When I attempted to interpret her rage and hatred towards her children for 'frustrating her love' she experienced me as hating and shaming her. Swamped with maternal persecutory anxiety, she offered me the following image:

> The children remind me of a litter of kittens. They would rather have a starving, dead mother than allow the cat to go and feed. It doesn't matter how long that cat has been lying there without feeding, when she gets up and moves away, the kittens feel she's a bad mother . . . And she feels she's a bad mother.

As I shall discuss below, maternal ambivalence entails both persecutory and depressive anxiety. Sylvia was both the persecuted cat and the abandoning cat because, in her mind, the longing to hide from the children, instituted by shame, meant she was a cat who longed to desert the kittens. Shame, however, not only institutes concealment but also threatens loss. Sylvia described her feelings when Eve was four:

> I remember, very clearly, standing in the garden with her. She was asking me all sorts of questions that I simply couldn't answer. I looked down and thought 'I'm not clever enough to have a child like this.' I had this fear that if it was discovered that I couldn't manage her and that she was too clever

for me, I would somehow lose her, that she would be taken. It terrified me
because though she drove me mad I thought she was absolutely wonderful.

At that moment, standing in the garden, Sylvia faced both the loss of
her internal good object – in this context her sense of self-esteem
and belief in her capacity to mother – and also her external good
object, the child. It was this threat of loss that turned her into what
she described as a slave to the girl. In such circumstances, hate
constitutes a barrier against dependence, precisely against despondent
dependence (Balint 1952). Sylvia felt dependent on her children for
her sense of well-being because, given her idealisation of maternity,
she had corrosive doubts about her capacity to mother. Thus she
both hated her children and loved them.

In our work together, I was for a long time witness to the prosecution; the recipient of endless narratives of Eve's appalling behaviour.
At times I feared I was simply collusive, but the therapeutic alliance
thus established enabled Sylvia to gain a strengthened sense of self as
subject. Accordingly her shame diminished and very slowly, she
began to use me as someone to whom she could safely acknowledge
hostility towards her daughter. Initially the acknowledgement
repeatedly instituted narcissistic defences against shame with splitting and projection: Eve was perceived as the all-bad daughter and
Sylvia as the good, ill-used mother. At one point when Eve, by now
15, again ran away from home, Sylvia exclaimed, 'I'm thoroughly
glad she's gone. I wish she would leave altogether, in fact I wish she
would live anywhere except in my house, creating chaos.'

Eve's disruptive behaviour was not limited to home. As Sylvia put
it, she was constantly being 'hauled up to school' to answer for her
child's sins. Shame almost completely isolated her. She felt ashamed
in front of the teachers and ashamed amongst other parents from
whom she hid. She resorted to reading endless parenting manuals,
which seemed to hold out impossible ideals and served only to
increase her rage and despair. Had her husband not worked abroad,
he might have mitigated shame by acknowledging and sharing all
that she had to contend with. But he was away from home for long
periods.

Phil Mollon (2008) writes that 'shame is associated with whatever
is outside the discourse, whatever cannot be spoken of' (p. 31).
Verbalising her conflicts with me had an impact on the intensity of
Sylvia's shame. The psychotherapeutic relationship finally created a

space for understanding instead of judging and her shame slowly diminished to the point where it began to provide insight and she began to acknowledge the element of love and hatred in maternal ambivalence. She was able to say, 'I realise why we have rows whenever Eve goes out. I just don't want her to leave. I don't want her to go out. I miss her.'

With self-knowledge came a capacity for mentalisation – an issue to which I shall return. It's well illustrated by the following incident:

> I expected Eve to be home by eight, She said she'd be in by eight. At ten when she wasn't home I went over to the funfair and there she was sauntering out of the gates. I lost my temper and started shouting at her. She told me to stop. So I explained to her that I was shouting because I was so anxious – the funfair is a dangerous place to be in the evening. To my amazement, instead of the usual stand-up fight, she apologised. I think she saw that my anger and anxiety belonged to me and wasn't an attack on her which she had to fight off. It made me realise that she had stood back, and that I ought to stand back. But it's difficult when it's your 15-year-old daughter.

Slowly she recognised that her compulsion to be an omnipotently powerful, perfect mother in itself constructed her sense of herself as an inadequate mother – and led her to resent her children. Once the shame generated by her sense of powerlessness and helplessness ebbed, she experienced a new ease with them – and they with her:

> I realised I had changed towards my kids when I stopped minding the way they borrowed my clothes. I feel now they can take what they want bar a few precious things. I no longer feel ripped off, resentful and guilty. And they have started asking first!

In the transference/countertransference Sylvia no longer needed to buttress herself against shame by anticipating interpretations and I ceased to have the sensation – bred of fearing to shame – of walking on eggshells. Challenge and disagreement became possible. The panic attacks became rare. Sylvia likened herself to a caged bird who had fallen off its perch. It had been an enormous strain sitting chirping and singing loyally and lovingly. On the other hand, the pleasurable aspects of idealisation had undoubtedly been lost while gaining the freedom to 'fall silent' and admit to maternal hate as well as maternal love.

Sylvia's response to motherhood is explicable in terms of her personal patterns, with the particular meanings love and hate carried for her. However, the intensity of humiliation and fear of loss occasioned by her dawning awareness of ambivalence need to be placed in the wider cultural context. The particular representation of motherhood which I term the 'maternal ideal' functions to deny maternal ambivalence at the level of the social. Shame – provoked by aggression and hatred in the context of a cultural idealised hate-free image of motherhood – with its panoply of destructive defences, thus renders maternal ambivalence unmanageable.

Distinguishing shame and guilt

Michael Lewis (1992) suggests that 'shame and guilt are confused because of their common origin as modes of correcting lost affective bonds' (p. 32). Where mothers are concerned, the confusion is created because, in maternity, shame and guilt are particularly closely interrelated. Before bringing them together to demonstrate the ways in which they inflate maternal ambivalence to unmanageable proportions, it is necessary to distinguish the two affects. Shame is understood to focus on the self while guilt on the thing done. Shame involves a conviction of failure and weakness. Guilt provokes a sense of wrongdoing. Cultures are contrasted according to the dominance of guilt and shame. A guilt culture is one in which authority is based on punishment, sin and forgiveness. In a shame culture, by contrast, ideas of honour and disgrace, renown and contemptibility, respect and ridicule dominate (Hultberg 1988).

An important aspect of the shame experience is that it entails the dominance of the objective sense of self. This is because the capacity to experience shame first appears in connection with the realisation that the self can be seen from the outside: 'the thinking about others thinking about us . . . excites a blush' (Probyn 2005: 45). The mental capacity to move back and forth and to maintain the tension between a view of self as object and a view of self as subject (Aron and Sommer Anderson 1998) is stalled in shame situations. The shamed mother views herself as the baby's helpless object with little or no sense of herself as author or agent in her life with the child. At that point rage and/or sadness shortcircuit empathy.

95

Developmentally, shame is considered to be the earlier affect, emerging pre-verbally, while guilt becomes apparent in the verbal child. In the case of Sylvia, she was so steeped in silent and silencing shame that her conflict and anxiety could only be expressed physiologically through panic attacks, and warded off by defences associated with paranoid schizoid processes. Shame is a global affect. The individual conceives of himself or herself as all bad and the subsequent pain prompts defensive splitting and projection. With guilt, good and bad are conceived as held within the same person and healthy splitting between the individual and their action enables the reparation characteristic of the depressive position. Hence guilt can potentially lead to corrective behaviours while shame prompts concealment and hiding.

Where maternal development is concerned, this neat bifurcation of the affects breaks down. In mothers, guilt and shame fuel one another. The two affects are often subtly fused, or function as a defence against each other. Guilt can be used to bypass shame since it is a less acute, less all-encompassing emotion – focusing on action rather than on the entire self. The words of the following mother, clearly illustrate the coexistence of guilt and shame:

> I can remember hurling the baby down on the pillows once, and just screaming, and not caring. I wanted to kill him really. I think it was being so tormented, worried and guilty. You know, the anxiety and guilt at feeling I was getting it all wrong, and that I was bad and useless. I just wanted to get away from the situation. I felt unable to tolerate it. I hated the baby for constantly being there.

One reason why shame develops such a powerful hold over mothers is that being a mother is an identity – involving the whole person – as well as a set of behaviours. This mother felt guilty (I was getting it all wrong) and she felt shame (I was bad and useless). The defences called forth are the defences of shame. She wants to flee – to escape the eyes of the shaming other. And she wants to kill the baby. Either violent rage or incapacitating sadness can be mobilised as defences against intolerable shame.

The intensity of the shame is dependent on the legitimacy of the judge. Sylvia looked down at her baby, Eve, and it seemed that the baby was regarding her with a look that said, 'Is this the best you can do?' Internal objects marry with the external source of condemnation (the baby) and to a shame-prone mother there can be no better equipped judge than the baby who was once part of her. In D. H Lawrence's (1913) *Sons and Lovers*, Mrs Morel looks down at her baby in terror:

> Did it know all about her? When it lay under her heart had it been listening then? Was there a reproach in the look? She felt the marrow melt in her bones with fear and panic.
>
> (p. 74)

Wurmser (1981) has described a shame–guilt dialectic. This is particularly relevant to mothers. There is an oscillation between the danger of weakness and failure – the position of shame – and the danger of exerting power and hurting the other – the position of guilt. Ambivalence both provokes and magnifies the oscillation; a mother loves the child whom she hates for rendering her guilty and ashamed. And, in addition to the conflict between love and hate, simply recognising that she is ambivalent instils both guilt and shame.

As significant as the guilt–shame dialectic for mothers is the pride–shame dialectic. That motherhood constitutes an identity leaves a woman open to the pleasure of pride – which of course magnifies the pain of shame. That new mothers are conventionally offered congratulations on the birth of a baby speaks for itself.

Proneness to shame-free guilt is considered to be the 'more adaptive affective style across many different aspects of functioning, as shame means overwhelming self-contempt and disgust, and a self that is considered defective at its core is much more difficult to transform and amend, whereas guilt offers opportunity of redemption' (Tangney *et al.* 2007: 359). To my mind, 'shame-free guilt' is an impossible ideal for mothers. Guilt repeatedly triggers and nourishes shame by promoting feelings of maternal inferiority, while shame can function as a defence against guilt. For example, a depressed mother may experience the reparation associated with guilt as beyond her capabilities. Hence she dismisses herself wholesale as a bad mother because passive, shameful resignation can seem preferable and safer to an active, guilty focus on transgression.

While intricately and constantly connected to guilt, the intensity of the presence of shame does, I believe, determine whether maternal ambivalence remains manageable or becomes unmanageable. We could see with Sylvia how shame at inevitably failing to provide unconditional love inflated the conflict of ambivalence. But, bearing in mind the concept of maternal development, the degree of shame dominating a mother can change over time depending, for example, on her history, living conditions, or the age and state of the child.

The aetiology of shame

Above I described the development of infantile ambivalence and then the specificity of the development of maternal ambivalence. It is necessary to do the same with shame. Children experience shame – through childhood and adolescence – especially in relation to their parents, whom they may feel to be peculiarly embarrassing. This is an example of shame as an aspect of manageable ambivalence, and prompts the child toward separation and autonomy. However, if shame is excessive, its 'hiding' defence will lead the child to with-draw into shyness, or to conceal themselves behind bravado, or into utilising other forms of denial, hiding what is felt to be their real experience and their self. Hidden shame demands to be dealt with, and it is possible that when the child grows up into a shame-prone mother, she will project shame on her child, who will then have to deal with it, in a recurring cycle from mother to daughter.

Two developmental lines have been identified in the growth of shame: one involving narcissism, and the other concerning instincts and control (Miller 1985). Where mothers are concerned, it really is impossible to distinguish the two.

Both Sigmund Freud and Anna Freud viewed shame as a servant of morality. 'Shame, disgust and morality are like watchmen who maintain repressions, dams that direct the flow of a sexual excitation into normal channels instead of reactivating earlier forms of expression' (Freud 1909: 45). Freud (1908) considered shame to be a reaction formation designed to maintain the repression of forbidden exhibitionistic instincts. Later theorists have understood shame as a failure of the ego to achieve a narcissistic ideal, in other words, shame emerges in response to an awareness of a discrepancy between the ego ideal and the perceived self when goals and images represented by the ego ideal are not achieved. Guilt, on the other hand, corresponds to an attack upon the ego by the super-ego. The ego ideal, built upon positive identification with parental images, stimulates an awareness of potential and a wish for competence, progress and development.

With mothers, the two developmental lines (instinctual and narcissistic) merge. Freud (1914) considered parental love to be essentially narcissistic. He wrote: 'Parental love, which is so moving and at bottom so childish, is nothing but the parents' narcissism born again' (p. 91). While usefully highlighting the presence of narcissism in parental love, this obscures the aspect of reciprocity in the relationship. The child who was once literally a part of a woman, is out in the world relating to her, exhibiting her, revealing, so she feels, her worth or lack of worth – her innermost being – to public gaze. Part of her is visible, on display and out of her control. A shame-prone mother – a mother who suffered early shaming – can feel painfully shown up by her child. Yet a mother also wants to exhibit her child, longs for approbation and applause for the child, and hence for pride in herself as a mother. Freud (1914) himself acknowledged the complex combination of infantile wishes and adult desires driving parenthood: 'in the child which they bear, a part of their own body confronts them like an extraneous object to which, starting out from their narcissism, they can give complete object-love' (pp. 89–90).

Experiencing a sense of failure to achieve the goals and images of the ego ideal is complicated by three separate but interrelated maternal dynamics. There is the mother's identification with her child and the associated regression. Then there is the determining impact of a mother's relationship with her own parents (both actual and in terms of internal objects). And there is a mother's response to current cultural representations of motherhood which crucially outlaw maternal ambivalence. Where identification with the child is concerned, a mother's desire for competence, progress and development becomes lodged in her child and we hear from the child about the burden of parental expectation. Mothers, however, do not simply imagine that their worth is measured by their children's achievements – or lack of achievements. We live in a mother-blaming, mother-idealising and mother-denigrating culture that views the child as the unmediated symptom of maternal psychopathology. Therefore, along with her personal ego ideal, a mother has to contend with a cultural maternal ideal. Thinking about mothering demands our holding in mind many complex interactions of internal and external reality. Cultural expectations of good and bad mothering interact with the unique meanings that mothering has for a woman. Mothers both reproduce and resist assumptions of what it means to mother – but these assumptions cannot be escaped. Our culture permits flexibility in other activities that involve intimacy, some heterogeneity, some diversity of style, but hardly any at all when it comes to mothering. A sense of the rigidity imposed on mothering can paradoxically be gauged from the schism that opens up between different generations of mothers. Yet alongside prescriptions on mothering there flourishes the assertion that mother knows best, with the implications that there can be no hard and fast rules for mothering, which is an essentially instinctive, intuitive affair. Despite changing beliefs about babies' capacities and thus childcare priorities, the representation of ideal motherhood is still almost exclusively made up of self-abnegation, unstinting love, intuitive knowledge of nurturance and unalloyed pleasure in children. With Sylvia, the maternal ideal married up with disastrous results to her unconscious reaction to being mothered and to being a mother. In the words of another mother, whom I shall call Naomi, we can see how the personal and public ideal together stir shame and render ambivalence unmanageable:

> The ideal mother is calm, patient and rational, at one with the children but firm, not letting them be wild. She stops them going into shoeshops and sweeping shoes off the shelves. Yesterday my kids did just that and I was told off for not being a proper mother. I also feel that I should be able to control them in a calm, rational way without screaming at them, without hitting them. Doing it almost by magic. But I don't manage that. I do get freaked out. I do shriek, I do feel like I'm going to explode, and I do feel this imperative from outside to control them. There are times when I think it would be OK for them to be a bit more relaxed in a public situation – but I feel the pressure. There is pressure from the children and pressure from the culture. I'm caught in the middle.

She remembers how her own mother's irritation and irascibility was a response to a similar desire to conform to a world of good manners. She describes her mother as 'very controlling, it mattered a lot what people thought of my sister and me. It was "don't stare, don't point," all the time'. Thus, when Naomi was reprimanded by the man in the shoeshop for her children's bad behaviour, part of her rebelliously identified with the 'bad children', while part of her felt humiliated and convinced she was not a proper mother, not adult or orderly enough. Tellingly at such moments she relates to her children as if they were her mother pointing out her unacceptable behaviour. Freud (1932) commented: 'Under the influence of a woman's becoming a mother herself, an identification with her own mother may be revived, against which she has striven' (p. 235). In other words, a woman can feel drawn back into an identification with a being from whom she may have long struggled to separate – with all the contradictory feelings which that inevitably entails. Long-buried fears, desire and resentment in relation to competing with her own mother may be reactivated by her own mothering. While acknowledging the impact of her own experience of being mothered on a mother, I do not believe it determines, in any straightforward way, the nature of her mothering. Her feelings towards her mother and her infant self will inflect a woman's mothering, but not in any predictive way. A whole clutch of circumstances combine to affect a woman's response to mothering, ranging from her unconscious processes, her physical health, her economic, social and family situation, the availability of emotional support and, of course, the specific contributions of her children. Naomi, cited above, told me:

> I was really prepared for the worst when I decided to get pregnant. I dreaded damaging the child. I worried that I would be like my mother – become her, in a way. But to my surprise I got immensely excited during pregnancy. I had this tremendous sense of potential. And when Jonathan was born I found I had something to offer. It seemed magical to me that I had milk the baby could make use of. I could satisfy the baby. It was such a pleasure.

Mirroring and shame

Naomi experienced herself as receiving benign 'mirroring' from her children when they were breastfeeding babies. I use the term mirroring because the basic processes of interaction at the non-verbal level remain similar across the life span. For infants and adults alike, face-to-face communication involves influencing and being influenced by the other, matching the expression of the other and

101

being matched, to produce similar physiological states in one another (Beebe and Lachmann 2002) Hence, when thinking about maternal shame we need to bear in mind the complex interaction of both a woman's early mirroring and the mirroring she receives from her child.

The aetiology of shame-proneness is understood to lie with early mirroring. Infant observation has identified shame in babies. The 'still face' experience demonstrates the manner in which babies avert their eyes when mother's do not respond as expected. Shame develops in response to an empathic break between the mirroring object and the self. The experience can construct a primary, internal shaming eye focused on the depleted, fragmented self with its believed failures and inadequacies (Ayers 2003).

Reversing the theory of infant mirroring to illuminate maternal subjectivity, I am suggesting that it is through the mirroring look of the baby that the mother is brought into being. But how she receives the look is over-determined. She receives the mirroring in the context of her own early mirroring under the impact of the regression induced by identification with her baby, as well as being influenced by her ego ideal in conjunction with the cultural maternal ideal, the circumstances of her mothering and the disposition of the baby. Hence, the baby who looks away from the mother while feeding, for whatever reason, all too easily stimulates shame in a shame-prone mother.

Of course, it is not so much the actual childhood experience that makes for shame-proneness but how it was understood. Susan Miller (1985) warns against drawing a simple links between shame and unempathic parenting. Citing Kohut she considers that unempathic parenting needs to be seen as only part of the 'decompensation of self-esteem and self-organisation that occurs in adults whose histories make them vulnerable to severe strain whenever self-esteem is not supported by the people or events in their lives' (p. 172).

Moreover, it is important to bear in mind that a mismatch of attunement, with the emergence of shame, is an inevitable aspect of development, because it is through the mirroring look of the mother, and the equally necessary turning away of her gaze, that self-consciousness is constructed.

Fonagy *et al.* (2004) have discussed the impact on the baby when a mother reflects not the baby's feelings but her own. The baby internalises the object's state of mind as an 'alien' and disruptive part of the self, leading to constant need for projective identification in order to establish self-consistency. We can see this at work in mothers' later adult experience of being mirrored by the baby. 'I felt that baby hated me,' a mother told me. 'He would bite me, but not with a twinkle in his eye. He'd be breastfeeding and he'd just bite me.' Another mother said of her child, 'I feel abused by her. I always have done. As a baby if you changed her nappy before she had her feed, she just got full of rage.' Melanie Klein (1937) wrote: 'We so much dread hatred in ourselves that we are driven to employ one of our strongest measures of defence by putting it on to other people – to project it' (p. 341). Hence these moments when mothers, in the course of being mirrored by their babies, project on them highly disruptive feelings of their own, and perceive the babies as malevolent opponents. Yet it is a perception weighted with the shame of being unappealing to the object, of failing to please.

Constructive shame

Shame in the context of mothering is not simply destructive. It has a protective role to play. Ana-Maria Rizzuto (2008) distinguishes normal shame from pathological shame. Normal shame relates to consciously identifiable experiences while pathological shame relates to the unconscious connection between an actual and an imaginary event and pre-existing beliefs and unconscious fantasies about one's own worth, defectiveness or unloveability. Donald Campbell (2008) sees normal shame as having a protective role. He writes of the shame shield which 'prevents further exposure and weakness or lack of control, and restores the self to a safe, private hidden place where it can be re-constituted' (p. 77). Mothers long to retreat from the shaming baby but the exigencies of care prevent it. And as Campbell points out, the 'protective function of shame as a shield between self and object depends for its success upon the object perceiving the external manifestation of shame as a shield between self and object which the object recognizes as a signal of failure and respects enough to react sympathetically to the self' (p. 78). Babies, of course, are incapable of acting as containing partners in shame, and shame in mothers is generated precisely by the sense of being 'shown up' by the child.

Nevertheless, shame, founded as it is upon relationship, does potentially protect a child. Jacoby (1994) describes shame serving the interests both of individuality and conformity, safeguarding boundaries, mediating closeness and distance, and controlling intensity of interest. Probyn (2005), writing as a sociologist who holds a particularly positive image of the workings of shame, claims that shame illuminates our intense attachment to the world, our desire to be connected to others, and the knowledge that we will sometimes fail in our attempts to maintain these connections. As Lynd (1958) puts it: 'experiences of shame confronted full in the face may throw an unexpected light on who one is and point the way to who one may become' (p. 20). Fully faced, shame may become not primarily something to be covered, but a positive experience of revelation. The following mother describes how shame fostered self-knowledge:

> I support pacifism. I'm opposed to all forms of violence yet now I know there is violence in me. My children have shown me what I am capable of. Yesterday I slapped Sam. He had promised to take Sally to her piano lesson and there he was still in bed. I poured cold tea over him and I slapped him. I do feel terrible about it.

She reflected over time on the rage stimulated by her son and was finally able to recognise aspects of herself that were denied, glimpsing in herself the 'laziness and irresponsibility' that she had projected into Sam. But, as with Sylvia, it was a long struggle to diminish shame to the point at which, in concert with maternal ambivalence, insight could be achieved.

At times, however, child–mother mirroring can directly heal shame, providing a woman with evidence of her capacity to love and be loved:

> I did not anticipate the intensity of the feeling: the enormity of the experience. I was overwhelmed by love. I had never been loved like that. She was ecstatic when I came into the room and miserable when I went away. It wasn't that I became more loving, it was that there was more to love.

Motherhood and the experience of reciprocal love in this case healed a lifetime of shame. Insofar as the child is experienced as loved and loving, motherhood can, thus, enhance a woman in her own eyes, but given that motherhood inevitably entails anger, irritation, disapproval and antagonism, motherhood can constitute a serious depletion of healthy narcissism. Some mothers react by omnipotently trying to control the child and change it; others respond by trying to achieve impossible levels of self-control, many veer between the two positions.

The very experience of ambivalence can undermine a mother's hope and expectation that here at last is someone to love unreservedly and wholeheartedly. Ambivalence (or so she assumes) denies her the chance to heal her own childhood disappointments. Her ego ideal, in conjunction with the cultural maternal ideal, represents ambivalence as a failure to love. As Freud (1914) commented: 'the realisation of . . . one's own inability to love . . . has an exceedingly lowering effect upon self regard' (p. 98). Ambivalence is emphatically not synonymous with the inability to love, but in a society wedded to the maternal ideal, it can seem that way to women.

Defences against shame

Given the positive possibilities inherent in shame, how are we to understand the development of pathological shame in mothers, the times when shame, in association with maternal ambivalence, stimulates not thought or self-knowledge but mindless violence?

The dynamics of maternal shame and ambivalence vary according to the age of the child. When a child reaches adolescence, as with Sylvia and Eve, a mother's capacity to bear hatred and shame is often tested to the limit by the necessary aggression entailed in the processes of separation, and mothers often regress to the infantile/ adolescent part of themselves in response. Describing her adolescent son a mother says, 'It's the silence, the closed door, the not saying anything. It enrages me.' It is the gaps and failures in human communication, the misconnection of expectation that one has of one another which augments shame (Mollon 2008). The inability to elicit similar affects, complementary messages in the other, is hence deeply shameful. Yet finding a sense of themselves which is distinct from their parents and their childhood selves is one of the central developmental tasks of the age group. The tools employed include opposition, evasion and a necessary questioning of all their parents stand for. A mother describes a son who very recently reached puberty: 'Dean holds my hand as if it was a chair – there are no messages going back and forth, and it is driving me crazy.'

Narcissistic rage functions as a defence against shame. The impulse is to destroy or annihilate the shaming other. A mother told me, 'I want to really hurt them, and to hurt them in the way which is most hurtful – getting rid of them, rejecting them, pushing them away.' Another said, 'I have wanted to hurl her across the room – erase her.'

Rage is often stimulated by helplessness: 'It's the desire to push him away that I find most upsetting. It usually happens when I am tired.' In redirecting the anger outside the self, the shamed mother is attempting to regain a sense of agency. Loss of control and feelings of helplessness are central to the shame experience, provoking intense anxiety.

Whatever a mother does, she is going to be experienced as denying and frustrating. Even the most devoted mother will be felt to be rejecting at times by her child because its demands are limitless, because life outside the womb is unavoidably frustrating (Anna Freud 1954). A child's cry can sound like a furious reproach making a tired mother feel inadequate and helpless, while at the same time the intense intimacy of the mother and child – the unconscious to unconscious communication between them – provokes a mother's own infantile needs and her infantile neediness merges with her adult needs as a mother to have a satisfied baby.

Intense shame generates both maternal persecutory anxiety and maternal depressive anxiety. The following mother illustrates the dominance of depressive anxiety with a sense of being ineffectual, a failure and worthlessness:

> She wasn't a particularly difficult baby. I just never felt I knew what the matter was. I don't think I felt hostile towards her: I turned it against myself. It was my failure to understand what was needed; my inability to cope. In a way it was easier to blame myself and to think of it in those terms, although it made me terribly helpless.

Unable to bear shame, she was overcome with depression and anxiety. A degree of depression is an inevitable concomitant of motherhood and implies a recognition of aggression, an acceptance of both responsibility and fallibility. Yet the interplay of psychical and social conditions of mothering with regard to the component of hatred inflates shame and militates against depression remaining a manageable, creative condition. Helplessness begets shame which in turn inflates helplessness. And a sense of severe helplessness is a major component of post-natal depression (Raphael-Leff 1991).

By contrast maternal persecutory anxiety involves a mother's fantasised experience of herself as punished and tormented by her infant – no matter the difference in power between them. Denial, idealisation, splitting and control are all employed by the ego to counteract persecutory anxiety – and to a lesser extent depressive anxiety. Once again, in motherhood, there is no neat bifurcation of affects. The two states of mind can alternate. As Melanie Klein (1937) writes: 'The desire to repair and revive a loved object may turn into the need to pacify and propitiate a persecutor' (p. 37). But common to both forms of anxiety is the driving presence of shame:

> When Martin was a year old he would only go to sleep if he could hold my hand. I would sit there by his cot and lose all sense of myself. My physical boundaries would feel to be disintegrating. I would want to scream at him 'Give me my space.' I felt desperate for physical space, let alone time for myself. Looking back I do feel tremendously guilty about that. I think the desire to push him away made me feel so terrible because it rekindled my own experience of rejection, I found that the most awful thing to see myself doing.

This mother, capable of insight, describes guilt coexisting with, even outweighing shame. Recognising the origin of the affect that swamps her as she sits by her sleeping son, checks the global nature of shame. She went on to tell me that she considers her impulse to retrieve her hand from her sleeping son must have damaged the child. She says, 'I am sure my rejecting response escalated his desire to cling.' What she does not consider is the possibility that her desire to pull back, to reclaim her sense of bodily boundaries, may also signify an appropriate and productive move towards separation on her part as a mother. Instead there is the automatic self-condemnation characteristic of shame as past bereavements, rejections and losses are evoked. In fact maternal ambivalence is vital for the project of separation – the aggressive component in ambivalence is central in the process of parting. But, at the same time, precisely because separation entails a sense of sense of destruction and aggression, ambivalence and the attendant shame can make separation too dangerous to contemplate. Separation becomes equated with loss.

Shame and loss are intimately related as described above in the case of Sylvia and Eve. Discussing the aetiology of shame Ana–Maria Rizzuto (2008) writes: 'Behind negative self-evaluation lurk the fears of the loss of the object and of loss of love' (p. 61). A child skips off the pavement. Its mother yanks its arm and brutally slaps the child. For, as the child steps into the gutter, the mother has a terrifying intimation of loss and her helplessness to prevent that loss. In the slapping moment, she experiences her own destruction of the good internal object that has been nourishing her from within, enabling her to care for her child. She hates the child for threatening her with loss, for turning her into a monster, and obscuring the love that is obviously also there. Her dependence on her relationship with her children is denied and they are omnipotently controlled and treated with triumph and contempt. She experiences herself as wronged and the child as utterly in the wrong. She can then feel permitted to mobilise sadism as a defence against shame.

Diminishing shame

So far I have been illustrating the role of shame in inflating the element of hatred in maternal ambivalence, rendering the affect unmanageable. But what of shame and manageable ambivalence? What are the conditions necessary for shame to act 'as a deterrent to enacting conscious and unconscious fantasies' (Campbell 2008: 78)?

Fonagy *et al.* (2004) have coined the term 'unmentalized shame' for shame which remains unmediated by any sense of distance between feelings and objective realities, describing the intensity of humiliation experienced when trauma cannot be processed and attenuated via mentalisation. They suggest that 'the ability to mentalise would mitigate this process, permitting the individual to continue to conceive of himself as a meaningful, intentional subject in spite of lack of recognition from the attachment figure' (p. 425). Adapting this to maternal experience we can see that the ability to mentalise enables a mother to regain a sense of self as subject preventing shame from escalating ambivalence from manageable to unmanageable. The following mother puts it well:

> Sometimes I can step back and see things from the children's point of view and understand how it feels to reach a point where nothing satisfies. If I

can unhook from feeling the source of their frustration, I can feel saddened rather than maddened. At those moments I can respond with 'I haven't got what you need' (nice and gentle) rather than 'I haven't got what you need' (through clenched teeth).

It can be the child's own behaviour which facilitates a mother's capacity to mentalise. Another mother describes such a process:

> I used to get much angrier with Laurie than with Matt. He wouldn't allow me to get angry. He would stand there and say, 'Don't hit me, don't hit me.' When he said that it made me aware that I didn't want to hurt inside, and I didn't want it to happen to him either.

The capacity to mentalise diminishes the global character of shame by affirming the subjective sense of self. Humour, confession and verbalisation all reduce shame by diminishing the dominance of self as object. We can see the process at work not only in the clinical situation where speaking shame mobilises the subjective sense of self, but also in the endless humourous/confessional maternal narratives in newspaper columns, magazine articles and books.

The mother cited above describes how the capacity to think, to verbalise and to feel for one another enabled her and Laurie in late adolescence to emerge together from global, divisive and destructive shame:

> Laurie came to see me. We had two days of misery and agony, but we sorted it out, and finally had a really lovely time together. He thinks I'm horrible, judgmental and dissatisfied with him – which I am. But I also think he's wonderful, and I don't feel him to be as bad as he thinks I do. The fact that we could speak it was an amazing thing.

We could understand the underlying dynamics in the situation between Laurie and his mother in terms of the mother moving between paranoid schizoid functioning and depressive position functioning. When in the grip of paranoid schizoid processes, she would experience a sense of self as object while depressive position processes would enable a sense of self as subject – a historical interpreting agentic self – to emerge (Aron and Sommer Anderson 1998). But I think it is more helpful to think of the vicissitudes of maternal ambivalence fluctuating under the impact of shame. Verbalisation enabled the mother to use shame-driven insight to engage in her battle with ambivalence rather than wanting above all to escape the shaming other.

Conclusion

I have argued that maternal ambivalence can have an enormously creative impact on a woman's evolving capacity to mother, sparking the impulse to give, understand, construct and mend, if the associated guilt and shame remain at manageable levels. When, however, the intersection of psychic reality and external reality magnifies shame, the conflict generated by ambivalence becomes overwhelming and ambivalence becomes unmanageable. Defences then instituted range from violent aggression to incapacitating depression. If shame can be diminished, a mother can retrieve a sense of self as subject as opposed to the sense of self as object, which dominates in shame experience. Mentalisation then becomes possible and mothers, prompted by the painful conflict of ambivalence, are able to think about both their children's and their own internal processes.

References

Aron, L. and Sommer Anderson, F. (eds) (1998) *Relational Perspectives on The Body*. New Jersey and London: Analytic Press.

Ayers, M. (2003) *Mother–Infant Attachment and Psychoanalysis: The Eyes of Shame*. New York: Brunner-Routledge.

Balint, M. (1952) 'On love and hate'. *Int. J. Psycho-Anal.*, 33: 355–362.

Beebe, B. and Lachmann, F. M. (2002) *Infant Research and Adult Treatment: Co-constructing Interactions*. New Jersey and London: Analytic Press.

Campbell, D. (2008) 'The shame shield in child abuse', in C. Pajaczkowska and I. Ward (eds) *Shame and Sexuality: Psychoanalysis and Visual Culture*. London and New York: Routledge.

Fonagy, P., Gergely, E., Jurist, E. L. and Target, M. (eds) (2004) *Affect Regulation, Mentalization and the Development of the Self*. London: Karnac.

Freud, A. (1954) 'The concept of the rejecting mother', in E. J. Benedek and T. Anthony (eds) *Parenthood: Its Psychology and Psychopathology* Boston: Little Brown, 1970, p. 385.

Freud, S. (1908) 'Character and anal eroticism'. *S.E.* 9: 169.

Freud, S. (1909) 'Five lectures on psychoanalysis'. *S.E.* 11: 45.

Freud, S. (1914) 'On narcissism: an introduction'. *S.E.* 14: 89–90.

Freud, S. (1915) 'Thoughts for the times on war and death'. *S.E.* 14: 273–300.

Freud, S. (1917) 'Mourning and melancholia'. *S.E.* 14: 25.

Freud, S. (1931) 'Female sexuality'. *S.E.* 16: 235.

Freud, S. (1932) 'On femininity'. *S.E.* 22: 133.

Hultberg, P. (1988) 'Shame – a hidden emotion'. *J. Anal. Psychol.*, 33: 109–126.

Jacoby, M. (1994, 2003) *Shame and The Origins of Self Esteem: A Jungian Approach.* London and New York: Routledge.

Klein, M. (1937) 'On the theory of anxiety and guilt', in M. Klein *Envy and Gratitude.* London: Hogarth Press.

Klein, M. (1940) 'Mourning and its relation to manic–depressive states', in M. Klein *Love, Guilt and Reparation and Other Works.* London: Hogarth, Press 1985, p. 349.

Lawrence, D. H. (1913) *Sons and Lovers*, Harmondsworth: Penguin, 1989.

Lewis, M. (1992), *Shame: The Exposed Self.* New York: Free Press.

Lynd, H. M. (1958) *On Shame and the Search for Identity.* London and New York: Routledge.

Miller, S. (1985) *The Shame Experience.* New York and London: Analytic Press.

Mollon, P. (2002) *Shame and Jealousy: The Hidden Turmoils.* London: Karnac.

Mollon, P. (2008) 'The inherent shame of sexuality', in C. Pajoczkowska and I. Ward (eds) *Shame and Sexuality: Psychoanalysis and Visual Culture.* London and New York: Routledge.

Nathanson, D. N. (ed.) (1987) *The Many Faces of Shame.* New York: Guilford Press.

Parker, R. (1995, 2000) *Torn in Two: The Experience of Maternal Ambivalence.* London: Virago Press.

Probyn, E. (2005) *Blush: Faces of Shame.* Minneapolis and London: University of Minnesota Press.

Raphael-Leff, J. (1991), *Psychological Processes of Childbearing.* London and New York: Chapman and Hall.

Rizzuto, A.-M. (2008) 'Shame in psychoanalysis: the function of unconscious fantasies', in C. Pajoczkowska and I. Ward (eds) *Shame and Sexuality: Psychoanalysis and Visual Culture.* London and New York: Routledge.

Tangney, J. P., Tracy, J. L. and Robins, R. W. (eds) (2007) *The Self-Conscious Emotions: Theory and Research.* New York: Guilford Press.

Yorke, C. B. (2008) 'A psychoanalytic approach to shame', in C. Pajaczkowska and I. Ward (eds) *Shame and Sexuality: Psychoanalysis and Visual Culture.* London and New York: Routledge.

Winnicott, D. W. (1949) 'Hate in the countertransference', in D. W. Winnicott *The Maturational Processes and the Facilitating Environment.* London: Hogarth Press, 1974.

Woolf, V. (1941) 'Moments of being', cited in E. Abel, *Virginia Woolf and the Fictions of Psychoanalysis*. Chicago: University of Chicago Press, 1989, p. 109.

Wurmser, L. (1981) *The Mask of Shame*. Baltimore, MD: Johns Hopkins University Press.

4

The pregnant mother and the body image of the daughter

Rosemary H. Balsam

This chapter is about the place of the pregnant maternal body in the developing body image of the daughter. Adult examples from two cases are offered to demonstrate its lingering effects on the women's perceptions of their shapes, sizes, abdomens, breasts, and buttocks. Attention is drawn to its neglect in our formulations. It is suggested that the whole exterior of the body of the female is as important to her as the outer and inner genitals, and makes a vital contribution to the final shape of her gender role identity.

It is surprising that the body of the pregnant mother is so neglected in our literature about unconscious fantasies that inform the body image of her daughter. The vast belly, the bounteous breasts, the swayback posture, all create an arresting new outline for the usual form of the grown woman. This symbol of fertile maternity is a major conscious and social focus of attention for adults and children of both sexes. It requires hard work to ignore a pregnant woman in the environment. The body outline captures in a moment's glance the epitome of female biological prowess, all the more so when seen nude. The erect phallus of the grown man is a familiar, visible, similar, nude icon of biological power, promise, and destiny. This latter symbol has been granted much more focus in the minds of both female and male analysands as reported in our literature and in our clinical and developmental theory, particularly about gender differentiation. This paper will attempt to address several questions. Why is the topic of the pregnant body *per se* virtually

113

absent from most written accounts about patients' preoccupations as they lie on the couch? What can this phenomenon mean, given the frequency of the occurrence in many people's early childhood? If the topic has been unrecognized or glossed over, does it manifest itself in unrecognized ways? If encountered, how does it yield to interpretation? And is it indeed important in the formation of a daughter's body image? One long case example and one vignette will be offered here to suggest the place in mental life that the mother's pregnant body can assume in the analyses of adult women. Let me note that I wish to differentiate entirely all the following ideas from any implications for general "normality" or "fulfillment" of womanhood. Only an individual woman can arrive at such a judgment.

Relevant literature

I detect five important trends in the literature about female psychology. Because of the historical development of each, I believe that the issue of a female-to-female body comparison inherent in a woman's emotional growth has fallen by the wayside. The topic has not readily fitted into the five agendae. Mayer (1995) begins to offer a way out of the dilemma, but does not go quite far enough. She articulates *dual* developmental lines in women, one line emanating from primary femininity and one line involving phallic concern. In her case study, she demonstrated how an impasse in an adult female's analysis occurred around the patient's phallic castration attitudes, a situation that yielded to forward movement only when the analyst began to take note of an underlying but repressed primary feminine constellation. Mayer offers that this analytic work suggests evidence of an interrupted line of development from the patient's core primary femininity, which had interwoven with her more evident phallic body concerns. Mayer's consideration stops with genital comparison and the stage of anatomical distinction. I wish to extend the territory of primary femininity to include from early on, a *whole* female-to-female body comparison which would then naturally include the small girl's fascination with the pregnant female body, the breasts, abdomen, buttocks, and all body parts including skin and hair as well as genitals. I believe that this developmental trajectory provides many clues to a woman's final body image, to its pleasures as well as

114

to the kinds of fears of inferiority that beset many females in our consulting rooms.

I shall now summarize the five trends.

1. Genital issues

Laqueur (1990) points out that Freud's idea of the girl starting as a little boy belongs in a tradition of a "one-sex" theory of humans, i.e., ". . . woman was understood as man inverted" (p. 236) for two thousand years till about the eighteenth century. Freud therefore reintroduced an atavistic element in the sex and gender debate by separating the clitoris (male) from the rest of female genitalia. For him, the female genitals were then "an anatomical marker of woman's lack of what man has" (p. 233). Yet by suggesting a universal libido and elaborating dominance of vaginal orgasm over clitoral orgasm in adult females, Freud also demonstrated an incomplete struggle toward a two-sex model, Laqueur argues, one in which adult females are sexually capable but different from men in "every physical and moral aspect" (p. 5). Men and women were still closely compared. Freud thus collapsed the two models in his thinking and his focus remained on the genitals. Young-Bruehl (1990) contends that Freud's abiding contribution of universal bisexuality still stands. It allows for a complex concept of gender identity derived from traits of one or the other sex in patterned form in an individual woman. Early psychoanalytic dissenters to the one-sex model were Jones and Horney. Most writers, however, followed Freud in comparing the woman's sexual organs closely with those of men, but many continued also to develop and describe the female in relation to her own body. Thus there are papers over the years pointing to early vaginal awareness, infantile masturbation, a female sense of inner space, reactions to sphincter control, the introitus, e.g., Erikson (1968), Kestenberg (1982), Richards (1992). Descriptions of the adolescent girl's reactions to her rapidly changing body and onset of menses have been richly rendered (Ritvo, 1976; Shopper, 1979). But here too the focus is on the genitals and abstractions about their integration into body image; little is said about, for example, the budding breasts. After her initial confusion about comparison to males, *the girl develops more or less as girl, but the genitals and her internal awareness are the main focus of these texts.*

115

2. *Woman as separate*

Deutsch (1944, 1945) pioneered a view of women through the life cycle. The female as menstruating, becoming pregnant and menopausal, highlights the difference of the female, even though Deutsch does not question a beginning embedded in one-sex ideas. This literature progresses, often subsequently enriched by a two-sex model. Pregnancy is a specific topic of Bibring *et al.* (1961), Benedek (1970), Pines (1994), Raphael-Leff (1995). Women analysts, too, were described as different from male analysts in some ways. Papers on the pregnant woman therapist belong here, Nadelson *et al.* (1974), Balsam and Balsam (1974), Uyehara *et al.* (1995). A male analysand's erotic transference, or paternal transference to a woman analyst were further explicated by Goldberger and Evans (1985).

Feminist critics contributed to a social debate toward the equality of women, decrying Freud's one-sex originary model of female development as a social construct. The biological body becomes lost in most of this writing. Chodorow (1978) discusses the mother's pregnancy importantly as part of the social oppression of the heritage of girls, but not otherwise as part of psychological development. *The fate of the woman herself is the focus.*

3. *Children and mothers*

The effects of mothers on their children as the latter progress through the psychosexual phases is explored extensively in the child literature, mainly in terms of their functioning as nurturers. I find few references to the girl's specific reaction to the mother's pregnant body *per se*, but I stand to be corrected because there are so many single case histories. I think it is fair to say that the topic has not been singled out. Freud (1933) developed late an awareness of the importance of the mother to the girl child's first desire to produce a baby, and Mack-Brunswick (1940) detected the preoedipal girl's wish for a baby, antedating her awareness of her genital difference from boys. Focused here are purely the child's wishes. The child's conception theories are familiar. Anal, male-derived, and oedipal fantasies about the child's wished-for "pregnancy" are recorded. The mother's reactions to genital difference is cited as contribution to the girl's reactions to her own genitals (Lerner, 1976). Much attention accrues to the new-born rival. Perhaps these complex factors overshadow the child's reaction to the maternal body. *The child's reaction to the pregnant maternal body remains slighted.*

4. *Female gender studies*

By now the concept of core gender identity is established (Stoller, 1968; Kleeman, 1971; Tyson, 1982; Tyson and Tyson, 1990). Gender role identity and sexual partner orientation are conceived as developmental additions to this basic building block. An unusual paper by Kleeman (1971) attends specifically to a two-and-a-half-year-old girl's comparisons to her pregnant mother to help her sort out anatomical difference, in addition to her comparisons to the male. My present paper belongs in this tradition for a search for detail of female comparison to female, to enrich the concepts of body image development and later to be fitted into the concepts and guidelines suggested by the Tysons in the trajectory of gender role identity formation.

5. *The Kleinian and object-relations tradition*

Klein (1928) certainly views the mother's body as equally weighted with the father's in a child's development. Phallus, vagina, body cavity, pregnancy, breasts, and parental intercourse are of equal fascination. Attention to body surface has not drawn interest because the focus is so internally derived from originary fantasy. Body specificity, I think, requires an underpinning of an ego-psychological orientation which has not easily fit with an exclusive object-relations perspective.

None of these five kinds of studies has been attentive to female-to-female body comparison. Yet obviously, a pregnant mother is inescapable to the eye, to the touch, and to the imagination of her daughter. In order to attend to this issue psychoanalytically, one requires aspects derived from each of these five categories of contribution. Thus, an analyst needs a two-sex model, an acceptance of the girl's body as productive of its own sensation, interest, and imagined future, a view of men and women as equal but different, and an

117

acceptance of the prime significance of the mother to a girl's development.

Case 1

Ms. A. was a forty-eight-year-old interior decorator, divorced five years previously. She had two adult, professional, single daughters in their late twenties. She turned to analysis to address a few questions that had long irked her. Why, she mulled, did she turn out to be the "spitting image" of her mother, with a short temper, a perfectionism that drove others to drink (a wry reference to her ex-husband), a need to nag her daughters about their weight, a grumbling obsession about her own weight, and an uneasy sense that her work was never good enough? She had hated these characteristics in her mother. Ms. A. believed she was hard to live with. "I pick at people. I pick and pick. When my mother was dying and she was half-conscious, I was sitting up with her during the night. I was stroking her hand. She opened her eyes for a moment – just long enough to growl at me – 'For God's sake Georgina, you're putting on weight again. Your hands are pudgy.' I felt so, so [she gasped back a sob] hurt. It was four a.m.. She died at dawn." Ms. A. did not want to continue to be enslaved to this relentless ritual of complaint.

Ms. A. was a fresh-faced, crisp little woman with a pear-shaped figure, dressed in a business suit. Her five-year analysis dealt with many issues common in the lives of women – questioning self-esteem, relationship problems, inhibition of aggression, inhibition of sexual feelings, and body image concerns.

The family history as it related to figures for identification involved this domineering and critical mother who was yet not devoid of warmth, especially for babies, and a working-class, steady father who held benign ideals of "betterment" for his two daughters and one son. My patient was the eldest. The sister, Estelle, was two years younger, and the brother, Eric, six years her junior. The patient and her sister Estelle were born during hard times in the Great Depression. The peak developmental moments of significance in the analysis of Ms. A.'s character and interwoven depression circled around the birth of each sibling – one at her anal stage, when she struggled with mother over constipation, the next at the height of her oedipal striving. Ms. A.'s marriage at eighteen years suggested an

118

effort at a precocious push into adulthood. The figure that loomed largest in her analysis was her mother.

The opening gambits in the analysis suggested a transference where I was a female friend and confidante. Excitedly, she shared with me her secrets, hopes to impress clients, disappointments. I heard about the details of her 25-year marriage, the high-school romance with the football hero, and her social success as Queen among the seniors, deteriorating to her gradual disillusion at how hard it was to have babies with a husband who was terrified that domestication would undermine his manhood. Fighting, back-biting, and his alcoholism marred their years together. Their sexual relationship was poor to nonexistent latterly. She attended art school in her thirties. As soon as she could support herself and her daughters were independent, she fulfilled a long-held promise to herself: she separated from and subsequently divorced her husband.

I watched the sting of Ms. A.'s tongue at first from a distance: this neighbor was callow in matters of taste; that co-worker lacked a sense of design; the other was laughably obese. Another was a "circus dwarf." How long, I wondered, could her contentment with me continue? Her talk to me echoed her experience with a high-school clique of nasty "popular" girls. Mutual allegiance had operated within the inner sanctum of approval. High school was her favorite time in life.

One day, about nine months into treatment, she saw me make my way toward the office, hunched against the cold, an old hat pulled over my ears, picking my path with caution over patches of ice. I preceded her, not noticing her at some distance behind me. Once established in the room, she said that I had slammed the front door in her face. What was wrong, she wanted to know. Hesitatingly at first, and with my help, though pointing out how she was holding back criticism of me, possibly sensing danger, she began to elaborate. How could I wear that old hat? The coat, too, looked worn and awful. It was too big for me. Or perhaps not, maybe I had put on weight? It was hard to get a full look at me. At the beginning of the analysis I had looked neatly dressed, she thought, more like her. I seemed bigger now – bigger and fatter than she was. I looked like a bag lady. What was I hiding?

A paradigm for the unfolding pattern of her inner conflicts was forming. Two themes will be isolated at this point. (1) "You ignored me. Then you slammed the door in my face. You hurt me

119

and make me mad. You disappoint me." (2) "Your body looks changed. How does your body compare to mine?" The conscious level of this sequence appeared over and over in the analysis. The unconscious underpinnings belonged to the eras of both of the mother's pregnancies.

Maternal preoccupation

At later junctures also the patient was exquisitely sensitive about my failures to see her in public places. She disliked any evidence of my preoccupation with my inner world. At these moments she described me as "dreamy and far away" and "spacey." I was "in a fog," "out to lunch," "distant," "in a world of your own."

Ms. A.'s language conjured up a transference creature adrift in internal contemplation. She denied that my actual attention to the details of her associations in the sessions had shifted. My behavior as I crossed paths outside the sessions was the stimulus. Because of her simultaneous references to my "baggy" clothes in these sightings, I asked about the connection between my look and her inference about my mental state when I failed to see her. "I can see your whole shape outside. I can tell how you're feeling when I see you from a distance," she explained. "When you're tentlike, you're too dreamy to notice me." She built many scenarios of my "troubles" and mental state based on these moments. She was worried that I was short of money. Was my husband out of work? That was the first clue to the time frame of the regressive material that began to emerge. Imaginatively, we were back in the Great Depression. The following dream also alerted us both further to the events of the time.

> I am walking in a street, and the lights are bright. It seems to be Christmas. I am very happy and expecting Santa Claus. I have on a green velvet dress. I smoothe down the front nice and flat. My parents were around someplace.
>
> The scene changes. Somebody in a big brown cloak has her back to me. I'm in a toilet, in a stall sitting on the toilet and feeling all swollen up. My mother turns out to be in that cloak, bears down on me and starts screaming at me. I start to cry and I wake up with my heart pounding.

120

The associations began with the figure in the cloak – like me, she said – turning my back. This was a symbol of my preoccupation.

Given the next scene depicting the cloaked figure's screams, Ms. A. began to wonder if her urgency about my inattention "cloaked" a terror that I was in fact enraged at her. It was like sitting on the toilet before Estelle was born, trying to "poop" while mother, with her own "fat" belly, got frustrated. Her sensitivity to my preoccupation and shape were therefore especially reminiscent of her mother's pregnant state at the time of Ms. A.'s constipation. Mother, however, was always somewhat irritable about physical closeness. "You had to watch her hairstyle, or her lipstick. I did sit on her knee – it's just that I had to be very careful. I liked to sit and play with her necklaces, and touch her breasts, and I fiddled with the buttons down the front of her dresses. I used to count them and examine spaces – like I knew when her breasts were getting bigger, before Estelle's birth. And I could feel the big lump under her dress. I believe she did breast-feed me for a bit – not long. I remember her throwing me off her knee in a rage when she got so bulky, and she told me I was too heavy." We had evidence of little Ms. A.'s attempts at close physical proximity, affectionate and hostile scrutiny of the mother's body, which were nevertheless tentative due to mother's irritability and self-involvement. Ms. A. had had to curb her curious and exploratory maternal touching early. We believed that mother's pregnancy, reduced lap, plus the wrangling over the constipation added an extra blow that created more uneasy distance between them. The quality of Ms. A.'s sudden concern about my keeping her at bay because of my money worries, my unemployed husband, and the simultaneous growth of my girth reconstructively placed us in reactivated concerns from that era. "Mothers who change shape can change mood too, and get very, very mad!" she averred. "You have to watch out." Ms. A. now no longer felt safe with me.

The changed body and the mother–daughter comparison

In the initial girl-to-girl transference, Ms. A. related to me as if I were separate but equal and possessed body similarities to herself, even if they were not brought to consciousness in analysis. The subjective realm of "shared" feeling tones, outlook, and imagined experience dominated the associative field. Others were outsiders, yet unconsciously compared to her own body as bigger than "us," uglier than "us," more grotesque than "us".

Cast out of my circle of intimacy, overt body talk was ushered in. First the clothes were the emotional trigger. These, she felt, had changed for the worse. Her own miserable feelings and my perceived ugly looks were meshed. "I feel closed out and hurt, and you are in a big, ugly coat" associatively came together. In her dream, mother's vast brown cloak – associated with mother's pregnant state and "a color I really hate" – was featured side by side with childhood memories of her own constipation, her enlarged, swollen belly and weeping because her stools were stuck inside and would not come out. The phrase she used, "She bore down," yielded also associations of the births of Ms. A.'s own children. The patient had dreaded pregnancy and had expected her body to be ruined due to uncontrollable abdominal swelling. Her first baby had been large, and had taken many hours to deliver. She remembered vividly screaming at the midwife and cursing the doctor who had to use forceps. It was an immense relief finally to get the baby out of her body. The mother figure in the dream she was analyzing now was furious, screaming, and conveyed an image of pushing something down upon her. Ms. A. recalled her childhood fantasies about mother's screams as she gave birth to Estelle, much like Ms. A.'s own reactions to her constipation and her own subsequent childbirth experience. The dream child was overwhelmed and afraid. "It was all a nightmare," she sighed. "You shouldn't wear those baggy clothes. It makes me scared you're pregnant too. And I can't stand you not seeing me."

One can see in these sequences an interchangeability between the affects, fantasies, and body experiences of the girl child, constipated in this case, blended with her experiences of the body and affect of the adult woman, pregnant in this case. Later we understood that in part the constipation episodes, like her angry response to me at the front door, probably were designed to pull mother out of her "dreamy" pregnant states.

When Ms. A. spoke of the green dress in her dream, she used her hands to smooth down her abdomen as she lay talking, a gesture signaling the current liveliness of the topic in my presence. The velvet dress had been a precious Santa gift from her father. She looked "gorgeous" in her new dress. "Then I was so nice and thin. Not like that heap of a mother. I was so flat in those days – not like now, when I'm so lumpy." Mother, by her own self-description, was tall but always wanted to be thinner. Frequently the mother compared their bodies while taking showers together, telling the child to cherish always her slender lines. Ms. A. recalled uneasily crawling into bed beside her pregnant mother, feeling very superior to the rubbery, "lumpy" (her word earlier for her own abdomen), yet "cushiony" form that she surreptiously tried to snuggle into. She would poke mother's body and say, "Lumpy, gooey, ucky!" Mother would push her away, telling her she "couldn't help it." The patient's unconscious ambivalence toward mother's belly, echoing the mother's own ambivalence toward her increased weight, pregnant abdomen, and breasts could be appreciated in Ms. A.'s memories and her contemporary words describing her own figure. In the analysis, fears of an increase in my belly and a shift in my affect were now in focus, and gauged by comparison to hers.

Ms. A.'s mother's dresses were a theme in the analysis. There was a red polka-dot silk cocktail dress. It was slinky, with a frill around the hem – "like a mermaid." Ms. A. stressed that it was flat in front. She imagined herself, this time enviously, watching mother put it on to go out with father. "She pulled it up from the feet over her great slim legs that she said Daddy said were like a ballet dancer's. We both looked in the mirror, and thought she was gorgeous."

"That word again, 'gorgeous,' comes together with 'being flat,' or like a mermaid," I reflected. She responded, "That makes me think of another dream. I'm a grownup. I am preening in a mirror and smoothing down the front of myself, in a blood-red satin dress, and I like what I see – slender hips and abs of steel," she said longingly, "so far from this pudgy shape I'm stuck with ever since my babies came." By the elucidation of these references, we appreciated again the red dress and her body image at one with her favored internal vision of the most admired shape of her mother, the version of her body between pregnancies. The story of the red dress continued in another session.

At age ten, as punishment for fighting with both siblings, mother banished her to the parental bedroom without dinner. After her tears had dried, the child took mother's sewing shears, opened her closet, pulled out the red dress and systematically cut it into shreds. She had no memory of the repercussions. This deliberate destruction was a complex act of vengeance wreaked on both herself and mother. "I cut up her favorite dress. It was my favorite dress of hers

123

too. I think I was trying to destroy her thin, flat, beauty to pay her back. She could never have the satisfaction of wearing it again. I felt hopeless about ever having a figure like that myself, and I was mad about being constantly pushed away by her. I was tubby around the middle at ten, and I was scared of having periods. I knew they had something to do with being able to get pregnant. She must have so resented being pregnant with me as well as Estelle and Eric. She hated us kids fighting." One could also detect here the fear of what fate awaited Ms. A.'s enlarging prepubertal body and a dread of future body swellings.

Throughout the analysis, Ms. A. regularly noticed and spoke about my clothes. Most of these comments would be followed by references to her own wardrobe, suggesting to me ongoing scrutiny of body comparison. Often it measured who was superior and who inferior in thin/fat terms. Her own body seemed always perceived by contrast or similarity to another woman. Tent shapes on me or herself were "like haystacks." A–line dresses were "cutsey little girls playing at being pregnant." Long skirts were fine, as long as the waist was visible. If the blouse flowed to the top of the legs without definition, it was deemed "frumpy." Trouser suits were not especially noted, perhaps because she once said that her mother never wore them.

Male influences regarding body image

The male comparisons for Ms. A., as often noted in case studies, focused on the genitals. In her ex–husband's drunken, disinhibited states she had seen him late at night, in underpants, with his large, flaccid organ hanging out as he dozed in the living room. Memories of her father came back. She used to sneak peeks of him in the bathroom, in underpants, the clear bulge of his genital being her fascination. Disgust, fear, as well as excitement were registered. "They did something dirty at night. I thought he poked it into her hole," she giggled, "like poking a stick into a car tailpipe with stinky fumes . . . [She sighed and nervously touched her abdomen] making damned babies again." Her emphasis was on largeness, bulge, ugliness, and a primal scene with an anal cast. I looked in vain for some connections, for awe and admiration of images of the adult phallus, perhaps leading her to an internalization of classical ideals of a "phallic" body image.

124

Her brother's tiny penis was the major focus for her male-oriented envy when she scrutinized their respective endowment. She thought it would be fun to play with such a dainty little stick. Secret genital play had occurred with brother. Masturbation fantasies involved "taking" his organ and putting it on her mons pubis. She admired latency-boy figures and connected her aspiration to be thin and flat also to acquiring brother's body outline. These conflicts were vivid for her at puberty. As she struggled with breast growth, growing hips, putting on weight at age twelve, and the initial horrors of menstruation, his seven-year-old body seemed enviable to her. The early adolescent closeness to peer girls, who characteristically compared their bodies, helped her to assume more comfort with breasts that were envied by other girls, and helped her appreciate her nubile body that brought excitement from peer boys. Interest in the technicalities of sexual intercourse and her female power to promote arousal and popularity with boys went side-by-side for her with temporary repression about the implications of her body for procreation and pregnancy, which, as we saw in the analysis, held a rush of horror, ambivalence, and expectation of ugliness. Adolescence was also a time of safer distance from mother. Not so, once she married. The unfinished internal work about her own body as compared to her mother's procreative body took on new life.

Ms. A.'s own experience of pregnancy and childbirth had a flavor of being "visited" upon her. At times she blamed her husband for his desire to prove his manliness by impregnating her. Once the girls were born, she was a passable caretaking parent. To say simply that she suffered from a denial of femininity did not do the situation justice. She wanted to be a mother in the executive sense. She could separate her feelings of bodily grotesqueness from her interest in the children's welfare. She recalled just "waiting out" the pregnancies, feeling depressed, and hiding from company the larger she became. Her first delivery was long and painful; she was grateful for a spinal block for the second.

A dream in which she ran through mud puddles, tearing the hem of a fancy pink dress, evoked a fantasy that she had glimpsed a torn hem on my dress the previous day. Perhaps my husband had ripped my dress off in a fit of passion, she mused. That made her think of me being torn apart giving birth. "Women aren't big enough to let out a baby," I said. "Yes . . . well I think that happens. I used to think that that must be the only way. You had a ragged and torn

125

vagina forever after. I imagined my mother was torn inside. In fact I saw her vagina once, and it looked like a jagged black hole with fur. I thought that's what made her cross all the time with us kids. She must have been ripped when giving birth. I was certain that I would end up torn like her. I guess I still think that . . . I just said you are torn too." At one point, while working on these issues in analysis, she reported using a mirror to examine her genitalia. She detected surprise in her reaction that she still looked intact. I felt that Ms. A.'s "castration" anxiety represented much about the fear of the fate of the female vaginal canal in childbirth. Her level of association seemed to support this anxiety rather than a more classical reference to a "missing penis."

The baby

For Ms. A., the wish to have a baby was expressed in two modes, a caretaking mode of maternal identification, which she preferred, and the bodily mode of carrying and giving birth to a baby. Envy of her mother for taking charge of the little ones, as well as a wish to join her and thus gain approval, was expressed in the former mode. We appreciated that her proclivity to criticize her children and others actually held a positive valence, and was part of a strong childhood picture of the behavior of any competent mother worth her salt. Turning out the "spitting image" of mother, in spite of contrary wishes, encoded the "spit" and "spite" of her early vision of an angry mother with three children under six years old.

The embodied mother, not surprisingly, was a largely negative construct for her. I can best show how Ms. A. reworked some of her own bodily anxiety together with her projected worries that mothers and mother/analysts hated being pregnant and delivering, by relating some unusual regressive events in my office, late in the analysis.

Consonant with her profession as an interior decorator, the patient often seemed visually compelled by the decorations on my walls. Her eyes would travel from picture to picture, while she would critique the merits and demerits of each work of art. Her gaze of me had shifted from the sightings in the street, to a closeup view of my surround. "I always feel that a person's decor is the same as their body," she said repeatedly. I understood then that her comments about the office were close displacements from her fantasies about my body. At times this was interpreted. For example, she said, "I hate that tapestry of the squirrel. People who like tapestries like dark, old, twisted things." "Perhaps something about me is dark and twisted today, and it seems easier to talk about the tapestry?" I asked, hoping to address the resistance. "What is twisted is that we both know that I'm talking about you, but I'm an artist and I just need to use this space to explore some things. Please let me do this in my own way! You have to understand that the interior of the room *is* you – as I lie here it's how I *know* your insides." She was fervent. I decided to accept her symbolism and enter into it with her, instead of insisting on secondary process.

A colorful Matisse poster from his Moroccan period particularly captured her eye. As she stared at it she reported a swelling sensation in her abdomen, "coming up like a balloon" and a tingling sensation of growing very large, extending over the end of the couch. "I feel myself inside the room in the painting, with you, looking into the distance. How can I get through the window and onto that beach below? Would I push the flowers on the windowsill aside and jump? Are there stairs hidden and leading down to the beach? The outside is sunny and there are little people on the beach below, but inside this room is blue and dark." She sighed sadly. I wondered out loud if she felt trapped. Her eyes traveled to a watercolor. "Now I am going through the woods and pushing through the black furry underbrush [I thought of her previous description of her mother's vagina]. I could swim down that brown river." Her gaze moved on. "The path down over there is hilly. The landscape is covered with little round hills. Maybe I could scramble down the bank? It's so hard," and she sighed again. I found myself in a responsive daydream. It was no accident that I, too, should have experienced my own regressive pull at those moments, for the landscapes in which she was now wandering were ones from our family place in Ireland, where I grew up. There is not an inch of the territory that surrounds me in my watercolors that I have not trodden, and there is not a "little round hill" that I have not clambered upon. I am, in effect, surrounded by my own Mother Earth, and it is the soil belonging to my father.[1] The whole room seemed to become my own vast imagined pregnant belly. It was as if she were imagining herself as my internal fetus becoming too big for the space, as if she were viewing from the inside the obstacles of my womb, inspecting the territory and wondering how to escape into the world. At a previous point Ms. A. reported a dream where she was first in a basket of a hot–air balloon, hovering uneasily over the earth. She became transfixed with the primary colors of the balloon and, in the dream, became anxious as she was gradually sucked up into the cavity of the balloon, being first long and thin and then expanding again. In her associations she had referred to the vivid primary colors of the Matisse painting and spoke of a parallel feeling of being "sucked into" the painting. Pregnancy and birth had occupied her associations that day. More anxiety had accompanied the association then, and had been interpreted at the time. She had spoken of the balloon as a uterus, and declared a fantasy of becoming sucked into my "womb." There had been Matisse prints in her childhood home. She associated primary colors to her children's bedrooms.

Based on her own comments about how the room was symbolic of my insides, my own regressive experience, and the memory of her balloon dream, I offered an interpretation. I spoke of her wish to exist inside my body and look at it from the inside. I proposed that she feared the power of her wish because it would mean that I could suck her into myself to make me big, and she feared it would be very hard to get out. She was quiet for a bit. "I do want to become like you," she said slowly. "I want to *be* you. I want to be your baby, right inside you. I want to be part of you. And I don't want you to push me away like mother, before I'm ready myself. But I want to get out, too. . . . I want to be your big girl too . . . It will be very hard to stop coming here." She recalled days on the couch when she would sit up slowly, experiencing dizziness. "I was angry then. I didn't want to get sucked in and be dependent . . . Now that's okay . . . but I also want to be free. I can imagine you looking at me through a window now. It is sunny and I fancy you'd approve of me playing on the beach." She ultimately translated this experience as a constellation of previously repressed fantasies, embodying both her desire to be inside the big belly and her desire to emerge, empowered to feel that she too could potentially become the possessor of the big form and belly. She later spoke of how important it was that I tolerate this regressive experience and not push her away as she felt mother had done when she snuggled up to her pregnant form in bed, to fantasize about her past and future as a woman, and to explore her mother's body further. It had been painful for the girl to hear her mother say about her pregnancy that she "couldn't help it." By listening to her regressive fantasy about birth, she extrapolated that I did not object to her position on the couch, in front of me, in my room, enacting a symbolic representation of being pregnant with her awaiting "delivery" (which turned out to be termination thoughts). Ms. A. was working through primitive guilt about a masturbation fantasy that involved my adult "pregnant body" (the room, the painting, and herself supine on the couch) and a fantasized trajectory of her fate as a girl infant who could also grow into a woman and be pregnant and deliver, with my blessing.

At times in the termination phase Ms. A. would wear bright blues and reds. She adopted more of a Bohemian style, "not like yours and not like mother's," with looser and flowing pants and dresses. It was an era of fashion toward the less form-fitting. But she and I interpreted her responsiveness to this shift as consonant with more ease about her underlying shape. It mattered less to appear "flat" all of the time. We terminated as she approached menopause. Her depression had lifted, and she had less fear of the physical changes she anticipated in advancing age. "Some day I hope my daughters will be pregnant and that I'll be a comfortable grandmother. I hope I'll have a granddaughter, and I suppose I'll redo the history of my body all over again." As I trudged through the snow in my old hat and coat, I hoped she would have the opportunity.

Case 2

Ms. B. was a thirty-one-year-old loving, if anxious, mother of a two-year-old boy, and wife of a scholarly graduate student of physics. She was a high-school teacher. She suffered from "underachievement," and wanted to explore her urgent competitiveness in analysis. Compared to her academically successful husband, she felt inadequate.

It was a functional marriage with mutual encouragement and passion. They were both entranced with their little boy. Ms. B's parents were a traditional couple from the Midwest, her father a businessman. Her sister, Frances, was four years younger.

The analysis lasted four years. The first year unfolded themes about Ms. B.'s competitive feelings with her husband. She felt her father had wanted his oldest to be a boy, to keep the business in the family. A tomboy and athletic, she still enjoyed coaching field hockey. There was evidence of a classical phallic oedipal striving; she tried to become father's best boy while at the same time covertly

129

wooing him to become his best girl. The route to a fantasy boyhood seemed more open because, as she said, "there seemed to be too many females to compete with in the household." The birth of her own boy and her marriage to a man her father admired provided an outlet for some transformation of these issues, if at times she felt rivalry with them both. She had unconscious fantasies of attempting to possess a penis, one way or another.

Male body themes became more peripheral as her specifically female body took center stage. Even from the beginning, Ms. B.'s breasts were a matter of pride and hope for body self-esteem. They did hold some phallic significance, too, for example, in such comments as, "Why should I care what the men have, when I have two beauties of my own?" All curves of her female body were of interest to her, but the breasts were predominant. Avid competition with women emerged. She was of medium height, trim and muscular, with a blonde bob. There was a bouncy air to her carriage. She had large breasts, which she talked about initially as needing special "cradling" in athletic support bras when she ran on the hockey field. Her words first attracted my ear because they were so tender, like words she used for her little boy, and they seemed offered in a slightly yearning tone: "my boobies," she called them affection-ately. At menstruation, when they became engorged, she declared that the slight ache was pleasant. "My great big titties are really gigantic today," she would giggle, "I'm glad I'm on my back here – they look like they're sitting up all by themselves today. Do you look at them? I wonder what you can see from where you sit?" And she would push them up further, inviting my fuller inspection. As these moments were full of teasing giggles, one day I ventured naughtily, "All the better to see you, my dear!" entering into her playfulness. "What big eyes you have, grandma!" she flashed back. "Oh I do feel like Little Red Riding Hood with her goodies, coming to see grandma . . . I feel like I'm offering you my breasts – maybe to eat, but more to show them and take them away. I have something you'd like, but they're mine, and I can take them home with me." "I guess you're teasing me with your goodies," I said. This led to associations about being teased at school by "drooling" teenage boys and being lustfully stared at by older men. She agreed with my interpretation that it was a reference to her "drooling," Grandma Wolf/analyst/father. It was a response to my enactment, but with its own internal significance. We were shifting ground between male and female.

She grew sad and serious. "Big breasts and looking make me remember that I used . . . every excuse to watch Mother breast-feed Frances. I thought they looked luscious to suck. I envied the baby. But I urgently wanted to know what it was like to have big breasts myself. Mother's breasts were great . . . awesome . . . like the universe or something," and she sighed wistfully. Ms. B.'s flirtation and cheeriness always markedly ceased when these themes of oral desire and envy and admiration of the mother's breasts came up. Talking about women was less playful than talk about men. She was in a state of deep awe observing her mother's body.

In the last two years we spent most sessions on herself, me as woman (as opposed to me as a man), her mother, and Frances, a stereotypically "frilly" girl. Ms. B. spoke of looking at women's magazines and other women in the gym as she worked out. She searched the torsos for "boobs" – the bigger the better. She constantly compared sizes of women's "rear ends." Spandex and skintight workout gear were her specialty. She watched my body especially for low necklines and declivity. She declared my breasts small. Her gaze also included the lower body.

"You sit all day. Your behind is big. That reminds me of a dream. I was in a zoo. There was this mammoth kangaroo. It was like a huge pyramid, and it had a little baby in its pouch. How do they give birth anyway? Do they have a big hole under there? Ugh! Imagine they'd lose all their control – they're such athletes, jumping around usually. They must pour their 'do' when they give birth – so gross! [a cloacal theory of birth, I thought]. Maybe their little Frankie, no, Joey – Frances! – comes out of their bellybuttons, right into the pouch? It would be neat to have a pouch in front like that. You could see everything then."

Later she spoke of thoughts about her mother's body and her pregnancy with Frances. She returned to puzzles about the kangaroo. Ms. B. expressed such concern about the perineum of the kangaroo that I told her I was reminded of her telling me she had worried the nurse would forget to let her look in the mirror when she herself was giving birth. "It used to be a mystery what was hidden down under," she said. (I refrained from interpreting the meaning of the choice of kangaroo as Australian, for her "down-under" references. The mood of the moment was somber, and I felt this intervention would be distracting. I fancied that my word play would invite her back into her teasing, phallic–competitive mode.)

131

After a pause, Ms. B. continued: "My father used to entertain me by taking me to the zoo to make me laugh when mother was pregnant." (I realized that I may have been about to do the same thing in the analytic process, now that the child's view of the topic of pregnancy and birth was graphically in the atmosphere. I noted to myself that there really is something anxiety- and guilt-provoking about staring at a pregnant body and wondering about the birth process in a sustained way, at close quarters, through the eyes of a curious onlooker. I had wished to dilute the moment in word play. Perhaps this reticence may be more widespread among analytic couples? Perhaps this was a clue to why people do not note this kind of material very often.)

Ms. B. went on in many other sessions to recall her views of mother's pregnant body in various lingerie, in different color large dresses, in the bedroom or bathroom. She had wanted to touch her mother's belly and breasts, but instead had eyed her constantly, viewing her mother's entire body, with special attention to her huge breasts and hips. She thought the buttocks might grow out in two mountains, to match the breasts. She connected her current attraction to looking at the female behind with a hope to see varying buttock size.

"I used to look at myself when I was seven or eight and worry that I would grow big, big buns. The big boobies were okay. How I yearned for the day when my little nothing chest would grow. I waited and waited. Yet I had a very unstable sense of what it would be like to change. As Mother grew, I thought it would never stop. And then she got flat again – but she still had those big, delicious breasts for a long, long time. God, how I wanted to *be* her and have those pillows myself."

Nature was kind in at last providing little Ms. B. what she wanted. She won the competition in body contour with her analyst, and apparently her mother and Frances, too. Ms. B.'s spirited competitiveness was therefore importantly fed by her female body comparisons, in my opinion even more prominent than her male body comparisons, but they were woven together.

Discussion

Does clinical material exist, in the associative process, that concerns primarily identification with the physicality of the mother? I believe

132

that it does, and that it deserves a place in our theory of female development as it relates to psychosexuality, gender role identity, and body image. The pregnant body, for example, would seem to be a natural apex in a theory of female development which claims that "the ego is first and foremost a body ego" (Freud, 1923, p. 27). I would therefore like to separate and bring into the center for consideration specific visual, kinesthetic, and tactile perceptions of female body-to-body comparison. Such cognitive registrations of body surface can serve as an external starting point for the kernel of fantasy life integral to interiority.

I have been particularly struck by ongoing and at times insistent reference to same-sex body comparisons that are frequent in the adult female patient talking to the female analyst. A male analyst may also hear these themes, but they are inescapable with a female dyad. Women like Ms. A. and Ms. B., of different ages and life experiences, are typical in their concerns as to the form and shape of their own exteriors and those of other women.

On hearing such references, which are additionally loaded with affect, such as envy or triumph, one rapidly listens on the plane of interior life and meaning. If one moves back a notch, as it were, concentrating on the description of exterior form and shape, joining the patient on the visual plane, then one begins to wonder about the origins of the heightened visual acuity for the human body that these fellow adults possess. Looking at shapes – not necessarily the detailed contents – and dressing with other women in mind seems a prominent preoccupation. The target of the eye is often other women, with a compared vision of how each appears in exterior outline. These images are often registered in comparison to the perceived outline of the subject herself.

A woman talking about another woman in analysis has often implied latent reference to "the mother." Developmentally, a dyadic object relation as opposed to a triadic situation can be implied, so that the analytic listener may become taken up with expectation of more primitive material and assumption than is the case when attending to the psychic plane of triadic object relations. I suggest that if this is the case, the therapist may almost automatically be attuning for merger phenomena accompanied by primitive fantasy, and thus perhaps may listen less for the surface quality of visual and tactile registration and its mental representation. A patient's ability to verbalize these phenomena suggests a capacity for separateness in

133

a woman when talking about her mother. It is true that Ms. A. showed primitive merger phenomena regarding the mother/analyst in her analysis, but only at one point, while deeply engaged in the analytic process prior to termination. The literature has stressed a continued internal focus on the mother, for women, as encompassing a "fixation" on her, implying a state to be hurdled if development is to proceed. This attitude could cause the analyst to try to "help" the patient too rapidly past the inevitable fascinations I dwell upon here. Mention of the same-sex body, too, is often related with alacrity to the erotic trend. Since homoeroticism is a difficult subject for patients who consider themselves heterosexual in orientation, the therapist is on the lookout for the disavowed and latent unconscious underpinnings. This listening stance could shift the attention away from granting phenomena concerning the surfaces of the body a history of their own.

"How do I occupy space as compared to other women?" seemed the underlying question as an originator of feelings, fantasies and memories that sharpened in the transference. "How do I shape up?" is a preoccupation that implies built-in comparison. "How is my body like my mother's?" is a question for a girl that encodes a present and future of changing shapes. I suggest that the questions, "Who's pregnant, who was, and who is not?" are a special unconscious dimension.

It is probably no accident that women's magazines have wide circulation in our culture. The pictures of other women in clothes of varying shapes are of endless fascination to fellow women. Tight forms, loose forms, emphasis on one curve or another concavity, colors and textures, and cosmetics draw women because of the shifting complexity of what may fit with any individual woman's visual necessity. The forms of naked women in men's magazines, which are more static, are perhaps of less interest to these manifest and latent concerns of women about fluid forms. This topic, of course, touches on the erotic response, which is a different but related question and is a complex one for women with regard to the respective visual lines of other females. I include it less here.

The attention to the analyst's clothes, the patient's own clothes and those of other women that appear in these case examples is testament to the importance of garments and their meaning to females. There is certainly a competitive element about how they will attract the male gaze.

Mirror, mirror on the wall
Who is the fairest of us all?

speaks profoundly to the intergenerational as well as the cross-generational beauty contest that exists for the erotic admiration of the King and the Prince. Dressing to optimize or conceal body configuration can represent this quest. Interior oedipal themes are easy to detect when such competition is in the atmosphere. Dressing for the Queen and Princess holds a separate interest.

What emotional valences "joined in the conversation" at the exterior of the body – to quote Freud's (1894, p. 180) useful way of thinking? Ms. A. ushered in her body talk by enacting with me the scenes of feeling acutely shut out of her mother's central focus, it turned out, especially at the periods of mother's pregnancies. She was chronically frustrated in her exploratory desire to touch and feel her mother, particularly when mother was pregnant. Joining the mother in her own self-perception, she grew first to admire visually the mother's nonpregnant or "flat" state, and later to search her own body for visual and tactile signs of this ideal. The pregnant bulge, the tired body and maternal preoccupation joined forces with her anger and hurt and repulsion. It is interesting how visual and kinesthetic sense becomes amalgamated with affective response and colors the response to shapes perceived in the object. Synesthesia is a concept in cognitive psychology to capture a joining of the senses, e.g., "the taste of the smell" of something. Grammatically, the phenomenon is known as "transferred epithet," e.g., "the green joy . . . [of the pasture]." This phenomenon must happen frequently in childhood when the attachments to the continuities of body form are less fixed, less predictable, and less knowable, and the interactions with adults are so intense. Convexity of the abdomen had vehemently retained for Ms. A. a sense of ugliness, anxiety, and despair. This was projected onto other shapes of women in her environment, with constantly comparative overtones. One can appreciate also how sublimation had turned into professional virtue. As an interior decorator, Ms. A. used her visual and imaginative proclivities for comparative assessments of the shapes and forms of material objects.

Ms. B., by similar mechanism of amalgamating visual stimuli with affect, had positive associations between fantasized delights of breast-feeding and the enlarged arc and circle or oval of the breast.

Convexity and largeness of the anatomical form accompanied by softness or firmness to the touch were her themes. Her focus on the buttocks seemed quite similar in quality to her focus on the breasts, but her responses were more ambivalent. Her reactions to rear ends conveyed overtones of both attractive and repulsive anal function. Her dream of the kangaroo located her body fascination with pregnancy. What a kangaroo hides under its "huge pyramidal shape" was a mystery. She admired the notion of a special pouch in front. One can hear, here, the often recorded wish of the girl to *see* the internal genital and womb, a wish often associated with envy of the boy's ability to clearly see the penis. Ms. B. seemed to have displaced upward some aspects of the swelling, growing pregnancy in the belly to her proudly held twin cupolae of the breasts. Perhaps her anxieties about the birth itself and how the babies would get out motivated her vision away from the belly toward the upper torso. Her feeling of having "nothing at all" in front, as a child, as well as comparison to mother's anatomical display arose also in comparison to her husband's and her father's sex organs. As suggested by Mayer (1995), Ms. B. could be thought of as having two interwoven developmental lines – one in consort with male body comparison, and the other in consort with the female body, including its capacity to bear children.

Conclusion

These are examples of women who compare themselves very closely with the mother. I think that these comparisons are probably not confined to actual experiences of mother's pregnancy, but may represent a wider scope of female preoccupation with the female body potential in general. By definition, a mother is the creature who bore the child, and the child is aware of this fact. A mother can also be pregnant or nonpregnant. It seems natural and expectable that a baby who is labeled "female" by the visual perception of her genitals by the grownups around her is going to be inculcated by virtue of mother's identified same sex and same gender with visual images of comparison. The genitals have traditionally been the main locus of definition in our literature for sorting out reactions and fantasies that build the girl's gender identity.

My material suggests that we have not sufficiently developed reactions in developmental progress about aspects of the female body other than the genital. Little has been written about the budding breasts, for example. My beginning contribution concerns the mother's pregnancy, an aspect more visible and I contend, at least as compelling for the growing girl as her own genitals. Granted, for a growing girl, it is a futuristic image, compared to the immediacy of her genitals. Her special physical interest in the body that swells up to deliver and to feed the child that she wishes or fears too, for whatever reason, may be at least as vital to a line of primary femininity as her comparative physical interest in the male.

Note

1 For a detailed description of a similar regressive transference/counter-transference, see Peto (1959).

References

Balsam, R. M. and Balsam, A. (1974) 'The pregnant therapist', in R. M. Balsam and A. Balsam *Becoming A Psychotherapist: A Clinical Primer.* Chicago, IL: University of Chicago Press, 1984, pp. 265–288.

Benedek, T. (1970) 'The psychology of pregnancy', in E. J. Anthony and T. Benedek (eds) *Parenthood, Its Psychobiology and Psychopathology.* Boston: Little Brown.

Bibring, G., Dwyer, T. F., Huntington, D. S. and Valenstein, A. F. (1961) 'A study of the psychological processes in pregnancy and of the earliest mother–child relationship'. *Psychoanal. Study Child*, 16: 9–72.

Chodorow, N. (1978) *The Reproduction of Mothering: Psychoanalysis and the Sociology of Gender.* Berkeley, CA: University of California Press.

Deutsch, H. (1944, 1945) *The Psychology of Women: A Psychoanalytic Interpretation*, Vols 1 and 2. New York: Grune and Stratton.

Erikson, E. H. (1968) 'Womanhood and the inner space', in E. H. Erikson *Identity, Youth and Crisis.* New York: Norton.

Freud, S. (1894) 'Further remarks on the neuro-psychoses of defence'. *S.E.* 3: 43–61.

Freud, S. (1923) 'The ego and the id'. *S.E.* 19: 3–59.

Freud, S. (1933) 'Femininity'. *S.E.* 22: 136–157.

Goldberger, M. and Evans, D. (1985) 'On transference manifestations in patients with female analysts'. *Int. J. Psychoanal.*, 66: 295–309.

Kestenberg, J. (1982) 'The inner genital phase: prephallic and preoedipal', in D. Mendell (ed.) *Early Female Development*. New York: S. P. Medical and Scientific Books.

Kleeman, J. (1971) 'The establishment of core gender identity in normal girls. 2. How meanings are conveyed between parent and child in the first three years'. *Arch. Sex. Behav.*, 1, 2: 117–129.

Klein, M. (1928) 'Early stages of the Oedipus conflict', in M. Klein *Love, Guilt and Reparation and Other Works: The Writings of Melanie Klein*, Vol. 1. London: Hogarth Press, 1975, pp. 186–198.

Laqueur, T. (1990) *Making Sex: Body and Gender from the Greeks to Freud*. Cambridge, MA: Harvard University Press.

Lerner, H. (1976) 'Parental mislabeling of female genitals as a determinant of penis envy and learning inhibitions in women'. *J. Am. Psychoanal. Assoc.*, 24: 269–283.

Mack-Brunswick, R. (1940) 'The preoedipal phase of the libido development'. *Psychoanal. Q.*, 9: 293–319.

Mayer, E. (1995) 'The phallic castration complex and primary femininity: paired developmental lines toward female gender identity'. *J. Am. Psychoanal. Assoc.*, 43: 17–38.

Nadelson, C., Notman, M., Aarons, E. and Feldman, J. (1974) 'The pregnant therapist'. *Amer. J. Psychiat.*, 131: 1107–1111.

Peto, A. (1959) 'Body image and archaic thinking'. *Int. J. Psychoanal.*, 40: 223–231.

Pines, D. (1994) *A Woman's Unconscious Use of Her Body*. New Haven, CT: Yale University Press.

Raphael-Leff, J. (1995) *Pregnancy: The Inside Story*. New York: Jason Aronson.

Richards, A. K. (1992) 'The influence of sphincter control and genital sensation on body image and gender identity in women'. *Psychoanal. Q.*, 61: 331–351.

Ritvo, S. (1976) 'Adolescent to woman'. *J. Am. Psychoanal. Assoc.*, 24: 127–137.

Shopper, M. (1979) 'The (re)discovery of the vagina and the importance of the menstrual tampon', in M. Sugar (ed.) *Female Adolescent Development*. New York: Brunner/Mazel.

Stoller, R. J. (1968) *Sex and Gender*. New York: Science House.

Tyson, P. (1982) 'A developmental line of gender identity, gender role, and choice of love object'. *J. Am. Psychoanal. Assoc.*, 30: 61–86.

Tyson, P. and Tyson, R. (1990) *Development: An Integration*. New Haven, CT: Yale University Press.

Uyehara, A., Austrian, S., Upton, L. G., Warner, R. H. and Williamson, R. A. (1995) 'Telling of the analyst's pregnancy'. *J. Am. Psychoanal. Assoc.*, 43: 113–137.

Young-Bruehl, E. (1990) 'Introduction', in E. Young-Bruehl, *Freud on Women: A Reader*. New York: Norton.

5

On motherhood

Erna Furman

In working with mothers' responses to the total or partial loss of their child, it becomes evident that, at one level, they experience such a loss as an injury to the integrity of their body ego, which includes the child. Their capacity to invest the child as a bodily part of themselves as well as to release him and transfer bodily ownership to him in the course of personality growth necessitates flexible body boundaries. This characteristic of the female body ego is both gratifying and threatening to the mother as well as to others. It also has a profound impact on the growing boy's and girl's attempts to differentiate themselves from the mother bodily and to delineate their own sex-specific body ego. The nature and outcome of this difficult process has a significant effect on women's and men's attitudes to motherhood. These attitudes contain many defensive measures against the primitive anxieties of this early level, contributing perhaps also to the frequent neglect of motherhood in theories of female psychology.

I shall focus on an aspect of female psychology that has been sidestepped, more often than not, in analytic contributions to this topic, namely the fact that the potential for being a mother and its realization, or lack thereof, forms the genetic core of womanhood and plays a crucial role in the development of boys and girls from the very start. The widespread neglect of the central role of motherhood – exemplified, for example, by Tyson's (1994) review of contemporary contributions to female psychology – is in striking contrast to our clinical experience which has shown us that: the female and male body ego develop by differentiation from that of a mother (not just a woman); girls and boys perceive their mother as a mother first and only later as a woman; their mother (in her mothering rather than womanly function) is their first object of identification; little girls want to be a "Mommy" long before they want to be a "lady" and refer to their doll as their "baby" long before it is given a special name; and, not least, the conscious and unconscious feelings and concerns about being or not being a mother (and what kind of a mother) remain a crucial part of being a woman throughout every woman's — and possibly every man's — life.

In keeping with this neglect, much of the controversy about sexual phallic monism has focused on establishing a concept of bedrock femininity characterized by a sense of bodily wholeness from the start and reinforced by identification with the mother's female genitals, without reference to motherhood. The emphasis, instead, has been on showing that little girls do not define themselves as lacking or inferior, but actually feel safer and more comfortable with their female genitals than boys do with their exposed vulnerable penis. Summarizing contemporary views, Tyson (1994) points out that establishing core gender identity is easier for the girl by virtue of her anatomy as well as through identification with her mother. The girl's "genitals and associated diffuse, whole body sensations are experienced as an integral and protected . . . part of her body from the beginning. . . . Therefore, defining a sense of body integrity is normally a smoother process for the girl" (p. 452). At the same time, identification with her mother provides "an experiential sense of being female, like mother, with female genitals" (p. 454). With motherhood left out, these considerations remain limited to boy–girl comparisons and the related phallic–narcissistic question of who is "better" or "better off."

It is noteworthy that the many analytic contributions that focus on the basic role of motherhood and the "inner space" as part of it, remain as isolated and neglected as the topic itself, especially in the USA. Among these are contributions by Chasseguet-Smirgel (1976), Erikson (1956, 1964), T.-B. Hägglund *et al.* (1978), T.-B. Hägglund *et al.* (1980), V. Hägglund (1981), Horney (1926, 1932), Kestenberg (1956a, 1956b, 1968), and Torsti (1993). In her 1976 paper, Chasseguet-Smirgel suggests that sexual phallic monism wards off the boy's double narcissistic wounds sustained in the relationship with the mother, i.e., his helplessness and dependency on her at first, and his oedipal disappointment and sexual inadequacy with her later. She finds that a powerful, envied, and terrifying maternal imago lies behind the defensive scorn of female inferiority. I do not dispute this insightful observation, but I think it does not explain everything.

Since boys *and* girls, men *and* women, find it so difficult to accept that the "psychological striving for motherhood is the core of femininity" (V. Hägglund, 1981, p. 143) and are so ready to exclude it from its role in male and female gender development, motherhood must imply additional deepseated early concerns. Over many years I have struggled to learn about these concerns and formulated some of my findings (Furman, 1982, 1984, 1992, 1993, 1994). I shall now retrace my steps in the hope of clarifying these inherently difficult issues.

The child as part of the mother's body ego

In 1969 I described the parents' special investment in their child as a hallmark of their entry into the phase of parenthood. In contrast to the investment of all other object relations, that of the parents in their child is characterized by a narcissistic cathexis, the child as a part of the self, which, to start with, far outweighs the concomitant object cathexis, the child as a loved person. As the child grows, there is a relative shift in the balance between these two kinds of investment, but the narcissistic one is never fully replaced and always remains a significant factor, qualitatively and quantitatively different from narcissistic elements in other relationships. I noted at the same time that, just as the parental investment of the child differs from other object relations, so the maternal investment differs significantly from the paternal one. Both parents include the child in their own mental self, but only the mother invests him also as a part of her bodily self, i.e., he is included in the boundaries of her body ego. The physiological and biological givens of pregnancy parallel and facilitate this latter process but they do not guarantee it. Some biological mothers fail to integrate their baby into their body ego or achieve it only partially; some adoptive mothers, though by no means all, succeed in this respect.

Although, at the time, I did not appreciate the full implications of the mother's bodily investment in her child, it proved to be a crucial and most helpful concept to me in understanding motherhood and is pertinent to the present discussion.

Mother's responses to the death of their baby

My first dramatic encounter with the manifestations of the maternal bodily investment came through my work with perinatal loss, mothers who lost a newborn or very young baby through death (Furman, 1980). Along with their conscious and very understandable feelings of distress, sadness, anger, guilt, despair and unconscious defenses against them, they complained of symptoms which disturbed them but which they in no way associated with their loss or, at best, vaguely related to the aftermath of a difficult pregnancy or delivery. Most often they experienced abdominal sensations which felt to them either like a growing cancerous tumor or like a strange "hole," "like something's all wrong with my insides," "some awful illness." Quite often too, they described radiating aches in their arms, a strange heaviness and difficulty in lifting or extending them. Occasionally, they attributed the disconcerting experience of "something all wrong" to their minds, fearing they were falling apart mentally and going crazy, and sometimes they could neither localize nor find words for their worry. Since others seemed not to take their complaints seriously, did not even want to hear about them, or told them to "pull yourself together," they felt even worse. Despite the intense anxiety, some of these mothers did not seek medical help and those who did were not reassured by the negative findings.

They were, however, greatly helped by two interventions: (1) My putting into words for them that the baby had been an integral, most important part of their body; that its removal from their inside (the hole) and lack of restitution by being also unavailable on the outside (the arms intended to hold him) were therefore experienced as an amputation of a vital body part or as the loss of a vital function, such as vision. They were feeling crippled and undone and, as with a real amputation or loss of function, would take a long time to adapt to the loss and repair their sense of bodily and mental wholeness without the baby. And because this experience was different and separate from the loss of the baby as a loved person, and represented, instead, a major injury to their bodily integrity, it was something that, like the sight of cripples, disturbed others and made it hard for them to empathize or even listen to their distress. (2) A concerted effort on the part of hospital staff as well as in working with the bereaved parents to afford them postnatal contact with the baby, even the dead baby, and to enlist their active role in arranging a funeral and burial or cremation. This facilitated the process of the mother transferring her cathexis of the inside baby to the outside baby and provided some opportunity for object cathexis. The more object cathexis, the greater the opportunity to mourn the child as a separate loved one – a difficult task in itself, but much easier for others to support than coming to terms with a shattered body ego.

Mothers' responses to the developmental loss of their child

During the subsequent years I could increasingly compare my child analytic findings with data from my work with mothers of infants and toddlers. I came to realize that the deeply shattering breach to the integrity of the maternal body ego accompanies not only the total loss of the child through death, but each developmental step in his personality growth and resulting increase in self-sufficiency (Furman, 1982, 1984, 1992, 1993, 1994).

The difference with the "ordinary devoted mother" of the living growing child is that she usually uses immediate and effective defenses against the threat of these primitive anxieties. During baby-hood, turning passive into active is most commonly used. I have described some of the many instances when the mother shifts the "trauma" of weaning from herself to her baby: she responds to his signs of readiness for self-feeding and rejection of the breast by leaving him first – by going to work, going on a trip, going out one night in such a way that he wakes up to an unexpected sitter, i.e., leaving him just enough to convey the terror of abandonment (Furman, 1982). These ways of leaving him first around the time of weaning often mark the start of the many sleep disturbances during the latter part of the first year.

These sleep disturbances, however, result as often from another maternal defense, namely transferring her hold on the child's body from nursing to sleeping. While letting go of the former, mothers tighten the reins on the latter as they unwittingly interfere with the child's "not needing" them during his night or nap time (Furman, 1982). Indeed, changing the form or area of owning the child's body is as common a defense as leaving him first. For example, spoonfeeding or rigid control of the types and amounts of food offered easily nullify the child's potential independence resulting from weaning; similarly, mother's ownership of nursing (what goes in) is often transferred to elimination (what comes out) which tends to be rationalized as related to the changes in digesting new foods.

During the toddler phase, the child's second and third years, mothers face the most concentrated task of changing the balance of their investment in the child, from predominantly narcissistic to object–oriented, in keeping with the child's personality growth. For mother and toddler this process focuses on the transfer of bodily ownership from her to him. She who heretofore gauged and met all his needs is expected to yield to his demand for bodily self-care and ownership, for it is mainly through the bit-by-bit process of owning, gauging, and ministering to his own bodily needs that the child differentiates himself from his mother and defines his body ego. This includes protesting pain, learning to avoid common dangers, washing, dressing and undressing, gauging hunger and self-feeding, gauging elimination and keeping clean, recognizing fatigue and putting himself to sleep.

I have described the arduous steps by which mother and child negotiate the transfer of bodily ownership – doing for, doing with, standing by to admire, doing for oneself – and I have described how extraordinarily difficult it is for mothers to do their part (Furman, 1992, 1993). They repeatedly ignore or deny the child's signals of readiness, they prolong the first two steps and, with the third of standing by to admire, tend to turn away, feeling no longer "needed." In doing so they have passed on the skill, the knowhow of self-care, but reneged on graciously handing over the gratification they experienced in performing it. By keeping that for themselves, they deprive their child of the most valuable part of owning his body. Once again, they leave him before he can leave them. The mothers' denials, delays, and reluctance are all the more striking when contrasted with their frequently expressed wishes for the child to do for himself, complaints about the tiring job of doing for him, even pride in his achievements of self-care, and often lavish support of the child's nonbodily skills, such as his motor activities, speech, block-building, or interest in puzzles. The same child whose small muscle dexterity is praised and admired may be deemed quite incapable of learning to wipe his behind.

144

Some mothers avoid being "left" by taking active control of their toddler's steps toward bodily self-care. Instead of heeding and responding to his signals of readiness and self-initiative, they are intent on teaching him each skill, and insist on his doing his "chores" when they consider it the right time, i.e., their time. In doing so they both push him away and retain ownership of his body because the process proceeds at their behest, while the child feels the threat of abandonment and need to satisfy mother rather than himself by performing for her.

All these maternal defenses protect her from the threat of losing the part of her body ego that is invested in her child. Unfortunately, they also constitute considerable interference in the child's ability to differentiate and integrate his own body ego and to invest it and his caring for it in an optimally pleasurable, gratifying way.

Many mothers are well aware of the wrench caused by the child's becoming his own person, be it his weaning, dressing himself, entry to nursery school, leaving for summer camp or college, getting married. They feel and verbalize their pain and sadness and, since they are also happy with and proud of his achievements, experience it as a bittersweet time that still allows them to support rather than impede his growth. Yet their awareness, though helpful to them and their child, derives from the more mature parts of their personalities. The primitive anxieties about bodily loss and disintegration surface in the form of sudden unwarranted panic states about losing something, which they in no way connect to the current situation of loss of the child. Let me add a couple of examples to several cited previously (Furman, 1994).

Example A

Following my presentation of this topic to an analytic group, an experienced analyst confided this episode: That very morning she had looked in vain for the sweater she was now wearing. As she rummaged through her drawers a panic seized her, quite disproportionate to the value of the sweater. She feared she had lost it for good. It finally occurred to her that her married daughter and grandchild had left that morning after a nice visit, and she became convinced that her daughter, who liked the sweater, had taken it with her. She found herself quite angry at her adult child, then opened once again the drawer where the sweater was supposed to be – and there it was.

145

She could not think how she had overlooked it, but she realized now that its presumed disappearance stood for the more profound loss of her daughter.

Example B

The mother of a two-year-old arrived to our appointment late and distraught. She had been "out of it" during the last four days because she had lost her wallet. She was without cash, credit cards, driver's license. She had searched everything in vain and spent her time telephoning around to stop misuse of the lost documents. She felt she was going crazy, could not function, and she also felt guilty for not being available to her little girl. As she retraced the events, it turned out that the night before the disappearance of the wallet the child had, at her own request, slept in a big bed for the first time, did so with pleasure, and wanted the crib removed. Mother had been pleased and appreciative of her daughter's developmental step but had reneged on removing the crib "in case she changed her mind."

Since the various effects of developmental loss on this mother had been a topic of our work in the past, I wondered with her whether perhaps, in addition to her positive feelings about her child's progress, there were also feelings of losing something very basic to her own self, so basic that it felt like she could not function without it. She connected the losses at once and cried out, "Oh my goodness, the wallet!" On returning home she called me, greatly relieved. She had found the wallet. It was where she had looked for it before.

Instances of pseudoloss are more or less effective ego measures to bind the emerging primitive experiences occasioned by body-ego loss of the child. We are alerted to them by the primitive panic the mother experiences temporarily and, often, by the accompanying anger at the child who, one way or another, is unjustly blamed for the loss or unwittingly "punished" for it, such as by mother's emotional withdrawal. It is only when mother and child reach an impasse during the transfer process or when the child reacts with symptomatic behaviors that upset the mother enough to request help that the ensuing therapeutic work reveals a glimpse of the forces that underlie mothers' manifest idiosyncrasies.

Example C

One mother came for help with her eighteen-month-old's persistent sleep disturbance which manifested itself in not going to sleep, waking repeatedly, and getting up very early. It "ruined" mother's life and she was also concerned for him, fearing she was doing something wrong. She was not concerned about his still frequent nursing, lack of self-feeding, and showing no initiative in other areas of bodily self-care. We came to understand that his sleep trouble related on one hand to his total dependence on her ministrations, without any means of self-comfort (thumbsucking, transitional object, or soft toy); on the other hand, it related to her many irregular absences during the day as well as emotional withdrawals when she was physically present. With closer observation we learned that her absences often appeared to be prompted by her son's even minor steps toward independence.

When his sleep trouble improved with the help of her increased insight and changes in handling, it suddenly got worse again. It turned out she had just begun an exercise program in the early mornings which made it necessary for the father to attend to the boy on his waking up. She felt she had to exercise "to get myself in shape and put my body together" – a rather common maternal response to the loss of the child as part of her body. With further insight into their mutual conflict about bodily ownership and delineation of body boundaries, she stopped the exercises, remained available in the morning, and his sleep again improved.

Then the following episode took place which frightened mother and child: She had always carried him downstairs, considering his learning to negotiate the stairs too unsafe. He had wanted to walk on his own on several occasions, but she reneged. That morning she again carried him downstairs, stumbled under the weight, and both fell headlong, sustaining minor injuries. She found herself in a rage and lashed out at him with, "See what you've done! You are much too big and heavy to be carried. From now on you will just have to get yourself downstairs on your own." She was chagrined and puzzled about her outburst and later apologized to him. She could begin to recognize that her need to thwart his "leaving" her and to push him away instead of supporting his independent steps warded off her sense of panic and rage at being "cut off."

She was not an abusive mother. Her anger was usually in good control and she wished for and appreciated her child's achievements in many areas. His bodily independence, however, constituted such a threat to her bodily integrity that her experience of it overtook the more mature aspects of her personality and allowed primitive panic and rage to surface.

147

The nature of the maternal, female body ego and some consequences

Some mothers can never allow their child to delineate and own his body ego for fear of what it would do to themselves and what they would do to him. Some can, with much effort, take the necessary steps if they are helped to gain sufficient insight into the nature of their predicament and if this work takes place in the context of a containing, supportive relationship. With less vulnerable mothers, such support does not need to be available through a therapist but can come through the relationship with an emotionally available husband, grandmother, or close friend (Furman, 1994).

The mother's psychic state at the time of these shattering experiences of bodily loss resembles those of an older infant or young toddler during the period of initial differentiation from the mother when his primitive, incomplete body ego is overwhelmed from within or without, or when the still essential parts of his mother's ego have disappeared, such as through her physical or emotional unavailability. He can only reconstitute his body ego by being bodily contained within the mother's, such as through her empathic holding and soothing of him. The extent to which the early states of bodily disintegration were effectively contained and repaired will determine how quickly and well he will later be able to use his own more mature personality parts to protect himself from such overwhelmings and/or to contain and repair them when they occur.

I have come to understand that the maternal body ego, and therefore motherhood itself, is characterized by never fully delineating itself. The female body ego is flexible, adapted to include a baby within its boundaries not only during pregnancy in its inside space, but also after birth when the child is physically outside the mother. This so essential extension of the mother's body ego to her child (how else could she care for him round the clock, often sacrificing satisfaction of her own bodily needs?) does, however, need to be renounced bit by bit and handed over to the child when he wants it as his own.

Graciously to surrender and even support and enjoy his taking away, as it were, now an arm, now a leg, now a need or function, renders her bodily integrity extremely vulnerable. No wonder mothers want to hold on to these outside parts of themselves or at least control the timing and form of the bodily transfer. No wonder they feel shaken to the core at times when they are not ready for it and are taken by surprise (Furman, 1994).

Many mothers experience difficulty in including the baby within their body ego when it grows inside them. Glenn's (1993) description of his pregnant patient's bodily sensations could be regarded as exemplifying this. Many avoid getting pregnant or carrying through a pregnancy because the attendant changes in their body ego are too threatening to their sense of bodily wholeness. Many experience great difficulty in letting the inside baby go (which contributes to prolonged labor). Many more find it difficult to effect the body ego changes by which the bodily self-invested inside baby becomes the bodily self-invested outside baby (which contributes to mothers' postnatal depressive or paranoidlike anxieties and is, in part, related to postpartum psychosis).

The lifelong process of "being there to be left" is, however, the hardest and most threatening aspect of motherhood (Furman, 1982). It never ends. It is repeated with each child. When one speaks of it with mothers they feel deeply understood and tend to respond with tears – not with words because these experiences predate words, predate symbolic representation, predate sexual gender experience in the usual sense of the term.

The maternal capacity to include the inside *and* outside child within her body boundaries and also to respond to his need for release by allowing him to own this most treasured part of herself constitutes the mixed blessing of motherhood – its primitive gratifications and dangers. As boys and girls, men and women, we all once were, and to a variable extent remain, a part of our mothers. Our earliest bodily unit with and differentiation from her leave us with a sense of the power and vulnerability of her flexible, undelineated body ego. This engenders awe, envy, terror, and all the defenses against them. It is a part of the way our own body ego is formed and maintained and serves as the matrix for sex-specific gender development.

Delineating and investing one's own body ego

Since the early seminal contributions by Winnicott (1941) and Hoffer (1949, 1950), there have been many studies of the ways infants and toddlers use their sensations and perceptions to form

149

their own body ego, to delineate it as an increasingly complete entity, including the genitals and their sexual function, and to invest it narcissistically. Much less has been said and understood about how protracted and difficult this process of integration is and how much it depends on the role of the mother. Katan (1960) describes a thirteen-month-old offering pretend food to his penis, much as, at that age, youngsters indiscriminately feed mother and themselves. His penis, like his mother, were part self and part other, or perhaps also still part of his early narcissistic milieu and body ego which includes body parts outside his own bodily limits. Katan goes on to describe cases in which the mother's handling of the boy's body and needs interfered with his ability to own and use his penis as an adult, i.e., to integrate his penis fully within his own body ego and to delineate his body ego from that of his mother.

We know, similarly, that a mother's insistence on inserting a pacifier can interfere with hand, mouth, and ego integration, or that her attitude to the older infant's transitional object can render useless his attempts to use it as a step in self–other differentiation (Furman, 1992, 1993). At the Cleveland Center for Research in Child Development, reports of the analyses of young children who were nursed through the toddler and preschool years have repeatedly shown how such prolonged breast-feeding not only enables the mother to continue owning the child's body, but how it also allows the child to continue owning his mother's body. After weaning, these boys and girls feel depleted and dissatisfied with their own bodies. They are enraged at mother for taking away the breast they considered theirs and have difficulty in investing and delineating their body ego.

Example D

A four-year-old girl felt forever incomplete bodily and incapable mentally, with rages of irrational demandingness. She had been nursed till almost three years and had only just begun to master other areas of self-care. Early on during her analysis, she showed her underlying conflict in this episode: She tore a nipple-shaped rubber doorstop from the wall and bit it excitedly, provocatively disregarding her mother's alarmed commands to stop and hand over the doorstop. Finally she threw it across the room and, when asked to pick it up, yelled, "You can pick it up yourself. It's yours anyway!" The mother, usually patient, became uncharacteristically enraged and spanked her daughter. She was puzzled and chagrined by her primitive outburst.

Tustin (1973) found autistic pathology to be caused by the rupture of the early mother–child unit which confronts the child with a traumatic sense of separateness and the lasting experience of a hole.

In the Hanna Perkins Toddler–Mother Group (Furman, 1992, 1993) we frequently observe how mother and child own each other's elimination, affecting the child's mastery of toileting and body ego differentiation. The toddler's manifest urinary and anal withholding often prompts the mother to use the toilet. For some toddlers this solves a beginning inner conflict, as if mother's mastery substituted for their own. With others, mother's going to the bathroom brings on loud, angry protests, as if her letting go interfered with their own withholding. When we can help mothers understand this, they let their child know that Mommy's going to the bathroom does not help *them* to be clean. The toddlers' responses are immediate: the relieved toddler resumes being conflicted; the protesting toddler calms down. Similarly, some mothers become quite distraught and are in tears at their toddler's trouble with toileting. They are often instantly relieved when it is pointed out that *they* achieved toilet mastery long since and it is now their child's turn. One little boy came to a mutually satisfactory arrangement with his mother: *she* used the toilet and *he* flushed it.

Anyone working closely with mothers and their toddlers can cite similar examples and ways in which the mother–child bodily unit gropes its way uneasily toward bodily differentiation and new body ego boundaries. I merely want to use these illustrative vignettes to underline that the primary mother–child joint ownership of their bodies involves flexible, unstable body ego boundaries for mother and child, that self–other differentiation implies renunciation of some parts of the extended body ego – especially for the mother, but also for the child – and that the child's progress toward owning and investigating his own circumscribed body ego depends crucially on the mother's capacity to facilitate, or at least to tolerate, this development. As noted above, it proceeds most markedly through their interactions around needs and the related impulses during the transition from mother's care to self-care.

The mother's vulnerability and difficulty in surrendering her narcissistic investment of the child's body and retracting the boundaries of her body ego accordingly have already been described. The healthy child's striving for autonomy is usually zestful (he has more to gain than to lose), but for him, too, there are satisfactions in owning mother's body and being owned by her. Being one's own separate person means relinquishing her omnipotence, having to make do with one's limited capabilities and bearing the frustrations of working toward mastery. Just as the mother never fully withdraws her cathexis of the child's body, so the child too retains a measure of his early bodily unit with the mother. Depending on the relative success of mother's facilitation and the child's self-delineation, the remnants of the primary bodily unit with its unstable boundaries of encompassing the mother and being encompassed by her, can serve boys and girls adaptively or become a lasting threat to the integrity of their basic body ego – a dread of mothers and of mothering. Such dread, primitive as it is for both sexes, is, of course, warded off by an array of defenses. This becomes incorporated in later characterological or symptomatic attitudes to mothers and women, including avoidance, denigration, idealization, and phallic monism. It affects later conflicts and compromise formations. It also plays a marked part in anorexia and bulimia and contributes to homosexual orientation in men and woman.

Some differences between boys' and girls' body ego

In keeping with the different biological roles of men and women, boys' and girls' body egos develop along different lines. Among the several authors who have, as mentioned, studied the girl's recognition and investment of her inside genital organs, destined to become child bearing, Kestenberg (1956b) views the girl toddler's early doll play as an externalization of her internal sensations and means of mastery as well as a preparation for motherhood.

My observations of toddlers and data available through treatment-via-the-parent and the analyses of girls confirm Kestenberg's findings, and provide some additional material (Furman, 1992, 1993, 1994). Just prior to and often overlapping with the adoption of the baby doll, toddler girls tend to adopt a container – a bag, purse, little box – which they treasure and fill with precious items. Mothers vary in supporting this activity. Sometimes they give their little daughter an old purse of their own to use; sometimes they provide special items to put into it to keep. Insofar as they are comfortable with their own motherly body, they at least regard the child's behavior with bemused appreciation. I have come to view this developmental step as a sign of the inside space being integrated into the growing body ego and serving as a precursor to the doll play – the transition from the inside baby to the outside baby. Sometimes this transition is made quite explicit, for example, when the treasured container is filled with a little figure or soft toy. Sometimes all containers have to be filled with a potential baby, such as when little Mary inspected her childless aunt's pretty bowl on the coffee table and then, just before leaving, placed a little teddy in it, molding it into the concave space.

I (1994) describe elsewhere how the baby doll and the maternal caring activities performed with it become such an invested part of the girl's body ego that she spontaneously remembers it, talks about it, worries about it when they are separated, and rushes to embrace it on their reunion, such as on returning home after a walk without the doll.

In other words, in normal body ego development, given mother's facilitation and absence of bodily overwhelming (illness, abuse, medical-surgical treatments), the girl toddler's body ego integration allows for the potential of including an inside and outside baby, retains flexible boundaries and tolerates, by virtue of same, a measure of bodily interdependence with her mother. Her maternal development is part and parcel of her gender identity. As little Mary, by then a bit older, put it one day seemingly out of the blue, "Mommy, when you have your next baby, will you please give it to me." Mary had not been in the company of babies, and her parents intended her to remain the youngest. Winnicott (1964) describes the maternal capacity for changeable boundaries as woman always being also someone else, with mother, grandmother, and little girl interchangeable within her, whereas man is all unto himself.

The boy's body ego integration and related narcissistic distribution is indeed quite different. He too grows out of the joint mother-child bodily matrix, reflected perhaps in "feeding" his penis and owning mother's breast or elimination. He too includes items outside his body as part of himself as he carries around a briefcase or tool box, becomes absorbed in big machines and how they work, or feeds his soft toys. But when he takes his teddy along, he either pushes it in a stroller or holds and drags it Christopher Robin fashion, in contrast to the girl who cradles her doll tightly in her arms. And his precious items do not go into treasured boxes but into his pockets. As he assumes ownership of his bodily functions and their care, including his penis, he encloses them within the clearly delineated boundaries of his body ego. This is often reflected in his play (so different from the girl's) which focuses on creating a circum-scribed space, such as the circular or oval train track or block-built corral for the toy animals. I view this as a sign of body ego integra-tion, comparable to the girl's treasured box. One toddler showed this achievement explicitly by asking his parent to draw the outline of his body on the pavement with chalk, to which he added the outline of his penis in the correct place. His proud achievement as well as his remaining vulnerability showed in his concern that the rain might destroy his representation and in accepting his parents' reassurance that it would only affect the picture, not his body (Furman, 1992).

With the boy, as with the girl, a measure of mutual bodily invest-ment remains part of him and of the mother–child relationship. Insofar as his body ego outlines achieve sufficient stability and narcissistic self-investment, these remnants will serve him adaptively – to be attracted to potential mothers, to allow temporary loss of ego boundaries with them in sexual intercourse, and to value, empathize with, and appreciate their mothering.

The role of the father

Boys especially, but girls too, are greatly helped with the differentia-tion and boundaries of their body ego by being able to relate with their father. Among the many benefits of the father–toddler relation-ship, I want to underline a specific one, pertinent to this context. It is the fact that the father's body ego is clearly and stably delineated, however much he may want to include the child as a bodily part of himself and be motherly in this sense, and however much the child is tempted to effect such a bodily unit with him. It is a big help to sense that fathers are and remain physically separate, can therefore support the child's separateness and can, at the same time, relate with and tolerate mother's relative lack of separateness. I am speaking, of course, of the role of the father in addition to the mother and do not wish to imply that body ego formation is facilitated by not experiencing a bodily unit with the mother to start with (Furman, 1992, 1993).

Some implications for later development

As with all areas of personality, the development of sexual gender is made up of a series of interrelated steps. The earliest strata described above are as significant in affecting the subsequent ones as the latter are in modifying and integrating the preceding ones. To understand the relative contribution of each we have to be in feeling touch with all. Our difficulties in recognizing and appreciating the role of the bodily mother–child matrix and its effect on body ego and gender development are, inevitably, handicapped by the fact that these experiences are preverbal and preconceptual and arouse very primitive annihilation anxieties. It may therefore be easier for us to identify women by their lack of a penis or to prove that women do not lack anything, and to disregard the role of motherhood. Yet these views may owe their intensity and persistence to the fact that *women do lack something, namely, clearly delineated, stable body ego boundaries.*

Lack of a penis brings the threat of castration fear. Lack of body ego boundaries brings the much more overwhelming, primitive threat of annihilation anxiety. This danger, to an extent, is part of motherhood. It is a very immediate threat to all men and women who encountered difficulty in differentiating and investing their body ego. The greater the threat, the stronger are women's defenses against owning and using their maternal body ego and men's against empathizing with and appreciating mothers and their mothering (Furman, 1994). Inevitably, this threat also contributes to difficulty in resolving later developmental conflicts and shapes the resulting compromise formations. Colleagues who analyze adults have personally shared such findings and found it helpful to trace and interpret the early origins of these pathologies. I hope they will, in time, publish their material and that others will contribute to the further elucidation of the links between the investment and differentiation of the basic body ego and later disturbances.

155

References

Chasseguet-Smirgel, J. (1976) 'Freud and female sexuality'. *Int. J. Psychoanal.*, 57: 275–286.

Erikson, E. H. (1956) 'The problem of ego identity'. *J. Am. Psychoanal. Assoc.*, 4: 56–121.

Erikson, E. H. (1964) 'Womanhood and the inner space', in E. H. Erikson *Identity, Youth and Crisis*. New York: Norton, 1968, pp. 261–294.

Furman, E. (1969) 'Treatment via the mother', in R. A. Furman and A. Katan (eds) *The Therapeutic Nursery School*. New York: International Universities Press, pp. 64–123.

Furman, E. (1980) 'The death of a newborn: assistance to the parent', in E. J. Anthony and C. Chiland (eds) *The Child in His Family: Preventive Child Psychiatry in an Age of Transition*. Yearbook Int. Assn. Child Psychiat. and Allied Professions, Vol. 6. New York: Wiley, pp. 497–506.

Furman, E. (1982) 'Mothers have to be there to be left'. *Psychoanal. Study Child*, 37: 15–28.

Furman, E. (1984) 'Mothers, toddlers and care', in S. I. Greenspan and G. H. Pollock (eds) *The Course of Life*, Vol. II, *Early Childhood*. Madison, CT: International Universities Press, 1989, pp. 61–82.

Furman, E. (1992) *Toddlers and Their Mothers*. Madison, CT: International Universities Press.

Furman, E. (1993) *Toddlers and Their Mothers: Abridged Version for Parents and Educators*. Madison, CT: International Universities Press.

Furman, E. (1994) 'Early aspects of mothering: what makes it so hard to be there to be left'. *J. Child Psychother.*, 20: 149–164.

Glenn, J. (1993) 'Developmental transformation: the Isakower phenomenon as an example'. *J. Am. Psychoanal. Assoc.*, 41: 1113–1134.

Hägglund, T.-B., Hägglund, V. and Ikonen, P. (1978) 'Some viewpoints on woman's inner space'. *Scand. Psychoanal. Rev.*, 1: 65–77.

Hägglund, T.-B., Hägglund, V., Ikonen, P. and Piha, H. (1980) 'The inner space of the body imago'. *Psychoanal. Q.*, 49: 256–283.

Hägglund, V. (1981) 'Feminine sexuality and its development'. *Scand. Psychoanal. Rev.*, 4: 127–150.

Hoffer, W. (1949) 'Mouth, hand, and ego integration'. *Psychoanal. Study Child*, 3, 4: 49–56.

Hoffer, W. (1950) 'Development of the body ego'. *Psychoanal. Study Child*, 5: 18–24.

Horney, K. (1926) 'The flight from womanhood: the masculinity complex in women as viewed by men and women'. *Int. J. Psychoanal.*, 7: 324–339.

Horney, K. (1932) 'The dread of woman. Observations on a specific difference in the dread felt by men and by women respectively for the opposite sex'. *Int. J. Psychoanal.*, 13: 348–368.

Katan, A. (1960) 'Distortions of the phallic phase'. *Psychoanal. Study Child*, 15: 208–214.

Kestenberg, J. S. (1956a) 'Vicissitudes of female sexuality'. *J. Am. Psychoanal. Assoc.*, 4: 453–476.

Kestenberg, J. S. (1956b) 'On the development of maternal feelings in early childhood. Observations and reflections'. *Psychoanal. Study Child*, 11: 257–291.

Kestenberg, J. S. (1968) 'Outside and inside, male and female'. *J. Am. Psychoanal. Assoc.*, 16: 457–520.

Torsti, M. (1993) 'The feminine self and body image'. *Scand. Psychoanal. Rev.*, 16: 47–62.

Tustin, F. (1973) *Autism and Childhood Psychosis*. New York: Jason Aronson.

Tyson, P. (1994) 'Bedrock and beyond: an examination of the clinical utility of contemporary theories of female psychology. *J. Am. Psychoanal. Assoc.*, 42: 447–467.

Winnicott, D. W. (1941) 'The observation of infants in a set situation', in D. W. Winnicott *Through Paediatrics to Psycho-Analysis*. New York: Basic Books, 1958, pp. 52–69.

Winnicott, D. W. (1964) 'This feminism', in C. Winnicott, R. Shepherd and M. Davis (eds) *Home Is Where We Start From*. New York: Norton, 1986, pp. 183–194.

PART TWO

Subfertility and reproductive technologies

Paola Mariotti

Difficulty in conceiving causes great emotional distress. Patients who turn to psychoanalysis or psychotherapy because they appear unable to conceive need to find a space to contain their emotional turmoil. They also, consciously or unconsciously, want to find a reason for their predicament, desperately wishing that, once this is found, they will be able to become pregnant. The concept of 'psychogenic infertility' supports this view. Some psychoanalysts whose subfertile patients have conceived following a particular piece of work done in treatment, have suggested that psychic conflicts can result in an inability to conceive. I have used the word subfertility to imply a difficulty to conceive, reserving 'infertility' to patients who cannot conceive at all.

Subfertility has been studied from different points of view, and different psychoanalytic models have highlighted various aspects of it. Langer for instance, in her 1958 paper 'Sterility and Envy', posits that in sterile women there is a failure of identification with a good fertile mother. She reports that, in the history of several infertile patients, traumatic events in the relationship with the mother can be found. She observes that in such cases it is possible to discern the way the patient typically had experienced her mother as weakened or destroyed by the child's own envious attacks – now adult, the patient

159

identifies the wished-for baby with an envious and destructive object and unconsciously rejects the baby, through vaginismus, infertility, or miscarriage.

More recently, Allison (1997) has suggested a different set of problems. He agrees that traumatic events are often present in the infertile patient's childhood. In particular he notes the significance of the loss of a sibling, or of having a disabled (male) sibling. This, he suggests, precludes the development and working through of jealousy and competitiveness and interferes with the capacity to become independent from mother, who is seen as in need of mothering from the patient. Sylvie Faure-Pragier, a French psychoanalyst who has written extensively on subfertility, also underlines the difficulty in separating from the maternal object that is often present in subfertile women. She describes (Faure-Pragier 1997, 2003) the clinical vicissitudes of patients whose original link with the mother has never developed in a triangular situation: 'Failing the development of an early triangulation, the excessive closeness with the mother occupies the representational space which is not free and available for conception' (2003, p. 55, my translation). She introduces the idea of passivity, which in French psychoanalysis has a much more positive connotation than it has in the Anglo-Saxon literature. The capacity to be passive in this sense is considered necessary in order to allow an empty space to remain so until something new develops, and Faure-Pragier refers both to the conception of a baby and to the conception of intellectual creative work: 'The subject must accept an unforeseen development which disrupts one's old representations so that new ones can emerge' (p. 72, my translation). Where the emotional link to the mother is all-consuming, and the Oedipal father is somehow absent, there is no mental/bodily space available for conception of something new.

Leuzinger-Bohleber in Chapter 6, on the Medea fantasy, reports that her patients suffering from frigidity and/or infertility, had a particularly difficult early childhood. She finds that they equate maternality with the presence of an omnipotent and dangerous mother, whose unbridled passions may lead her to give life and to take it away. However, she suggests that this fantasy has a more ubiquitous connotation and thus transcends specific situations: it can be present in women, and perhaps in men, who do not have specific fertility issues. Her use of the Medea myth captures this well because Medea was not a barren woman, and yet her maternal capacities were undermined and perverted by an unbearably wounded sexual

narcissism, by jealousy and envy, by revengeful hatred, all of which left no space for love or indeed for life. Her children were an extension of herself, perhaps containing goodness and love, which she would not allow her unfaithful husband to enjoy.

Psychological issues and infertility: causality or correlation?

In a well-argued review of the psychoanalytic literature on infertility, *Psychoanalysis and Infertility: Myths and Realities* (Apfel and Keylor 2002), the authors caution against assuming direct causal links between psychological issues and infertility. The authors stress the importance of psychological difficulties in women who are subfertile, but they question the concept of psychogenic sterility. They write: 'the subjective experience of infertility is central to psychological treatment and need not be confounded with psychological causality or treatment' (p. 86). They found few prospective longitudinal studies on the psychological aspects of infertility. Of note in their review is a Finnish study involving 180 subfertile women (Vartiainen *et al.* 1994). It was begun before the women attempted to become pregnant and 'no significant association was found between later fertility problems and personality factors' (p. 90).

As psychoanalysts we are interested in reports that do not necessarily have a statistical significance but throw light on to a patient's state of mind. We may find convincing Langer's (1958) thesis that envious attacks on a damaged mother may interfere with the development of maternality, or we may recognize in our patients the lack of separation from the mother as described by Faure Pragier, or find the Medea phantasy a very good representation of our patients' predicament. This does not necessarily imply that there are causal relations. Apfel and Keylor (2002) point out:

> The older literature is replete with efforts to translate bodily states directly into the language of emotions. . . . In our time we are rightly less confident of . . . one-to-one correspondences as we contemplate the bi-directional influence of mind and body, or of any important relational dyad, including the therapeutic relationship.
>
> (p. 88)

Joan Raphael-Leff implicitly supports this view in 'The Baby Makers' (Chapter 7). Raphael-Leff is a sociologist and a psychoanalyst and has published extensively on the subject of pregnancy and mothering. In her chapter she describes the treatment of a woman undergoing fertility treatment. The patient explores in her sessions what maternity means to her, and what it meant to her mother. As the patient goes through a seesaw of hopes and disappointments in her fertility treatment, with her work in analysis she achieves a sense of inner development and freedom – it is clear that, at least in this case, there is no point-to-point connection between worked-through conflicts and successful conception.

There are no doubts that the diagnosis of infertility has a traumatic effect for a patient. Leon (2010) underlines the loss of self-esteem suffered by the person who has been diagnosed as infertile, the damage to their self-image, and the sense of having lost a sense of control over their life on which they had relied until that point. A woman may feel she is being thrown back to early childhood, as a powerless, helpless creature who cannot do what her mother has been able to do – envy may well be present, directed to women who have children and felt deeply towards her own mother of whose fertility she is the living proof.

Apfel and Keylor (2002) confirm that 'numerous longitudinal studies demonstrate that infertility stress has a reliable and deleterious impact on both physical and mental health' (p. 90). And they add:

> The stress factor is most apparent in women who have a hormonal basis for their infertility. . . . This indicates that women with greater hormonal dysfunction leading to infertility may also have increased hormonal responsivity to stress. This specific subgroup is one in which emotional responses may both contribute to the infertility and to the desirability of psychological intervention.
>
> (p. 91)

Providing a space to enable the patient to tackle her emotional responses is therefore very helpful and valuable. In some cases treatment can influence, to an extent, the woman's reproductive potential. In other situations, as Raphael-Leff shows, one can offer a possibility of real psychic development, whatever the results in terms of conception and pregnancy, by allowing the patient to explore the issues triggered by the diagnosis of infertility and by reproductive technology itself.

For the analyst, there may be difficulties in the countertransference. There may be an implicit belief that psychoanalysis should be able to vanquish the power of the body – almost its very existence, rather than taking it into consideration, even (especially) when it represents an obstacle to one's omnipotent wishes. For instance, cases of infertility due to the male partner have been attributed to the woman's psychology. Apfel and Keylor (2002) examine Benedek *et al.*'s (1953) study 'Some Emotional Factors in Infertility'. Being aware that five out of six infertile patients had husbands with low sperm count, Benedek still proceeded to refer the women for psychoanalysis. Of the six patients, the only woman who conceived was the one whose partner had a normal sperm count, but the successful conception was attributed to psychoanalytic treatment.

Countertransferential inclination may lead the analyst to regard a patient's choice not to have children as resulting only from psychic problems. Chodorow (2003), for instance, describes 'how a constellation of unconscious mother–daughter–sibling fantasies, anchored by a deadened aggression against both self and object, destabilizes and undermines fertility and maternality' (p. 1181). When the woman at last realizes that she would like to have children, it is too late – her age does not permit it. However, in some cases the ambivalence that obstructs motherhood is the outcome of unconscious but realistic doubts about one's mothering capacities or desires.

The idealization of motherhood as the absolute best for all women may be rooted in the young child's real or imaginary love affair with his or her mother, to which, for the infant, nothing can compare. If this belief is defensively held on to, any woman who has no access to mother–baby bliss is deemed to be suffering from an unredeemable loss, maybe from a shameful or guilty disability. But when childlessness is the result of choice or of thoughtful acceptance, it may denote a woman's maturity and wisdom, in taking into serious consideration her limitations and/or her aspirations. If a woman has no choice, the mourning for much desired motherhood contributes depth and strength to a woman's personality. In the open space of a consulting room, a woman may find and bring together aspects of herself which might have been overlooked throughout her life, as shown in Raphael-Leff's paper – a space to which Medea had no access, with tragic consequences whether or not she has babies.

Medically assisted reproduction

'No sperm, we get sperm. No eggs, we get eggs. No uterus, we rent a uterus' – says a reproductive endocrinologist, quoted by Ehrensaft (2008: 4). This sums up the attitude of some professionals working with infertile women or couples: in this way they may unwittingly encourage their patients to believe in a magic omnipotent technology that will deliver whatever is requested. The painful working through of anxieties and fears can apparently be sidestepped. But if the medical interventions fail, the patients may be totally unprepared to deal with the disappointment, and even if they are successful, omnipotent beliefs will make it harder for the couple to negotiate their relationship to each other and to their child.

Reproductive technology has delivered astonishing results but the available opportunities awaken primitive phantasies and anxieties. The interventions consist of a vast range of complex, sometimes invasive and expensive procedures. From fertilization with a donor's sperm, to in vitro fertilization (IVF), to IVF with a donor's sperm, to surrogacy with the patient's egg or with the surrogate's egg, with the husband's or with a donor's sperm, or implantation of a donor's egg pre- or post-fertilization in the mother's uterus, the multitude of procedures aiming to make procreation possible is in continuous evolution. In many cases one partner is not able to produce the required gametes or to host the embryo, in others the couple is fertile but belonging to the same sex, or it may be a single mother who wishes to be inseminated. Their experiences will depend on their conscious and unconscious fantasies, fears, anxieties, aspirations, but in any case these medical procedures have a tremendous emotional impact on the individual or the couple. Raphael-Leff's chapter vividly describes the spiral of hope and disappointment, and the increasing stress as the technology that should lead to conception becomes more medicalized and farther removed from the sexual act.

In order to deal with the emotional onslaught, patients may reduce procreation to a kind of adult part–object interaction. And indeed sometimes parents relate to what Ehrensaft (2008) describes as the 'birth other' as if she or he were a 'part-object': the donor is not seen as a person but as sperm, eggs, or uterus. Alternatively, drawing from her psychoanalytic experience, Ehrensaft describes how the 'birth other' can be idealized, and all negative feelings toward him or her are erased from the parents' consciousness: but of course 'he or she is not a body part; he or she is not a parent or lover. Psychoanalytic exploration that brings the unconscious to consciousness is often necessary to address the part/whole-object reversals and to bring parents to this middle ground' (p. 11). The image of the 'birth other' is inevitably the object of projections and fantasies: she or he may be seen as a generous helper or as an envied interloper, or both.

In a case of surrogacy, Lester (1995) describes the boundary confusion in a patient whose child was carried by another woman. She illustrates how identified the patient was at times with the surrogate mother, and with the baby, and how she felt envious of both, wishing to carry the baby herself, and also to be carried in the safe womb.

Countertransferential issues can be particularly relevant when choices have to be made, as it happens when a subfertile patient begins her progression through the procedures of medically assisted reproduction. Questions of omnipotence in regard to making babies, or of envy and competition, beliefs as to the 'suitability' of the patient as a mother, and to the desirability of having babies, and one's opinions on the available procedures may all interfere in the analyst's mind with her desire to provide the best psychoanalytic space to her or his patient. Similar problems have been encountered well before these technological advances in relation to adoption – an important topic that is however beyond the scope of this book.

Zalusky Blum in Chapter 8 describes the analysis of a patient undergoing medical procedures to conceive. The analyst had to examine her own ideas about the patient's decisions, being aware that the patient may pick up subtle clues to her feelings and be influenced by them. In her paper she pays particular attention to the countertransference, and reports discussing her response to the patient's pregnancy with a donor's egg with women colleagues who had patients undergoing a similar treatment, and finding that all had been reflecting on their emotional reaction. Male analysts would probably be less directly affected by their female patients' predicament, but not immune to it as, of course, procreation touches on a universal concern.

Lester describes how she felt that her patient, who had recourse to surrogacy, needed a safe place in the session, but she insightfully concludes:

On reflection, I wonder whether my strong empathic stance was not, partly, a countertransference enactment, representing my awe of D's most unusual experiences. Furthermore, it is possible that my own uneventful experiences with pregnancy made me somewhat vulnerable to D's demands for support and nurturance. Unconsciously, like M [the surrogate mother], I became the generous, repairing mother, to avoid D's envy.

(Lester 1995: 332–333)

Different yet similar countertransferential issues may have to be confronted if the patient is in a homosexual relationship, or is a single mother. The analyst may have to consider, for instance, whether her interpretations convey a subtly negative judgmental message, or if on the contrary she is congratulating herself on her own open-mindedness, whether she feels perhaps threatened by her patient's decision, or if she is projecting on the patient her own forbidden wishes.

Corbett (2001) points out the importance of recognizing the existence of fantasies relating to the primal scene and of helping patients to acknowledge those fantasies. However:

These contemporary realities [of reproductive technology] require that we begin to distinguish heterosexual penetrative union from primal scene fantasies [and] from conception fantasies, which to date have been considered as one and the same, revealing yet again an assumed correspondence between heterosexuality, reproduction, family, and reality.

(Corbett 2001: 618)

Reproductive technology is a comparatively new area of medicine, and impacts on core phantasies that are part of the very structure of one's personality, phantasies about origin and creativity, gender and maternality, sex and relationships. Psychoanalysis is uniquely placed to help patients to express and integrate those unconscious phantasies with the new opportunities.

References

Allison, G. H. (1997) 'Motherhood, motherliness, and psychogenic infertility'. *Psychoanal. Q.*, 66: 6–17.

Apfel, R. J. and Keylor, R. G. (2002) 'Psychoanalysis and infertility: myths and realities'. *Int. J. Psycho-Anal.*, 83: 85–104.

Benedek, T., Ham, G. C., Robbins, F. P. and Rubenstein, B. B. (1953) 'Some emotional factors in infertility'. *Psychosom. Med.*, 15: 485–498.

Chodorow, N. J. (2003) 'Too late'. *J. Amer. Psychoanal. Assn.*, 51: 1181–1198.

Corbett, K. (2001) 'Nontraditional family romance'. *Psychoanal Q.*, 70: 599–624.

Ehrensaft, D. (2008) 'When baby makes three or four or more'. *Psychoanal. St. Child*, 63: 3–23.

Faure-Pragier, S. (1997) *Les bébés de l'inconscient. Le psychanalyste face aux stérilités féminines aujourd'hui*. Paris: PUF.

Faure-Pragier, S. (2003) 'Défaut de transmission du maternel. Absence de fantasme, absence de conception?', in J. André, (ed.) *Mères et Filles – La menace de l'identique*. Paris: PUF.

Langer, M. (1958) 'Sterility and envy'. *Int. J. Psychoanal.*, 39: 139–143.

Leon, I. G. (2010) 'Understanding and treating infertility: psychoanalytic considerations'. *J. Amer. Acad. Psychoanal.*, 38: 47–75.

Lester, E. P. (1995) 'A surrogate carries a fertilised ovum: multiple crossings in ego boundaries'. *Int. J. Psycho-Anal.*, 76: 325–334.

Vartiainen, H., Saarikoski, S., Halonen, P. and Rimon, R. (1994) 'Psychosocial factors, female fertility and pregnancy: a prospective study – Part I: fertility'. *J. Psychosomatics and Gynaecol.*, 15: 67–75.

Zalusky, S. (2000) 'Infertility in the age of technology'. *J. Amer. Psychoanal. Assn.*, 48: 1541–1562.

The 'Medea fantasy'

An unconscious determinant of psychogenic sterility[1]

Marianne Leuzinger-Bohleber

Introduction

Oedipus and Narcissus are two male protagonists of Greek tragedies who, as we know, stood sponsor to Freud when he wished to draw attention to ubiquitous conflicts of human mental life. Freud postulated that myths, as narrated to us by creative writers in every age, continue to fascinate us today because they portray central unconscious human fantasies and conflicts, as a rule connected with our repressed, early infantile sexual fantasies. These fantasies are preserved in our own unconscious minds and, in projecting them on to the main figures in these tales, we unconsciously recognise our own destiny in them: 'It may even be that not a little of this effect [of an imaginative work] is due to the writer's enabling us thenceforward to enjoy our own day-dreams without self-reproach or shame' (Freud, 1908, p. 153).

There are of course also female Greek mythological figures who still fascinate us today and have inspired creative writers down the ages to depict and recreate their fate in ever new forms. One such figure is Medea, who, it seems to me, has become particularly relevant to our time, characterised as it is by migrations of ethnic groups, high divorce rates, new forms of neglect, and the recurring murders of children reported voyeuristically in the media (see, for example,

Kämmerer *et al.*, 1998). Medea's fate surely confronts us unconsciously with one of the most profound taboos of our western civilisation, a form of female destructiveness in which intense unbearable counter-transference reactions arise in us analysts, making it hard for us accurately to perceive and recognise this dimension of the 'dark continent' of femininity in our female analysands. We are often at a loss for images and words to help us even begin to grasp our horror of such situations, which at first floods and confuses us. In our struggle for visualisation and verbalisation, myths present themselves as a helpful, neutral 'third party', on to which we first direct our own projections of what we can neither grasp nor bear, thus enabling us subsequently to recover our bearings in the images, utterances and narrations of the protagonists. We are then in a position to reflect critically on analogies and differences between the clinical observations and the mythical figure, with a view to gaining a better understanding of the unconscious dynamic operating in the analytic situation.

This paper gives an account of such a progressive process of discovery, in which I found it particularly helpful to think about 'Medea'. On the basis of an analytic session followed by a longer case history, I shall illustrate the way in which this tragic ancient woman's destiny reflects central unconscious fantasies of female generativity and destructiveness that stem, like the Oedipus complex, from early infantile sexual and object-relations fantasies. My reports are based on clinical observation of a specific group of female analysands who had unconsciously sought psychoanalytic treatment for the same symptoms: psychogenic frigidity and sterility. In the six psychoanalyses and four long-term therapies, we finally discovered that a central unconscious fantasy, hitherto unrecognised, had determined all these women's experience of their femininity; with the myth in mind, I called it the 'Medea fantasy'. Pivotal to this fantasy was the unconscious conviction that sexual passion carried the risk of existential dependence on their love partner and of eventual deception and abandonment by him. These women were unconsciously convinced that they would not be able to endure such an abandonment and would react to it with lethally destructive impulses constituting an existential danger to the self and the love object – as well as, in particular, to the products of the relationship with him: their children. For this reason it seemed to them psychically imperative to forgo any creative unfolding of their femininity and symbolically to 'deaden' themselves and their bodies.

In their long and difficult treatments, it emerged that all these patients had sustained severe traumas in their early object relations, with consequent excessive stimulation of archaic fantasies about the female body and about characteristic modalities of the early relationship with the primary object. For example, it turned out that all these women shared the striking biographical fact that, during their first year of life, their mothers had suffered from severe depression and been treated with antidepressants. As a result, the mothers had presumably lacked an adequate capacity to present themselves to their babies as helpful, reliable and indestructible objects that could thereby have come to their aid in, for example, the progressive integration of archaic destructive fantasies. These had consequently been preserved in the form of split-off, unconscious 'Medea fantasies'. While the traumatic quality of their early object relations had undoubtedly favoured the formation of this unconscious fantasy in the analysands, I now wonder whether the Medea fantasy might possibly constitute a ubiquitous unconscious fantasy of femininity. According to my clinical experience, it is observable in milder form in most female analysands, because it is based on infantile sexual fantasies (e.g. oral fantasies connected with breastfeeding, as well as fantasies about the female body, pregnancy and birth), as well as on frightening modalities of early object-relating experiences with the maternal primary object.[2]

Women (mothers) are experienced here not only as omnipotent givers of life who provide invulnerability and paradisal-orgastic unification but also as furies and avengers who, if wounded in the extreme, put out the life to which they themselves have given birth. It is in my view plausible to assume that, given reasonably normal development, these archaic fantasies of femininity can be differentiated, cultivated and ultimately integrated into a mature female self with a stable identity as a sexually active woman and good-enough mother. The knowledge of one's own potential destructiveness – which might in an extreme situation even be directed at one's own children – is psychically present in a stable female core identity. Hence a reflexive dialogue with the shadow side of one's maternality appears to be one of the prerequisites for an appropriate capacity for mothering (including the holding function, containing, etc.), and for deriving mature narcissistic and libidinal satisfaction from it.

In attempting to explain the clinical observations outlined above, I find myself in agreement with analysts of a wide range of theoretical persuasions for whom the concept of unconscious fantasy[3] remains paramount today, who consider that unconscious fantasies determine present thinking, action and feeling, thus making for an unconscious continuity between past and present (for a summary of the relevant discussions, see Beland, 1989; Inderbitzin, 1989; Ogden, 1992). With regard to the genesis of unconscious fantasies, apart from the above considerations derived from object–relations theory, account should be taken of the view of the Kleinian and other analysts that ubiquitous early bodily experiences and the associated fantasies also mould one's unconscious 'truths'. For instance, my analysands experienced their female bodies as devouring, destructive and lethal – as a source of uncontrollable libidinal and aggressive impulses. In addition, their unconscious bodily self-image was distorted by projective identifications with the depressive maternal primary object, which was experienced as destructive. Finally, the archaic oral bodily fantasies had become mixed with later anal–destructive and, in particular, oedipal fantasies, such as the wish to kill their female oedipal rival. In my view, therefore, ubiquitous early bodily fantasies on the one hand and idiosyncratic, specific object–relations experiences on the other have come together in the unconscious Medea fantasy: both the specific object–relations trauma and the 'ubiquitous biological' elements in the body have become a source of unconscious emanations.

The analogies between the fate my analysands feared, in their unconscious fantasies, might befall them and the 'actual', female destiny of 'Medea' as narrated in the myth are demonstrated below, with reference to the ancient Greek portrayal of 'Medea' by Euripides in his eponymous tragedy. This work is cited by various psychoanalytic and psychiatric authors. Freud himself mentions Medea only once, in the 'Dora' analysis (1905, p. 61), when he likens her relationship with Creusa to Dora's with Frau K. Wittels (1944) was the first to invoke a 'Medea complex', which he defines as the mother's unconscious hate for her maturing daughter. E. S. Stern (1948) objects that Medea had no daughters but two sons, and himself characterises the Medea complex as the mother's death wishes against her own offspring in general, coupled with vengeful feelings towards the child's father. Rheingold (1964) presumes that all mothers, to some extent, nurture impulses to kill their children. Orgel and Shengold (1968) concentrate on Medea's fatal gift, emphasising that Creusa cannot resist the oedipal seduction and atones with her death for the transgression of the incest taboo. Greenacre (1950) stresses that not only oedipal but also pre-oedipal traumas favour the development of the 'Medea complex'. Friedman (1960), too, in her case history of a woman obsessed by impulses to kill her youngest child, mentions low self-esteem and narcissistic neediness, which she also attributes to pregenital disturbances, principally in the patient's early relationship with her mother. Babatzanis and Babatzanis (1992) give two detailed case histories. One concerns the psychotherapy of a mother who murdered her 6-year-old son in a psychotic depression, while the other describes the therapy of this woman's 7-year-old daughter. Referring to the drama of Medea, the authors here concentrate on the transgenerational transmission of female violence and destruction. Finally, Warsitz (1994), with respect for example to the psychoanalytic structuralism of Anne Juranville (in the tradition of Lacan), adduces the Medea of Euripides to facilitate understanding of the psychodynamics of female melancholia. I believe, however, that no psychoanalytic author has yet connected psychogenic sterility with the unconscious 'Medea fantasy', as I shall attempt to do below (see also Adorer, 1998).

'O LOVES OF MAN, WHAT CURSES ON YOUR WINGS': THE MEDEA MYTH AND CLINICAL ILLUSTRATIONS OF AN UNCONSCIOUS FANTASY

Introduction illustrating the clinical material: analysis of a dream

Let me begin with an account of a psychoanalytic session, which briefly illustrates certain clinical observations and my attempts to understand them in more detail with the aid of the Medea myth.

In the third year of her treatment, the analysand concerned is standing outside the door of my office together with a young anorexic woman who has mistaken the time of her appointment. Seeing that I have to send this patient away, she enters the consulting room with a smile and says after a long pause how pleased she is that I preferred her to the other woman. After a further silence, she recalls that she has had an 'oddly confused, incomprehensible and frightening dream'. The dream is as follows:

I was driving a car. My husband and three brothers were with me. We were going on holiday. We came into a peculiar town, Gordes, which is actually in France – but in the dream it was in Italy. Everything was wrong. We wanted to have a meal, but I did not want to drive into the town, but to go round it. I had a detailed plan in my hand, with a square blob that clearly represented a bog we had to drive to. Immediately beyond it was the sea.

I can't remember any talking in the dream. The weather was terrible. I drove into a cul-de-sac and had to turn back. The ground was muddy and slippery and the road winding. Oh, yes, I've just remembered something else: suddenly the ground was full of lettuces – no, they were little houseleek plants with hard slabs in between them. I zoomed along in a mad frenzy – and then, yes, suddenly there was a bend, and I was overtaken by a black sports car that harassed me. It was too late to get out of the way and I drove at a furious pace over the plants, squashing them all flat. Mud and clay flew into the air. Then came an expanse of very blue water. It wasn't the sea yet, but only Lake Maggiore – we had not yet reached the end of our journey.

Her first association was that Italy to her meant remoteness, nature in the wild, wind and sea. She had often spent her holidays there as a young woman; and once, when she was 17, accompanied by a girl-friend, she had fallen head over heels in love there. She had felt a powerful sexual attraction for this young man, but had broken off all contact with him for fear of a boundless passion. Unlike her companion, who moved abroad to be with her 'Italian boyfriend', she had returned 'home', to her little village in Austria.

I know from the treatment that Mrs M experienced the aggressive impulses aroused by the adolescent process of detachment as archaic internal destruction – a crisis that culminated in a suicide attempt and a stay in a psychiatric clinic. Having overcome this severe crisis, she moved abroad. She now lives a long way from her home village, in a foreign country. I think of the scene with the adolescent anorexic at the beginning of the session and wonder what Mrs M is trying to communicate to me with these associations.

She now speaks at length about her stable marriage, which is quite unlike the situation of the girlfriend mentioned above. Hearing recently that this friend has given birth to a son although she lives alone, the childless analysand was filled with envy. The matter of children reminds her of 'Gordes' – of a Gordian knot in the treatment so far.

At an unconscious level, the patient's childlessness was her main motivation for embarking on an analysis. During the initial interviews she was in a severe suicidal crisis. As the analysis reveals, she was then aware of her unconscious fantasy that the 'intellectual products' of her creative activity as a writer were 'her child'. In the last few weeks, moreover, I have realised from various transference observations that by choosing me (a working woman and the mother of small children) as her analyst, she was also attempting to preserve this fantasy in her mind in a different way by identifying with me. Despite powerful resistances, her painful envy of my being a mother has moved in the last few months to the focus of our analytic work and ultimately confronted her with her own desire for children, hitherto intensely defended against.

P. (*after a pause, in a thoughtful tone*) bog – something dangerous you can sink into, but also fascinating – the beautiful bogs of Finland – nature . . . the symbiosis of water and land . . . the strange flora and fauna (*after a pause*) – the bog body – there is no solid ground in the bog – you sink into it quite slowly – the bog bodies are preserved for centuries, like people who have fallen into a crevasse.

A. And we talked in the last session about your petrifaction, your 'playing-dead reflex', which you use to immunise yourself against the powerful, painful feelings you found yourself confronted with in the quarrel with your husband over having children. You said you would rather 'put these feelings on ice . . .'[4] (*pause*). Strange, this contrast between the silence and timelessness of the bog and the frenzied movement in the other part of the dream . . .

P. (*now thinking of the 'sports car'*) It was black – not a hearse, but a very smart model . . . (*pause*) . . . I'm just thinking, it must have been my husband at the wheel.

She now tells me that this sports car is threatening to put her in a situation she cannot avoid, in which she 'squashes life flat'. She felt enormous rage at this driver, because he put her in such a dependent position with no way out. Mrs M then remains silent for a long time, finally commenting that the houseleek plants she flattens are called semper vivum.

This reveals to us that the subject matter of the dream is connected with the present conflict in her marriage. The recurring wish for

175

children mentioned above has led to massive marital problems, because her husband, a successful film-maker, is dead set against having children. (As it happens, she experienced this wish for children – as well as myself, because I persisted with the subject, thereby bringing her construction of life as a woman into the analytic discourse – as 'harassing', 'throwing her off course', etc.) In the quarrel mentioned above, which had been followed by weeks of 'petrifaction' in the analysand, her husband had told her again in no uncertain terms that his only wish was 'to get through life more or less decently and not to pass on the misery of this world'. Consciously, Mrs M had accepted her husband's decision. However, it had become evident in the last few months of the analysis that she now saw it as a sign of severe depression in him. Her associations to the 'sports car/hearse' that was partly responsible for her squashing the 'semper vivum' flat betrayed her anger, and indeed death wishes, towards him. She gradually became aware of her own part in this 'marriage conspiracy'. Her choice of partner had unconsciously been motivated partly by the fact that this man was dead set against having children, thereby protecting her from archaic anxieties to the effect that she might herself – in a 'mad' frenzy – become the murderess of her own children. As the later course of the analytic work was to show, this fantasy was multi-determined, connected as it was, among other things, with powerful death wishes towards her younger siblings (the three brothers in the dream), as well as with the fantasy that her mother had killed the two stillborn children who had preceded her. She was the replacement for the second of these dead babies. Of course, I inevitably thought of all this immediately I saw the two women outside the door before the session and had to send one of them away. I therefore regarded the dream as a gift to me: I keep her, and not the sister/brother, but, during the session, I was also absorbed by the fantasies that might have been triggered in my analysand by my sending away ('killing') an anorexic (needy, sick) patient. I mentioned this at the end of the session: 'In the dream you destroy the "semper vivum" – and I sent away a needy woman who wanted to come to me'. Although Mrs M did not respond directly to this interpretation, her associations in the next few sessions confirm the hypothesis inherent in it. She reported a telephone conversation with her mother, who told her that she had become severely depressed after the two stillbirths and had been treated with drugs for two years. After that, it had been only with great difficulty that she had become pregnant again. The pregnancy with the patient had been marked by complications: owing to the threat of a miscarriage, she had had to stay in bed for months on end. In the patient's first year of life, too, 'her depressions had caught up with her', and she had been treated with antidepressants.

Many months later Mrs M brings another dream, in which she has to get rid of a dead body in the long, dark hulk of a ship and discovers that there are many other corpses in there as well – thus revealing infantile fantasies about the mother's female body, her own body, and also her own birth. The mother, lying in bed suffering from depression and migraine, had told her pre-school child that she had almost bled to death with her afterbirth. Telling me this in the session, Mrs M said spontaneously: 'Although I came out undamaged, she still had the earlier afterbirth inside her . . .', but then immediately corrected herself. We presume that this bizarre idea stemmed from an infantile fantasy in which she imagined that a part of her dead brother or sister had been preserved in the mother's body in the afterbirth. Hence birth was closely connected with the subject of death (or, if you will, with the question: 'Who kills whom in that situation – does the mother kill the child, or the child the mother?'). Mrs M returned to these dreams again and again in later sessions. It turns out that both the 'lethal bog' and the 'ship's hulk' have to do with unconscious bodily fantasies about the female genitals. She unconsciously experiences the womb as a 'dark, devouring cave' – bottomless – in which men's semen, as well as countless children, can be stored dead (on this point, see also Hagglund and Piha, 1980; Jordan, 1990; Bernstein, 1993).

It becomes clear in the analytic work – for the first time through this dream, but also later from a large number of clinical observations – that Mrs M's psychogenic sterility also constituted an unconscious protection against sexual passion and against fantasied murderous impulses towards potential children, as well as against profound, humiliating feelings of dependence on her love partner – all of which are characteristic features of the Medea drama, which I shall now briefly summarise.

Summary of the tragedy

In his tragedy, first produced in Athens in 431 BC, Euripides takes up the myth of Medea and modifies it characteristically. My summary singles out the main aspects of the plot relevant to an understanding of the analogies with the unconscious fantasies of my ten woman patients.

Jason will get his father's throne in Iolcus back from his uncle Pelias only on condition that he brings him the Golden Fleece from Colchis. Together with the most famous heroes of Greece, the 'Argonauts', he embarks on the dangerous voyage to the Black Sea.

Colchis is ruled by King Aeëtes, the father of the enchantress Medea. When Medea, a priestess and daughter of the demigoddess Hecate, first sets eyes on the stranger in her father's palace, Eros is, according to the legend, standing behind the hero and shoots his arrow right into the heart of the king's daughter. Struck by the arrow, she struggles with all her might against the overwhelming passion, cursing the stranger and his appearance, but in vain: her love for Jason finally wins the day. She is therefore unable to turn down Jason's request to ally herself with him against her father, and gives him a lotion that endows him with superhuman strength and makes him invulnerable. She sings the dragon to sleep, so that Jason can kill it and snatch the fleece away from it. She tells him what he must do to tame two wild bulls and yoke them to the plough, and how to subdue the armed men who sprout from the furrows, by casting a stone quoit among them to sow dissension in their ranks and make them kill each other. Medea then flees with Jason. When the Argonauts are surrounded by their pursuers, led by Medea's brother, she lures him into a trap and delivers him up to Jason's sword. Hearing of the successful escape and of his son's death, her father tears himself to pieces in his rage. In the legend, the tragic fate of Medea that now ensues is the revenge for this double murder.

Back in Iolcus, Medea first rejuvenates Jason's old father, by cutting him up and boiling him with magic spells in a cauldron, and entices the daughters of Pelias to do the same with their father. However, to avenge herself for the wrong he inflicted on Jason's house, she gives them the wrong herbs, so that Pelias never returns to life. Jason and Medea must then flee, and are taken in by King Creon in Corinth. To assure himself and his two sons by Medea of a permanent refuge, Jason abandons Medea and proposes to marry Creon's daughter Creusa. Medea pretends to accept this, but sends Jason's new wife an enchanted robe and carcanet. When Creusa dons them, both she and her father, who rushes to her aid, are consumed by fire. But this is not enough to quench Medea's thirst for revenge: to hurt Jason to the quick, she finally kills both her sons and, at the end of the tragedy, flies away with their bodies in a chariot drawn by winged serpents. It is her grandfather Helius, the sun god, who thus rescues her from the land of her enemies. In her dialogue with Jason, she is filled with simultaneous pain and grief at her children's death, but also with the satisfaction of having avenged herself on her husband. (For a complete account of the myth, see, for example, Kerényi, 1992.)

A tentative psychoanalytic approach to the myth of Medea

Like many myths, that of Medea begins with a transgenerational theme: Jason demands his father's throne, to which he is entitled, back from his usurping uncle Pelias. By a stratagem, Pelias tries to send his nephew to his death: he is to bring him the Golden Fleece – the skin of the ram that had long ago borne Phrixus and Helle to Colchis on their flight from their stepmother. For this purpose, he appeals to the young Jason's thirst for adventure and his narcissistic neediness. This puts us in mind of the Laius complex, in which fathers despatch their sons (possibly out of envy of their youth) into warlike adventures, in an attempt to avoid relinquishing their power to the next generation and being confronted with their own old age and approaching death. Jason, we presume, is unable to see through his uncle's stratagem and murderous intent because of his own oedipal guilt feelings and castration anxieties, which he defends against by adolescent fantasies of omnipotence.[5]

The same theme now unfolds further, this time applied also to Medea. In Colchis, the adolescent Jason encounters another (oedipal) father, Aeëtes, the 'father of the enchantress Medea . . . priestess and daughter of the demigoddess Hecate'. Eros shoots off his arrow of passion, thereby uniting Jason and Medea, the young generation – the symbol of the sexual excitement and passion that (in adolescence) become the powerful, 'ineluctable' motivation for turning away from the oedipal couple to the new, heterosexual love object. However, the myth presents an extreme variant: Medea has a presentiment of mortal danger and struggles with all her might against the overwhelming passion, curses the stranger and his appearance, but in vain. In psychoanalytic terms, what is here portrayed is an irresoluble inner conflict: Medea experiences the adolescent turning away from the oedipal couple as threatening the loss of her self and her internal objects. The irreconcilability of cultures in external reality stands for her irresoluble situation of internal conflict: for her, there seems to be only an 'either-or' – the token of an archaic world of internal objects from which the adolescent self can detach itself only by killing them off psychically. Aeëtes stands, in the legend, for a wrathful, patriarchal ruler who demands total subjugation even from his daughter – in other words, who abuses her as an archaic selfobject. If adolescent daughters experience their real and internal fathers in this way, the representations of these fathers fuse regressively with those of the archaic, pregenital mother – so that neither an early nor an oedipal or adolescent triangulation is possible! The formation of any inner room for manoeuvre, or intermediate space (Winnicott, 1971), then becomes impossible and the only psychic alternatives are subjection to the primary (maternal or paternal) object – that is to say, fusion with that object – or abrupt detachment and forced individuation. This means that there can be only one survivor in this struggle: either the self or the object, and individuation becomes a murderous affair. This 'inner truth' unfolds in the continuation of the myth.

Medea now regresses into an archaic world of objects, dominated by splits and fragmentations (paranoid-schizoid thinking and feeling). Having fallen in love with Jason, she fuses with him, and fuses unconsciously with the 'good, idealised primary object', her mother, the demigoddess of fertility. She now possesses magic powers, makes Jason invulnerable and – like the good, early primary object – 'sings the dragon to sleep'. Medea, in addition, possesses wisdom: she divulges to Jason the stratagem of 'how to tame two wild bulls and yoke them to the plough' – in other words, how to gain control over the animal, sexual drive impulses by force, so as to place them in the service of the work in hand – the ploughing of the field (of transgenerational fertility: Medea later bears him two sons!). Moreover, the theme of splitting appears again at this point in the story: thanks to Medea's wisdom, Jason can avoid murdering the armed men directly, so that he can remain the 'pure hero' – by sowing dissension among them, he causes them to kill each other.

However, the conflicts do not end there. The oedipal father fails to keep his promise: although Jason successfully performs the tasks assigned to him, he gives him neither the Golden Fleece nor his daughter, and the only course open to the pair is flight. The murderous struggle begins: Medea must now decide between her lover on the one hand and her father and brother on the other. Once again the triangulating third party is lacking: the mother does not appear. Medea resorts to a stratagem to lure her brother into a trap, and betrays him. Jason kills the brother. The father, overwhelmed with narcissistic rage, 'tears himself to pieces' (possibly a depiction of the fragmentation that befalls a fragile – paternal – self as soon as the – archaic – selfobject is withdrawn from it). Medea's tragic fate is 'the revenge for this double murder' – a portrayal of a situation of archaic guilt feelings in which the internal objects become murderous persecutors from whom there is ultimately no escape.

Medea's first action in Iolcus, the 'rejuvenation of Jason's old father', therefore gives the impression of an attempt at reparation. At the same time, however, she transgresses the barrier between generations and fulfils some of her oedipal wishes. The daughters of Pelias thereby succumb to temptation, 'dismembering' their own father, but, to avenge herself, Medea denies them the 'right herbs' that would have caused the fragmentation to lead to a 'rejuvenating reintegration'. In other words, the fragmented, early infantile father representation cannot be recreated and reintegrated on a new, living level. In terms of Medea's own internal situation, revenge stands in the way of her attempt at reparation: the father representation remains fragmented, and the inner state of persecution (represented by the external flight) persists. It is worth mentioning that Jason plays hardly any part in this: he now seems to be substantially depotentiated and, for Medea, forfeits both the function of the (adolescent) new love object and his triangulating role in the detachment from the oedipal and pre-oedipal parental couple. Instead, he now becomes the passive victim of the 'poisoner Medea', the 'bad mother': on her account he is banished from his homeland, the world of the 'good mothers', and flees to an alien land – Corinth. Jason restores his narcissistically wounded self by turning to a new (oedipal) love object: Creusa, Creon's daughter. Fused with the new 'good object', he hopes to save himself and his sons. He separates abruptly and radically from Medea, whom he now experiences as a 'bad object', the representative of a barbaric, savage, uncivilised world on the Black Sea, who does not fit into the 'bright, pure' Hellenistic culture, from which, split off and despised, she must be kept apart.

Medea's immediate reaction to this abandonment is a 'draining' of her self: she becomes suicidal, her murderous aggression and revenge being directed against her own self. But she then collects herself, restoring an archaic pride by fusing with her archaic internal objects:

> so but one thing reach me not,
> The laugh of them that hate us . . .
> For never child of mine shall Jason see
> Hereafter living, never child beget
> From his new bride, who this day, desolate
> Even as she made me desolate, shall die
> Shrieking amid my poisons . . . Names have I
> Among your folk? One light? One weak of hand?
> An eastern dreamer? – Nay, but with the brand
> Of strange suns burnt, by hate, by God above,
> A perilous thing, and passing sweet my love!
> For these it is that make life glorious.
> When the leader of the chorus warns:
> Thou canst not kill the fruit thy body bore!
> Medea replies:
> Yes: if the man I hate be pained the more.
>
> (Euripides, 1910, p. 46f.)

The restoration of Medea's regulation of her narcissistic self-esteem by the destruction of the object now becomes her primary – and ultimately sole concern. First, impelled by her unbearable envy, she revenges herself on her rival Creusa, who is narcissistically seduced by her gifts and fails to see through her stratagem. The fact that, for this purpose, Medea has at her disposal poison (a symbol of the early mother's power) and fire (a symbol of sexual passion), and thereby destroys not only her rival but also the rival's oedipal love object, is a further indication of the depth of her regression into an archaic world governed by one principle alone, the lex talionis. The only alternatives are life and death.

This regressive process can also be traced in the change in Medea's relationship with her children that now ensues. At first she still experiences her children as a token of hope, as a transgenerational link with Jason, as a sign and product of the genital love she wishes to regain. Gradually, however, they become for her mere archaic selfobjects – means of avenging herself on Jason. Medea cannot bear to be excluded from the (oedipal) couple; she lacks sufficiently stable internal objects to permit mourning for the lost love object, whereby she could have protected her children, as symbols of the next, coming generation and of life itself. Unable as she is to integrate the new, painful experiences (e.g. the loss of her sexual attraction and passion) into her self and object representations through the work of mourning and memory, she falls victim to a regressive process in which the paranoid-schizoid position prevails. The self, it seems, can now survive only by killing the 'bad object', or, if you will, by destroying it in a fit of archaic revenge, through the murder of the link to it, namely the children. Narcissistic triumph – fusion with her divine grand-father Helius – gains the upper hand over mourning for the loss of her generativity.

Description of the Medea fantasy

In accordance with their idiosyncratic, traumatic early object-relations experiences, each of my female analysands had developed different forms of the Medea fantasy, which I observed in various details of the Medea myth recounted above. However, the following characteristics of this 'unconscious truth' seem to me to be common to them all.

Their own femininity, to them, unconsciously means 'power over life and death'. This is connected with archaic anxieties about their own destructiveness – including the potential impulse to kill their own child. The female body is experienced as highly ambivalent or is substantially rejected, associated as it is with predominantly negative bodily fantasies. The female body functions are perceived not as potent and pleasurable but as uncanny, unreliable and potentially destructive. The female genitals are unconscious symbols of 'bloody destruction', of a secret doom that will overtake not only them but also the penetrating penis and potential children. Furthermore, their own female body is unconsciously felt to belong to the mother and not to themselves. This is also the context of unconscious attacks on the generativity of the maternal body and – in identification with it – on the (potential) products of these women's own femininity.

In addition, the fact of being a woman (in terms of both sexual passion and motherhood) is experienced as existential dependence on their male partner and father of their own (potential) child. This makes for an experience of impotence and profound injury, often occasioning intense penis envy (as in the case history of Mrs B presented below) and panic-anxiety at the possibility of being betrayed and abandoned. Both sexuality and motherhood are therefore conflictual and seem to be associated, in fantasy, with the danger of loss of the boundaries of self and objects, and of being flooded with intense libidinal and/or aggressive affects. The combination of sexuality and motherhood, in particular, is experienced as a threat to both self and object, and is associated with 'death' and 'depression' (loss of self). All the women were unconsciously convinced of the 'truth' that there could be only one unscathed survivor of pregnancy or birth: either the mother or the child; either the self or the object.

Psychogenic sterility and frigidity were possible consequences of the unconscious Medea fantasy in the group of women described here.

The following account is intended to illustrate, at least fragmentarily, how this unconscious fantasy unfolded in the transference, and how its subsequent understanding and working through in the psychoanalytic process led to a change in a woman's experience of her femininity and to a new blossoming of her creativity (see also, for example, McDougall, 1991).

The unfolding of the 'Medea fantasy' in the analytic process: fragments of a psychoanalysis

When Mrs B, a strikingly beautiful, fashionably dressed, 30-year-old student, arrived for her first interview, her thick, black hair and good-looking, pale, somewhat rigid face reminded me of 'Snow White' – an association repeated at the end of our talk after she had told me of her father's death, which had driven her, as a 6-year-old princess, out of her still pristine early infantile realm.

Mrs B needed psychotherapeutic help because she was suffering from a severe phobia: she was almost unable to leave the house and attend her lectures and courses, and had cut herself off totally from all social contact. At night she was overcome by fits of panic anxiety, which left her unable to sleep and 'wandering about her apartment like a caged animal'. Her husband, who was twenty years her senior, was unable to calm her down, although he was a professor of neurology. She also suffered from a range of psychosomatic symptoms, such as migraine, stomach pains, sleep disturbances and eating problems. It was only in the fourth year of her analysis, however, that it emerged that her main analytic motivation was her psychogenic frigidity and sterility.

In the first interview, I learned practically nothing of her life story, except, as already stated, that her father had died suddenly of heart failure when she was 6 years old, and that she had subsequently been plagued by the obsessive idea that she too might succumb to sudden heart failure.

I was impressed by the fact that, almost throughout the interview, tears streamed down Mrs B's totally expressionless, mask-like face – without any visible connection with what she was describing. It seemed to me that she was quite remote from her own emotions and bodily sensations; not even her language seemed to be her own, for she resorted substantially to her husband's highly abstract jargon.

Here are some of the most important biographical facts (most of which emerged only after the third year of her analysis).

The patient's mother had lost her first husband in an air raid in 1945. She herself had been able to escape by running into the house, but he had been killed outside the door. After this she had developed a severe phobia that had left her unable to work and caused her to lead a restricted life close to her parents. She had met Mrs B's father at the beginning of the nineteen fifties; according to the family romance, she had become pregnant the first time she had slept with him and given birth to an illegitimate, Down's syndrome daughter. Mrs B told me that, because of this daughter's feeding problems, her mother had left her at the clinic, where she had died a few weeks later.

According to the mother's account, a heavy burden had weighed on her pregnancy with the patient, as she had been very afraid of having another disabled child. The birth had been dramatic – a matter of life and death. It had, again according to the mother, been followed by a depression, for which she had been treated with drugs for eight weeks. The patient had had virtually no breastfeeding, but had been fed in a 'rigid four-hour cycle'. When the patient was 5 years old, her mother had undergone a radical hysterectomy for a carcinoma. A year later, the patient's father had died. After his death, the mother had led a withdrawn life at home, without 'work in the outside world' and without a fresh relationship with a man. The patient had shared her mother's isolated life; having virtually no childhood friends, she had developed an infantile neurosis, which had been neither diagnosed nor treated. At puberty, she had still slept in the same room as her mother; and her mother would read her diaries. A frightened Mrs B told me of an impulse she had had one morning to strangle her mother in the bed next to hers. At 14, the patient's phobia had become so intense that she could no longer attend school, and she had gone into psychiatric treatment. A therapy group had provided Mrs B with limited contact with other young people. She had begun an apprenticeship, but could sit examinations only in her mother's presence. At the age of 19, her phobia had made it impossible for her to leave the house, and she was admitted to a clinic in Zurich as an in-patient. There she had met her husband-to-be, who, finding this young woman attractive, had fallen in love with her. The in-patient psychotherapy and the relationship with the husband enabled her to leave her mother and move to another town, where she had belatedly taken her school-leaving examination and gone to university. After the marriage, however, her symptoms had caught up with her one after another; this had badly wounded her and ultimately motivated her to embark on a psychoanalysis.

In the present context I can give only an outline of this six-year, four-hour-a-week analysis, concentrating on the points most relevant to our subject. Although long stretches of this analysis were very difficult for me, I found it at the same time interesting and impressive.

Owing to the intensity of the analysand's defences against archaic fantasies about femininity and her inability to become pregnant, it seems to me by no means coincidental that these did not become the focus of our attention until the fourth year of the analysis. Before that, she appeared to be absorbed predominantly in her infantile conflicts, doing her best to get herself cared for, comforted and loved. Her marital situation was also very difficult, characterised as it was by, for example, her narcissistic functionalisation of her husband. Without manifest guilt feelings, Mrs B could spend huge sums of his money and take possession of his car, time and feelings. She often treated me in the same way in the analytic sessions, taking it for granted that she could dispose of me as she wished. For instance, on one occasion, without prior notice – and without a trace of perceptible guilt feelings – she returned from holiday four weeks later than the agreed date.

In the first two years of treatment, she would often bring dreams of an almost psychotic quality. Once she dreamt that she was looking out of the windows of an ice palace, watching emotionlessly as some dwarfs outside fried parts of her husband's body on a giant grill (cf. Langer, 1988). On seeing my little daughter bathing in the garden, she had a detailed fantasy in which, beside myself with rage and anger after a quarrel with my husband, I struck out at my daughter and killed her. She would recount these fantasies in an oddly cold way, as if petrified and emotionally frozen This manifestly enabled her to project her own frightening unconscious Medea fantasy wholly on to me, so that she could deny that she might have anything to do with such ideas. Again, when she developed powerful phobic symptoms after this session, she could not see any connection whatsoever between them and the material of the session.

In retrospect, one of the functions of these defensive strategies was to help her disavow her feelings of archaic dependence on others, which were an unconscious determinant of her phobic symptoms: in her phobic 'attacks', she felt – consciously – totally dependent on her environment, husband, mother, analyst. Finally, however, her fantasy that no one could help her in her symptoms led us to the opposite unconscious wish, namely, to be dependent on no one, not to need anyone, to cold-shoulder everyone – an unconscious compromise formation that had arisen during her adolescence. The analytic work on this complex exposed her archaic anxieties about dependence, which were due to the deficiencies in the formation of her self and object boundaries. This work led not only to an imperceptible loosening of the narcissistic defence and its associated substitutive satisfactions but also to a diminution of her need to flee into a 'unique' phobic world. This was followed, in the treatment, by the appearance of the theme of sexuality. In the fourth year of her treatment, she brought the following dream.

'I am in our bathroom checking whether Mrs W [her cleaning lady] has cleaned everything properly. I lift up the lino and see some verminous bugs crawling out; I feel nauseated, squash these horrible creatures and am incredibly peeved that Mrs W did not make a better job of the cleaning.' Since the second year of the analysis, Mrs B had repeatedly made the same conspicuous slip, calling me by the name of her cleaning lady, which had a variety of meanings. These associations as a rule led to feelings of triumph over, and devaluation of, myself – especially, as it happens, if she had perceived me as an empathic, maternal woman emotionally involved in the sessions. Further associations led to expressions of Mrs B's identification with her mother's rigid defence against sexuality: sexual fantasies were 'dirty' and had to be 'got rid of'. Like Mrs W, I, as her analyst, was 'accused' of not making such 'unclean thoughts' disappear, but of taking an interest in them instead. In the ensuing sessions, furthermore, it became clear how much Mrs B had also unconsciously identified with her oedipal mother's 'defective surgically mutilated belly'. In a subsequent session she remarked that she had no feelings of any kind in this region of the body: 'It might as well be dead in there . . .!' After this session, Mrs B was admitted to hospital as an emergency with a suspected Fallopian pregnancy. She reacted with panic anxiety to the prospect of having a general anaesthetic, and telephoned me in utter desperation from the hospital, filled, as she said, with the fear of death! She manifestly associated the loss of control under the anaesthetic with the conviction that she would thereby also lose control of her body and her life. She discharged herself early from the clinic, against medical advice. In the next session, she resentfully reproached me: 'Look what happens when we focus on this part of the body. I would rather go on anaesthetising my belly and "keeping it dead".' It became clear that she was unconsciously experiencing my analytic contact with her body as intrusive – and indeed, as though I had 'taken possession' of it, effacing the boundaries between our bodies. Many new memories emerged in Mrs B in the ensuing weeks – how her mother had told her, as a pre-school child, all the details of her illness, her operation and her bodily feelings during radiotherapy – memories that now became mixed, often in odd ways, with her own surgical experiences. This ultimately led us to presume that the 'deadening' of the belly was not only, as stated, an expression of her identification with the 'defective' female body of the mother, connected with the 'dead' introject of the depressive mother, but that the withdrawal of cathexis from these parts of the body also implied a 'turning away from the female body', which was in addition a (neurotic) attempt to separate the mother's body from her own (see, for example, Pines, 1988).

A further theme later emerged in the wake of the dream mentioned above: Mrs B associated the verminous creatures crawling out from under the lino not only with 'dirty, male semen' but also with her half-sister's two children, who had seemed to her, on a recent visit, to be untamable, 'crawling vermin'. In the manifest dream, she killed off this 'vermin'[6] in a state of utter nausea – something we could now see as part of the unconscious 'Medea fantasy', traces of which we were to encounter again and again in the ensuing months. A vital element in the formation of this fantasy in Mrs B was the part of the family romance connected with the death of the Down's syndrome sister. Evidently the analysand had later fantasised that the mother had 'left the sister to die' in the clinic because she did not want her, because her disablement was a nuisance to her and wounded her narcissistically. In these fantasies, Mrs B experienced her mother as endowed with the power of decision over life and death![7]

However, the dramatic tales about her own birth also stimulated the Medea fantasy. Her mother had told her that she had almost bled to death during her birth. She had survived only because her husband, who fortunately had the same blood group as hers, had been able to donate blood for her. The treatment revealed how far such tales had aroused the patient's magic fantasies and contributed to the unconscious 'truth' that birth was an event in which either the mother or the baby (she herself had been almost asphyxiated by a twisted cord) – or indeed both – might die: birth and death were intimately connected. We now understood that Mrs B was again and again staging this central fantasy and her associated unconscious convictions in the transference; the transference phenomena of the first two years of treatment were also connected with this, as well as with other factors. Until the third year of treatment, Mrs B seemed to forget everything we had discussed in the sessions, as if she were obliterating me and our analytic work. During this period, I often doubted the point of the treatment and the appropriateness of analysis, and contemplated breaking off – 'aborting' – the treatment, partly in order to protect myself from her 'destructive abuse'. In retrospect, these fantasies also reminded me of the following theme: who is to survive; who is to kill whom; who is to decide whether a life (or an analysis) can come into being and grow?

Furthermore – again as revealed by hindsight – the analysand was seeking to project her still unbearable feelings of dependence and impotence, as well as a profound depression, on to me, and to perceive helplessness, failure and dysphoric affects in her analyst – in order to control them in me (projective identification). In the transference, I became the 'dead object', the expression of an early mother transference, in which Mrs B felt me, in this phase of the analysis, to be her depressive ('dead'), 'cold' and unresponsive early mother. However, as Bollas (1995) stresses, this projective identification ultimately proved extremely helpful to the analytic process, since we were (progressively) able to discern, in these transference phenomena and the analysand's projections on to me, her split-off identifications with the 'dead mother' – a trace that led back to her traumatising early object relationship.

In addition, in this early phase of the analysis, the mechanism of projective identification constituted an attempt to establish a hard and fast boundary between Mrs B and myself – which she did by making me the stranger who ipso facto experienced completely different emotions from herself! The intensity of her anxieties about fusing with me, putting herself at my mercy – 'turning into your product', as she once put it – became clear to us in the later stages of the analysis. This was another reason why intimate themes such as sexuality and femininity were not broached directly in the treatment for so long. She was afraid that I might thereby get too close to her – something her dreams portrayed repeatedly in various guises. In the manifest dream content, I would often transgress boundaries, be unempathic and intrusive, accompany her to the toilet, wipe her bottom, or persecute her in her flat. As in these dreams, I seemed (in the mother transference) to be able to dispose of her body as I wished.

I was impressed to find that the analytic work on these components of the 'Medea fantasy' manifestly led to a deepening of the analytic relationship and a parallel relieving of the burden on her relationship with her husband. Looking back in the fifth year of her analysis, Mrs B once mused: 'It is funny – I can now let my husband get closer to me without immediately being afraid that he might slip inside me or that I might have to push him out again. It is as if I felt a secure skin between him and myself, so that I don't need to erect a protective wall between us any more.' This sense of having secure boundaries between herself and the object resulted in a moderation of her intense envy of men, which, although it had often put me in mind of Freud's concept of penis envy, was no doubt also connected, in Mrs B's case, with the feeling that, because of their anatomical difference, boys could separate more easily and more completely from their mothers (see, for example, Grossman and Stewart, 1976; Chasseguet-Smirgel, 1988).

With these gradual changes, a new closeness arose between the couple, especially in the sexual field. For the first time in her life, Mrs B discovered pleasurable and passionate sensations in and with her female sexual body. The intensity of her fear of these passionate feelings hitherto now became clear in the treatment. One 'symptom' disappeared at this time: until then, she had had a compulsive need to bite her husband when he kissed her (thus causing him to recoil, and unconsciously confirming to her that she was not fused with, but separate from, him in sexuality). These new sexual experiences now led also to an intense wish for a child, which brought out many new anxieties and conflicts in the analysand in the ensuing months. While a detailed account is beyond the scope of this paper, I should like to conclude with two important dreams that illustrate the extent to which she was here concerned, among other things, to establish an inner boundary between her own female body and her mother's.

The first dream was triggered by an overt conflict with her mother, who abruptly terminated a visit to her daughter because – as Mrs B saw it – she could not bear it when her daughter preferred to sleep with her husband rather than have breakfast with her.

> I was pregnant and very happy; I already had a big belly. My husband and I wanted to go into town to buy something pretty for the baby. We went into a baby shop. We were served by an old woman, but she brought me nothing but rubbish, and never what I wanted. I became quite desperate. She kept disappearing into the back of the shop. Finally she brought me a frying pan, which she wanted to force on me. I got terribly angry and yelled at her. My husband had already left the shop. I slammed the door shut and ran after him, but I couldn't find him and had a fit of panic. And I think I didn't have a big belly any more . . .

She associated to her inner struggle over the ownership of her body ('her round belly'): was it hers, her husband's or the old woman's (the mother's – and mine in the transference)? She herself made a connection with the scene mentioned above: 'I imagine I now have to pay for the fact that I sided with my husband and threw my mother out of my bed – for that I now have to give up my unborn baby to her!' Another element to emerge was that she experienced the loss of the baby as revenge for the oedipal triumph over her maternal rival in the above scene.

In the ensuing months the analytic work again came to focus on the intense conflict of separation and loyalty with the mother and on oedipal (and pre-oedipal) envy and rivalry, in the form of trans-ference fantasies connected with the forthcoming termination. In her fantasy, I would be left behind, like her mother, emptied out, depressive and 'with my insides drained of blood' if she terminated her analysis, felt healthy and became a mother herself. Through a psychic umbilical cord, goaded on by her destructive envy, she would deprive the maternal body of nourishment, fertility and life, leaving it destroyed. 'Your mother almost bled to death when you were born, and now you are afraid that you might have damaged me too, leaving me behind drained of blood, destroyed and plotting revenge, if you are reborn psychically and separate from me.' After this interpretation had been tossed back and forth between us over a number of sessions, Mrs B brought the following dream:

> It was a dream full of anxiety. I had a child, but it was absolutely tiny, and I looked after it tenderly and with every care. That was very necessary because it was so small. But [laughing] it had a tooth and could bite me.' Her associations led first to a dream that a woman friend of hers had had: this friend had told her she had dreamt that the two of them had given birth to one child together, which aroused very ambivalent feelings in her. 'On the one hand it was very disconcerting to me, because it was not clear which hole the child had come out of and who it belonged to, but, on the other, I was also very touched by my friend's desire to stand by me like a midwife [holding her in her arms – M.L.-B.].

She then recalled that the child had a tooth:

> P.   It is tender and cuddly, yes, but at the same time already capable of defending itself and not completely at my mercy . . .
> A.   That sets your mind at rest – it is also not completely at the mercy of your destructive side, although it very much needs your loving, caring side.
> P.   Yes, and it is also something special, like Princess Sissi,[8] who, if I remember rightly, also came into the world with conspicuous teeth . . .

The fact that she was capable of having this dream towards the end of the analysis, even if the child featuring in it was still very small and in need of abundant care and attention – although at the same time naturally endowed with means of defending itself – was seen by Mrs B as a sign that she could now dare to terminate the analysis and proceed along her feminine path by herself. The shared 'analytic baby', while itself still rather small, was capable of developing, and she would take good care of it in the future too . . .

We ended the treatment after just over six years. Three years after the termination, Mrs B telephoned me: she was four months pregnant and proud of 'having been able to be fertile'; most of the time she enjoyed her state. Thinking back to the treatment, she felt very grateful. 'When I sometimes have anxieties and physical troubles, I try to remember my dreams – and then I can be my own analyst,' she said self-confidently, although one could at the same time feel a bond with me. Shortly before the birth, she telephoned me in some anxiety to say that, partly because of her high blood pressure, the doctor was afraid that she might develop toxaemia of pregnancy. She herself could not decide whether this was a psychosomatic symptom (her mother suffered from hypertension) or something organic. A Caesarean section proved necessary; although she experienced this as a massive wound, she soon got over it without the need for professional assistance on seeing her healthy son. She reported all this to me in a further telephone call when her son was about 6 months old. She was able to experience to the full the ups and downs of early motherhood without being drawn into the archaic abyssal maelstrom, and to discover herself, her son and her husband as a 'unique trio'.

Discussion

It gradually became clear in the initial phase of Mrs B's psychoanalysis that her apparently narcissistic defence had the function of holding back massive anxiety about dependence on the object. At the same time we were ultimately able to discern in it manifestations of the analysand's unconscious identifications with her 'dead mother'. Her extreme dependence anxieties were partly determined by her insecure self and object boundaries, resulting from her traumatising early object-relations experiences. Succumbing to her depression, the patient's mother had probably functionalised her daughter for the purpose of narcissistic regulation of her self-esteem; she had probably done this already in the first year of Mrs B's life, as well as later, after the death of her second husband. In her depression, the mother had probably not been able adequately to reflect back her baby's childish needs and to achieve an understanding of her little daughter's mental processes good enough (in Winnicott's sense) to allow her to develop the capacity to understand mental states in herself and others, accompanied by a stable core sense of self, and psychically to integrate and cultivate archaic aggressive and destructive impulses. At the same time, the father had been insufficiently available to Mrs B during the early phase of triangulation. Released from captivity as a prisoner of war, he had returned with a severe heart condition and, although, according to the family romance, he constantly reforged a tender relationship with his little daughter, he would withdraw abruptly if conflicts arose between her and her mother. For this reason, he was virtually unavailable to the patient as a 'third party' in the process of detachment from the primary object during the first phase of individuation. The internal and external experiences associated with his death, as well as the mother's radical hysterectomy during the oedipal phase, were further severe traumas for Mrs B. She had thereafter contracted an infantile neurosis, which, following more traumas in adolescence, led to a psychic breakdown when she was a young woman and consequent admission to a psychiatric hospital.

When the analytic work had provided Mrs B with a 'psychic skin' between herself and her love objects (and/or the analyst), when her pre–oedipal and oedipal envy problems had become accessible in the transference, and when the archaic aggressive impulses associated with her basic pathology seemed to have become more psychically integrated, it was possible for the analysis to concentrate more on her problems of female identity (including her frigidity and psychogenic sterility). The 'Medea fantasy' now unfolded clearly in the transference, and it became progressively possible to identify and work through its individual components. As a result, Mrs B ceased to be afraid of sexual passion and became capable for the first time of having satisfying and blissful sexual experiences. She was increasingly able to integrate 'good' and 'bad' elements of her sexual impulses and experiences into her female core self and to feel them to be aspects of her own feminine identity. She then became more and more able to tolerate ambivalences in the current object relationship with her love partner. As these inner experiences progressively stabilised, Mrs B conceived an intense wish for children, which she was ultimately able to fulfil with her husband after the termination of the treatment.

Conclusion and discussion

On the basis of clinical observations from six psychoanalyses and four long-term psychoanalytic psychotherapies with female patients who had unconsciously sought psychoanalytic help mainly on account of their childlessness, some characteristics of a central unconscious fantasy – the 'Medea fantasy' – are outlined with reference to Euripides's version of the Medea myth. An analytic session (Mrs M) and an extensive case history (Mrs B) exemplify the extent to which this unconscious fantasy determined these women's subjective experience of femininity. Forming an unrecognised part of their own female self-representation, it was responsible both for the profound splits in their perception and experience of their own identity as women and for their anxiety at their own unintegrated destructive impulses. All ten patients had previously been incapable of sexual passion, which, to them, was associated with the danger of fusing with the love object and, should they be deceived and abandoned by that object, left at the mercy of uncontrollable, archaic drive impulses, which were experienced as a threat both to the autonomous self and to the object. The fantasy of endangering the love object through 'female destructive rage' was also connected with the issue of having children – for example, with the unconscious conviction that they would impulsively kill any child of their own. The psychogenic sterility thus partly constituted an unconscious protection from this risk. As outlined in the case history of Mrs B, the 'Medea fantasy' unfolded progressively in the transference, and it ultimately proved possible, through the projections on to the analyst, to discern and work through its individual components; Mrs B could not otherwise have regained her capacity for sexual experience, engaged in professional activity, and ultimately satisfied her wish for a child.

Attention is drawn to the surprising fact, revealed by the psychoanalytic treatments of these ten women, that they shared a number of conspicuous biographical features – traumatic experiences that had over-stimulated their unconscious, early infantile fantasies and associated libidinal and aggressive impulses. These experiences included severe traumas during the oedipal phase (loss of the father, abrupt banishment from the oedipal paradise, 'damage' to oedipal rivals due to illness, destructive divorces and the like, narcissistic abuse by the mother during adolescence and so on). Another surprising common thread that emerged during the course of these long treatments was that the mothers of all these women had suffered from severe depressions during the first year of the patients' lives and had undergone long-term treatment with antidepressants. These

195

serious depressive illnesses had impressed a powerful stamp on the patients' early self-development and the integration of archaic libidinal and aggressive drive impulses. Fonagy *et al.* describe in detail the pathologies of the self that babies born to depressive mothers must develop as sheer survival strategies:

> Pathology of the self arises out of an intensification of defensive aggression, and the incapacity to tolerate one's own destructiveness because of the perceived fragility of the object . . . It is the combination of the object as both fragile and dangerous which limits the child's opportunity to internalise a reflective or intentional stance. The absence of such a stance further reduces the child's capacity to contain his own aggression.
>
> (1993, p. 480)

As the clinical material shows, my analysands had unconsciously identified with the 'dead, female bodies' of their depressive mothers, and this had been a determinant of their psychogenic sterility. They had in addition split off their archaic libidinal and aggressive impulses, thereby excluding them from the process of further, differentiating psychic development. These impulses combined – in the unconscious Medea fantasy – with early ubiquitous bodily fantasies of a primitive, devouring, envy-driven, destructive self. The patients subsequently (in fantasy) ascribed their mothers' depression to these destructive impulses of theirs: they imagined that they had destroyed the feeding maternal object by their envy, rage and despair. The split off, psychically unintegrated impulses and fantasies determined their subsequent psychic development. For example, against this initial background, the early process of individuation and separation became a life-and-death struggle: on the one hand, in the case of birth (and pregnancy), either the self or the object but not both could survive; and, on the other, separation from the primary object signified destruction either of the individuating self or of the (depressive) primary object. For this reason, at an unconscious level the patients' own bodies still belonged to their mothers, self and object boundaries having remained relatively undeveloped.

D. Stern (1995) also describes early identificatory processes of this kind on the basis of direct observation of interactions between depressive mothers and their babies. Because the children of depressive mothers cannot totally do without close contact with their primary object, the only course that remains open to them is identification, so that they ultimately align themselves with the mother's depression in terms of facial expression, gesture and affective behaviour (an example is Mrs B's 'petrified' expression in her initial interview). Stern here also mentions the 'dead mother complex', the reference being to André Green's 'dead mother' concept (1983, 1999). However, the group of patients described by Green (1999) differ from those discussed in this paper. The mothers of Green's patients had suddenly become depressive after the loss of an important person in their lives while the child was under 2 years old. Having abruptly lost the capacity to engage in a responsible, satisfying emotional dialogue with their infants, they were subsequently experienced by their children as 'emotionally dead'. As a result, these children formed an internal representation of a dead mother who could, without warning and unpredictably, cut off their children's sunshine and make their lives meaningless. These children therefore unconsciously yearn for the 'lost early paradise' with their mothers, but are at the same time compelled by panic anxiety to shun close relationships, which are unconsciously associated with an early 'total' object loss. Unlike this group of patients, the analysands described here seem to use their bodies as a protection from further trauma: their psychogenic frigidity and sterility prevent 'fusional' physical proximity to a love object, which is associated with traumatic experiences in the early object relationship in the fields of sexuality, femininity and motherhood.

Another point worth mentioning is that it was virtually impossible for these patients to compensate for the early traumas sustained with the unempathic, 'dead' primary object because the fathers were insufficiently available to them during the early triangulation phase. This further impeded the process of separation from the primary object (see, for example, Rotmann, 1978; Herzog, 1994). Many biographical details suggest that these analysands' mothers had begun to overcome their depressions during their daughters' second year of life, and were then able to facilitate a premature, compensatory development of autonomy in their daughters, so that the archaic destructive conflicts in these women seemed to be confined predominantly to their fantasies of femininity. For example, all the analysands showed good cognitive development (cf. Medea's 'wisdom'). As toddlers, they exhibited a conspicuous interest in 'masculine games and activities' rather than feminine ones (cf. Mayer, 1991) – no doubt

197

indicating the pregenital roots of these women's pronounced penis envy. The 'world of fathers and men' appeared to them in many respects safer than that of 'mothers and women'. As we saw in the case of Mrs B, these girls nevertheless sought to separate from the 'dangerous early mother' by an identification with the pregenital father: the paternal (anal) penis became a symbol of the restoration of a narcissistic perfection, of an undamaged object (on this point, see, for example, Chasseguet-Smirgel, 1988). However, the fathers, who were in reality often absent or weak, probably offered their daughters too little for these compensatory archaic fantasies to become progressively differentiated. Oliner (2000) has described similar processes of identification with the pre-oedipal father in another group of women, whom she characterises as 'bad mothers'.

The traumas thus sustained during the oedipal phase once again upset these girls' fragile psychic equilibrium: the split-off, archaic impulses were reactivated, endowing the oedipal conflict with a similar quality to that portrayed in the Medea myth. Its focal points again became murder and suicide – due to revenge, jealousy and narcissistic rage. The only way out appeared to be flight from the 'oedipal triangle': like Mrs B, all my analysands had already developed a pronounced infantile neurosis during latency. However, it was only in adolescence, owing to the intensified pressure of the drives and to the process of detachment and individuation during this phase, that psychic breakdown occurred, as in Mrs M and Mrs B. The latter now developed a manifest phobia, while the former became suicidal. Any adoption of a heterosexual love object would unleash panic anxiety and was therefore avoided by means of these symptoms (just as Eros represents a deadly peril in the Medea myth). Through therapeutic help, both women ultimately succeeded in achieving a fragile psychic equilibrium, but this proved inadequate in late adolescence for the development of a stable female identity. It is therefore no coincidence that what motivated these analysands to embark on a psychoanalysis was the unconscious wish for children. This represented a wish to free themselves, with external help, from the transgenerational fate of their mothers and fathers – a desire to work on their traumatic infantile conflicts in order to extricate themselves from the pathological position they occupied as daughters. These patients longed to develop an intermediate space (Winnicott, 1971) in a psychoanalysis, to enable them to decide finally on a real or fantasied motherhood of their own – i.e. on their individual generativity.

This process of finding an identity was connected, in these patients, with the appropriation of their own history in all its traumatic and intolerable aspects. There are many possible approaches to explaining how the severe traumas described above were preserved in these women's memories, but a full account is beyond the scope of this contribution. I could only postulate that, in the genesis of the Medea fantasy, early traumatic experiences (stored in pre-verbal, sensorimotor-affective schemas) interacted with later traumas in the development of female identity (after the acquisition of the capacity for symbolisation). That presumably led, by constant 'rewriting' of bodily and relational experiences, to the formation of this unconscious self-representation, which had (in a manner hitherto unrecognised) been constantly repeated according to the mode of the dynamic unconscious (cf. Leuzinger-Bohleber *et al.*, 1998). I thus found it helpful, as an analyst, to reflect on Medea, the literary representation of a woman's fate, in the process of progressively linking the sensorimotor-affective bodily perceptions in the countertransference with images and language, and connecting them with projections of my analysands on to me as their analyst. My analysands had projected intolerable (feminine) parts of their selves that they had banished from consciousness on to me, the analyst, where they had localised and controlled them 'as seemingly alien entities'. As described by Bollas (1995), these projections and projective identifications proved to be an indispensable psychoanalytic aid in allowing unconscious elements to be expressed in the analytic process at all. When it eventually became possible for analyst and patient together to perceive and understand these projective processes in detail in the transference, my analysands progressively became capable of drawing close to the hitherto split-off 'bad' and 'dangerous' components of their female selves and ultimately to integrate them into a more mature, ambivalent sense of female identity (see also Kernberg, 1987). This led, as illustrated by fragments of the case history of Mrs B, to a change in the experience of female sexuality and potential and actual motherhood. It therefore proved essential to recognise the unconscious fantasies if a permanent change in the female sense of self and identity was to be achieved. This paper is therefore also intended as a contribution to the debate aimed at securing a deeper understanding of the 'dark continent' of female sexuality (Freud, 1926, p. 212), which, widely documented (Shengold, 1963; Resnik, 1970; Piers, 1976;

Stoller, 1976; Blum, 1977; Giovacchini, 1979; Sugar, 1979; Schaule, 1982; J.-M. Quinodoz, 1986; Koster-Sanders and Groen-Prakken, 1988; Escoll, 1991; Tyson, 1991; Young-Bruehl, 1991), is currently being conducted on an interdisciplinary basis. Since it is beyond the scope of this essay to discuss the results of these studies, the reader is referred to the excellent review by Cherazi (1988), which compares early psychoanalytic theory with present-day conceptions of the development of femininity. Other significant contributions are those of Bernstein (1993), Chasseguet-Smirgel (1976, 1988), McDougall (1991), Pines (1993) and D. Quinodoz (1991), all of whom discuss unconscious bodily fantasies relevant to our context.

Similarly, I have been able only to touch upon the controversies surrounding the theoretical understanding of unconscious fantasy in the psychoanalytic literature (on this point, see Beland, 1989; Inderbitzin, 1989). The 'Medea fantasy' is considered in this paper from the standpoint of object-relations theory because, as the clinical observations show, it incorporates both early ubiquitous bodily fantasies and traumatic object-relations experiences. It proved just as important to establish a patient's individual, split-off object-relations history as to bring out 'ubiquitous biological' bodily fantasies. Progressive insight into their biological and biographical roots thus enabled the ten patients ultimately to discover and hence to moderate their unconscious feminine self-image, the 'Medea fantasy' – a self-image that is reflected in Jason's characterisation of Medea:

> Tigress, not woman, beast of wilder breath
> Than Skylla shrieking o'er the Tuscan sea . . .
>   (Euripides, 1910, p. 74f.)

Notes

1 Translated by Philip Slotkin, MA (Cantab.), MITI.
2 The action of the myth centres on a pair of lovers, Medea and Jason, which suggests to me that the tragedy here portrayed concerns both sexes. However, I shall concentrate in this paper on unconscious fantasies of this kind in women.
3 For example, Ogden writes: 'The patient unconsciously holds a fierce conviction (which he has no way of articulating) that his infantile and early childhood experiences have taught him about the specific

ways in which each of his object relationships will inevitably become painful, disappointing, overstimulating, annihilating, unreliable, suffocating, overtly sexualised, etc. There is no reason for him to believe that the relationship into which he is about to enter will be any different. In this belief the analysand is of course both correct and incorrect. He is correct in the sense that, transferentially, his internal world will inevitably become a living intersubjective drama on the analytic stage. He is incorrect to the extent that the analytic context will not be identical to the original psychological-interpersonal context within which his internal object world was created, i.e., the context of infantile and childhood fantasy and object relations' (1992, p. 235).

4　It emerged much later from the analytic work that this dream image was also a reference to an unconscious body schema: she experienced the female genitals as something 'bottomless', 'into which you can sink', in which the man's semen and countless children are stored dead.

5　Such attempts at interpretation are of course always fragmentary and problematic, as they often express the author's projections on to the myth rather than motifs 'objectively' contained in it. However, we are specifically concerned here to identify projections of (ubiquitous) unconscious fantasies on to the myth, and not to find the most appropriate historical or literary interpretation of the tragedy. For this reason, I seek in my interpretations to concentrate on the parts of the Medea fantasy that I encountered in the patients presented here and which proved to be of central importance to the therapeutic work. I attempt to illustrate this by a session in which a dream is interpreted (see pp. 173–177 above).

6　This kind of dream symbolism already appears in Freud's Introductory Lectures: 'They [dreams] treat children and brothers and sisters less tenderly: these are symbolized as small animals or vermin' (1916–17, p. 153).

7　During their treatment, all these patients had dramatic family stories to tell about birth (mothers dying in childbirth in three cases; replacement children in four cases; abortions in six cases). These had manifestly given rise to unconscious fantasies that the female genitals were destructive and destructible (see also Kestenberg, 1988; Bernstein, 1993). In this way they unconsciously experienced menstruation as 'proof' that something had been destroyed in their genitals – triggering intense menstruation-related conditions such as migraine, nausea or abdominal pain.

8　Translator's note: The reference is to a series of romantic German films from the nineteen fifties about the Habsburg princess Elisabeth, starring the young Romy Schneider.

References

Adorer, S. (1998) 'Impotence and frigidity'. (Panel report.) *Int. J. Psycho-Anal.*, 79: 152–155.

Babatzanis, J. and Babatzanis, G. (1992) 'Fate and the personal myth in Medea's plight: filicide', in P. Hartocollis and G. I. Davidson (eds) *The Personal Myth in the Psychoanalytic Theory*. Madison, CT: International Universities Press, pp. 234–254.

Beland, H. (1989) 'Die unbewusste Phantasie. Kontroversen um ein Konzept'. *Forum Psychoanal.*, 5: 85–98.

Bernstein, D. (1993) 'Weibliche genitale Ängste und Konflikte und die typischen Formen ihrer Bewältigung'. *Psyche*, 47: 530–560.

Blum, H. (ed.) (1977) *Female Psychology*. New York: International Universities Press, pp. 139–157.

Bollas, C. (1995) *Cracking Up. The Work of the Unconscious*. New York: Hill and Wang.

Chasseguet-Smirgel, J. (1976) 'Freud and female sexuality – the consideration of some blind spots in the exploration of the "dark continent" '. *Int. J. Psycho-Anal.*, 57: 275–287.

Chasseguet-Smirgel, J. (1988) 'A woman's attempt at a perverse solution and its failure'. *Int. J. Psycho-Anal.*, 69: 149–163.

Cherazi, S. (1988) 'Zur Psychologie der Weiblichkeit'. *Psyche*, 42: 307–328.

Escoll, P. J. (1991) 'Prologue and epilogue to: Contemporary issues in female psychology'. *Psychoanal. Inq.*, 11: 421–427, 602.

Euripides (1910) *The Medea*, trans. G. Murray. London: Allen and Unwin.

Fonagy, P., Moran, G. S. and Target, M. (1993) 'Aggression and the psychological self'. *Int. J. Psycho-Anal.*, 74: 471–485.

Freud, S. (1905) 'Fragment of an analysis of a case of hysteria'. *S.E.* 7: 1–122.

Freud, S. (1908) 'Creative writers and day-dreaming'. *S.E.* 9: 143–153.

Freud, S. (1916–17) 'Introductory lectures on psycho-analysis'. *S.E.* 15: 9–239; *S.E.* 17: 145–156.

Freud, S. (1926) 'The question of lay analysis'. *S.E.* 20: 251–258.

Friedman, A. R. (1960) 'Group psychotherapy in the treatment of the Medea complex'. *Acta Psychotherapeutica et Psychosomatica*, 8: 457–461.

Giovacchini, S. L. (1979) 'The dilemma of becoming a woman', in M. Sugar (ed.) *Female Adolescent Development*. New York: Brunner-Mazel, pp. 253–273.

Green, A. (1983) 'La mère morte', in A. Green *Narcissisme de vie, narcissisme de mort*. Paris: Minuit, pp. 222–253.

Green, A. (1999) 'The Greening of psychoanalysis: André Green in dialogues with Gregorio Kohon', in G. Kohon (ed.) *The Dead Mother: The Work of André Green*. London and New York: Routledge.

Greenacre, P. (1950) 'Special problems of early female development'. *Psychoanal. St. Child*, 5: 122–138.

Grossman, W. I. and Stewart, W. A. (1976) 'Penis envy: from childhood wish to developmental metaphor'. *J. Amer. Psychoanal. Assn.*, 24: 193–212.

Hagglund, T. B. and Piha, H. (1980) 'The inner space of the body image'. *Psychoanal. Q.*, 49: 256–284.

Herzog, J. M. (1994) 'Die Begegnung mit dem Vater in der analytischen Situation'. Paper presented to the Frankfurter Psychoanalytische Vereinigung, 9 May.

Inderbitzin, L. B. (1989) 'Unconscious fantasy'. *J. Amer. Psychoanal. Assn.*, 37: 823–837.

Jordan, J. P. (1990) 'Inner space and the interior of the maternal body'. *Int. Rev. Psycho-Anal.*, 17: 433–445.

Kämmerer, A. *et al.* (eds) (1998) *Medeas Wandlungen. Studien zu einem Mythos in Kunst und Wissenschaft.* Heidelberg: Mattes.

Kerényi, K. (1992) *Die Mythologie der Griechen. Band I: Die Götter- und Menschheitsgeschichten.* Munich: DTV.

Kernberg, O. (1987) 'Projection and projective identification: developmental and clinical aspects'. *J. Amer. Psychoanal. Assn.*, 35: 795–821.

Kestenberg, J. C. (1988) 'Der komplexe Charakter weiblicher Identität'. *Psyche*, 42: 349–365.

Koster-Sanders, T. and Groen-Prakken, H. (1988) 'Über die weibliche Identität und Sexualität'. *Zeit. Psychoanal. Theorie u. Praxis*: 113–123.

Langer, M. (1988) *Mutterschaft und Sexus. Körper und Psyche der Frau.* Freiburg: Kore Verlag.

Leuzinger-Bohleber, M. *et al.* (1998) 'Wo ist das Gedächtnis geblieben? Psychoanalyse und embodied cognitive science im Dialog', in M. Leuzinger-Bohleber *et al.* (eds) *Erinnerung von Wirklichkeiten. Psychoanalyse und Neurowissenschaften im Dialog.* Stuttgart: Verlag Internationale Psychoanalyse.

Mayer, D. L. (1991) 'Towers and enclosed spaces: a preliminary report on gender differences in children's reactions to block structures'. *Psychoanal. Inq.*, 11: 480–511.

McDougall, J. (1991) 'Sexual identity, trauma and creativity'. *Psychoanal. Inq.*, 11: 559–582.

Ogden, T. H. (1992) 'Comments on transference and countertransference in the initial analytic meeting'. *Psychoanal. Inq.*, 12: 225–248.

Oliner, M. (2000) 'Die schlechten Mütter'. Unpublished paper presented at the Sigmund Freud Institute, February.

Orgel, S. and Shengold, L. (1968) 'The fatal gift of Medea'. *Int. J. Psycho-Anal.*, 49: 379–383.

Piers, M. W. (1976) 'Das Problem des Kindermords'. *Psyche*, 30: 418–436.

Pines, D. (1988) 'Wozu Frauen ihren Körper unbewusst benutzen'. *Zeit. Psychoanal. Theorie u. Praxis*, 1: 94–113.

Pines, D. (1993) *A Women's Unconscious Use of Her Body. A Psychoanalytical Perspective*. London: Virago.

Quinodoz, D. (1991) ' "J'ai peur de tuer mon enfant", ou Oedipe abandonné, Oedipe adopté'. *Rev. Franç. Psychanal.*, 51: 1579–1593.

Quinodoz, J.-M. (1986) Identifizierung und Identität in der weiblichen Homosexualität. *Zeit. Psychoanal. Theorie u. Praxis*, 1: 82–95.

Resnik, P. J. (1970) 'Murder of the newborn. A psychiatric review of neonaticide'. *Am. J. Psychiatry*, 126: 10.

Rheingold, J. C. (1964) *The Fear of Being a Woman. A Theory of Maternal Destructiveness*. New York: Grune and Stratton.

Rotmann, M. (1978) 'Über die Bedeutung des Vaters in der "Wiederannäherungsphase" '. *Psyche*, 32: 1105–1147.

Schaule, A. (1982) 'Tötungshandlungen von Müttern an ihren eigenen Kindern unter besonderer Berücksichtigung des Medea-Komplexes'. Munich: Med. diss.

Shengold, L. (1963) 'The parent as Sphinx'. *J. Amer. Psychoanal. Assn.*, 11: 725–751.

Stern, D. (1995) *The Motherhood Constellation: A Unified View of Parent–Infant Psychotherapy*. New York: Basic Books.

Stern, E. S. (1948) 'The Medea complex: the mother's homicidal wishes to her child'. *J. Mental Science*, 94: 321–331.

Stoller, R. J. (1976) 'Primary femininity'. *J. Amer. Psychoanal. Assn.*, 24: 59–78.

Sugar, M. (ed.) (1979) *Female Adolescent Development*. New York: Brunner-Mazel.

Tyson, P. (1991) 'Some nuclear conflicts of the infantile neurosis in female development'. *Psychoanal. Inq.*, 11: 582–602.

Warsitz, P. R. (1994) 'Medeas Schwermut. Zur Psychodynamik der Melancholie', in M. Schuller and K. Dahlke (eds) *Melancholie und Trauer* Leipzig: Kassel.

Winnicott, D. W. (1971) *Playing and Reality*. London: Tavistock.

Wittels, F. (1944) 'Psychoanalysis and literature', in S. Lorand (ed.) *Psychoanalysis Today*. New York: Covici-Friede, pp. 338–348.

Young-Bruehl, D. (1991) 'Rereading Freud on female development.' *Psychoanal. Inq.*, 11: 427–441.

The baby makers

Conscious and unconscious psychological reactions to infertility and 'baby-making' – an in-depth single case study[1]

Joan Raphael-Leff

If I had a son! A little boy black of curls and
wise. To hold his hand and slowly step
down garden paths.
A little
Boy.

Uri I'd call him, my light:
Soft and clear, the short name is
A fragment bright.
To my darkhaired child
'Uri!' –
I call.

Still I'm embittered as Rachel the matriarch.
Still I pray like Hannah at Shilo.
Still I await
Him.
    Barren, the Hebrew poet Rachel, 1928 (my translation)

Poets and artists have a capacity to ingest, contain and absorb misfortune that invades the internal world, before spewing it out in a pearl-coated missive of pain. Most of us, faced with unremitting, cumulative trauma, merely attempt to shield our vulnerable inner selves by defensively hardening the social boundaries of external reality, establishing protective partitions deep inside between different facets of our psychic reality and using magical means to control the inexplicable.

The psychological trauma of prolonged infertility has an emotional impact which in the past culminated either in acceptance of childlessness or adoption. Recent interventive technologies of fertilisation (such as AIH, AID, IVF, GIFT)[2] have however brought in their wake new hopes; prolonged treatment itself seems to have resulted in a new syndrome of psychological disturbances in the consumers. A review of thirty research publications has found convincing evidence that patients treated in infertility clinics show significantly higher levels of psychosocial distress, among them females scoring higher than males (Wright *et al.* 1989). This raises the question of whether anxiety and emotional disturbances precede or even cause infertility, or whether infertility causes psychological disturbance. For many years studies focused on psychogenic components (Benedek *et al.* 1953) and emotional factors (Rubenstein 1951; Taymor and Bresnick 1979) or personality traits (Platt *et al.* 1973) in infertility. Others studied psychological differences between fertile and nonfertile individuals (Eisner 1963) or within infertile subgroups versus fertile (Callan and Hennessey 1989). However, findings have not always been replicated; reviews of studies indicate methodological flaws (Mahlstedt 1985) and many researchers have found no significant differences or patterns on personality variables, psychopathology, patterns of marital interaction and social support, on either matched couple (Mai *et al.* 1972) or prospective studies (Raval *et al.* 1987). Causal evidence is inconclusive and comparative findings of psychological dysfunction appear related to the duration of infertility (Edelmann and Connolly 1986).

Research into psychological stress associated with the impact of reproductive failure has isolated factors such as disappointment (Brand 1989), lowered self esteem (Kedem *et al.* 1990), identity readjustments following diagnosis (Raval *et al.* 1987), effects of interventive investigations (Pfeffer and Woolett 1983; Connolly *et al.* 1987), chronic anxiety due to uncertain treatability and/or success rate of some conditions (Edelmann and Golombok 1989), male, female or pair sexual problems (Elstein 1975; Berger 1980; Demyttenaere *et al.* 1989) and marital distress (Kaufman 1969; Connolly, Edelmann and

Cooke 1987). Elsewhere, I have suggested that the emotional trauma of the infertility diagnosis has repercussions on all levels: intrapsychic, interpersonal, psychosexual and occupational (Raphael-Leff 1986). In my clinical experience, oscillations of psychological disturbance associated with infertility and its treatment, manifest in symptoms as diverse as depression, low self-esteem, guilt, hypochrondria, derealisation, depersonalisation, paranoia, psychosomatic and anxiety reactions, and defensive manoeuvres such as denial, phobic avoidance and obsessional reactions with rumination, magical thinking and compulsive rituals (Raphael-Leff 1991).

One in eight couples is likely to experience trouble conceiving. While each person reacts to protracted infertility in a uniquely personal way dictated by his/her own psychological history and current socio-biological circumstances, in my dual capacity as both psychoanalyst and social psychologist I would like to delineate some areas of emotional difficulty commonly affecting most people undergoing prolonged treatment for problematic fertility. Later, by way of a single clinical example, I shall describe in more detail some specific dynamics underlying these.

1 The prime experience of infertility is that of *violation of the expectation of generativity* as a fundamental normal human property. Being branded 'infertile' constitutes an existential shattering of naive trust in natural universal order, unquestioned since infancy.

2 Couples diagnosed as infertile experience considerable interpersonal stress in their intimate relationship. As individuals, each member's insular pith is pierced by doubt. *Personal singularity is subverted* during investigations and/or treatment for subfertility, as the couple's *mutual creative reciprocity is evaluated* and their interdependence is constantly demonstrated.

3 Manifestations of *persecutory guilt, inferiority and shame* about past sexual encounters and current inability to conceive/impregnate mingle with accusatory blame. Past abortions, procrastinated family planning or conceptive hindrance are all grist to the mill and anger when one partner's incapacity forces the couple into 'artificial' reproductivity. Invariably, doubt and resentment fester below or break through the marital-surface, even when their common pain draws the couple together.

4 Each partner suffers a *corporeal disillusionment* in relation to the lack of control over their own body, no longer 'normal' and

taken for granted as a working creative component of self-image, but now proved 'inferior', non-functioning, sterile. Confusion between the inner world of the psyche and the inside of the body often leads to a generalised sense of being stuck, impotent and non-productive, which may affect work and social accomplishment.

5 *Sexual activity*, stripped of its potential procreative function, often feels sterile or mechanical. Infertility stress may result in orgasmic disturbances, impotence and premature ejaculation. Ironically, lovemaking cannot bring comfort and closeness to the estranged couple without poignantly also reminding them of their personal ineffectuality.

6 A deep narcissistic wound is experienced in relation to *core gender identity* as sexually-propagative man or woman. Resentment and shame may centre on the dependent sexual reliance on a third person, the virile doctor, interjecting in the intimate intercourse between two lovers. The *male–female gender divide* is highlighted by different treatment experiences they face and the focus on fundamental biological functioning.

7 Uncertainty, lack of control and biological dependency lead to *a heightened emotional attachment* to the Godlike 'Baby Maker'- infertility expert who has magical powers attributed to him and becomes imbued with special feelings originally associated with oedipal parents in childhood.

8 Motivation, nature and quality of proposed *parenthood*, taken for granted by most prospective parents, must be profoundly questioned and perpetually justified by couples who agree to go to great lengths to make a baby rather than just having one. Intracouple differences of motivation are starkly revealed and a flawed relationship will flounder. Temptation arises to treat each other as *substitutes* for the elusive baby as an escape route from the round of infertility treatment, resulting in a realignment of marital emotional forces.

9 *Everyday-life becomes split* between the ongoing activity of professional/social life in which they make choices and decisions and the permanent grief and secret yearning for realisation of a potential life now held 'frozen in cold storage' that is beyond their control and cannot be lived until conception is made to occur.

10 *Time*, takes on a triple quality:

calendar time: the observed life-march of other people's babies growing into children and becoming teenagers, leaving the static infertile person behind;

periodicity: the relentless biological clock racing on towards menopause, ticking away menstrual cycles of waiting and wanting, hope and despair, elation–deflation and treatment stops and starts,

posterity: the nightmare of broken lineage and unbearably slow passage of time spent in powerless yearning for genetic immortality, nursing the flame of faith in the sweeping trajectory of eternal linkage from past to future generations despite each recurrent transient amputating disappointment.

11 *Space*, too, becomes divided between *inner space* with its depleted powerhouse and a dangerous *outer space* peopled with threatening fertile-aliens – colleagues who make work demands when resources are so scarce; friends who catch one unawares by thoughtlessly quoting their kids; parents who ask for grandchildren; strangers who push prams in parks; pregnant women who steal infertile people's chances and babies in supermarkets who look good enough to eat, kill or kidnap.

12 Confronted by ordinary happenings in the outside world, the infertile individual encounters *primitive, raw emotions* she/he did not know were there – feeling singled out as not good enough to reproduce, feeling left out and left behind; flooded by envy, destructiveness, hatred, helplessness, greed, vengefulness, jealousy, bitterness, rage, spite, shame, panic and fear. Ownership of such reactions is difficult, and the bad feelings are often buried again, split off inside or deflected outwards and projected onto partner or others. *Vigilance* has to be maintained against further hurt, either by withdrawing and keeping people at a distance by hardening the outer shell or by creating internal barriers to protect the vulnerable self inside from the full impact of its own feelings.

It is these various defensive procedures that we encounter as psychological symptomatology. In this presentation, I will attempt to demonstrate some underlying unconscious phantasies and dynamic processes experienced during the course of protracted treatment for infertility. My general data are derived from an in-depth study of thousands of hours of listening to 19 infertile patients seen in psychoanalysis five times per week or less frequent psychotherapy, either individually or as a couple, for a period of up to seven years. In this paper (with her permission) I shall focus on one particular woman, seen twice weekly for five years, chosen not for her pathology but because her symptoms are so clearly a product of her infertility, albeit interacting with historic personal variables. I highlight both the vicissitudes of her emotional reactions to the ongoing infertility, and her personal growth during the therapeutic treatment. Attention will be focused on subfertile patients' special transference relationship to the medical specialist – as 'Baby Maker', and their own strange experience of 'making' a baby rather than simply having one. Wherever possible, I shall let you hear her speak her own words.

Waiting for the verdict

Eve, as I shall call her, sought psychotherapy during the six-month period of waiting for a diagnostic assessment of fertility following an ectopic pregnancy. Previously even-tempered and professionally productive, she had begun to experience both a sense of being stuck and paralysed and of boundary-slippage: some difficulty concentrating on her very demanding work accompanied by uncharacteristic feelings of depression, frustration, anger and resentment. In the therapy, as the weeks of suspense crawl past, we begin to unravel the bewildering irony of possibly having lost her fertility after actually being pregnant without experiencing it. Her dreams and waking preoccupation are with her much desired (ectopic) baby not having found a safe 'nest' inside her, just a 'bad, hollow, frightening place' in which it got 'strangled'. The undetected pregnancy, ectopic emergency and long vigil of waiting helplessly for an authority outside her to tell her what is happening inside her own 'tummy' leave Eve disillusioned with her previous naive trust in a 'harmonious relationship' between herself and her body. She now believes these events confirm her husband's secret lack of faith in her ability to be creative and her own fear that she will not be allowed to have children. Surrounded by demands to continue as normal, Eve feels the therapy offers the only place in which *the centrality of her traumatic experience* can be recognised: an oasis in which she can explore and express her confusion, sense of failure and ominous fantasies. Every day brings her a step nearer towards knowing whether her remaining fallopian tube is viable or whether she is doomed to be barren. However, the months in psychotherapy are used fruitfully and Eve begins to envisage a fresh phase starting in her married life. She now realises that, previously, her husband, Adam, had consented to her having a baby but had not shared in her 'almost overwhelming desire to have children'. Had pregnancy continued and the baby been born, they would have 'been entering parenthood from very separate and isolated positions'. However, she hopes that during these painful past few months they have achieved a better shared understanding of the 'chasm' of differences that split them.

The deadline arrives. The good news registers but Eve does not feel relief as expected, only a numbness which gradually gives way to new suspense. She wonders whether her own good news is Adam's bad news. Confidence in her body and innocent trust cannot be restored after the upheaval of the past months. Eve finds it difficult to feel 'uninhibitedly happy and deserving' having been told that the scarring in her tubes is due to a 'silent infection' years earlier. Guilt over sexual encounters during her late teens mingles with guilt over 'pushing ahead' with another pregnancy which Adam fears would dilute their special intimate relationship.

Ironically, now that she is released from thinking about the inside of her body, the focus is upon the transactions between them. Short of 'taking a leap in the dark' into the future, their conflict appears even more insoluble, since only parenthood will convince him that his trepidation of being overshadowed by a baby is unfounded. Eve decides to become pregnant despite reservations about overriding Adam, who was until now 'the powerful one' in the relationship. She looks forward to her fertile period during their holiday, feeling that demands of work prevent her from engaging fully in 'the counterscript' of wanting to conceive. It is now over a year since she first started trying to become pregnant, and she is tired of the uncertainty of not knowing how long she will be juggling her emotional energies and commitment between work and taking time out to have a child. However, making love is so 'good' again since they have discarded contraception, and Eve feels deeply liberated and tearfully moved by the doctor's verdict, indeed, his agreement, permission and blessing to 'enjoy themselves trying' after so many months of stern injunctions. She believes that making love means making babies, and special love-making will produce a special baby.

Trying to conceive

For the next seven months, Eve is powerless to stop the hopeful part of herself gathering force each month, then being sorely disappointed as her period arrives. She wonders:

What is this depth of desire in me to conceive? The shadow side of wanting so much is an anxiety that the more I want it the more it will be withheld from me. I can't shake the feeling that I won't be allowed to have a child. That it is forbidden. I'm flooded by envy and painful feelings watching my friend breastfeed her baby. The little gremlins in me can't bear others taking for granted what I can't have. It feels as if their success is depriving me of mine . . . my concentration is impaired. It's such an effort to concentrate single-mindedly when this powerful need to be a mother keeps grabbing my thoughts away. But I must get on with life regardless of my inner desire and terrible frustration . . . I feel my readiness and inner state of yearning for a baby, not knowing when I will connect with it. As if there is a child waiting for me somewhere: 'Where are you?' I ask, 'When are you going to come into our lives?' – as if it has a reality, is there but out of reach. 'Please come towards me because I'm receptive and want you!' It's ridiculous! This baby does not exist except in my own mind but when we make love I feel such a powerful rebirth of hope that surely out of longing and closeness our child will connect up and grow to be real.

Living in limbo

With the passage of time, Eve feels '*marginal and peripheral*' – belonging neither to work nor to people with kids. The 'insurmountable gulf' between mothers and childless women appears even less bridgeable than the divide between men and women. She observes superstitiously:

If I can't have my baby I feel I must hug my preoccupation to myself. If I get involved with other interests, it will detract from the vigilance. If I forget, it feels impious. As if I'm afraid if I stop waiting all will disappear. I have to hold onto the desire and hope and disappointment all the time, like grieving, otherwise it won't come true . . .

Eve finds herself in a state of suspension in *relation to her own mother.* Envying her mother's motherhood she feels she cannot be an equal with her Mum until she herself is a mother, and can begin to give out and give back some of what she has received. The void in her own life will not be filled until her baby comes, but paradoxically she also believes she cannot become pregnant until she has vacated a place for the new baby by mourning her losses – her dead foetus; her wasted pregnancy; the lost idealised relationship with her mother; her previous merged intimacy with her husband from whom she now feels separate in their male/female differences. She tells me:

> I need you almost on a fantasy level – to trust and wait with me, make it all better and use your fertile magic to turn me into a parent. I feel so deprived and doubly deserted – no one remembers I am vulnerable, hurt and different and there is no one to appeal to. I am grabbed by unpredictable sudden devastating sadness and I don't know when it will be triggered, by what or whom – as if I'd become a baby rather than getting one . . . But I need to keep up hope – be receptive on a physical level so as to conceive despite the risk of not conceiving, and on a social level, expose myself to people despite the risk of being hurt. I have no choice but to go forward, come out of my hole and even go and see my colleague's new baby.

The *anniversary* of the ectopic pregnancy comes and goes. Eve feels she inhabits a 'twilight world', believing that if she does not relive that precious eight weeks of unexperienced pregnancy of the previous year it will create a backlog of unlived time. She now feels she needs both to go forward and to go back and recapture: . . . 'catch up with myself and gather the scattered bits together as if I've become a watered down version of myself, cautiously safe and stuck in old patterns'. Gradually the realisation creeps in that she might now be missing out on the present as then she missed out on her unfelt pregnancy. As time passes she has 'such a strong sense of others moving on with their lives while . . . I'm just watching. I can't shift my own life up to the next gear . . . Other people have choices and make decisions and I just wish something special would happen to light me up.'

Her contact with pregnant friends seems bitter-sweet. It is distressing to watch them grow larger and she feels the need to erect a barrier so they do not fear her envy or miscarry because of it; but it is also reinforcing because it confirms that 'reality does happen' and reminds her that it is not a missed period she is waiting for but a baby. With a lot of therapeutic working-through of her acrimonious feelings, Eve begins to sense 'a great relief and gratitude' as she says, 'like a child emerging from a tantrum' to find that the world and mother/therapist and she herself still exist. Gradually optimistic, she now believes that 'having a baby will be a bonus, not the sole and total *raison d'être*'.

Consciously, Eve now wants to be 'released from the '*tyranny of conception*'. She is taking on a new position of authority at work and thinks of going back onto contraception when she starts her new job. If and when she becomes pregnant again she wants it to be in the right place in her body and at the right time in her life. She realises that so much of her life has been driven by a desire to satisfy her deprived mother, always feeling a 'profound sense of responsibility, wanting to repair her, and perform miracles for her . . . as if she needs my success like a mirror, a barometer to give her some meaning to hold onto for herself'. As the weeks pass, Eve begins to believe she can leave therapy. 'It has taken a long time to disentangle myself and know that my feelings are not my own but Mum's in me. Perhaps if I can convey to my mother that I'm no longer waiting for conception she too can see there is a life beyond motherhood.'

Listening to my patient as I have to other subfertile women, I feel confident that despite the prematurity of her conscious independence she is ripe to conceive, now that her identity no longer depends on becoming a mother.

Infertility

Two months later she is back on my couch after another ectopic pregnancy. 'I was going one way of inner relaxation' she says 'and my body just went its own way and played a malevolent trick.' For a precious moment remote Adam had put his arms around her saying 'I could get very excited about this pregnancy', but ironically, that night, after making it public by telling their best friends, the pain came on followed by bleeding and confirmation of a fallopian pregnancy. Eve fancies Adam's ambivalence had put the embryo in the wrong place. 'If he had accepted it from the first it would have gone to the right place. His acceptance came too late' . . . After he expressed his sorrow at having felt excluded from sharing the brief pregnancy with her, Eve dreams that Adam gave birth in the bathroom to a girl baby. 'It didn't seem weird that he had a vagina', she

214

observes, 'I fed the baby, I had milk.' The dream is about his brief retrieval of tenderness and a newfound mutuality in his emotional reparation for her solitary miscarriage in the bathroom. It is also about infertility. She has a waking image of her tubes 'as destroyed suspension bridges with the ovum just floating around'. Connection will have to be provided externally.

The following months are given over to exploring the idea of IVF. Watching a TV panel of experts, she feels a strange temptation to treat them as 'god-like', granting them all the childhood feelings of dependency on omnipotent parental power to grant or withhold: 'Having journeyed so long, with options falling off on the way, at this last stage, could I be saved by a special person who chooses me to be special?' After four months of deliberation Eve decides to apply for IVF treatment:

> As a healthy woman, it is an option. I should exercise my choice but I won't treat it as a be all and end all. I have come a long way in these two years of agony and raw suffering but I am stronger for it. I feel I've laid something to rest inside me – even if the answer I seek is negative and I am not accepted for IVF, I don't feel I'll regress. It is like the last station on a train line. I don't have to retrace my steps if the option fails. At times, I have an image of *a grille in the road*, as if I have dropped something valuable down it, just beyond reach yet visible. I need to get help to retrieve it rather than abandon hope without trying. I feel a revival of old hopes, as if making myself open and receptive again to the possibility of growing a child in my own body, yet it is so different from the simple hope I had when just the two of us were trying on our own.

Seeds of hope

The *first IVF interview* brings hopefulness, sadness and apprehension. Eve says:

> At any point the pack of cards could tumble. It is strange having a stranger intervene in my intimacy with my husband. So sad when Adam was taken away to produce a sperm-sample, alone where there should have been two of us. I'm glad he stayed for my examination. Since the ectopic pregnancies he feels a sense of danger lurking, lapping at our feet . . . We need to marshal our resources, separately and together to face this. Even

if I am accepted and do become pregnant I'm not sure I can keep the embryo safe. I need extra protection for a little while against something bad inside myself and just random tragic events.

Eve's father has another heart attack. Further treatment improves Adam's sperm count although motility is poor due to an asympto-matic infection. Yet more 'shattering of innocence', another example of bodily ignorance and lack of control. The metaphor of this micro-scope light showing up what has been there all along is applied to self-discovery and mutual revelation of all they had not known about themselves and each other and, now knowing, cannot be reversed. Adam is put on to antibiotics for 70 days. Once again help seems just beyond grasp, always retreating out of reach . . . more delays, doubts, difficulties and 'other people always holding the strings'. In the endless round of treatments to optimalise the condi-tions of their reproductive systems it is easy to lose sight of the baby. Eve finds herself always crying now when they make love – great raw sobs, like a form of orgasm, releasing throbbing pain deep inside her.

Another birthday comes and goes with the inward disappoint-ment that what she wants 'will not arrive wrapped-up like her gifts'. She still has the fantasy that her baby might be 'just waiting in the wings, wanting to be born', a phantom child kept alive by her yearning.

Therapy continues to focus on the struggle to disentangle her own needs defined in terms other than those of Adam and her mother. She has always felt the need to be caring and considerate of others before she could give to herself. Eve even fancies she was born prematurely because her mother was so desperately impatient to see her. Psychotherapy offers her permission to experience her denied, rebuffed neediness. Flooded with the realisation of her own lack of care for herself, Eve begins to nurture herself instead of only others. Entitled to be separate, to have and explore her own full range of emotions and fantasies, she begins to hear her voice for the first time, bringing long-buried feelings out into the open and creating space inside. She discovers layers and depths to herself that had been obscured by her mother's lifelong belief that one only became oneself when a baby arrived, and her own conviction that the primitive and fertile parts of her self could only be indulged vicariously by mothering a baby and needy others. Eve says: 'Had you told me a year ago that I would feel this way it would have meant nothing – then I was aching for a physical baby in my belly.' She now truly has achieved the *internal freedom to conceive of herself independently of physical conception.*

However, feelings fluctuate and there are still periods of anger with her body for not being able to do what is so natural that every animal can do it. At times Eve still finds herself in the throes of emotional turmoil and confusion: 'I'm overloaded with stuff running around inside colouring how I am at work, and making it difficult to remain rational and objective when I'm in the grip of the feelings brewing inside.' She marks the date her second baby would have been due, with subdued sadness.

After eight months of preliminaries, the couple is offered a final appointment at the hospital to determine whether they will be allowed to proceed with the IVF programme. 'My greatest need,' thinks Eve, 'is for *something definite* after all this waiting and uncertainty. Not a definite outcome but a chance to try.' A scan of her ovaries is 'excellent'. 'I was so pleased,' she tells me, 'after all the depressing things I have found out about myself and what is going on inside, I was irrationally excited seeing it clearly visible on the screen. The doctor said: "Well done!" and I felt I'd been a very good girl. I had an overly full bladder and was desperate to go to the loo but held on a little longer, pleased to let them get such a good picture.' She feels comforted and reassured that Adam is more involved and supportive. He has had his own 'exam' and is worried about his sperm count. Eve observes:

On one level we can't lose out – if IVF works we will have gone through it together and become parents as a unit. If it doesn't work, our sadness will be a shared one, not just me carrying it in isolation. With my first pregnancy Adam said he could just about bravely accept it although inside he felt very angry and persecuted by the whole idea of having a child. Yesterday, putting up with anxiety, tears, stress and worry, he said: 'Can't you see, isn't it obvious, I want to go through with it?' Yet I still need him to say: 'I'm in this with you right through till the end, whatever the end may be.' He now has a taste of what it is like to wait for your body to get healed and ready and be unable to influence the decision. It put me back in touch with how isolated I felt before, for being made to feel I was the greedy one who wanted this child when he was just on the sidelines . . . I find it a strange idea that he has an infection, like I had had – brings up thoughts of guilty secrets, where it came from, who gave it to whom, did I pass it on or are his and mine completely unrelated. There's an irony that something good is coming out of all that fucked-upness inside, we are better potential parents now. I'm aware of the mess we might have been in had I just straightforwardly conceived with nothing healed between Adam and myself. Our silence was the infection in us both, the malevolent toad waiting to jump out and wreak havoc . . . Our marriage seemed so good but we were ill as a couple, good in bits but stillborn and empty in others. Although we didn't know it, we were two very frightened people behind barriers, a silent chasm with Adam on one side and me on the other and no bridge other than a suicidal leap into creating a pregnancy because we could never move out of the endless, sterile futile conversations about whether to have children with the chasm yawning beneath us and me filling up with yearnings and fantasies about babies that I couldn't begin to understand, while Adam stood miles away. I pushed us both into it because I couldn't bear being stuck on the edge. But now, we can talk and share what really matters.

Three magic wishes

While waiting for the go-ahead for IVF, therapeutic work continues, guided by dreams and unconscious preoccupations as well as external realities. Eve emotionally relives much of her childhood relationship to both her parents and siblings, and begins to see the way these have been repeatedly played out in her present relationships. Eve is aware of living in a 'state of suspension' in relation to her mother, with a sense of 'bottomless grief' at being unable to pass on the much loved childhood rituals her mother taught her that she had learned from her own mother. She feels she is 'not really adult' until she can share in what her mother conveys is the most important experience of life – mothering. Eve believes her parents must feel profoundly let down by her inability to have a baby, and that a grandchild would have brought herself relief from her function of being the sole source of their satisfaction. Returning for the harvest festival in her parents' village where she grew up, she feels ashamed and different, childishly wishing her mother would gather her close and hide her. Gradually she becomes aware how much she actually envies her own parents their experience of having a child, her, and feels sorely deprived of the chance to be 'grown up', fruitful and proud to give back some of the special love and care invested in her.

Preparing for the *IVF briefing at the hospital*, she is again acutely aware of curtailed autonomy and adulthood: 'It feels like going back to the classroom at school, to be taught the facts of life by a teacher-guru, and having to wait my turn. I have no choice but I really don't want to meet all the other couples, and have to wonder: Which of all of us in this room will get what we want? Will they be called before us? Will they be the lucky ones? It feels like my brothers looking enviously at me – if I get the sweetie from Mum will they have to go without?'

In England, the free National Health Service programme offers three IVF attempts, with a minimum of three-month intervals between them. Eve says it is 'like three wishes in fairytales.' From now on she lives on *red alert*, a mixture of excitement, apprehension and suspense that any cycle could be the one. Her dreams reveal nightmarish anxious fantasies about dependency on autocrats, constipation and degrading things which will be done in the name of high technology to her defenceless body. The 'Baby-Maker' doctors have all the power and control over the resources and, in the transference, she is envious of my creative freedom and angry about her lack of say over 'feeding' and 'toilet' schedules and therapy times.

Despite Adam's greater involvement Eve still identifies the pain of the problem as her own. 'Adam might have his own feelings about wanting a child but I as a woman also want the experience of carrying a baby inside my body.' At this parallel point her mother has a hysterectomy. Eve feels an 'irrational sadness' as though she is losing an 'intimate place', the part of her mother where she began. 'Whatever your age or state of life,' she muses, 'it is so easy for woman's insides to have problems, they're hidden away in the dark. I have two sets of imagery – a magical place, fertile, swelling, creatively transforming, and the other image of technology, knives, surgery, bits being put down a sluice.' There is no longer an unfair discrepancy between them now that mother and Eve both are at the mercy of their reproductive systems, as if both are expiating guilt and living out terrible punishments, both awaiting informtion about their bodies, and each ultimately alone with her own separate experience. Eve feels a searing longing to go home but permits her father to look after her ill mother in her place, thereby changing the habitual family constellation of herself as saviour.

Eve's own first priority now is to the future – preserving her resources for IVF. She says:

It is like *a funnel*. When we started having a child, the options were wide open. Over the years they have been stripped away, options closing off as we go – the ectopic pregnancy, the discovery of my twisted, scarred, damaged tube; six agonising months of waiting later the verdict said I could still get pregnant. Still hope, but from the moment the doctor told me that the next ectopic pregnancy had destroyed the other tube there was no going back; then these long months of uncertainty about Adam's sperm and acceptability for IVF. Now we have the go-ahead, we're still battling on, but all our energies are concentrated on this last hope the bottom of a narrow funnel. We can't stay in the funnel and there is no going back to a time of plenty. It's paradoxical – the objective is so narrow but the hope and energy so very rich and concentrated and so pressing, immediate and urgent despite the long wait . . .

Once again she lives in the rhythm of her menstrual cycle, full of hope yet bracing herself with each period for rejection by the IVF programme. She sees this as more complex than simply trying to conceive – her concern is whether the eggs will implant: 'It is a paradox – now I feel my womb is safe and roomy but I feel I need a plug to stop them falling out. Only three chances – like something from the Bible – how will I feel when it is two down and one to go? What does it feel like to have the three chances just trickling away?'

On the threshold

Eve surprises herself with the degree of her involvement in her new job. She has grown in confidence, feels much less defensive and more able to take risks, has a clearer sense of overall perspective and asserts herself with inner conviction. With her internal 'opening up', she is aware of simultaneously being happier and stronger but also experiencing a whole range of new feelings, extremes of unhappiness, anger, anguish and homesickness that were previously inaccessible.

The hospital gives them *a green light* after a final scan. A lot is happening: Eve daily goes back and forth to her GP for drug injections. The doctor expects her back on Monday for another scan to check her response to the drugs, and if she's responding well she will have yet another scan on Tuesday to see if she's developing eggs followed by an operation on Thursday to remove and culture them and a 48-hour wait to see if they fertilise, then back the following weekend to have three embryos implanted. She takes it one day at a time, excited and apprehensive, thoughts chasing ahead to the next stage, yet living in a state of *transition between two worlds*. Adam has been 'great', very supporting and involved although initially startled and taken aback. He has been talking about their next holiday abroad as if wanting to preserve a 'corner of freedom'. Eve's initial anger and hurt feelings about this have given way to a recognition that 'he needs his fantasy that he is not 100% in the ring'. However, since Monday he has been fully behind her, protectively keeping external demands to a minimum and ensuring that she has enough space for herself and keeps 'a low profile' at work. Eve's overriding sense is of not knowing what is happening inside her body but, having seen her 'insides' on the screen, she tries to visualise them while in the bath, pressing her hands to her tummy and mystically willing her follicles to ripen. She walks around in a daze, feeling pumped up full of drugs 'sloshing about' inside her as her dose is increased to bring about a growth spurt in the follicles which are too small. There are a few days of nerve-wracking timing since the IVF team do not work on weekends; if her body is to respond it must do so now. She traipses off for her hormone injection at 12.30 mid-night to allow 33 hours before Friday morning.

Life is peculiar, quite surreal as her follicles are pinpointed on the ultrasound screen and a computer print-out reveals what she does not know about her body. At home she gives her follicles 'a jolly good talking to' trying to coax them into growth. Back in hospital, she lies waiting for the doctor's crucial pronouncement. 'Abandon treatment,' he says as her heart sinks through the soles of her shoes. But he only means on Thursday. Communication is easily mis-understood when she is so tense. Adam is quite tense too; it is both a comfort to know he is so affected but very painful when he is cast down and she feels guilty. 'We are two people holding our breath,' she says. 'Nothing else retains its ordinary significance – it's all in a state of suspension. I don't feel very much in touch with life at all, odd experience going home on the train, seeing people at work living ordinary lives. Inside I feel very separate from it – going through the motions but feeling dislocated, like somebody in a book. It's all happening but I can't fall back on anything familiar. Yet I desperately don't want ordinary life to come rushing back with a great thump because I've abandoned it, like waking from a dream. But there is no way I can be gradually let down. It's all such *a lottery so* much luck involved, each month is different; anyway, if I try again, we will have accumulated some helpful information about my responses to this time as a base-line for judgements, whereas this one is all trial and error.'

On the following Wednesday she reports that five eggs were fertilised after the operation to remove nine on Friday. The best three little embryos were implanted on Monday and now there is simply a period of waiting after the long week of excitement and attention. 'The doctor said: "We've done all we can, now its over to you".' She has been told to come to the hospital in two weeks for a very early pregnancy test if her period does not come. Having become a 'baby maker' herself, her relationship to the 'Baby Makers' undergoes a subtle change. In view of her previous fantasies, Eve is surprised at how personally involved the team seems:

They don't just forget you when they send you off. It is a strange process building up this close attachment to the hospital and the staff, coming in and out so frequently, and feeling so profoundly grateful for this incredible thing they have done for us. It was an extraordinary moment of trust when they replaced the embryos in through the cervix. I watched on the screen. I do wish I had seen them through the microscope. I keep wondering what is happening to them now. 'At least one of you just cling on,' I tell them. Adam is so delighted that the eggs had been fertilised – he was still quite worried about his sperm. When the hospital rang us at 9.30 on Sunday morning, he was very excited and it was so precious to me to see his face, such a contrast to his detached uninvolvement when I first told him I thought I was pregnant three years ago. I feel quite fragile now. I just want to be intertwined together and embedded at home, like our egg-and-sperm embryo. Most irrational things go through my mind – I woke with a wind-pain in my tummy after having beans for supper and was worried that would dislodge the little embryos if they are still alive. I've been clinging to your trust that my tiny scraps of life can cling on without me having to try too hard. I can't possibly do any more. I *feel fertile*. Going through this process has buoyed us both up, we both produced the necessary ingredients. We can't know if the combination is right but there is an abundance – a paradox at the heart of it all – and the doctors' excitement is quite infectious. We're so afraid to let them down. Although we have no direct control over producing eggs or sperm we both felt we'd done so well, they seem so pleased with us, as if we've been very clever. It is such a soothing compensation for the past three years of feeling my body is inferior and untrustworthy. Adam and I are very close, we have something so special at the moment, creating this feeling of warmth and togetherness and intimacy – IVF together is a very intimate thing, unusually private despite its very public nature. It has been binding.

Beginnings and endings

That same day Eve phoned in tears to tell me her father had died of a massive heart attack 'as if he had to go to make room for my baby'. Coincidentally, his first heart attack had happened when she was unknowingly pregnant (with the first ectopic pregnancy) and he'd recovered after her miscarriage. In the weeks that follow Eve is haunted by a search for logic in the coincidence of events, wondering why her life seems blighted and why she has been set apart and forbidden what everyone around her gets so easily. It feels as if 'everything has collapsed'. As Adam told her of her father's death she says she 'felt something snap' and when her period came it was 'not a big histrionic disappointment but a low key, resigned, quiet, sad, inevitable feeling'. Life feels as if catastrophes are there, just waiting to happen and the only way to keep them at bay is to be very still. Not rock the boat.

Therapy continues and in the months that follow Eve's bereavement she is aware of the biological clock not in a desperate way but with a perspective of growing older and needing to make the most of time. She is more realistic about her relationship with her mother. Wistfully restraining herself from 'bubbling over' and spilling out her frustrations and pain, she swallows it back, aware that it has always been so – her mother so wrapped around in love of her successful 'saviour' daughter that she is unable or unwilling to hear what Eve is really saying. However, Eve is now better able to mother herself and to love her mother without having to perform miracles for her. Eve's hairdresser mistakes her for somebody else and asks how her baby is. She is poignantly aware of the contradictions of going through so much to have a baby: 'It's at the nub of being infertile. Having kids is so commonplace, so natural, that if you're not part of it you feel singled out, excluded from all common assumptions – like being *blind in a seeing world*.'

It is six months before she reconsiders baby-making again. Both she and Adam are edgy and feel on trial until the eggs are fertilised.

Despite the previous experience it still feels strange: 'I am used to lying there with my legs open and them poking, pushing and prodding around but it is still an odd experience having a dialogue about what is happening on the screen.' She prefers it if there are no other couples waiting around – like *a production line:*

> Although I remind myself we're each unique it is strange that they're going through similar stages what should be so intimate ends up like a dentist's waiting room. And statistically, only one of us will get the baby. I wish *we* were the only special ones there. The doctor said they were having a 'good run'. I was touched by that, infected by the mood of optimism and success but also feeling as if his magic could wear off . . . Here I am back in this strange world, taking a urine container even when I go out to dinner or the theatre. It is intrusive to my physical, emotional, social, professional being as if I'm always tied by an umbilical cord. Sometimes it is so difficult to hold onto what IVF is all fundamentally about, not a way of life but just a means to an end. If this time does not succeed, neither of us want to embark on the third and very last attempt with its slender hope and full weight of longing. How marvellous it would be if this worked and we left with a sense of abundance – with yet another chance in the bag . . . The staff are so kind and encouraging, they stroke my hair and hold my hand and tell me about the eggs they are removing. I suppose it's not unlike having a baby – needing care and help when it hurts and trusting them. So tantalising – I so want to have something *real* at the end of all this, a pregnancy, a child. But all these complicated manoeuvres might just lead to a period. It is hard for us to imagine what it is like for each other – Adam's bit was over in 10–15 minutes. He was extremely anxious he wouldn't be able to do it to deadline. Whereas mine is all mapped out – not asked to do anything but the impossible – just to relax . . .

Three embryos were replaced but Eve feels pessimistic as fertilisation was late:

> I'd like to think these little specks are robust, with a drive for life, a powerful survival instinct, but I'm aware of how tiny and fragile and insubstantive they are, like us. I kept thinking they would just fall out when I went to the toilet – but I can't stop my ordinary life. This time I've gone back to work although I'm full of hormones and feel bloated and heavy and tender inside. It is such an achievement of synchronisation – me, Adam, clinic, embryos. Now that it is skewed I'm afraid it will fail although I have such

an incredibly strong urge of wanting to connect up with those little scraps at the right point. So near yet so far – just missing the boat; going through the whole process of being fertilised . . . so close yet miles away, slipping through my fingers like the ectopic pregnancy. Not for lack of wanting or trying or feeling or willing – just something I can do nothing about. My Dad could have made it work but he's gone.

The failure of the second IVF makes Eve feel her 'face is almost against the wall'. 'I will need to face my infertility, and nobody, not you or even Adam can experience what the loss of this will mean to me.' An *existential crisis* occurs in Eve's life as the bubble is pricked. She feels there is 'no benevolent force, no mysterious benign logic that will make things all right. No prayers, no miracles, no one to bail me out. I have to accept that misfortunes and difficulties affect people's lives. I ought to get on with putting my energies into life – my job, friendships but it is so hard to raise the strength to fight back. So much easier to just lapse into absorption, exclusion and a feeling of being locked out, left behind and abandoned.'

While discussing the implications of the IVF failure with the hospital team the doctor announces he is leaving. Shocked, Eve feels the thread is lost. He has been the key presence and although she understands about staff burn-out and his need to move on she is sad that the continuity is broken and that the people she trusts cannot see it through with them until the end. Eve wonders whether the 'magic' will work with a stranger.

The female chain

The third IVF is delayed while the possibilities of adoption are explored. She feels it is hard to convey the intensity of hunger pounding around in her head as she tries to wrench herself out of that level of reality. Adam is very keen to adopt a child. Babies are rarely placed for adoption. Eve desperately feels the issue is being pushed further and further away from what she has always wanted since childhood. She has a tragic sense of severing a primordial chain of womb-relatedness linked through blood: 'My mother and Dad were *real* parents because I was born to them. But I will have just married and adopted kids, and when Mum dies the age-old blood-thread will be broken.' Eve grieves her deprivation of a baby growing inside her body, mourning loss of the momentous experience of birth, and a downy head cradled against her cheek. The adoption agency advises them to take up their last IVF option now, as they soon will be too old to be assessed for adoption. Eve 'falls in love' with Adam's suggestion of adopting a sibling group of children since they at least would be blood-related to each other. They keep both IVF and adoption options in play feeling like 'people facing two directions at once . . . standing underneath a signpost but unsure which way it is pointing'.

Back to the 'excited, optimistic, hopeful, up-lifted feelings' which come crashing down as each period arrives just too late for the IVF-deadline of Monday by 12.00 noon. Back to the miserable, frustrated feeling of waiting for her body to perform, trying to synchronise her system to dovetail with that of the infertility clinic, and the seemingly insurmountable barrier of bringing period-IVF unit-ovum-sperm together. Ironically, the one month her period does come at, literally the eleventh hour, the hospital cannot accept them as they are fully booked. 'The last IVF is like a hysterectomy,' she says. 'Failure takes away hope of fullness – it pulls out the plug.' Eve feels hooked into the artificial sense of an 'internal gearing up to readiness, then having to be switched off again with a tremendous emotional effort and expenditure of energy, just to get back on to the plateau'. Yet her preoccupation with biology is counterbalanced by an inner awareness of personal growth and fulfilment. She believes she possesses purposeful capacities that are not dependent on having a child. It is an emotional struggle to hold onto these areas of satisfaction and self-control, which are always in danger of being swamped by the sense of endless aimless vacuum while waiting for a period. 'I do have a choice,' she declares: 'I won't allow myself to be defined as a set of ovaries waiting for hospital.' Nevertheless, she feels caught in between what she calls *the ongoing stream of life* and the 'primitive urge that feels a thousand million miles' away from her professional self, like *a call of the species*. On a very deep level, Eve feels a cumulative sense of human aloneness, awareness of mortality and fragility of life at its very beginning and end, and a tragic impression of her genetic connectedness to the future being uprooted and pulled away.

With passing time, Eve finds solace in solidarity among women:

I'm drawing on concentrated benevolent femaleness and being sustained by a very strong sense of relatedness to the whole range of women – black, white, older, younger, mothers and childless, all shapes and sizes – we can be all these things, different from each other, each with our own parcel of conflicts, dilemmas, losses and strengths, and then I am not singled out, cut off and deprived but just one of many, different but not foreign, in the middle not alone or in limbo . . . Some women are drained, exhausted and burnt out – I'm lucky, receiving a lot of nurturing and my resources are sufficient. I have been there, too, depleted, unable to think about myself, constantly giving to others, but I now feel on surer foundation with myself and my mother too. I used to feel personally responsible for her happiness. Now, she is learning to nurture herself and I hope she can enjoy this later stage of her life. Time is too precious to waste on negative nothingness and stagnant repetition. *I can* make things happen and life can be fun. I still have an empty hole in me – the lack of a child – but it is not the whole of me, just a space. I'm not an empty person inside. I am a strong person with good things inside and an empty pocket aching for a child.

The third IVF is jettisoned as Eve was about to be pre-medicated for egg-collection as a high percentage of Adam's sperm are found to be defective and immobile. He feels humiliated and angry while she has 'raw, uncivilised and punitively destructive feelings' wanting to let her fury erupt and spill out 'vomit all over his books' and to scream at the now-changed hospital personnel who could have spared her the drugged week of hope and preparation. 'What a waste! All my eggs were poised and ready. But his dead, sluggish, mishapen sperm were reluctant. It's like an uncanny mirror – as if I'm still dragging my reluctant husband into childbearing along with me. Our needs are out of step – I feel young and want to pass on what I've stored up; he feels depleted. But what I want is non-negotiable – I can't suppress it; it's like having an arm and a leg taken away. I've kept the hope alive in the face of daunting opposition from my body, his body, the hospital – I can't just bury it.' Yet, as the final check-up date nears, Eve is tempted to say 'Let's call it a day'. She refuses donor sperm, feeling that Adam and she have 'switched round'. Paradoxically, despite the sadness that sweeps over her intermittently, for the first time she experiences a sense of having a real choice:

I feel strangely uplifted, quite excited and more powerful – a definite sense of relief. We can make a responsible choice about how we are going to live a significant part of the next twenty years of our lives. We're both

227

depleted by the process of the past five years – it's almost been like going through the experience of having a child without having a child. Having yearned and wanted and allowed my life to be dominated by the gap and consciousness of what a child would have meant – so much worry and energy has gone into that, that we now relish our freedom like parents whose children have finally left the nest. I'll never be free of the grief that if I have a child it will not come out from between my thighs like I came out of my Mummy, like Russian dolls all fitting together . . . Whatever happens, this pain can't be outgrown. It is fundamentally a part of myself and, when it comes back, I cry and it still feels so intensely painful but I wouldn't want it to go away. I would lose part of myself. When I'm hurting most I'm also most alive and fully here in touch with all of me . . . Six years ago – all I had to do to have a child was stop the contraceptive. Now there is no avoiding anxieties. I've gained much more of a sense of my own depths but I feel older, old and wise and sad.

My narrative stops at this point in the therapy. At the time of writing Eve is becoming ready to end psychotherapy and awaits possible acceptance on an adoption list. If *you*, the reader, feel left in suspense and frustrated by this ending, you are sharing a little taste of the years of unrelieved uncertainty experienced by this couple, who also dearly wished they could peep at the answer at the end of the book.

Notes

1 An abridged version of this paper was presented at the International Congress on Pre- and Peri-Natal Psychology and Medicine, Jerusalem, March, 1989.
2 Since writing this paper, further innovations include egg donation, and more recently, egg freezing, with many emotional and ethical ramifications. See Raphael-Leff 2007, 2008 and 2010.

References

Benedek, T., Hame, G., Robbins, F. P. and Rubinstein, B. (1953) 'Some emotional factors in infertility'. *Psychosomatic Medicine*, 15: 485.
Berger, D. M. (1980) 'Impotence following the discovery of azoospermia'. *Fertility and Sterility*, 34: 154–156.

Brand, H. J. (1989) 'The influence of sex difference on the acceptance of infertility'. *Journal of Reproductive and Infant Psychology*, 7 (special issue on Psychology and Infertility): 129–132.

Callan, V. J. and Hennessey, F. J. (1989) 'Psychological adjustment to infertility: a unique comparison of two groups of infertile women, mothers and women childless by choice'. *Journal of Reproductive and Infant Psychology*, 7 (special issue on Psychology and Infertility): 105–112.

Connolly, K. J., Edelmann, R. J. and Cooke, I. D. (1987) 'Distress and marital problems associated with infertility'. *Journal of Reproductive and Infant Psychology*, 5: 49–57.

Cook, R., Parsons, J., Mason, B. and Golombok, S. (1989) 'Emotional, marital and sexual functioning in patients embarking on IVF and AID treatment for infertility'. *Journal of Reproductive and Infant Psychology*, 7 (special issue on Psychology and Infertility): 87–94.

Demyttenaere, K., Ramon, W. and Nijs, P. (1989) 'Sexual dysfunction in IVF women: a perinatal risk for the psychosexual development of the coming child'. *International Journal of Prenatal and Perinatal Studies*, 1: 187–194.

Edelmann, R. J. and Connolly, K. J. (1986) 'Psychological aspects of infertility'. *British Journal of Medical Psychology*, 59: 209–219.

Edelmann, R. J. and Golombok, S. (1989) 'Stress and reproductive failure'. *Journal of Reproductive and Infant Psychology*, 7 (special issue on Psychology and Infertility): 79–86.

Eisner, B. G. (1963) 'Some psychological differences between fertile and infertile women'. *Journal of Clinical Psychology*, 24: 369.

Elstein, M. (1975) 'Effect of infertility on psychosexual function'. *British Medical Journal*, 3: 296–299.

Kaufman, S. A. (1969) 'Impact of infertility on the marital and sexual relationship'. *Fertility and Sterility*, 20: 380–383.

Kedem, P. *et al.* (1990) 'Psychological aspects of male infertility'. *Journal of Medical Psychology*, 63: 73–80.

Mahlstedt, P. P. (1985) 'The psychological component of infertility'. *Fertility and Sterility* 43: 335–346.

Mai, F. M., Munday, R. M. and Rump, E. E. (1972) 'Psychiatric interview comparisons between infertile and fertile couples'. *Psychosomatic Medicine* 34: 431–438.

Pfeffer, N. and Woolett, A. (1983) *The Experience of Infertility*. London: Virago.

Platt, J. J., Fisher, I. and Silver, M. J. (1973) 'Infertile couples: personality traits and self-ideal concept discrepancies'. *Fertility and Sterility*, 24: 972.

Raphael-Leff, J. (1986) 'Infertility: diagnosis or life sentence?' *British Journal of Sexual Medicine*, 13: 28–30.

Raphael-Leff, J. (1991) *Psychological Processes of Childbearing*. London: Chapman and Hall.

Raphael-Leff, J. (2007) Femininity and its unconscious 'shadows': gender and generative identity in the age of biotechnology. *British Journal of Psychotherapy*, 23: 497–515.

Raphael-Leff, J. (2008) Emotional aspects of egg donation in reproductive technology. *Psychoanalytic Psychotherapy*, 16: 69–85.

Raphael-Leff, J. (2010) The gift of gametes: unconscious motivation and problematics of Transcendency. *Feminist Review*, 94: 117–137.

Raval, H., Slade, P., Buck, P. and Lieberman, B. E. (1987) 'The impact of infertility on emotions and on the marital and sexual relationship'. *Journal of Reproductive and Infant Psychology*, 5: 221–234.

Rubenstein, B. B. (1951) 'Emotional factors in infertility'. *Fertility and Sterility*, 2: 80.

Taymor, M. L. and Bresnick, E. (1979) 'Emotional stress and infertility'. *Infertility*, 2: 39–47.

Wright, J., Allard, M., Lecours, A. and Sabourin, S. (1989) 'Psychosocial distress and infertility: a review of controlled research'. *International Journal of Fertility*, 34: 126–142.

Infertility in the age of technology

Sharon Zalusky Blum

Rapid advances in medical and biological technologies are changing the ways we are born, live, and die. Biotechnology is pushing us in our notion of what is possible, and tapping into our most primitive omnipotent fantasies. For the most part these new techniques have not yet been integrated into a shared social consciousness. This paper examines, in a case study of a woman who eventually got pregnant with a donor egg and in a shorter case vignette, how the new technology impacts upon the analytic process. Attention is focused on the permeability of the boundaries between analyst and patient and between fantasy and action. The study shows how analyst and patient, together and often for the first time, must face the difficult moral and ethical issues stimulated by such procedures, as well as the anxieties and underlying fantasies they evoke. It is the uniqueness and the intensity of this experience that permeates boundaries, stimulates emotion in patient and analyst alike, and has the potential to deepen the analytic bond. The study underlines the need for the analyst to be flexible, moving back and forth between interpreting and creating a needed holding environment. Finally, the paper points out the tension between the traditional roles of motherhood, fatherhood, and family and those being created in this high-tech world.

The new technologies are forcing us to rethink what constitutes a self, a mother, a father, and a family. They are pushing us in our notions of what is possible, and tapping into our most primitive omnipotent fantasies. We are at the very beginning of what Jeremy Rifkin (1998) calls the Biotech Century. He states:

In little more than a generation, our definition of life and the meaning of existence is likely to be radically altered. Long-held assumptions about nature, including our own human nature, are likely to be rethought. Many age-old practices regarding sexuality, reproduction, birth and parenthood could be partially abandoned. . . . Our very sense of self and society will likely change, as it did when the early Renaissance spirit swept over medieval Europe more than seven hundred years ago.

(p. 1)

Within the last few years our preconceived notions of reproduction have already been challenged. First we were introduced to Dolly, the cloned sheep, and then to Dolly's offspring. In 1997 a woman in her sixties, using a donor egg, gave birth to a baby. That same year, in awe and disbelief, we followed the story of the McCaughey septuplets, which was followed by the unimaginable Chukwu octuplets a year later. Now scientists tell us that they are perfecting techniques that will soon allow women to freeze eggs for fertilization later. All of these events will have far-reaching developmental, psychological, and societal impact.

As analysts, we know that these extraordinary phenomena stimulate fantasies in patient and analyst alike. Ordinarily we try to make sense of new information by integrating what is new into preexisting templates. However, for many of these technological advances we have no templates. The facts, insofar as we are able to grasp them, intermingle with fantasy in our heads, much as facts intermingle with fantasy in the heads of children, who on the basis of limited knowledge develop their own theories about how babies are made. As Anita Hoffer, a biotechnologist in the area of reproductive medicine, has said, "The technology is simple. It's the psychological that's difficult" (personal communication).

As is often the case, technology advances faster than we can grapple with the deeper meanings it holds for us. Hearing of scientific feats, we are frequently left in an unsettled state of awe mixed with anxiety. What existed once only in fantasy suddenly has the potential of being realized. Omnipotent fantasies of destruction turned into reality with the atomic bomb. Omnipotent fantasies of self-creation are on the precipice of becoming real.

Psychoanalysis and technology

Psychoanalysis has not engaged directly with the greater implications of technology for the analytic process. A number of analytic papers have been written about organ transplants. One of these looked at issues of analyzability in a man who had received a renal transplant (Freedman 1983). Another examined the question of who would likely benefit from transplants (Basch 1973), and several more investigated the task of integrating the representation of the transplanted organ into the body ego. These studies concluded that intrapsychic integration of a new organ into the body ego is a difficult one, often fraught with major psychological complications (Castelnuovo-Tedesco 1973, 1978, 1981; Basch 1973).

At the time that these papers were written, the focus of analytic investigation centered almost exclusively on the patient's intrapsychic world. Little attention was paid to the analyst's own internal reactions to these exceptional procedures, beyond the usual countertransference considerations. Today society endorses organ transplants to extend or save the life of a human being, but that was not always the case. The impact of such procedures on the analyst, on the analyses, or on society in general was not examined in these studies, and it has not been examined yet in the psychoanalytic literature.

Furthermore, technology is now moving beyond extending life into the realm of creating life. Once again we are in uncharted territory. Patients and analysts both are being forced to confront increasingly complex human dilemmas. The way our patients resolve their conflicts around fertility will have ramifications that reverberate beyond themselves. Their decisions will affect the lives of others, their own future children, and society in general.

Contemporary psychoanalytic theory

The assumption underlying much contemporary psychoanalytic theory is that a continuous interplay exists between the subjective lives of the analyst and the analysand. Equally fundamental, however, although often not explicitly stated, is the notion that both participants exist within a larger social context, which exerts, at times, a

233

silent and indirect influence. Because analyst and analysand often share a similar social reality, its influence may go unexamined.

New techniques in reproductive medicine have not yet for the most part been integrated into a shared social consciousness. When our patients begin to think about procedures such as surrogate motherhood, fetus reduction, or egg or sperm donation, they compel us both as analysts and as individuals to confront difficult medical, moral, and ethical issues. What makes this unique for the analytic process is that we analysts must confront our own anxieties and the underlying fantasies stimulated by the new procedures at the same time as we are helping our patients analyze theirs. Patient and analyst alike become inextricably linked in an exploration that will ultimately have a profound impact on both participants. Regardless of theoretical position, we become a part of the process, willingly or not.

Psychoanalytic literature and infertility

The new reproductive techniques are transforming our concept of fertility. Psychogenic infertility, originally believed from the psychoanalytic perspective to be a major factor, is now understood to account for only five percent of the cases seen by fertility specialists (Apfel and Keylor 2002). In the past, psychoanalysts have reinforced the notion that infertility stems from early developmental pathology. Langer (1958) and Pines (1990) have pointed to the female patient's pathological envy at her mother's creative ability. They have suggested that infertility may be a result of the woman having destroyed in fantasy a fertile mother with whom she can identify. Infertile women have been reported to have had difficult and conflictual relationships with their mothers (Allison 1997; Deutsch 1945; Langer 1958; Pines 1990) or conscious and unconscious hostility toward a defective or deceased male sibling (Allison 1997), and it has been suggested that because of these factors, they have unconsciously repudiated either femininity or motherhood, or both. However, while the above dynamics may indeed be present in analysands who suffer from infertility, they are also often seen in men and women who are able to conceive naturally. We must be careful not to confuse correlational data with causality. Apfel and Keylor (2002) remind us how tempting, but how often false, it is to rely upon *post hoc ergo propter hoc* as the basis for our conclusions.

234

Recently the psychoanalytic literature on infertility has shifted its focus from uncovering etiology to understanding meaning. Apfel and Keylor (2002), after an extensive review of both the psychoanalytic and the psychological literature on infertility, have suggested that the term "psychogenic infertility" is at best questionable, and almost always unhelpful in treating people with fertility problems. They believe that it is anachronistic, fails to take into account the complexity of the problem, and should be retired. Lester (1995) also asks that psychoanalysts reconsider psychoanalytic thinking about the procreative wish, infertility, and the significance of pregnancy in mothering. She presents a case of a woman whose infertility was related to intrauterine exposure to her mother's treatment with DES. Her patient's egg was fertilized in vitro by her husband's sperm, and later implanted into the uterus of a surrogate. In her paper, Lester examines the psychological issues that developed with regard to the in vitro fertilization and the use of a surrogate to carry the fertilized ovum. Special attention was paid to the notion of boundary crossing between the surrogate and the genetic mother. Lester used the notion of boundary crossing to imply a sense of confusion in self–object demarcation: "the, mostly unconscious, fantasy of a part of the self becoming part of the object, or vice versa" (p. 327).

As analysts, I believe, we are on firmer ground if we examine the consequences of infertility, rather than making claims about its causality that we cannot prove. All the above authors seem to agree that the immense stress of infertility can and often does trigger regressions to earlier stages of psychological development. It can stimulate envy, and with it conflicts that have their roots in childhood. Infertility can evoke powerful and frightening fantasies and feelings that may reverberate to the person's core. As Freud stated, the ego "is first and foremost a body ego" (1923, p. 27). The earliest way we know ourselves is through our body.

In this paper I intend to add to the scarce literature on infertility by presenting first a short case vignette that looks at some unforeseen ramifications of frozen sperm, and then a complete case study of the six-year analysis of a woman who became pregnant by means of a donor egg. I will use these examples to illustrate how infertility in the age of technology impacts upon the analytic process. When technology enters our consulting rooms it forces us to accommodate to its presence and to integrate it into our clinical theory, at times by rethinking such familiar analytic concepts as boundaries and the relationship between fantasy and action (Zalusky 1998). I intend to expand Lester's notion of boundary crossing to emphasize the semi-permeability of the boundaries between analyst and patient.

The vignette

Rebecca, a single woman of thirty-five who had never wanted children, began a four-day-a-week analysis in an attempt to deal with her anger at her father. She complained bitterly of his narcissism and his self-aggrandizement, all the while holding him at the center of her emotional life. The essence of Rebecca's pain appeared to stem from her father's inability to maintain a sustained interest in his youngest child and only daughter. He had not always been like this, Rebecca told me. She explained that when she was little and adored her daddy unconditionally, he treated her like his little princess. When she became a teenager and put on weight, her father began to distance himself. It was an immense blow. Intermittently in her adult life, when her father needed her, she'd be the center of his attention, and then he would once again disappear.

Rebecca was ambivalently attached to me. Early in the analysis she missed sessions frequently. On the couch she would often complain that I was losing interest in her, and she would then defensively lose interest in our work. Her belief that I was indifferent to her always took me by surprise, as it could not have been farther from my subjective experience of her. I found her not only interesting, but fascinating. I identified with her on many superficial levels, all the while aware of how different we were. Clearly we were involved in some transference–countertransference enactment yet to be understood.

Next transpired a set of events that might have been invented by a science fiction novelist. Rebecca's father leaves his wife to marry a woman half his age, and then develops a rare disease. Knowing that he may soon be infertile, he has his sperm frozen, in order to have future children with his young wife. By a series of coincidences, the bill to keep the sperm frozen mistakenly gets sent to Rebecca's house: if the bill is not paid within a period of time, the sperm will be destroyed.

With this news, there is an immediate change in the tenor of the analysis. Rebecca, who up to now has been without enthusiasm for her analysis, comes to her sessions invigorated. She is now a person with a sense of purpose, having found her lost passion (Sones 1997). Delighted by the power finally to affect her father's life in a meaningful way, Rebecca tells me she knows what she must do. Naturally, I am hoping that she wants to analyze her feelings, but I know my patient better than that. She tells me with determination that she must not pay the bill. Her father's sperm is to be destroyed. He must not have any more children, especially with this woman young enough to be her baby sister. He's failed over and over again as a father and does not deserve another chance. As Rebecca recounts this set of events I experience my own anxiety rising. By the excitement in her voice, I know she is under the sway of a powerful fantasy. As analysts we have grown accustomed to dealing with our patient's repressed oedipal or sibling rivalry fantasies, but this is something different. It is my first introduction to the unforeseen ramifications of the new techniques in reproductive medicine.

Up until recently, unless a patient were psychotic or seriously disturbed, if she had a fantasy of having her father's baby, for example, or of destroying her parents' ability to have future children, we accepted the fantasy for what it was: an unconscious wish from the past that was becoming conscious. My patient's unusual scenario shows us how the new reproductive techniques have created a situation where there is now the potential to cross the established boundary between fantasy and action. Rebecca's hostility, fueled by oedipal themes and sibling rivalry, once would have been confined to the domain of fantasy, or some distant derivative thereof. But now it has the potential to be enacted in a concrete way, with serious life consequences.

Needless to say, the analysis takes on a sense of urgency, at least for me. I feel that we are in a rush with the clock, and that I am about to be a tacit co-conspirator in the plot to destroy Rebecca's father's sperm[1]. Obviously, I know that she and I are involved in enacting something powerful: not only between Rebecca, her father, and her stepmother, but also between Rebecca and me, between her father and me, and between my own conscience and myself. However, what it is has yet to be understood.

I know two things about Rebecca that stir my anxiety. One: during moments of overwhelming anxiety Rebecca's modus operandi has always been to act first and reflect later. Two: Rebecca prides herself on being a decent person; this is part of her ego ideal.

237

Any actions that she might take under the sway of such an intense vengeful and jealous fantasy would have the power to affect irrevocably the life of her father and his new wife, but they would also ultimately affect the way she viewed herself.

It was clear that both Rebecca and I were attempting to influence each other. The internal pressure I was feeling was based on many factors. On a conscious level I believed that the analysis itself had stimulated in her a regression that was fueling her sense of urgency. As an agent of the analysis, I did not want to become a silent conspirator. On another level I began to understand that my unconscious identification with Rebecca was connected to my past and present relationship with my own father.

Throughout the analysis I had identified closely with Rebecca. From the beginning it was as if I had already known her. She, on the other hand, was certain that we came from two different worlds. Both were true. Frequently when Rebecca was angry with her father I found myself identifying with him, thinking she was too hard on him. At other times when she spoke about him, he seemed to be warm and engaging. It was as if I knew him too. In many positive ways Rebecca's father reminded me of my own. They were both successful men, capable of meaningful involvement. Yet as time went on, I also understood that Rebecca's father, unlike mine, would invariably disappear, disappointing her. She would be left wondering whether he had ever really been there in the first place.

My father, on the other hand, had always been a faithful and devoted family man. That was the father I knew. But sometime during Rebecca's analysis my own view of my father began to change. My mother died. He, like Rebecca's father, surprised me by marrying a woman thirty years younger than himself. I would never have expected it from him, and it made me wonder who he was. Suddenly, from a deeper emotional level, I understood Rebecca's bewilderment, disappointment, and rage at her father. It helped me make sense of my previously unconscious identification with her. It became increasingly clear that in my wish to stop Rebecca from acting out, a part of me was also unconsciously hoping to stop myself. I believe that new techniques in reproductive medicine bring each of us closer to our own primal fantasies, and because of this we re-experience them with both intensity and anxiety.

Though I never explicitly expressed my feelings, Rebecca must have sensed my internal pressure to keep her from acting out these destructive fantasies. Worried that our analytic work might stimu-late in her some inner battle, Rebecca was conflicted. She attempted to block my effectiveness as an analyst. Knowing that I was in consultation, Rebecca gave me strict instructions: I was not to discuss the content of our sessions, though she saw no harm if I discussed the process.

Soon it became clear that Rebecca was trying to get between me and my consultant in much the same way she was trying to come between her father and his new wife. I interpreted this aspect of the transference to her, which succeeded in diminishing her call for action: the sperm would be allowed to live.

Over the next four years, as Rebecca was able to disengage herself from her unconscious struggles with both her parents, her desire to become a mother increased. By the end of the analysis she had married and had a child.

The case study

I will present the case of Diana for several reasons. First, it is the complete and successful case of a woman who through analysis uncovered a wish to be a mother, and in doing so discovered her own infertility. Our work together helped her develop the strength to endure many of the procedures necessary to maintain a viable pregnancy. Second, it illustrates the accommodations that her fertility treatments demanded of her analysis. Third and most impor-tant, it shows how the treatments impacted upon Diana, the analysis, and me as they became increasingly high-tech.

Diana came into a four-day-a-week psychoanalysis as she approached her fortieth birthday. She was experiencing an acute identity crisis. Recently divorced after an eighteen-year marriage, Diana had no children, no career, no long-term friends, few memo-ries, and few interests other than the men in her life. At that time motherhood was not consciously on her mind. She came to treat-ment in an attempt to find herself.

Diana, like Rebecca, described herself as a person without passion, either in life or in sex. She said, "I do what it is I need to do. I don't immerse myself in life. I can't just let go, in anything." Not too surprisingly, she also had difficulties feeling passionate about our analytic work.

Early on it became clear that Diana was unable to go after what she wanted, because she would not let herself know what she desired, other than to marry the man she was dating. And that she did. As the analysis progressed, Diana began to have glimmers of a career she might wish to pursue but, just as in her treatment, external events always managed to get in her way. By focusing on the many ways she distracted herself from her inner life, we learned that Diana tended to be self-critical, was plagued by self-doubt, and lacked faith in her ability to follow through.

Diana had many strengths; however, she could neither recognize nor nurture them in herself. She had had little experience of being nurtured as a child. She was intelligent, warm, and caring, but was continuously derailed by her anger at both her parents. Though she was an adult woman, she was still very tied to her family of origin, primarily through her disappointment in them. In many ways it was no wonder that she had not thought to have a family of her own.

Diana mentioned that she had just begun to talk to her present husband about his feelings about having children. He told her that he was not against the idea; he just wanted to wait. He liked the special attention Diana gave him, and was afraid that it would all change. She told me that she could understand that. So why not wait, she said. Since my friends, many of my patients, and I were all struggling with our biological clocks, I was surprised at Diana's denial of hers. I confronted her, asking her how on one hand she could be so worried about growing older, and yet feel no urgency about becoming pregnant though she was now over forty. Her denial could not be penetrated. It seemed to serve her acquiescence to her husband's desires. But why?

As the treatment progressed, we learned about Diana's relationship with her father, and with other men. During her childhood the family's attention centered almost exclusively on her father, whose career was skyrocketing. Handsome, brilliant, and charming, her father achieved success, power, and enormous wealth, and was often in the public eye. Diana remembered her father entertaining Nobel laureates, international dignitaries, politicians, movie stars, and athletes at their home from the time she was a little girl. She told me how insignificant she always felt in their presence. The same feeling of insignificance pervaded her life as a grown woman in almost every venue, including the analysis.

Diana's journey through infertility

As we began to work on how and why she denigrated her own needs, it struck Diana that this stance was no longer necessary. She had married a man unlike her father, who was capable of acknowledging her needs and accepting her feelings (even if it did take a little work). They soon began to talk about having children.

For a year they tried unsuccessfully. At the same time Diana was making tremendous gains in the rest of her life. She was in graduate school. She was learning not to give in to her fears. She was working hard, which was something new. As she allowed herself to get closer to me, for the first time in her life she also began to have close friendships with women. These were hard-earned accomplishments, but it was also beginning to dawn on Diana that she might never have a family. Diana complained of feeling confused, inadequate, and depressed. An old belief that good things weren't meant for her began to resurface. We examined how that belief had always gotten in the way of her moving forward.

Diana began to take a more active stance. She called a fertility specialist, and the process began: fertility drugs, laparoscopies (surgeries), and artificial inseminations. Suddenly the infertility process was affecting the analysis, creating technical dilemmas for me as the analyst.

Diana suddenly seemed so fragile. I wondered whether the fertility drugs themselves were having a destabilizing impact on her. If so, how much could be attributed to the hormones? Was the analysis itself becoming too stressful for Diana? What were the other factors? Clearly, Diana had a long history of giving in to herself, of falling apart rather than meeting demands head on. The physiological effects combined with the psychological created a very complex picture. The only thing that was certain was that Diana was in crisis. I concluded that it was wise to view the analysis as a holding environment until she herself was ready or able to work in a more traditional analytic way. There seemed to be no room for interpretation at this time. However, only a few days after this Diana brought in a dream: A valued mirror was broken, shattered. The dream was short, but as she began to associate to it, it became clear that the mirror represented her self: a self that was fragmenting under the stress of the drugs, the treatments, and the uncertainty. She no longer had a way of clearly seeing or knowing herself. Putting her feelings into words helped her.

After the inseminations proved unsuccessful, Diana and her husband tried in vitro fertilization (IVF). Though the procedure itself brought up fantasies both for her and for me, it did not create intense anxiety in either of us. IVF has long been integrated into the social fiber. She was still seeking to create a baby from her own egg, fertilized by her husband's sperm. The analysis was still proceeding like any other. The IVF was successful, and Diana became pregnant. She was delighted, and so was I for her. Suddenly another set of concerns came forth, typical ones for pregnant women and only indirectly related to the unusual procedures. Diana began to question whether she would be able to be a good mother. She worried about her body changing. What if she was pregnant with triplets?[2] What if her baby was a boy? etcetera, etcetera – all sorts of questions typical of pregnant women. We explored all her fantasies.

In the early weeks of her pregnancy Diana dreamt the following: "I gave birth to this little foetus. I kept forgetting to feed it. When I found it, I didn't know what to do with it. I was at a loss. It didn't look human. It looked undeveloped." It was clear that having a baby brought forth Diana's difficulty nurturing the vulnerable part of herself. In the dream, she identified both with the neglectful person, and also with the person who had been neglected, the person who wasn't fully developed. This dream brought forth genetic material. For the first time she told me of her mother's child-raising philosophy, which was to let the children cry. I also learned about her father, who was the parent more capable of nurturing but who was rarely home, and only inconsistently involved with the children when he was there. The dream brought forth memories of the many cruel and sadistic nannies in whose care she and her siblings had been left.

Shortly after becoming pregnant, Diana miscarried. She was naturally heartbroken, and retreated for a while. Again the analysis became a place where Diana and her pain were held symbolically until she was able to deal more actively with the meaning of her loss. Within a short time Diana became able to deal with her pain. She regrouped, began to pursue her career again, and soon felt ready to start fertility treatments anew – this time with a different set of doctors.

Diana tried alternative medicine, acupuncture, Chinese medicine, and herbs. Pines (1990) spoke of the role of the doctor in these fertility procedures, and how often the women patients idealize these doctors who create life. In the case of Diana, a more complex ambivalent picture emerged. Alternately she would trust her doctors and then not, in keeping with her fundamental belief, which she enacted over and over again in the transference and elsewhere, that caregivers really didn't care.

Eventually Diana got pregnant on her own. This time the pregnancy was a bit more frightening. She knew there was the possibility of miscarriage, and unfortunately that possibility was realized. She was depressed. Again she worried that she was not ever allowed to get what she wanted.[3] She felt as if the world was against her. She wondered whether her internal anger at her parents was killing off her chance to be a mother. To make matters worse, while she was mourning this new loss and dealing with the fact that she was aging, her father married a woman eighteen years younger than she. He and his new young wife effortlessly gave birth to a baby.

It was a terribly painful time. We learned about a fantasy that Diana had been harboring – she had hoped that her father would be a devoted grandfather to her child. In her fantasy, her child would be able to get from him what she had not been able to – his full attention. Diana would become special to her father by giving him his only grandchild. Now the fantasy was ruined. Diana felt angry, because a "normal" family life was now even further out of reach. She never had a "normal" father, and she would never have a "normal" grandfather for her child.

Through her disappointments, Diana began to come to terms with her childhood and how it affected her adult life. She stated, "My grief is with the choices I made with my life. I married some crazy person and stayed with him for nearly twenty years. I lived in avoidance. I postponed my development, my growth, my education, and my crucial childbearing years. I don't know whether I will be able to forgive myself. I wish I could get those years back. Age is so critical for me."

Through her grief, Diana was growing. She was using her crisis to come face to face with her life. Her attitude about the analysis had shifted. She was more engaged. She began to ask the difficult question, "Did my ambivalence about having a child affect my ability to stay pregnant?" This question raises a paradox. Our analytic patients naturally search for the psychological meaning of their infertility. That search offers hope, but there is something omnipotent about it too. It is as if we are saying, "If only you could discover that one unresolved conflict, maybe then you will be able to hold onto your pregnancy."

Obviously, no one has the answers here: we do know the mind can affect the body, but still, many ambivalent women get pregnant. Yet by analyzing her ambivalence, Diana did discover something very important. She learned that she was afraid that she could not sacrifice for a child or for anyone, never having had a role model upon whom to draw. Her mother, whom she loved very much, had been ineffectual and inconsistent in her ability to take care of Diana when she was young. Throughout Diana's childhood her mother had been desperate to hold onto the father, whose attention was regularly with other women. There was often subtle and not so subtle competition between mother and daughter for father's limited attention. Diana would frequently win out, which left her feeling both satisfied and guilty.

I began to notice that every time Diana was about to make a decision to move forward with a new procedure, she would miss a day or two of the analysis. I brought that to her attention. She began to wonder out loud whether I had children, though she told me she was sure I did not. It soon became clear that Diana feared that I might not want her to have a child. As we discussed what seemed to be an unconscious fantasy, she began to remember things her mother had said that implied to her that it might be better for Diana not to have a child. At first it seemed unimaginable to Diana, but she began to wonder if it was possible that she unconsciously, out of a sense of guilt, had complied by not wanting children.

Diana had another dream that gave us insight into her ambivalence. She was in a hospital bed with IVs. Her husband was there crying. Through her associations I learned that Diana had survived a life-threatening illness many years before. She then spoke of her husband's grief when his father died young, leaving him and his brothers to be raised by his mother alone. Diana was frightened that there was something wrong with her; she might die and leave her future baby and husband all alone. She had never dealt fully with the psychological aftermath of her illness, or how profoundly it had affected her emotionally. Talking about her fears gave her strength to continue.

Diana and her husband tried in vitro fertilization a second time. Same result – pregnancy then miscarriage. Though she was depressed and mourned the loss once again, she was amazed that she was not

244

devastated. The sadness was limited to her miscarriage. The pain was not as global as it used to be. Diana felt stronger. She was able to pursue her career and contemplate her future with or without child. We both agreed that she was ready to think about leaving her analysis.

The analysis, she told me, had helped her find herself. She knew she wanted to be a parent. She believed she had a lot of love to give, and wanted to care for another. The wish to have a child was no longer tied to the earlier fantasy of compensating for an unhappy childhood. We set a termination date, recognizing that she was going to continue to try to have a baby.

Decision to become pregnant with a donor egg

Diana had accepted that she would most likely not be able to have a biological child of her own. She had also accepted the possibility that they could adopt, but her husband had not yet reached that point. Together they decided to try one last procedure. Convinced that Diana's eggs were too old, they chose to use a donor egg. Psychologically Diana was ready to cross that boundary. I was not.

My feelings began to intensify. Up until now I would characterize my reactions in the analysis as usual countertransference reactions. When Diana wondered if I had any children, or whether or not I wanted her to have children, I knew that she was touching on something personal for me, but I was also convinced that the feelings evoked were part of our unique transference–countertransference configuration. For me there was something profoundly different about egg donation that fell outside of usual transference–countertransference enactments. This new procedure had potential meanings for me that conceivably were not related to my patient's issues. However, my way of managing my own feelings would ultimately affect my ability to help her analyze hers. I wondered if I would feel differently if she were contemplating sperm donation, or adoption. I knew that in embracing this new technique, I would have to examine my personal values privately, at the same time that Diana was struggling with her own. Clearly the stakes were different for each of us.

Initially Diana was uncomfortable about the process of selecting an egg donor. She wondered whether she was crossing some improper boundary – was she playing God? Both she and I had gotten psycho-logically used to the IVF procedure. However, this was different. Diana would be taking an egg from another woman whom she did not know, and would be fertilizing it with her husband's sperm. She would be carrying a fetus with whom she shared no common genetic material. It would be her husband's genetic child, but not hers. I wondered to myself what Diana wondered out loud: Was this an unthinkable omnipotent enactment – a disregard for age or limits – or simply the taking advantage of scientific advancement in order to accomplish an important life goal? We both seemed to accept the anxiety that goes with this extreme procedure that so fundamentally alters our traditional notions of motherhood, fatherhood, and family. Though I did not articulate my conscious anxiety with my patient, I believe that on some level she must have known.

Diana's way of choosing a donor turned out to be very touching to me. It was not the color of the woman's eyes or even her religious affiliation that Diana was interested in; instead she was looking for a donor whose life story evoked in her the wish to mother. While she told me what evoked mothering feelings in her, I began to feel warm and tender towards her, with motherly feelings of my own. I felt proud of Diana's maturity.

High technology at work

So much for the human story. What followed was high technology at its finest. It was also technology that was mainly under the control of male physicians. Diana's body had to be prepared for pregnancy. She had immunological treatments: leucocyte transfers. Her menstrual cycle needed to be in synch with the donor's, and they did that by injections of Lupron. The donor was also taking Lupron, and Perganol to stimulate ovulation. When ovulation occurred, the donor's eggs were fertilized by Diana's husband's sperm, and three days later five embryos were implanted in Diana's uterus. Diana injected herself daily in the hip with progesterone and estrodial, and twice daily in the abdomen with heparin. Periodically she had IVs of gammaglobulin to allow her to maintain the pregnancy. At the same time, she was taking a low dose of prednisone. It was ironic that Diana, who only a couple of years before had felt incapable of sacrificing, was enduring an intense physical sacrific in order to give life. We were both surprised at how well she tolerated the immense quantity of hormones and other drugs in her system. This time her determination had a stabilizing effect.

The pain she was experiencing, however, stirred up feelings in me. I felt both awe at what was possible, and terror at what was unknown. As Diana told me about all the shots, the bruises everywhere on her body, I felt as if my own boundaries were once again dissolving. Unconsciously I think I wished to mother her during this time, to protect her from the pain. I wondered how a lay person could make decisions about such complicated technical procedures, especially when she was paying such a huge price for her hope. I worried about whether there was a masochistic component in submitting to all these procedures, even though by now I realized that her major motivation was to have a baby. I found myself identifying not only with Diana in her pain, but also with the young woman whose eggs had been harvested. I wondered who that woman was. She was so young. Could she possibly understand the implications of what she was doing? Would there be an unforeseen psychological or physiological price to pay down the road? Would I be somehow complicit? Michels (1976) reminds us that therapists may be attacked for pursuing their narrow therapeutic aims without regard to the impact of their work on the values of society.

Naturally, the analyst in me wanted to be careful that neither my anxieties, nor the fact that I did not have any children of my own, would impact too greatly on Diana's feelings about what she was doing. I discussed my reactions with a female colleague who was also analyzing a woman pregnant by donor eggs. My colleague had a child, but was trying unsuccessfully to become pregnant again. She seemed more stirred up than I was. Then there was Eva Lester (1995), who wondered whether her own uneventful pregnancy had caused her to take a more empathic, generous stance in an unconscious attempt to avoid her patient's envy. It seemed that no matter what one's life situation was, it was impossible not to be affected in an emotional way. Becoming pregnant by a donor egg is a dramatic new phenomenon. Our attitudes may not affect the decisions our patients make, but they do affect the manner in which the patient's fantasies can be explored.

Initially, Diana sensed my protectiveness and asked if I was angry with her husband for putting her through all this. In fact I was, but I did not share it directly. In this case, I knew that her pains stirred up my own conflicts, but I also knew that this piece of our work was the kind of not-so-complicated transference–countertransference enactment that occurs in any analysis.

When we explored her fantasies, it became obvious that Diana wanted me to share her anger at her pain, but that she also wanted me to help her keep her resolve. She wanted me to know that this was an accommodation that she was making to have a fulfilling life: she could not have a genetic child of her own, but she could grow a baby inside her. She knew she could bond with her baby and protect it by eating well and by taking good care of herself.

Diana was delighted to find that all five embryos were growing strong in her body, and she accepted at least in fantasy the possibility that she would soon be the mother of five. But that happiness signaled the onset of the next drama. Her uterus was very weak, and embedded with fibroid tumors. The doctors told her that to have a viable pregnancy she would have to reduce down to two fetuses. It was traumatic and extremely painful for her to learn about the procedure, which would leave her with two fetuses. They were all five her children. Yet if she kept them all, it was certain that none of them would be born healthy, if at all. Diana had struggled so hard to create life. Now she was forced to go against her own values. She wondered if she and the doctors were playing with nature. So did I. She wondered whether she should take her doctor's advice or whether unconsciously this was one more time that she was unwilling to sacrifice. I tried very hard not to get in the way of her decision, which was immensely personal. We continued to analyze. Again she worried about whether she would be playing God, deciding who would live and who would die. I wished that she did not have to make such a painful choice. I also knew that my strong reaction to fetus reduction was tied to omnipotent fantasies on my part. I wanted to believe that she could have everything – that she was strong and powerful and would not have to suffer. In analyzing my own reaction, I got in touch with my wish to protect my own mother, who had lost a baby strangled by the umbilical cord, and to protect myself from the pain of mourning along with my patient.

Finally Diana decided she had no choice but to reduce to two fetuses. When she found out that she was going to have twin boys, for a moment she believed that she had killed her only daughter. She had dreams of killing other family members. I, too, was in her dreams, responsible along with her for all sorts of murder plots.

She was also sad for herself. The analysis had helped her to believe that she could have a mother–daughter relationship more fulfilling than the one she had with her own mother. And she wanted that experience with her own daughter, especially now that she was leaving the analysis. Each new development brought forward intense conflict and deep emotion in both Diana and me. I believe that the physical pain she suffered, the creation of life, and the uncertainty of the outcome all added to the intensity of our shared experience.

In her fifth month, Diana began to have premature contractions. Ironically, this complication helped her confirm that she had done the right thing in reducing down to two. Her suffering alleviated her guilt. Throughout this time Diana and I maintained our decision to keep the scheduled termination date. That Diana would end the analysis while giving birth added to the poignancy of our work.[4]

This story fortunately has a happy ending. After many years of aborted attempts, Diana gave birth to two healthy baby boys. When she brought them to meet me, she said with pride, "Look at my beautiful babies. Finally, I was able to work for what I wanted." Diana went from being a woman without passion to one who had found her capacity to love and to sacrifice.

When I asked her permission to present this material Diana told me about her experience as a mother. She said, "Often while I was struggling to have a child, we wondered whether the emptiness I was feeling was really about something else. However, shortly after my sons were born, I noticed the feeling was gone. Of course, I still have my issues, but the longing to be a mother was real, and it is now fulfilled."

Discussion

For many patients like Diana, infertility begins with the wish to have a child. Though it was clear in Diana's case that many psychological issues contributed to her having postponed the decision to become a mother, there were also many physiological factors that prevented her maintaining a pregnancy without the help of the new techniques in reproductive medicine.

Diana's analysis created support precisely because it gave her the opportunity to revisit in an emotionally charged way old familiar developmental crises. She had to deal with these conflicts in an intensified form, however. This was in part because of the extraordinary measures that her desire to give birth required, the perpetual sense of uncertainty in her precarious pregnancies, the conflict about transgressing the usual customs, and, most poignantly, the use of another person's body to fulfill her dream of being a mother.

Though many of us, at least intellectually, have become more comfortable with the thought of organ transplants, egg donation differs from organ transplant in two fundamental ways. The eggs are harvested from a live person in order create a new life, while in organ transplant the needed organ is often taken from a person who has died, in order to save or extend the life of the patient. The moral and ethical implications of life-creating procedures may create a psychological crisis in one or both of the analytic participants. Analyst and patient may find themselves struggling consciously and unconsciously with the meaning of such actions, which force us all to evaluate the fundamental value of creation. It is the uniqueness and the intensity of this experience that permeates boundaries and stimulates emotion in the analytic partners.

This shared experience also has the potential of intensifying the analytic bond. It underlines the need that the analyst be flexible, moving back and forth between interpreting and creating a needed holding environment during the various crises, the surges of hormones, and the extreme stress of multiple losses. Lester explained, "For long periods D used the analysis primarily as therapy. . . . I was aware of D's need for a nurturing relationship, the background safety she needed at this particularly stressful period of her life, and I went along with her. However, on reflection, I wonder whether my strong empathic stance was not, partly, a countertransference enactment, representing my awe at D's most unusual experiences" (1995, pp. 333–334). There seems to me to be no need to apologize for enacting a nurturing stance, or whatever stance the analyst takes. The issue cannot be whether this is analytic therapy or psychoanalysis. The enactment is the analytic process (Friedman and Natterson 1999; Renik 1994). It is to be understood and analyzed. It is impossible not to be moved by, or not to react to, these extraordinary situations. I do not think that nurturing is the only response an analyst might have; it happened to be Lester's. That was her way to mother her patient. Mothering may be a common role response (Sandler 1976) to a patient who is searching for a way to learn to be a mother. However, as we all know, mothering takes many forms.

There is a tension between the traditional ideas of motherhood, fatherhood, and family, and those being created in this high-tech world. Clearly, Diana was willing to take extraordinary measures to be a mother. In her wish to have a "normal" family she needed to create a special family, in which a third phantom person would always be present and tied to her, her husband, and her child. Ironically, at the end of the analysis, while Diana was working to take the analyst in symbolically, she was concretely taking into her womb another woman's creation. The juxtaposition and the tension between the two created an opportunity for Diana to learn about herself and to find and develop the mother inside her.

Because patient and analyst are different people with different life experiences, some aspects of the treatment may create more anxiety in one than in the other. I found myself more actively preoccupied than Diana with the unknown donor. Some might say it was projective identification, but I never felt that. Diana's preoccupations were more with her actual bodily experience. She was struggling with issues of omnipotence, of creating and destroying life. I am confident that when fantasies of the donor come up for Diana, and they will, she will be capable of understanding and dealing with them. It needs to be emphasized that Diana developed what appeared to me to be an excellent relationship with her husband, who is psychologically very sensitive.

Conclusion

In conclusion, technology is advancing faster than our mind can grapple with the meanings it holds for us. It is blasting open the frontiers of the possible. What was once imaginable only in the realm of fantasy now has the potential to be enacted in concrete ways. New technologies, until they are integrated into a shared social consciousness, may stimulate anxieties and omnipotent fantasies simultaneously in analyst and patient alike, creating unique challenges in the analytic process.

As psychoanalysts, we have always known that many of our limits are self-imposed. What Diana and I both discovered is that the process of opening ourselves up to new possibilities changed our perception of ourselves.

Notes

1 Destroying sperm is one of many scenarios that can be acted out. Apfel (1999), in a presentation at the Fall Meeting of the American Psychoanalytic Association, presented a case of a male patient who gave a sperm donation before each analytic session. First he kept this from his analyst. Later he rationalized it as a way to pay for a fee increase.
2 This fantasy was directly related to the fact that they had implanted three embryos.
3 Not an uncommon fear in women who are having fertility problems.
4 Termination issues are beyond the scope of this paper.

References

Allison, G. H. (1997) 'Motherhood, motherliness, and psychogenic infertility'. *Psychoanal. Q.*, 66: 1–17.

Apfel, R. J. (1999) 'Male infertility: shooting blanks'. Paper presented at the Fall Meeting of the American Psychoanalytic Association.

Apfel, R. J. and Keylor, R. G. (2002) 'Psychoanalysis and infertility: myths and realities'. *Int. J. Psycho-Anal.*, 83: 85–104.

Basch, S. H. (1973) 'The intrapsychic integration of a new organ – a clinical study of kidney transplantation'. *Psychoanal. Q.*, 42: 364–384.

Castelnuovo-Tedesco, P. (1973) 'Organ transplant, body image, psychosis'. *Psychoanal. Q.*, 42: 349–363.

Castelnuovo-Tedesco, P. (1978) 'Ego vicissitudes in response to replacement or loss of body parts – certain analogies to events during psychoanalytic treatment'. *Psychoanal. Q.*, 47: 381–397.

Castelnuovo-Tedesco, P. (1981) 'Psychological consequences of physical defects: a psychoanalytic perspective. *Int. R. Psycho-Anal.*, 8: 145–154.

Deutsch, H. (1945) *The Psychology of Women, Vol. II.* New York: Grune and Stratton.

Freedman, A. (1983) 'Psychoanalysis of a patient who received a kidney transplant'. *J. Amer. Psychoanal. Assn.*, 31: 917–956.

Freud, S. (1923) 'The ego and the id'. *S. E.* 19: 12–66.

Friedman, R. and Natterson, J. (1999) 'Enactments: an intersubjective perspective'. *Psychoanal. Q.*, 68: 220–247.

Langer, M. (1958) 'Sterility and envy'. *Int. J. Psycho-Anal.*, 39: 139–143.

Lester, E. P. (1995) 'A surrogate carries a fertilised ovum: multiple crossings in ego boundaries'. *Int. J. Psycho-Anal.*, 76: 325–334.

Michels, R. (1976) 'Professional ethics and social values.' *Int. R. Psycho-Anal.*, 3: 377–384.

Pines, D. (1990) 'Emotional aspects of infertility and its remedies'. *Int. J. Psycho-Anal.*, 71: 561–568.

Renik, O. (1994) 'Countertransference enactment and the psychoanalytic process', in M. Horowitz, O. Kernberg and E. Weinshel (eds) *Psychic Structure and Psychic Change.* Madison, CT: International Universities Press, pp. 135–158.

Rifkin, J. (1998) *The Biotech Century: Harnessing the Gene and Remaking the World.* New York: Tarcher/Putnam.

Sandler, J. (1976) 'Countertransference and role-responsiveness'. *Int. R. Psycho-Anal.*, 3: 43–47.

Sones, G. (1997) 'Paradise regained: the restoration of lost passion'. Paper presented at the Fall Meeting of the American Psychoanalytic Association.

Zalusky, S. (1998) 'Telephone analysis: out of sight, but not out of mind'. *J. Amer. Psychoanal. Assn.*, 46: 1221–1242.

PART THREE

When not all goes well

Paola Mariotti

The chapters in this section address the more problematic areas of motherhood: miscarriage and abortion, postnatal depression, and abusive parenting.

Miscarriages are frequent. Rates vary according to the woman's age, number of previous miscarriages, and whether or not unreported miscarriages are included. In what may be a conservative estimate, 15 per cent of all pregnancies end in miscarriage in the first trimester (British Medical Journal 2006). The loss of a pregnancy has a powerful impact on a woman and on her family. If the woman has other young children, they are often not informed, yet they will pick up something of the parents' sadness and of their unconscious reactions. The child has then to make sense as best she or he can of his parents' responses to this unknown but distressing event. Sometimes, its effects can be surmised in analysis when the child has become an adult.

One may see miscarriage as motivated by conscious or unconscious death wishes. But even when it is the result of medical complications, it may nevertheless trigger fears and phantasies that may be felt by the woman, consciously or unconsciously, to have had the power to cause the loss of the pregnancy.

Voluntary terminations of pregnancy are also very frequent: in 2009, the Department of Health have recorded 189,100 abortions in England and Wales. In the USA Remeikis (2001), in her review on the psychoanalytic literature on the subject, reports there are one and a half million abortions in the United States each year.

Dinora Pines wrote on women's lifecycle, including miscarriage and abortion. In her book *A Woman's Unconscious Use of her Body* (1993) she collected her clinical papers on the female reproductive cycle. She describes how her patients in childhood internalised the relationship with their mother, and how their experiences as adults were shaped by an 'interaction between Fantasy and Reality' (p. 59). Her paper on miscarriage and abortion, reprinted in this volume (Chapter 9), highlights the importance of ambivalence as a 'universal parental dilemma' (p. 270). In her clinical examples she illustrates the different meanings that pregnancy can have for different women. She also suggests that, in some cases, a woman's life may be happier and more serene if she allows herself to remain childless.

A consistent theme running through all the chapters in this section is the particularly intense and problematic maternal ambivalence. We are in the territory of what Parker in Chapter 3 describes as 'unmanageable ambivalence'. A frank acknowledgement of her reluctance to have children enables a woman to use contraception effectively. However, if her need to be pregnant overshadows her consideration for the foetus and for her own body, a woman may temporarily suppress her awareness of what conception entails, and may start a pregnancy that she cannot, all things considered, bring to term. But even when a woman feels sure that it was the right decision, a voluntary termination of pregnancy has a profound life-long effect. In her chapter, Pines mentions that one of her patients who had three abortions apparently without hesitations or regret, still 'remembered the dates at which these foetuses would have been born and how old they would have been' (p. 275).

Problems in early maternity

Postnatal depression (PND) is relatively frequent – occurring after 13 per cent of births (Musters *et al.* 2008). Like miscarriage and termination of pregnancy, its discussion is underrepresented in the psychoanalytic literature, perhaps, in part, because of patients' reluctance and shame about exposing their difficulties at a time of life when women are supposed to be blissfully happy. The impact of maternal PND extends to the infants who are at greater risk from depression in later life (Murray 2009).

A woman who feels, consciously or unconsciously, utterly devoid of resources may end up having a child as an extreme defence against being aware of her desperate psychological situation. If her experience of being mothered has not provided her with a nurturing maternal image, and she was perhaps traumatised by her parents' violent behaviour to each other and to her, a young mother may go to great lengths to split off her neediness, whether or not she becomes clinically depressed. She may be unable to ask for therapy because she cannot begin to consider the extent of her deprivations, needs, and rage. Alone, unsupported by an absent or violent partner, she will find it difficult or even impossible to reflect on the impact of her experiences and how they may shape her relationship to her baby. The sense of deprivation experienced by the young mother is poignantly described by Fraiberg and Adelson (Chapter 13) and by Lemma (Chapter 11), whose patient was not materially deprived but regarded her baby as withholding what the young mother needed.

The maternal experience of deprivation can be manifested through eating problems. Harold Blum (1978) describes a patient who had suffered from PND after the birth of each of her children, some years before starting the analysis. Blum writes:

> She constantly wanted to see herself as nurturant, yet identified herself with the hungry children who needed food and love. She was also envious of the affectionate care the children received, and again had to vomit back the food she in fantasy took from them since she had literally eaten off their plate. Finally, she ate not only their food, but symbolically the children themselves in an ambivalent mixture of primitive love and destruction. . . . If she did not vomit after incorporation, she might be devoured from within.
>
> (p. 344)

Blum quotes Freud's account of a pre-psychoanalytic, postnatally depressed patient, who had problems with eating. Freud's patient seems to express a central aspect of perinatal vicissitudes, namely the anxiety experienced by a mother who is afraid of not containing enough goodness for herself and her child. Freud's patient was unable to feed her newborn baby. She had attempted to breastfeed, but she had lost appetite, vomited her food, and became agitated when the baby was brought to her bedside. Freud's first attempt was not successful, but eventually he told her in hypnosis that she would become angry at her family and accuse them of not feeding her enough. This treatment was very successful. The patient's anger at her family supposedly not feeding her is seen as a displacement of her anger at a depriving mother, and it also expresses the woman's sense of deprivation and fear of being dispossessed by the baby of the little she has got for herself. This resonates with what women who cannot breastfeed their children sometimes say: 'I didn't have enough milk.' The newborn can be seen as 'the monster baby' who will eat up what little goodness the mother has got to nourish herself – the reversal of the Medea fantasy.

The myth of Medea as a phantasy active in the unconscious of women who have children, may be a factor in the child's maltreatment and abuse. A woman who has experienced her own mother as powerfully destructive may reproduce that image in her relationship with her own children, either by experiencing them as embodying the destructive and powerful figure, or by identifying herself with a wronged, revengeful and controlling maternal image.

In many cases of PND one finds that the young mother's relationship with 'the mother within' is extremely conflicted. Problems between the patient and her mother can sometimes be linked to known traumatic events in the previous generations. According to Halberstadt-Freud (Chapter 10), one 'has to take at least three (possibly four) generations along the maternal lineage into account, when interpreting pathology like postnatal depression' (p. 287). This is confirmed by the research mentioned earlier on the transgenerational transmission of depression (Murray 2009). The issue of unconscious communication between generations is an important aspect of the internalisation of maternality, and it has been discussed or at least alluded to by most psychoanalytic authors writing on this subject. There is a tension in a psychoanalytic treatment between the patient's psychic transformation of the maternal message, and her recognition of that message. Faimberg has tackled this tension in discussing what she called the 'telescoping of generations'; she does not refer specifically to a maternal line, but her concept describes well how a patient may feel identified with objects (or better, processes) which do not belong to her generation. She writes of a male patient:

> I am not simply stating that the patient has unconsciously identified himself with his father. I think that an identification involving a telescoping of generations is carried out with the object and part

of the attributes of the secret history and not only with the object in question.

(p. 13)

Faimberg (1981/1985) proposes that such identifications are 'alienated because they partially depend on conflicts of a generation that is not the patient's' (p. 11). What is the 'secret history' of women who suffer from PND, who reject their babies, who see their newborn as a monster, or see themselves as monsters from whom the baby has to be protected? Faimberg makes a very relevant point, when she writes that these 'identifications constitute a "link between generations" which are alienating and *opposed to any psychic representations*; therefore they are not articulated and are not heard by the analyst. The passage between identification to representation [. . .] became possible due to the interpretative construction' (p. 15, my italics).

If the woman is able to ask for help, psychoanalysis or psychoanalytic therapy can help a woman to find her 'secret history', which the patient may know already, but whose implications are the real secret. Hendrika Halberstadt-Freud discusses in this present book the psychoanalytic treatment of a woman who suffered from postnatal depression (Chapter 10). The patient was aware that in her maternal family there was a belief that if a child is born, either the child or the mother has to die. But she was initially unaware of how much she had internalised such belief in her relationship with her mother, and how this prevented her feeling angry against her mother, and she turned the anger on herself and her partner, and, for a time, on her child. The author has suggested in previous work (1989, 1998, 2010) that the concept of the Electra complex is useful in distinguishing the girl's development from the boy's: 'The girl must steer between the Scylla of a symbiotic illusion vis-à-vis her maternal object and the Charybdis of hatred of it' (1998). Her patient's capacity to work in analysis on her feelings and on her relationship to her mother led her to an appropriate sense of separateness from her mother and from her mother's history, and helped her to resolve her depression, which did not recur in the patient's second pregnancy.

In their papers Baradon (Chapter 12) and Fraiberg and Adelson (Chapter 13) give detailed illustrations of the interactions between mothers and their babies. Both papers convey the intensity of those subtle exchanges, the speed at which the communication takes place, and its all-or-nothing quality. The atmosphere in the dyad can change suddenly depending on a misunderstood gesture, on a perceived failure to respond, and warmth can return because of a loving smile.

Mother–infant psychotherapy is the setting of Baradon's paper. She illustrates the countertransferential challenges and pitfalls of working in a situation where a mistimed interpretation causing distress to her adult patient may lead to damage to her precarious relationship with her baby. In such cases, the support offered by colleagues is essential. Baradon's patient was able to use what was offered to her. She was in touch with her need for help, which is in itself a good prognostic sign. According to Lawrence Blum (2007), the inability to acknowledge one's dependency and neediness is a characteristic of postnatal depression. He suggests that conflicts relating to dependency, anger and the relationship with one's mother form a triad of issues typically present in this condition. Patients who resort to counterdependency to protect themselves from those conflicts may be particularly reluctant to request therapy and Blum surmises that this could be a reason why this pathology is scarcely discussed in the literature.

In 1998 Estela Welldon published a seminal book, *Mother, Madonna, Whore*, which put forward the notion that mothers can use their children to satisfy an unconscious sadistically perverse desire of power and control. In Chapter 14 in this volume, Welldon describes a young woman whose history of abuse and neglect started in childhood, and continued throughout her life. Her inner strength and courage in the face of such an abusive background is striking, and yet she replicated the parental brutality in her violent relationship with her partner, exposing her children to experiences similar to her own. Welldon underlines the difficulties for the mental health professionals working in those cases. To remove a young child from the care of his or her mother is very painful – and more so, I would add, when there are uncertainties as to the possibility of finding a good long-term alternative for the child. The mother may deny that she causes him or her any pain or distress: if not highly trained and professionally supported, those working in these cases may give in to a collusion with the mother that her care is essentially adequate, sometimes with tragic consequences for the child.

There are a number of babies and children at risk, not of brutal violence or sexual abuse, but of protracted physical and psychological maltreatment at the hand of their mother and father. This may range from verbal humiliation to various forms of physical punishment or sexual exhibitionism and lack of boundaries, unconsciously aimed at making the child feel inadequate and powerless, dependent on his or her mother and excited by her. While the important work of clinicians such as Welldon (1998) and Motz (2005) draws our attention to the extremes of cruelty of which parents are capable, it is important to keep in mind that subtler abusive behaviour, more difficult to recognise, may still have a devastating effect on the child, and indeed on the mother herself. Baradon's and Halberstadt-Freud's patients might have become such mothers, had they not had enough inner strength and external support, to seek psychoanalytic treatment.

Adolescent mothering

In Chapter 13, Selma Fraiberg and Edna Adelson address the problem of adolescent mothers. Fraiberg and her co-workers were pioneers of mother–infant psychotherapy and were addressing a population of sometimes extremely deprived women and families. They developed an approach based on psychoanalytic understanding, which took into consideration the potential and the limitations of their patients. They would visit their patients at home – as the mothers could not be relied upon to come to a clinic on a regular basis. With tact and persistence they were able to communicate with young women whose own mothers had received no support and had inflicted terrible traumas on their children. Fraiberg and Adelson show that if a baby at risk of neglect and abuse is to be left with his natural mother, the mother has to be supported – she needs a therapeutic input which will allow her to internalise a capacity to look after her child, even when the professionals are no longer involved. Their work, which took place in 1960s and 1970s, is still very relevant today, when solutions are being sought for mothers who seem unable to look after their children but do not want to be separated from them.

Adolescent mothers can have great difficulties. A young woman, little more than a child, fantasises that a baby will give her the love and intimacy she has never known. When a vigorously demanding baby is born, the disappointment and dismay may be enormous – far from providing what the girl needs, the nursling is expecting to receive from her what he needs. The young mother who already feels so depleted in herself, has now to provide nourishment for a hungry baby. Without support, or perhaps with a partner as young and confused as she is, she falls back on the mothering she has received, from a mother who, in many cases, was herself deprived and traumatised. The potential for the intergenerational transmission of the fear, insecurity, and emptiness that she carries in herself is considerable. Fraiberg and Adelson suggest that the young woman needs support and implicit reassurance that she has some goodness in herself, which will develop and help her to provide her baby with what he needs. Gradually the young mother can be helped to understand the complex psychic processes which render her relationship with her child so difficult.

These problems are not exclusive to materially deprived young women. Lemma describes in Chapter 11 the psychoanalytic treatment of an adolescent mother whose emotional deprivation (in the context of a materially privileged background), was contributing to a profound envy. Lemma shows how the psychic development of the teenager is crucial in shaping her response to her maternity. Much depends on whether 'the young mother . . . has some sense of herself and of having a mind of her own, even if projective processes still hold sway, as is the case for most adolescents as they struggle to discover who they are', even in this case, 'significant problems for both mother and baby can ensue. This is, nevertheless, quite different to experiencing the baby as getting in the way of the very psychic survival of the self'. She illustrates the latter situation with a patient who experienced her baby as a tormenting and withholding maternal figure keeping to herself whatever goodness the young mother desperately needed.

I have focused so far on the mother's contribution to the difficulties that may arise between mother and baby and how these often relate to the 'mother within the mother'. There is another aspect of problematic mothering that has been investigated, although without conclusive results: this is the contribution the infant brings to a difficult parent–infant bonding. A number of studies support the view that both members have an effect on the contact and on the communication within the dyad. Beebe and Lachmann (1988b) propose:

> Mutual influence refers to a communication process in which influence flows in both directions: both mother and infant systematically affect, and are affected by, the other. Mutual influence

does not imply equal influence. Each partner does not necessarily influence the other in equal measure or in like manner. However, each contributes to the regulation of the other's behavior.

(p. 4)

Introducing a paper discussing 'a complex and varied range of interactions of maternal impingement and infant avoidance' during videotaped face-to-face play, Beebe (2000) suggests:

Mother and infant coconstruct their interactions in two different ways. In a more general way, the mother brings transferences to the baby based on her own history, and the baby often brings self-regulation difficulties, such as difficulties in regulation of arousal, or unusual sensitivities to sound or texture, often referred to as difficult temperaments. Each, then, may contribute to an aversive interaction in this way. Second, each contributes in the sense that, moment to moment, both partners adjust their behaviors to the other. They adjust timing (rhythm, pausing, turntaking), spatial pattern (approach-avoid), facial and vocal affect, and arousal (behavioral activation/inhibition as well as physiological arousal), which constitute the primitives of the system.

(p. 423)

Beebe supports her work with research (Stern 1971; Beebe and Stern 1977; Trevarthen 1979; Beebe and Lachmann 1988a; Beebe *et al.* 1997; Field 1981) corroborating her findings. The mother–child interaction is examined mostly with the use of frame-by-frame videos, or with cameras synchronised into one split-screen view. This type of evidence is impossible to replicate in a home or in a consulting room, but the observations are a useful contribution to the understanding of difficulties in the personal relationship between a mother and her baby, difficulties that may rapidly evolve into major impasses. For instance, Baradon was treating a mother–infant couple where the baby had needed to stay at the special care unit at the hospital for some weeks after the birth. Subsequently, he was a tense, difficult to soothe baby. There is a possibility that some early maturational difficulties, added to the experience of the hospital in the immediate extra-uterine period, may have complicated the relationship between the infant and his already frightened and ambivalent mother.

263

Raphael-Leff (2003) suggests that infants with poor motor control 'find it more difficult to establish and maintain eye contact with their carers, and there may be fewer opportunities for parents to enjoy the normal interpersonal contacts and sense of relationship with the infant that can make child care so rewarding' (p. 266). If the infant has some difficulty in responding adequately to the mother, she may become unable to develop a confident and relaxed communication with her child. This increases her anxiety and possibly in some cases may set in motion a need to take over and intrusively control her baby's state of mind. In such a scenario, whatever problem the infant experiences in regulating his affects or adapting to external stimulation will escalate. At the same time the mother's incapacity to deal satisfactorily with her baby will feed into her deepest anxieties, and her responses may become more and more unhelpful.

However, psychoanalytic treatment offers an opportunity to rethink early difficulties in terms other than attack or persecution, thus mitigating the anxiety. Eventually, problems, conflicts, doubts and mistakes can be seen as inevitable elements of a loving relationship, which truly enrich it and contribute to its ongoing creativity.

References

Beebe, B. (2000) 'Coconstructing mother–infant distress'. *Psychoanal. Inq.*, 20: 421–440.

Beebe, B. and Lachmann, F. (1988a) 'The contribution of mother–infant mutual influence to the origins of self- and object representations'. *Psychoanal. Psychol.*, 5: 304–337.

Beebe, B. and Lachmann, F. M. (1988b) 'Chapter 1, Mother–infant mutual influence and precursors of psychic structure'. *Progress in Self Psychology*, 3: 3–25.

Beebe, B. and Stern, D. (1977) 'Engagement-disengagement and early object experiences', in N. Freedman and S. Grand (eds) *Communicative Structures and Psychic Structures*. New York: Plenum Press, pp. 35–55.

Beebe, B., Lachmann, F. M. and Jaffe, J. (1997) 'Mother–infant interaction structures and presymbolic self- and object representations'. *Psychoanal. Dial.*, 7: 133–182.

Blum, H. P. (1978) 'Reconstruction in a case of postpartum depression'. *Psychoanal. St. Child*, 33: 335–362.

Blum, L. D. (2007) 'Psychodynamics of postpartum depression'. *Psychoanal. Psychol.*, 24: 45–62.

British Medical Journal (2006) 332: 1223–1224 (27 May).

Department of Health. www.dh.gov.uk/en/Publicationsandstatistics/ Publications/PublicationsStatistics/DH_116039.

Faimberg, H. (1981/1985) 'The telescoping of generations: a genealogy of alienating identifications', in H. Faimberg *The Telescoping of Generations: Listening to the Narcissistic Links Between Generations*. London and New York: Routledge, 2005.

Field, T. (1981) 'Infant gaze aversion and heart rate during face-to-face interactions'. *Infant Behav. and Devel.*, 4: 307–315.

Halberstadt-Freud, H. C. (1989) 'Electra in bondage'. *Free Associations*, 1R: 58–89.

Halberstadt-Freud, H. C. (1998) 'Electra versus Oedipus: femininity reconsidered'. *Int. J. Psycho-Anal.*, 79: 41–56.

Halberstadt-Freud, H. C. (2010) *'Electra vs Oedipus: the drama of the mother–daughter relationship*. London and New York: Routledge.

Motz, A. (2005) *The Psychology of Female Violence*. London and New York: Routledge.

Murray, L. (2009) 'The development of children of postnatally depressed mothers: evidence from the Cambridge longitudinal study'. *Psychoanalytic Psychotherapy*, 23, 3: 185–199.

Musters, C., McDonald, E. and Jones, I. (2008) 'Management of postnatal depression'. *BMJ*, 337: 736.

Pines, D. (1993) *A Woman's Unconscious Use of her Body*. London: Virago Press.

Raphael-Leff, J. (2003) *Parent–Infant Psychodynamics*. London: Whurr.

Remeikis, G. V. (2001) 'A review of the psychoanalytic literature on abortion'. *J. Amer. Acad. Psychoanal.*, 29: 231–244.

Stern, D. (1971) 'A microanalysis of the mother–infant interaction'. *J. Amer. Acad. Child Psychiat.*, 10: 501–507.

Trevarthen, C. (1979) 'Communication and cooperation in early infancy: a description of primary intersubjectivity', in M. Bullowa (ed.) *Before Speech: The Beginnings of Human Communication*. Cambridge: Cambridge University Press.

Welldon, E. (1998) *Mother, Madonna, Whore: The Idealization and Denigration of Motherhood*. New York: Free Association Books

Pregnancy, miscarriage and abortion
A psychoanalytic perspective

Dinora Pines

Despite a growing interest in the psychoanalytical understanding of pregnancy there is as yet no literature regarding spontaneous abortion or miscarriage, although some attention has been paid to planned abortion. Analysis of women patients who have miscarried often reveals their sense of loss, prolonged grief and unresolved mourning many years after this event.[1] Analysis of these women frequently reveals a longstanding depression, a loss of self-esteem and hatred of their female bodies which do not bear live children as their mothers did. Their self-representation is damaged.

In this presentation I shall discuss miscarriage, i.e. spontaneous abortion, and planned abortion, their psychological antecedents and consequences. In both situations young women become pregnant, enter a normal further developmental stage of the life cycle but are unable to continue their pregnancy to become mothers and bring a live child into the world. Thus spontaneous abortion is frequently a threat to normal first pregnancy. The medical reasons are often difficult to diagnose and treat and do not necessarily recur in subsequent pregnancies. Most occur during the first trimester of pregnancy when the pregnant woman consciously experiences the developing foetus as an integral part of herself. Her dreams may reveal other aspects of unconscious fantasy and anxiety, such as whom the foetus represents, and who has fathered the oedipal girl's baby in a forbidden guilt-laden intercourse.

In analysing women's dreams I have been impressed by the influence of physiological bodily changes on psychic life. Dreams may reflect a woman's bodily hormonal change during a menstrual cycle. Mind and bodily changes influence each other in a woman's monthly and developmental cycle and the intimate link between them allows a woman unconsciously to use her body in an attempt to avoid psychic conflict. In considering women patients in my practice who have had miscarriages, I have come to speculate on some possible unconscious reasons for some spontaneous abortions, factors that might be considered in which analysis could be helpful. A first pregnancy, a move from childlessness towards parenthood, is a time of emotional and psychological upheaval. Yet it is a normal developmental phase despite the emotional crisis it provokes, and a valuable time of emotional preparation for motherhood. During pregnancy, particularly first pregnancy, conflicts belonging to past developmental stages are revived and the young woman has to achieve a new adaptive position within her internal and external worlds. We may therefore view first pregnancy as a crisis point in the long search for a feminine identity and as a point of no return.

Pregnancy is an important phase in a woman's life-long task of separation and individuation from her own mother (Pines, 1982). Childhood wishes to identify with a primary object, namely the powerful pre-oedipal mother are foreshadowed in play and fantasy long before there is any possibility of parenthood. A little girl's gender identity is established in early childhood and a young girl's sexual identity largely resolved by the end of adolescence. At this point the adolescent's physiologically mature body forces an important stage of separation and individuation upon her. The intense revival of sexual feelings drives the young girl towards her first intercourse, which confirms her right to take responsibility for her sexuality and ownership of her adult body as distinct from that of her mother. Her mother's ownership of her daughter's body has now ceased.

However, pregnancy, the next stage in a woman's life-cycle, offers an adult woman a further stage of emotional identification with the pre-oedipal mother. The unseen foetus, concretely within her body, enables her to re-experience a feeling of primary unity with her mother, and at the same time to identify narcissistically with that same intra-uterine foetus, as if it were herself in her mother's body. Such a symbiotic state in the future mother may well activate intense ambivalent feelings both to the foetus and to her own mother. For a young woman whose experience with her own mother has been 'good enough', the temporary regression to a primary identification with a generous life-giving mother as well as with herself, as if she were her own infant, is a pleasurable developmental phase. For others, where ambivalent feelings towards the mother have been unresolved, or where negative feelings towards the self, the sexual partner or important figures from the past predominate, the inevitable regressions of pregnancy facilitate the projection of such feelings on to the foetus. Thus the foetus may already possess a negative prenatal identity in the mother's mind long before the birth.

In a first pregnancy the young woman has two alternative means of resolving psychic conflict. The foetus may be physically retained, given life and cocooned or may be physically rejected as in miscarriage and abortion. A mother may thus either facilitate life and motherhood or destroy them both. Unfulfilled pregnancy and the failure to produce a live child, either because of unconscious reasons for spontaneous abortion, or conscious reasons for planned abortion, will affect each patient individually. Interaction between fantasy and reality in the pregnant woman's mind will affect the emotional outcome. For some women, from the moment that pregnancy is confirmed, the foetus is invested, in conscious fantasy and daydreams, or in unconscious fantasy and night dreams, with the physical appearance of a baby and even with a sexual identity of its own. These women look forward to becoming good enough mothers as they had experienced their own mothers. Miscarriage for them is a painful loss as if a fullterm baby had died and has to be mourned.

Other women regard the foetus as a part of their body which can be dispensed with as easily as an inflamed appendix. Their conscious wish to become pregnant does not have motherhood as its ultimate goal. Pregnancy for them may be an unconscious means of confirming a female sexual identity or adult physical maturity. The foetus is not represented as a baby in fantasy, dreams or reality but rather as an aspect of the bad self, or as a bad internal object that must be expelled. Analysis of such patients reveals an early relationship with the mother which is suffused with frustration, rage, disappointment and guilt. Loss of the foetus either by miscarriage or abortion is experienced as a relief, rather than a loss, as if the continuing internal bad mother had not given permission for the child to become a mother herself. It is possible that the pregnant woman's unconscious anxieties connected with the fantasy of the foetus, representing a bad and dangerous aspect of the self or of her partner,

269

may be a contributing factor to the stimulation of uterine expulsive movements, which end in miscarriage. The analyst is experienced as this malign internal mother in the transference. Analysis of these aspects of psychic life may enable a woman to maintain her pregnancy and become a mother herself.

Freud's predominant attitude towards motherhood was that the mother's first child was the extension of her own narcissism, and thus her ambivalence towards her living child would be positively resolved. Her child would feel wanted and loved. Her love for this living child would elicit guilt about her negative feelings and prompt her toward reparation. However Freud also acknowledged maternal ambivalence and the difficulty for a mother in having a surviving yet unwanted child. 'How many mothers, who love their children tenderly, perhaps over-tenderly . . . conceived them unwillingly and wished at that time that the living thing within them might not develop further!' (Freud, 1916, p. 202).

Clinical experience leads us to recognize that ambivalence, whether latent or manifest, is present in all parent–child relationships and much depends on the relationship between the biological parents and with their future child. The biblical myth of Moses, the Greek myth of Oedipus and the Celtic legend of Merlin, all babies abandoned by the parents after their birth, illustrate the universality of this theme. Clinical experience bears out the universality of the temptation to be physically or emotionally cruel to a helpless demanding baby or to a difficult growing child. This universal parental dilemma may be highlighted in our counter-transference feelings when a patient's behaviour may run counter to our personal standards of morality. In these circumstances, particularly with perverse or sadistic patients, the neutral stance of the analyst may be particularly difficult to maintain. The analyst may have to monitor his own position in order to withstand the temptation to take on the role of the parent who judges and maintains standards of morality for the recalcitrant child.

I shall illustrate my view regarding the universal dilemma of maternal ambivalence and its varying solutions by presenting material from three patients. The first patient was a victim of the Holocaust, and her traumatic experiences led her to miscarry several times. The second patient had an extremely difficult relationship to her own mother and, despite a conscious wish to have a child, analysis revealed her unconscious ambivalence towards the foetus but also helped her not to miscarry. The third patient had intentionally aborted three pregnancies and felt relieved when her menopause approached and she could no longer be pregnant.

Clinical illustration 1

Mrs A was a survivor of the Holocaust. One week after her first period had started she was sent to Auschwitz. Her parents perished there. After her release from the camp, Mrs A emigrated to England and married. Her periods returned irregularly. Mrs A longed to become pregnant and bring a new life into her new world which was no longer dominated by sadism and psychic and physical death. For her, as for many survivors of the Holocaust, babies represented the restoration of normality from a psychotic world and the re-establishment of family life. Unconsciously, Mrs A's future children were to replace her dead parents. Mrs A, who was desperate to have a child, joyfully became pregnant several times, but each time miscarried. Each miscarriage was physically unbearable. She took a long time to recover physically and frequently remained huddled under her bed covers in a darkened room.

Mrs A was living in her present reality, as well as in the past reality of Auschwitz where she had spent so much time hiding under her ragged bed covers. Her past had not been integrated and mourning for the murdered past objects had not been achieved. Two vital aspects of emotional identification in pregnancy were impossible to achieve; identification with her own mother and identification with the foetus as if it were herself. Although Mrs A had seen her dead mother's body she could not let her die in her mind and thus mourn her, for that involved her own guilt at surviving her. Identification with the foetus as a representation of herself was too traumatic to bear. Her wish to become pregnant also contained Mrs A's unconscious wish for rebirth and for a new self. Yet there was no viable alternative in Mrs A's mind for a murdered mother and a traumatized child. Thus, while pregnancy satisfied her wish to become a mother, miscarriage enabled her to avoid her own mother's fate and spared her unborn child from the fate that had been her own. Analysis enabled Mrs A to begin mourning her past and to fight for her right to emotional survival. Her acceptance of her analyst as being a strong life-giving mother in the transference

271

encouraged her to bring new life into a safer world. Mrs A eventually had a family of three children, although she never forgot the age that the miscarried babies might have been had they survived.

Clinical illustration 2

Mrs B had married late in life, and consciously longed to fulfil her childhood wish to have a child in the short time that was available to her before the menopause. She was the only daughter of a professional woman who devalued her own femininity and that of her little girl. Mrs B's mother doted on her two elder sons and constantly praised their physical and academic achievements, while Mrs B's own achievements appeared to her to remain unnoticed. Mrs B's father was ill and retiring, so that the mother's idealization of her sons influenced the solution of her daughter's oedipal conflict. Mrs B knew she wanted to be a boy throughout her childhood in order to gain her mother's love, as her brothers had done. Her quick intelligence enabled her to achieve high academic rewards, which eventually gained her mother's admiration, but Mrs B's femininity and pleasure in her female body remained unsatisfying to her, since her mother had not valued it or her own. However for several childhood years a secret relationship with her younger brother, consisting of mutual masturbation, had enabled her to enjoy giving and receiving sexual pleasure with a male which raised her self-esteem. Nevertheless the underlying difficult early relationship with her mother, in which she felt neither of them to be satisfying or satisfactory to each other, led to an unstable basic sense of well-being and narcissistic difficulties, which Mrs B attempted to solve by a series of heterosexual relationships. These were physically satisfying but emotionally painful. Her first lover was old and gentle, as her father had been, and those who succeeded him were younger and treated her badly and scornfully, as her brothers had done.

During the course of her analysis, Mrs B's initial transference feelings towards her female analyst, originally seen as the projected terrifying powerful mother of her internal world who could neither give nor receive love, were modified. A warmer and easier relationship both with her mother and her analyst ensued. Mrs B, now more capable of giving and receiving love, found a caring partner. She married him and became pregnant. Consciously she was delighted and yet it became clear as the pregnancy progressed that she remained unconsciously ambivalent towards her future child. She did not look after her own health nor that of the foetus which the scan had revealed was a boy. The earlier conflicts and difficulties that appeared to have been previously worked through in her analysis re-emerged during her pregnancy, as if the new identity of future mother to a child threatened her old identity. Her mother showed no enthusiasm for her daughter's pregnancy. Several times Mrs B bled but would not rest in order to save her pregnancy.

A dream, after a short break when I had cancelled three sessions, revealed her conflict. In the dream she was walking with her mother and felt she was in danger of miscarrying. Her mother said nothing could be done, but Mrs B knew that she must hurry to the hospital where the doctor would save her baby. Her mother said there was no point and did not help her or give her permission to bear a living baby.

Mrs B knew that the hospital doctor represented her analyst whose positive response to her pregnancy reinforced her husband's confirmation of herself as a woman. Analysis had shown her that something could be done in the past and she was impatiently waiting for her analyst to return. Mrs B did not miscarry in reality.

As her pregnancy proceeded and the reality of the kicking baby inside her impelled her towards her new identity, a series of dreams revealed the compelling re-emergence of her analytic themes.

In the first dream she was applying for a new passport; in another she was at a swimming pool where the big boys were rough with a little boy and pushed him under the water. Another woman jumped in and saved him. Mrs B was relieved to see him alive.

In her associations Mrs B remembered being pushed under water by her brothers when a woman nearby had shouted and made them stop. She was dismayed that even in her dream it had to be her analyst who saved the boy foetus and not herself, as if she was identified with the mother who did not save her. She was relieved that her ambivalence could be calmly accepted by her analyst, her unconscious guilt made conscious, and her pregnancy kept safe. In other dreams Mrs B's childhood envy of her brothers came to the fore. She dreamt that she was a hermaphrodite and allowed herself to remember that, as a small girl, she had thought of herself as a brain-damaged small boy.

This new material enabled a further working through of her ambivalence towards boys and towards her unborn baby boy. Finally it became clear that for her the unseen foetus was an oedipal child, and thus evidence of her fantasized incestuous relationship with her brother. Resolution of so much unconscious guilt during the course of her pregnancy has helped Mrs B to become a good mother to her baby boy, with whom she is closely identified.

Clinical illustration 3

My final case illustration[2] concerns a patient whose conscious negative feelings towards her mother and her own motherhood and mothering were enacted in planned abortions. Yet each time pregnancy confirmed that her feminine identity was important to her.

Mrs C was the eldest of a large family. Her father, a passive and retiring man, had died when she was 14 years old and she was shocked when her mother, a vigorous, attractive woman, married her lover immediately after her husband's death. Mrs C's separate emotional needs and ambitions were never acknowledged by her mother, although she had always cared for her daughter's body. Her mother had told her that it had been a long and hard labour when she was born, since her body was too big for her mother to give birth to her easily. She told her repeatedly what a bad child she was and finally angrily told her that even in the womb she had defied her, when she tried to abort her during pregnancy. She was thus left with an image of herself as a bad child and with a potentially murderous internal mother. These stories had reinforced Mrs C's feelings that her body and her character had never satisfied her mother.

Adolescence enabled her to find an alternative way of dealing with her painful situation. By using her physically mature body and her adolescent sexuality, she could bypass the painful affects of mourning her father's loss as well as the narcissistic rage evoked by her mother's involvement with her lover. Her relationships with boys provided her with the regressive, primitive satisfaction of the mother–baby relationship, in which she sought the comfort always denied her by her mother. Mrs C's mother was angry at her daughter's attempts to separate from her and contrived to make her feel guilty. Eventually the situation became so intolerable that Mrs C made an abortive suicide attempt. The policeman who saved her and took her back to her mother severely reprimanded her and told her that she was her mother's property until she was 18 and had no right to kill herself. This confirmed her conviction that her body belonged to her mother and was not her own.

Mrs C's relationships with men were always stormy as they had been with her mother and she unconsciously provoked them to violent anger, although she herself showed none and felt she was their victim. She could thus break off and abort each relationship. In this way she was, in fantasy, not only the baby who has to cling on to keep alive but also the mother who had to abort the foetus in her turn. The fantasy of clinging to life, in spite of her powerful mother's attempt to abort her, had become the basis of a narcissistic, omnipotent fantasy which she enacted by making decisions of life and death for the foetus.

During the course of her analysis, Mrs C disclosed that she had had three planned abortions during her adult life, and that she had each time become pregnant with a man whom she had seduced into the relationship. Shortly after aborting the foetus she aborted the relationship with the man, and repeated this pattern when she aborted two previous attempts at therapy. It emerged during her analysis that the emotional closeness with others, in which she sought and regained the earliest pleasure of the symbiotic, mutually satisfying relationship with her mother, also revived primitive fears of merging, since her mother could not recognize her as emotionally separate with needs of her own. Emotional separation from her mother was not achieved. Once her sexual identity and separateness from her mother's body had been concretely established by a pregnancy, she could abort the foetus as if it were a meaningless part of her body. Yet Mrs C remembered the dates at which these foetuses would have been born and how old they would have been.

We gradually understood Mrs C's unconscious use of her body to seek revenge on her dominating mother. Her sexual exploits were enjoyed with black men, whom her mother disapproved of, and were designed to use her body as if it were an extension of her mother's and thus subtly to humiliate her mother. Mrs C's mother frequently criticized and reproached her, saying, 'How can your body which was once in mine, feel anything for a man I cannot tolerate?' In this way we could see that Mrs C's mother reciprocally shared her daughter's fantasy of not being bodily separate from her. We understood that by aborting the foetus, her relationships and her previous attempts at analysis, Mrs C had felt herself to be even more grandiose and omnipotent than the bad and murderous aggressor-mother with whom she was identified.

Mrs C's use of her body was also subtly reflected in the transference. Interpretations that showed understanding aroused her fears of fusion with me and she used her body, in order to remain separate from me, by having intercourse with her lover before every analytic hour. In this way the excitement of good emotional closeness with me and the fear of merging was defused by a physical experience of orgiastic fusion with a man. Each time I had hope of creating a healthy analytic baby Mrs C was impelled to abort it. This was reflected in Mrs C's work, where she could create lively ideas which she felt obliged to pass on to others to fulfil. In this way her inability to produce a live baby was complemented by her inability to allow her brain babies to grow. She projected her destructive wishes on to the outside world in which every reader was the critical, sadistic, aborting mother with whom she felt fused in her internal world.

Mrs C was relieved when her menopause approached and she could no longer become pregnant.

Conclusion

Women who miscarry or consciously abort a foetus may have unconscious difficulties in identifying with a generous representation of their own mother and her capacity to mother. For the nutrient mother may be seen as a Januslike figure; on the one hand that of a powerful generous nourishing life-giving object or as her fantasized opposite face, the witch-like murderous mother, who will bring retaliation to bear upon her daughter. Difficulty in integrating these two polarized aspects of the mother and her mothering into that of a 'good enough mother', may lead to a negatively ambivalent relationship between mother and daughter, to difficulties in emotional separation and identification with the murderous mother and infanticide, rather than towards identification with the positive nurturing mother that gives life to her child. Fathers of these women may often have been dead, absent or emotionally detached, unable to influence the difficult relationship between these mothers and daughters.

These women may have unconsciously somatized their childhood emotional difficulties by using their bodies to avoid unconscious affects and fantasies which have felt overwhelming to the young child's ego. Thus, for some women, the small girl's wish to bear a child in identification with the fertile mother may be difficult to fulfil, since the child's early sexual wishes and fantasies are invested in a forbidden object; mother's sexual partner. In the child's psychic reality the oedipal wishes have become so traumatic and guilt-laden that they remain unconscious, unacknowledged and unresolved in adult life. They are therefore unavailable in adult heterosexual relationships, although the pervasive ill-defined sense of guilt may lead to an unconscious need for punishment, such as masochistic submission to a sadistic partner, or to self-punishment by miscarrying a longed for pregnancy. The pregnant woman's normal ambivalence towards the foetus and whom it represents may be reinforced by the small girl's unacknowledged and unresolved guilt-laden wishes towards a forbidden sexual object.

Spontaneous abortion which denies life to the foetus may provide a psychosomatic solution to this psychic conflict. If the patient is in analysis during pregnancy, analysis of her conflicts may in some cases lead to a successful pregnancy and to the birth of a baby.

Summary

This paper examines some of the unconscious reasons that may lead to unfulfilled pregnancy, either by means of spontaneous abortion, or by conscious planned abortion. During pregnancy the universal dilemma of maternal ambivalence towards the foetus and whom it represents may be strongly influenced by unresolved conflicts and anxieties belonging to earlier stages of a woman's psychic development. Spontaneous or planned abortion, which allows the woman who has become pregnant to deny life to the foetus, may provide a psychosomatic solution to this psychic conflict.

Notes

1   It should be noted that one first pregnancy in four ends in miscarriage.
2   I have described this patient more fully elsewhere (Pines, 1982).

References

Freud, S. (1916) 'The archaic features and infantilism of dreams'. *S.E.* 15: 199.

Pines, D. (1972) 'Pregnancy and motherhood: interaction between fantasy and reality'. *Brit. J. Med. Psychol.*, 45: 333–343.

Pines, D. (1982) 'The relevance of early psychic development to pregnancy and abortion'. *Int. J. Psychoanal.*, 63: 311–319.

Postpartum depression and symbiotic illusion

Hendrika Halberstadt-Freud

A review of the literature reveals how little has been published by psychoanalysts about the important subject of postpartum depression. This article offers a way of looking at the phenomenon from a transgenerational perspective. The concept of symbiosis is taken from the mother's point of view as well as from the baby's. It is defined as a delusional two-person fantasy of mutual dependence rather than as a normal phase of development. The analysis of a case of postnatal depression is presented to illustrate the clinical and theoretical implications of this viewpoint and how it was applied in treatment.

Current estimates are that about one mother in ten experiences some form of depression after giving birth (Gavin *et al.* 2005) but definitive data are still lacking. The emotional consequences for mother and child are serious and deserve treatment.

Traditionally in psychoanalysis, motherhood and the early mother–child relations have been studied from the infant's side, the fantasies and feelings of the mother often remaining a 'dark continent'. It is proposed here that separation and individuation are not only an important phase in the life of the child but are also highly significant from the mother's point of view. I suggest that the woman's unresolved *symbiotic illusion* (Halberstadt-Freud 1989) with her own mother can play a central role in postpartum depression.

The case of Ernestine

Of the patients with postnatal depression whom I have treated, Ernestine is the most colourful. She has a South American background and her confusion between fantasy and reality, hovering between symbol and act, recalls the Gothic atmosphere of García Márquez's novels.

When Ernestine is referred for analysis, she is 37 years old and has a 4-month-old boy. She looks extremely worried and run down. She is casually dressed, looking more like a boy than a mature woman, suggesting that her sexual identity is conflicted. To her great dismay, her life changed totally, after giving birth to a baby who had not been planned.

Ernestine is inconsolable and cries for hours every day, without understanding what is the matter with her. She tells me she feels intermittently desperate and angry. When she realized she was pregnant, she considered an abortion without informing her partner. Later she changed her mind and decided she wanted to keep the baby. Now she fears she is a bad mother who does not take proper care of her child. She once had the murderous fantasy of throwing her baby out of the window. She worries a lot about what he eats, whether it is safe or poisonous for the infant – she even fears poisoning him with her milk.

Though Ernestine and her partner, who are not married, have lived together for over twenty years she never consciously wished for a child and according to her she seldom gave motherhood a thought.

Ernestine's mother has always warned her not to become pregnant. She used to tell her daughter what an unpleasant and depressing experience it had been for her to be pregnant. The implication was that a child might harm the mother and as we shall see later this was reinforced in many ways during the patient's childhood. Not surprisingly, being this 'monster' that became a demanding toddler fostered a profound sense of guilt in the patient.

Ernestine's conflicts around femininity have always found expression through physical symptoms. Anxiety, stress and emotional pain have been played out via the body. During menstruation, she habitually suffered heavy headaches, which, she insists, have nothing to do with emotional problems, but are purely physical.

It came as a great surprise to her that being pregnant gave her an exhilarating feeling. She felt, for the first time, like she was a superwoman and supermum, proudly showing off her pregnancy and swinging her heavy belly around for everybody to see. The shock after delivery was all the greater. The physical separation from her baby made her feel empty, flat, lonely, and totally deprived. Since his birth she has been mourning her lost unity with the baby.

Unacknowledged feelings of ambivalence toward her mother, Mrs A, surfaced for the first time during Ernestine's pregnancy. She is disappointed by her mother's negative reaction, but instead of setting limits to her mother's demands she directs her anger at her partner. She admits being chronically and unreasonably angry with him. Although he is a caring father and a helpful partner, she feels lonely, as if neglected by him. She fights him wherever she can and claims his attention like never before. They fight about every detail of their daily life and particularly around issues concerning food. She reacts very emotionally when she thinks he might use food that is beyond the sell-by date and she is preoccupied with the question of when to throw food away in order not to be poisoned by it. Concerning the care of their son, she is sure she knows best what to do and leaves no room for the father who she fears might harm the child or even poison him. Although she can be argumentative and vindictive, more often she tends to be resentful, complaining and crying. She feels oppressed and victimized. As this couple was quite happy when they lived together before the patient's pregnancy, the change has been striking and clearly connected to the baby's arrival.

During the analysis the negative feelings towards her mother, who is not at all pleased with her grandchild, are quickly becoming more manifest for the first time. Although Ernestine is desperate enough to agree to my proposal of analysis, she insists that she doesn't have any problems, while tears pour out of her eyes, demonstrating a clear tendency toward splitting and denial. From the start of her analysis, her ambivalence about being a mother is clear. On the one hand, she defensively idealizes motherhood and makes excessive demands on herself. On the other hand, being 'opposed to the role of women in our society', she rejects her femininity. In her present predicament, she 'feels hooked and a slave'.

Ernestine's anger about the fact that having a child changed the course of her life, dissipates quickly in the first few months of analysis. Her son seems to have become a narcissistic self-object, who is part of her body, and whose well-being gratifies her sense of self. The maternal lineage, especially well-suited to the perpetuation of either positive or negative attitudes being transmitted from mothers to daughters, is broken by a male child. A male child does not automatically inherit the angry feelings toward the mother, enabling Ernestine to have positive feelings about her son. During the analysis she quickly changes into an overprotective, solicitous mother who loves and enjoys her baby.

Ernestine's personal and family history

Notwithstanding her initially telling me about her happy memories, growing up on an isle in the West Indies, my patient turns out to have had a very troubled childhood and family background. Her parents formed an unhappy couple always at odds with each other, with Ernestine mostly taking her mother's side. There was great emphasis in the family on food and eating habits. Conflicts tended to centre on what and how to eat. Daily angry scenes took place at the dinner table.

My patient was the first child of Mrs A, an unhappy, depressed mother who felt overburdened by having to look after her baby and her own dying stepmother simultaneously. Like her daughter, it seems she experienced an undiagnosed but severe postnatal depression. Mrs A did not breast-feed her children, as she claimed her breasts were inflamed.

To her mother's great dismay and irritation, Ernestine was a hungry, skinny, and very unhappy baby who, according to her mother, cried all the time. Moreover, she was allergic to milk and had to be fed a soya-based diet, which, she was told, left her starved. The problems around food and eating point to an early disturbance in the mother–child relationship in which oral conflicts are prominent.

Mrs A was extremely troubled by the birth of a second unwanted child, another girl, when the patient was about 3 years old. She had herself sterilized, without informing her husband. By this act she went squarely against his wishes as he hoped to have other children, and especially a son.

My patient, as a toddler, followed her mother everywhere and reacted to being rejected by physically clinging to her mother and throwing temper tantrums. According to her mother she would follow her to the bathroom and when Mrs A shut the door on her, the child would bang desperately at the door. As she was recounting this in the sessions I got the impression of a desperate child needing contact with her mother and, on the other hand, of a mother who experienced her daughter as a persecuting monster. As she grew up Ernestine tried to please her depressed and chronically irritated mother, by being extremely compliant and well-behaved. She recounted how at the dinner table she would behave politely and with good manners, while her father attacked her mother and her sister – he would let out his frustration by attacking his wife about trivialities, like 'the food lacks salt', and be angry at his younger provocative daughter's poor eating manners.

Beneath her politeness Ernestine felt great anger against her sister whom she considered responsible for all the arguments, conflicts and unbearable scenes at the dinner table. She saw it as her role to try to keep the family together by being 'good'.

Ernestine's relation to her father was characterized by the fact that for him, she replaced the son he never got. By being athletic and tomboyish she succeeded in becoming the successful 'good' daughter. Her younger sister became the 'bad' one, always protesting and provoking arguments. Her father constantly persecuted and criticized her during meals. The tendency to use the defence mechanism of splitting, e.g. differentiating between the 'good' and the 'bad' daughter, was well established in this family early on.

Ernestine's mother and sister were the martyrs of the family, exposing the father as a tyrant, by their passive resistance and/or provocative behaviour. However Ernestine was his favourite. She denies ever having been jealous of her younger sister, whom she hates to this day. She claims she has no reason to be jealous because she always felt superior in every respect.

She reserved her empathy for her mother, with whom she has always secretly colluded against the father. The father was chronically angry at his wife, a 'tyrant' frustrated by his wife in his desire to have more children, and especially sons. There was a vertical split in the family. The patient would agree with mother about father being domineering and ill-tempered. Mother and Ernestine were meant to be 'good' and well-behaved, not 'difficult and provoking' like father and sister.

Ernestine harbours several incompatible ideas, kept separate in different areas of her mind. She idealizes motherhood, but pregnancy means to tread in your mother's footsteps, something she has always tried to avoid. Unwittingly she is strongly identified with her mother as victim. She discovers she hates her mother for being such a martyr, a role she hates and always strove to avoid. Although her maternal identifications are so contradictory and conflictual she is not at all separated from her mother-imago. Until the analysis mother and daughter are fused and together considered the father the bogey man. At the same time Ernestine has a strong masculine side to her personality. She has always identified with her father through sports and shared physical activities.

Three generations of mothers and daughters

Ernestine's traumatic background stretches over at least three generations. During her analysis she begins to question her mother, whom I shall call Mrs A, about the past. Mrs A was born in the South American wilderness and was cared for by strangers after her own mother's death when she was a toddler. Her father was mostly away, crossing the jungle to trade horses. She seems to have been a traumatized child, lacking maternal care and neglected by her father. Did Mrs A as a child unconsciously think that her father blamed her for the death of his wife? Did her mother suffer from loneliness and postnatal depression, was there an unspoken implication in the family that she might perhaps have committed suicide? We will never know the facts.

The traumatic event of Ernestine's grandmother's death gave rise to fantasies and family myths being carried over from one generation to the next. The family myth concerning this tragic event linked the cause of death to overeating. Anxieties about food and poisoning and perverse rituals around eating have remained prominent ever since. Over the generations, the matrilineal link seems to be marked by primitive fantasies around killing and being killed through oral greed and cannibalism. 'A mother either kills her child or is eaten during pregnancy by the little monster in her belly', seems to be one of the fantasies passed on from mother to daughter.

Unconscious fantasies seem to have magically linked birth and death The birth of a child will cause the death of its mother, or more generally, as Ernestine would put it to me, 'when one comes, the other has to go'.

Mrs A told her daughter that she was frightened to have children. When she became pregnant for the second time, she panicked and went through what seems to have been a hypochondriacal crisis. She was complaining of terrible stomach pains, suspecting a tumour or an intestinal obstruction, which led her to seek and to obtain, albeit pregnant, a pointless operation on her stomach, as if she had to symbolically abort the foetus. This acting out resembles the later infanticidal fantasies of her daughter. Ernestine, at the beginning of analysis, was very worried, because she fantasised she might kill her baby by throwing him out of the window. Later she projected her aggressive fantasies onto her partner, who she feared would kill the child by poisoning him with out–of–date food, and at some point she was extremely concerned that the poisonous laburnum tree in the garden would kill the child. 'To kill the child before it kills me' seems to be a fantasy which sometimes afflicts women suffering from postnatal depression.

Ernestine felt that her mother, Mrs A, had loathed motherhood, and hated her as a child, feeling overburdened and hopelessly depressed. In this tale of death and guilt there was perhaps a sugges-tion that Mrs A was attempting to repair her unconscious guilt vis-à-vis her own mother who had died when she was still a baby, by caring for her dying stepmother. Feeling stretched and pulled from two sides she emotionally neglected her own baby. When Mrs A's stepmother died, shortly after Ernestine's birth, the birth of a child and the death of a mother were linked once again in the history of this family.

When she had her baby, instead of receiving the care a young mother needs from her own mother, Ernestine was forced to empa-thize about 'the terrible time she had given her mother' in the past. According to the patient, it is clear that Mrs A feels vividly resentful to this day of the patient having been such a burden to her, and she talked to the 'good' daughter about the 'bad' baby she once was.

From the moment my patient had a baby, her mother has become more demanding. She becomes ill, with severe hypochondriacal complaints, even threatening to die. She insists on being cared for and pitied by her daughter. To Ernestine's great anger and disap-pointment, her mother does not show interest in the baby. The patient can no longer bring herself to function as her mother's mother, a role she has dutifully fulfilled over the years since she was very young. Ernestine, with the vertical split in her ego loosening during analysis, begins to realize to what degree she hates her mother.

In the analysis we wondered whether Mrs A is reacting strongly to the loss of her daughter's motherly affections and is suffering a

285

serious recurrence of her own postnatal depression of 40 years before. My patient thus feels very guilty and has compelling fantasies that her mother will die as a consequence of her having a baby.

Once more the fantasy reappears: *when a child comes, a mother goes.* Ernestine experienced this family myth as psychically real, and she conveyed to me that for her at times there was no distinction between fact and fantasy. This seemed to be the result of real life events, in combination with imagined ones. It is as if reality has interfered with symbol formation. Fantasies are so real and vivid, they have to be acted on. For example, Ernestine has to chop down the laburnum tree in her garden after she hears its flowers are poisonous because she vividly imagines her son being poisoned and dying when he sits under this tree. Besides the theme of oral destruction, this might also point to her castration wishes – as we'll see Ernestine seems to have a strong masculinity complex related to her father's wish for a son.

It becomes clear in the analysis that the patient needs to work through the dramatic events of a generation ago as the problems encountered by her mother are transmitted to her (Kogan 1995). What seems to have been deficiency in mothering, combined with her own feeling that it was up to her to save her mother from death – a feeling which, we thought, was implicitly shared by her mother – seems to have created a reversal of roles, which began one generation before. It is not rare for a daughter to look after her mother and thus, as it were, become her own 'grandmother' (Freud 1988). It has been observed that postnatal depression tends to recur over generations (Asch 1966; Asch and Rubin 1974; Bouchard 1979; Anthony 1983).

Multigenerational links and symbiotic illusion

Linking my work to the existing literature, I want to suggest two points. First one needs to consider the multigenerational involvement in health as well as in pathology, especially in regard to reproductive issues, between mothers and daughters. The second point regards symbiosis and what I have called the symbiotic illusion (Halberstadt-Freud 1989), which can play a vital role in postnatal depression.

Mothers form an essential link in the carry-over from one generation to the next. Motherhood is a three-generation experience, accompanied by a revival of past conflicts and anxieties (Pines 1972).

The feminine lineage, by its strength and direct carry-over and without the intervention of gender differences, makes it easy to pass on assets as well as weaknesses.

The primordial homosexual bond between mother and daughter can have powerful effects on female development. 'The relation between mother and daughter is handicapped from the start . . . due to the sexual identity between mother and daughter' (McDougall 1970a: 98). Girls are born in a same-sex relationship in which a woman creates her own likeness by having a daughter. From some points of view she can project herself more easily into a daughter than into a son. Mutual identification creates more closeness, more ambivalence, more hatred and more longing for maternal love in women.

'The roots of feminine erotism are laid down in early infancy' (McDougall 1986: 228). Women struggle with the problem of how to integrate the profound homo-erotic tie to one's mother. The need for a girl to identify with her mother, added to her being of the same sex and gender, breeds likeness and the consequent illusion of sameness. Moreover it is important to remember that a woman's reaction to her offspring has to be seen in the context of her relationship to her mother, and of her mother's relationship to her own mother. The therapist has to take at least three (possibly four) generations along the maternal lineage into account, when interpreting pathology like postnatal depression.

Symbiosis, as Mahler (1968) admitted, is not to be meant literally, as mutual dependence, when used to describe the normal mother–child situation. 'The term symbiosis is a metaphor. It does not describe, as the biological concept of symbiosis does, what actually happens between two separate individuals. The essential feature of symbiosis is the delusion of a common boundary of the two actually and physically separate individuals' (1968: 9). The baby, in his or her illusion of omnipotence, can imagine being one with the mother and partaking of her greatness and power, but normally mothers do not need their babies to the same extent as a support for their narcissism.

The idea of symbiosis is an imaginary ideal from the child's point of view. 'Blissful symbiosis' is an idealized view of the baby's feelings. There is no evidence of a positive symbiotic phase (Brody 1982). According to Stern the baby is not fused with the mother in the sense of not having boundaries: 'the experience with a self-regulating other . . . does not breach or confuse the sense of core self and a core other' (Stern 1985: 105).

A two-sided dependency, a pathogenic reciprocal symbiotic illusion, not at all rare between mothers and daughters, is a defence mechanism and a sign of disturbance. The 'imaginary baby' – the mother's fantasy about her unborn baby – is a normal phenomenon. It becomes pathological when a mother harbours the fantasy that all her unfulfilled desires and aspirations will be met by her baby. If a mother is insecure, narcissistically vulnerable, and/or depressed, she risks losing sight of the real baby and its needs. She tends to imagine the child as part of her physical and emotional self, and as indispensable to her well-being. She cannot see it as a separate person with needs of his or her own. A situation arises in which she needs the baby to need her, as is seen in infants' sleep disturbances (Lebovici 1983). Becoming a mother and having power over a child can give rise to a perverse mother–child relationship, e.g. a symbiotic illusion, where the mother perverts her love for the child into a self-serving relationship.

In these cases the mother needs constant confirmation that she is the good beloved parent. She demands likeness and sameness – for instance she may believe the infant to be hungry when she is. As we shall see this situation arises when a mother is not separated but still merged with her own internal maternal imago. She tends to use her baby from its birth onward as a transference object on whom she projects her fears and hopes – in fact her image of herself as a baby.

Ernestine alternates between being identified with her crying baby (Blum 1978; Zachary 1985), representing herself, and seeing her child as an accusatory figure representing her guilt-inducing mother. As Ernestine felt accused by her mother, she now feels blamed by her crying baby. She hates her child for any sign of independence or autonomy, signifying separation, and she is unable to confront her hatred. But gradually, anxious that he might die, she replaces her wish to get rid of him and becomes overprotective – a reaction formation which on the one hand indicates the strength of her hatred at her mother/child, but on the other it also indicates her capacity to love and protect her baby.

Mothers like Ernestine resent their child and feel threatened by its demands unless 'blissfully' merged in a mythical union over which she has full control. Consequently, they cannot afford to allow anything resembling separation or individuation to take place

Their infantile primary homosexual bond with their own mothers persisting in the unconscious has not allowed their Oedipus complex and their relationship to men to develop properly. Males are resented as disturbers of the homosexual bond with the mother. These women remain caught up in a dyadic rather than a triadic relationship. For a mother such as Ernestine merging with her mother or her child is a lure and a threat. Her heterosexuality is weakly developed. As her father has played a minor role in her life, so does her husband, especially after the birth of a child. As a mother, she tends to become totally involved in her baby, without a life of her own and without enough interests apart from her child. The child senses this symbiotic need and, for its survival, tries to comply. Locked in a symbiotic idyll the mother as well as the daughter has a vital interest in keeping up the illusion of a happy bond for which they pay a high price. As we know, being 'condemned to each other' fosters hostility that has to be suppressed and denied. As a child she misses out her pubertal protest against her mother and is unable to set limits. If she becomes critical of her mother, she fears she will kill her by the sheer wish to separate from her. These deeply held beliefs are, to an extent, unconsciously passed on through the generations and therefore shared – and confirmed – between mother and daughter. For instance, another patient who also came to analysis suffering from postnatal depression, had succeeded in confronting her mother and being critical of her for the first time in her life. The following day her mother, who had been severely depressed for a long time, committed suicide. The daughter felt she had murdered her mother, and at the same time the mother's suicide can be seen as a desperate punishment for her daughter's attempt to be independent.

An increase in guilt feelings is to be expected when autonomy is experienced as hostility. Disavowal of anger and frustration can lead to splitting and projection of the negative feelings outside of the dyad. Because the father's image tends to be excluded, he can easily become the receptacle of hostile fantasies, especially because mother and child will do everything to keep their false idyll intact.

In this family constellation, where the father keeps his distance and the mother needs repeated proof that she is a good mother, she provides love and care on condition that the child gives up its independence. This is illustrated in Marcel Proust's famous novel *Remembrance of Things Past*. He describes a goodnight kiss episode in which the mother 'abdicates' by giving in to her son's childish wishes. The boy is desperately crying as he cannot go to sleep without a long session of kissing with his mother. He is so wretched that she decides to give up her demands on him and gives in to his wish to be consoled. She spoils him, on condition that he gives up his independence. Her 'abdication' means that he will remain for ever tied up to her, and to her mother, the narrator's beloved grandmother. 'It struck me that my mother had just made a first concession . . . that it was a first abdication on her part from the ideal she had formed for me, . . . that I had succeeded . . . in relaxing her will . . . and that this evening opened a new era' (Proust 1981: 41). She spends the night with her son and the father goes to bed alone (Halberstadt-Freud 1980, 1991), a false and perverse mother–son idyll is created which will mark forever the child's future love life (Welldon 1989).

In the symbiotic illusion, mother and child strike an unconscious deal to oblige one another in endless 'bartering' (Khan 1962/1979). As described in Proust's brilliant example, the child may become a willing partner, requesting and offering to mother exclusive dependence and blurring of boundaries. When tokens of dependence are not given by the child, maternal love turns into hatred. The result is 'symbiotic anxiety', with its archaic fears of either loss of identity through fusion with mother, or risking loss of love. For the daughter, having a baby of her own breaks the spell with the mother and the resulting confusion may end in postnatal depression.

The difficulty in separating from her mother hinders the daughter in forming a triadic relationship. When she becomes a mother, she feels burdened by two competing dyadic bonds, one with her mother and the other with her child. Her husband, a denigrated object like her father, is not allowed, or is unable, to alleviate her plight. Her (internal) mother figure is imagined as envious and demanding, in competition with the baby. She tries to solve this conflict by hating either her mother, her baby, or herself, as was the case with Ernestine. Identification with the baby and its crying gave rise to an intensification of her own baby wishes and desires vis-à-vis her (internal) mother. Under the influence of reaction formation, Ernestine turned hatred into loving care. She became so utterly devoted that she became mentally and physically exhausted.

Symbiotic illusion, the Electra complex, and Oedipal feelings

The problems around female development are far from settled and they are not free from the historical burden of having been often

290

studied from a male perspective. The pre-Oedipal girl, remaining attached to her mother longer than her male sibling, is supposed to experience a belated Oedipus complex, a concept derived from male development. For women who struggle with their maternal image (the internal mother projected on the external one), the term *Electra complex* complements the Oedipal paradigm (Halberstadt-Freud 1989, 1993).

The Electra complex, named after the classical mythical figure of that name, is characterized by hatred for the mother and idealization of the distant father. Electra's father Agamemnon was away for ten years fighting the Trojan war. She had always felt emotionally neglected by her mother and now blamed her for being unfaithful to her father by taking a lover after he left. When Clytemnestra killed her returning husband, Electra decided her mother and her lover had to be killed. She engaged her brother to perform this cruel act. This myth has been taken up by many authors, from Euripides and Sophocles to Eugene O'Neill, and is paradigmatic of female pathology. Reproaches centred around lack of maternal love and care can develop into hate and murderous fantasies in the daughter. Women have to sail between the Scylla and Charybdis of a relationship that can become either too close or too distant to permit harmonious female development to take place. Moreover, the myth of Electra highlights the importance of the relationship with the mother, which the classic Oedipus complex tends to neglect.

While Ernestine experiences an Electra complex, she is more preoccupied with hating her mother than longing for her distant father. Her symbiotic wishes and desires for merger had to be denied after she became a mother herself. The maternal representation became split into a longed for caring image and a dangerous threatening object.

She re-experiences her own early rapprochement crisis, a normal conflict in the first few years of life around approach and avoidance of the maternal figure. The early experimenting of the small child with moving away from mother and back to her, the desire for individuation and at the same time the need of closeness, becomes loaded with ambivalence and fear of loss of love when the mother does not allow distance, like Mahler's case of Wendy illustrates (Mahler *et al.* 1975: 153–168). Ernestine, after the birth of her son, moves away from her mother and turns to her father. Becoming a mother, while stimulating regression and pre-Oedipal conflicts, has given Oedipal

291

dynamics a renewed chance. She feels that her father always wished her to be a boy, and she strove to accommodate him. She did not feel valued by him as a girl (Schwartz 1986) and tried to be as competitive and as good in sports as she possibly could.

But having become the mother of his longed for (grand)son, she experiences her father as being more sensitive to her Oedipal wishes by showing appreciation for his daughter. He becomes more chivalrous toward her and regularly brings her flowers. He is proud of her ability to produce the son his wife did not give him. When they meet he greets his daughter with an almost painful blow on the shoulder, 'knighting' her as a 'wo-man', thus stressing his bisexual vision of her.

Her father strongly suggests to give his grandchild his family name, as if it were his son, thereby excluding the biological father. She resists his Oedipal seduction, though having a son is a triumph for her. The downside is that it resuscitates her Oedipal rivalry and guilt vis-à-vis her mother. She says she sometimes feels as if she stole the baby boy from her.

The positions of the protagonists in this drama have changed with the baby's arrival, largely through splitting – a traditional defence mechanism in this family. The father of the baby has become the bad man; Ernestine is angry with him most of the time, and she does not allow him to look after the baby. Her father and her son become her new love objects. The baby, hated at first and envied for the attention he gets, has become her idol. It is as if the grandmother has become the hated baby who should not be looked after and should be left to die. Ernestine develops an aversion to her, showing all the hallmarks of a mother-phobia, by no means unusual in postnatal depressions. The former symbiotic illusion has to be denied and a flight from engulfment takes place.

In this situation, mother has to be kept at a distance. Clare, another patient suffering from postnatal depression I treated psychoanalytically, clearly showed this fear of her mother coming near her or the baby. Hatred and a strong aversion, to the point of not being able to touch her mother, took the place of former pseudo-closeness. The baby daughter became her idol, but her ambivalence showed itself in not being able to talk to the child at all. She felt accused when the child cried and reacted by becoming an obsessional and perfectionist mother, not unlike Ernestine. This child developed digestive problems and required a diet which included the withholding by the mother of the food the child liked best. A similar developmental interference happened to Ernestine as a baby.

Transference and countertransference

Ambivalence, stemming from the simultaneous wish to fuse with and avoid re-engulfment by the mother, is well-known in postnatal depression. Blum (1978), in his paper about a patient who had much in common with mine, mentions the demand for and struggle against dependence and concomitant denial of dependent affectionate feelings. 'Ambivalence is intensified, and clinging to and coercion of the maternal object may be associated with strenuous efforts to protect the relationship from the child's hostility' (p. 353).

The self and object representations are split in good and bad parts. Ernestine's compliance and acceptance of my interpretations is coupled with stubborn denial of her need for help. She experiences severe problems admitting her need for (the benign part of) the object. Her identification with the crying baby gives rise to regressive wishes towards the analyst, which have to be denied. She can admit that she misses the care she feels she had a right to expect from her mother, but she does not allow herself the necessary regression in the transference, except by crying profusely. She vigorously fights dependency by saying she doesn't need analysis. Her adequate, grown-up part, and her crying, baby part are in conflict. To need the analyst means to be dependent and less than perfect, an unbearable idea for Ernestine, who seems in a life-and-death struggle of independence from and competition with the analyst.

Before her pregnancy she would satisfy her need for support by projective identification. She used to project her needy self onto her friends and in looking after them she vicariously enjoyed the care she gave them. She was the 'helper' and the 'therapist' of her mother and various other women. She was satisfied with this role until the regression that accompanied the birth of her son made it impossible for her to keep it up. Now that she realizes how they made use of and exhausted her she has come to consider them all egoists. She tells me repeatedly about her strong aversion to her unhappy mother and her troubled friends. She avoids contact because she feels persecuted by them. She fears the 'shit' they put into her will 'poison' her child and hates them for trying to lean on her. Anal and oral sadism

293

are reinforced by her regression. The theme of food and poison resurfaces on every occasion.

These processes are repeated in her transference feelings toward the analyst. She fears that I would want to lean on her like her mother does. This will happen whenever she has the weakness to show her affection for me and her need for consolation and comfort. The burden of being responsible for the analyst is all the heavier as she can't allow herself to lean on me. The conviction that I would like to have her full attention for myself is almost delusional and does not seem to respond very well to my interpretations. Her latent but stubborn resistance succeeds in eliciting feelings of helplessness, hopelessness, and anger in me. Those are exactly the feelings that her mother stirs in her, leading me to a better understanding of this re-enactment and more complete interpretations of it.

She unconsciously repeats the destructive interaction with her mother via enactments in the transference. We are the new mother–daughter pair. My countertransference reflections enable me to sympathize with her feelings towards her mother, as we regularly change roles, and I become the helpless child while she is the powerful mother who can withhold her love. She reacts as if my interpretations are useless and rejects them. Her mother does the same, first asking for advice and then rejecting it when given. She tries to enact the same mother–daughter deadlock with me. She pretends to be too self-effacing to make demands, and, like her mother, too demanding to be satisfied. Her manifest attitude toward me is one of submission, even slavishness, all the while trying to make me feel as useless as her mother makes her feel. She benefits from re-enacting the coercively demanding bond with her mother with me in the transference. Thus becoming more conscious of this interaction enables her to loosen the suffocating ties that bind her to her mother.

Despite her not showing any feelings towards her analyst and her avoidance of intimacy I can feel there is another more unconscious emotional side to her. She is devoted to her treatment, never misses a session and in her own way she works hard and towards the end verbalizes her gratitude towards me.

Gradually she comes to experience her mother as someone who wronged her, used her, and does nor did give her what is a child's due. Nevertheless, she resists my suggestion of a connection between her anger vis-à-vis her mother and her avoidance of closeness to the analyst. She has to split the good analyst from the bad one, and distinguish the bad mother from the good analyst. Libidinal as well as aggressive fantasies concerning the analyst remain repressed. She is angry and frustrated, mourns the mother she missed, cries profusely while the spell of her symbiotic illusion is irreparably broken.

But to admit an emotional relationship between us remains impossible for her. She insists that there is nothing between us and that she doesn't want to have anything 'personal' to do with me. She does not at all miss me during holidays, implying that she doesn't need me – consciously, she perceives me more like a burden than a helper. Meanwhile she tries to repair this negative attitude by expressing her admiration for the fact 'that you are always there for me'. She is sure I have done much to improve her condition, showing she split me in an idealized and denigrated object. She can eradicate me from her consciousness as she cut down the laburnum tree. But like the tree, which she carefully wrapped up and put on the street as a foundling, an abandoned child, she saves a hidden positive part-image of me. She denies having any thoughts or associations pertaining to my person. No wonder that she is quite unable to associate freely. Her thinking is very organized, and has an obsessional tinge. Feelings are isolated from facts which are related in great detail.

In hindsight it seems that the burden of looking after her mother left no room for her wish to have a child of her own. When she becomes pregnant for a second time – unplanned again, like with her first pregnancy – she is anxious it will be a daughter. She fears that she will hate her and will be unable to bring her up properly. How can she teach a daughter to become a woman, she wonders. She moreover fears she will die after the baby is born, which seems a magical repetition of what took place with her grandmother when her mother was born, and with her step-grandmother when she, Ernestine, was born and what perhaps nearly happened to her mother after her son was born. She then has a dream that her son will be eaten by a crocodile, aptly symbolizing her active and passive oral sadistic and cannibalistic fantasies vis-à-vis her mother. She fears her mother will die and be reborn in the person of a daughter, whom she then will have to kill or be killed by her. I propose that she fears a daughter might also stir her own wishes to be a baby again, which she denies. At the height of her ambivalence towards her children her son has his first asthmatic episode and nearly suffocates because she can't make up her mind and call the doctor.

She decides she cannot have a baby and be in analysis at the same time. She rationalizes this in terms of the time needed to look after two children. She would feel too much burdened with demands from all sides and she decides, after two years, to leave treatment before the baby is born. The resurgence of old problems, in quick succession, at the termination phase of analysis, is a helpful development. I speculate that she has to symbolically abort her analyst (like her mother symbolically tried to abort her sister) instead of her imaginary baby daughter, acting out the hostility she is unable to experience consciously. Maybe, she tries to save her foetus, her child, her mother, or herself from an imagined deathly fate? Or is she fleeing from dependence, satisfying her narcissistic need to be self-sufficient? Is she taking revenge for having been left alone by her mother when in need of support?

Whatever her reasons for stopping her analysis, she has achieved her aim of overcoming her depression. My concern over her chances to remain healthy might be exaggerated. She feels that her condition has improved due to her analysis and she sounds quite confident about the new baby. She has apparently worked through her former fears well enough to look forward to having another baby and to look after two children without fearing a recurrence of her depression. She shows she is grateful and appreciative by sending me a big bunch of flowers after leaving.

Two years later, she calls me, giving me the permission I requested, to publish her case history and telling me she is doing well. Her depression has not returned, and she has two thriving sons. She talks about her partner in a positive tone, and thanks me once more for what I did for her.

Discussion and conclusions

Puerperium is a period of rapid transitions allowing for change through therapeutic intervention. The bodily and emotional turmoil of the woman before and after childbirth increases her sensitivity and opens up chances for psychological change as a new equilibrium has to be found. It can be considered the third separation/individuation phase of women, after the very early stage and adolescence, offering an opportunity to reinforce one's dependency or to develop autonomy. In the period after delivery the emotional sluices are wide open, creating possibilities for renewed personal growth, as clearly shown in Ernestine's case. The puerperium can not only be a period of regression but of progress as well. My patient succeeded in resolving her rapprochement (approach–avoidance) conflicts enabling her to loosen the ties with her maternal object. Massive anger at her mother became conscious and was partially worked through in the transference. Ernestine's ending the analysis during her second pregnancy must have been a triumph for her and punishment for the mother figure in the person of the analyst, but it helped her to achieve more separation and autonomy. Her leaving treatment is reminiscent of adolescent patients who suddenly feel the need to be independent and leave before the analyst considers their treatment finished.

As pointed out before, the suffering of mother and child would justify devoting more attention to postpartum depression than the subject has received from psychoanalysis so far (Asch 1966; Asch and Rubin 1974; Blum 1978; Fraiberg 1980; Anthony 1983). This fact has its historical roots. The Oedipus complex was conceived according to male development. If the founder of psychoanalysis had been a woman, she might have chosen Electra as an example of female pathology instead of Oedipus. For women, the fateful combination of love and hate for the same object is the kernel of conflicts, so well expressed in the myth of Electra.

For a long time, female development was understood in the light of drive development and the Oedipal stand vis-à-vis the father, to the detriment of the study of the mother–daughter relationship. Following Freud, the baby was seen for a long time as a substitute for the woman's missing penis (Zilboorg 1929, 1931; Deutsch 1945). As a consequence of seeing the female as an '*homme manqué*,' a castrated male, disturbances were often interpreted as being caused by frustrated phallic Oedipal strivings in women. As Chasseguet-Smirgel (1985) has so aptly pointed out, phallic sexual monism, as adopted by psychoanalysis, belongs to the vision of the male fetishist.

Postnatal depression doesn't figure in the index of the *Standard Edition of the Complete Psychological Works of Sigmund Freud*. As a consequence of Freud's theoretical and clinical inclination, mothers and maternity have long been neglected. Postnatal depression has seldom been elaborated theoretically or illustrated clinically, either before or after Blum remarked on this state of affairs in his 1978 paper. Infant research has provided new evidence about the devastating influence

297

that the mother's depressed mood has on the baby (Brazelton 1983; Cramer 1983; Lebovici 1983; Soulé 1983; Field *et al.* 1985, 1988). Psychoanalysis traditionally considers mothers from the vantage point of the child, avoiding the question: What does a mother want?

I have introduced two theoretical concepts and their interaction, the first being the 'symbiotic illusion' used as a defence mechanism (Halberstadt-Freud 1989, 1991). The second one is multigenerational involvement in pathology like postnatal depression.

The female dyad that a woman forms with her mother can lead through several phases in her life and over several generations to suppress aggression and obliterate differences. I have suggested that a symbiotic phase does not exist as such, as there is normally no phase in which the mother needs her child as it needs her. Some narcissistically vulnerable mothers need their child more than it needs her. Symbiosis becomes a euphemism for pathology: if the child is needed for the satisfaction of its mother's wishes, and the father is not functioning as the third person, the mutual dependency creates an unwholesome dyad. The father's absence or exclusion risks perpetuating symbiosis in mother and child. The clinging within the mother–child couple demands the banning of aggression from the dyad. In this parasitic relationship, the child has to serve the needs of its mother in order to survive psychically, and both parties in this bond have to evade or suppress anger and hostility for the sake of continuing a peaceful symbiosis. Thus an illusion of mutuality is created, differences are obliterated, there is a pervasive assumption that they both share the same feelings and thoughts, and this is never challenged. The false idyll between mother and child remains quasi-intact at the cost of much psychic pain, as the dependent daughter suffers diminished self-esteem and misses out on normal pubertal protest, a precondition for individuation and autonomy. The topic of matricide, avoided in the psychoanalytic literature, is pervasive in fantasy life, especially when hostility is being barred from expression.

Regression threatens every new developmental phase of the female life cycle as progression means renewed identification with the maternal figure. The events of pregnancy and giving birth not only mean following in the mother's footsteps but also imply identification with the baby (Deutsch 1945; Bergler 1959; Hayman 1962; Benedek 1973; Pines 1982). Renewed symbiotic fantasies in relation to the mother stir old wishes of fusion and concomitant fears of re-engulfment. In other words, approach–avoidance conflicts typical of the rapprochement phase are common in the puerperium. After delivery, the loss of oneness with the baby can give rise to separation fears, ambivalence and regression in the mother. Ego regression and identification with the 'oral existence' of the crying baby, being in conflict with superego identification with the powerful and punishing mother image, leads to depression. The fear of being a bad mother may bring about the impulse to kill either oneself or the baby. The baby may be seen as a monster eating up the mother and consuming her whole life. Guilt feelings tend to be projected, and, like in Ernestine's case, the husband gets blamed for not providing the love and attention the puerperal woman missed from her maternal object in the past as well as in the present.

The temporary regression implied in the 'primary maternal preoccupation' (Winnicott 1956/1958) can endanger a woman's equilibrium. She identifies with the maternal role while part of her has to identify with the needs of the baby. The revived desire to be a baby herself, like in Ernestine's case, has to be repressed and denied. She resented the baby who once more forced her to take responsibility instead of being taken care of. She tried to banish her envy and hatred of the baby, who upset her entire life, by reaction formation. Ernestine became the more than perfect mother. Analysis helped her to be freed from the conflicts with her mother, competing with the baby and threatening to die if not getting the attention she demanded from her daughter. Ernestine became able to withstand her mother's claims and realized how much she hated her for being so demanding.

The woman who becomes a mother is strongly confronted with her inner mother, the maternal image she carries inside. In postnatal depression, she mourns the mothering she missed and falls prey to a paradox: As she cannot direct her anger at mother image, split into a powerful and a vulnerable part she is afraid to kill, she will tend to direct the freed hostility and aggression at herself, her partner, or her child. The Oedipal rivalry with the mother is revived and dyadic functioning can become triadic.

Though gender identity is not as threatened by the mother–child bond with girls as it is with boys, individuation and separation are endangered by the absence of sexual difference. These developmental milestones have failed to take place to a sufficient degree in the female lineage in women falling prey to postnatal depression. When the spell is broken, which inevitably happens after giving birth, the daughter is suddenly confronted with her ambivalent feelings toward her mother.

This illusion of imagining oneself being one with the mother, crumbles during the puerperium. The pact is broken, hostility is freed from repression, and fear of being close or becoming (like) the hated mother emerges. Aggression – so far safely split off and projected onto the outside world (e.g., the father) – threatens to re-enter consciousness. This shattering of the false idyll with the mother, at a time when emotional support is needed in becoming a mother oneself, can easily prompt a breakdown. A 'mother phobia' or 'allergy' can result, expressed in fears like having the mother near, an aversion of touching her or being touched by her, and generally a need to keep her at a distance. She is not allowed to approach the baby, or else . . . evil will happen, a theme which often surfaces in fairy tales, involving evil stepmothers or wicked fairies.

Postnatal depression is a multigenerational problem. The woman who lives with an unresolved imaginary bond with her mother tends to repeat this problem with her child. She recreates symbiosis as an illusion, which can easily become a delusion. If the child complies with the mother's unconscious needs, the child's autonomy and her future successful motherhood are in jeopardy. This process tends to repeat itself over the generations. As in the case of Ernestine, familial mythology and fantasies explaining traumas and disasters in the past result in magical thinking, confusion and shared delusions. Unconscious conflicts are more easily transmitted along the straight female line of descent, as matrilineal identification is not diluted by sexual difference.

Although problems in relation to the woman's mother have been noted by most authors on postnatal depression, whether the authors are psychiatrists or psychoanalysts (Jones 1942; Lomas 1960a, 1960b; Hayman 1962; Douglas 1963; Molinski 1972; Pines 1972; Roth 1975; Bieber and Bieber 1978; Ketai and Brandwin 1979), the multigenerational links have received scant attention. Ernestine's case demonstrates how fantasies and projections are carried over from grandmother to granddaughter and beyond. In this case magical ideas around food as poison, and oral anxieties around devouring and being devoured, were prominent, illustrating the regression of the young mother to the phase of oral sadism.

Ernestine could not get support from her mother after the birth of her baby. On the contrary, the mother's own postnatal depression (we supposed she had experienced) was revived, and she began to lean more heavily on her daughter. She wanted to be the baby, creating a total reversal of the generations. Women with postpartum depression often feel caught between saving their mother and saving their child, feeling guilty of abandoning, even killing either.

As it is characteristic, there was no history of adequate mothering as a reference point in this family. Severe trauma had haunted motherhood for several generations. The fathers through the generations, remained background figures, creating a void where caring maternal and paternal objects of identification should be. Ernestine's identification with her father was always already clear in her dress and manner, from childhood on she tried hard to replace the son the father missed. This way she received love and attention from him that her mother couldn't give. This created difficulties in her heterosexual development as she tended to be the male instead of desiring him. McDougall (1970b) writes about the wish to be and to have the object of the other sex. After the birth of her child, her partner of very long standing and mutual understanding became devalued, like her father has been. She had always colluded with her mother in denigrating talk about 'that brute of a father'. The paternal object is consequently split in her mind, like the mother is, into a role model and a denigrated man.

If treatment is successful, which is often the case in this period of rapid changes, Oedipal feelings will get a renewed chance to develop. Having a baby is, like adolescence, another chance to prove that a woman's anatomy is far from being her destiny.

To sum up my findings. Ernestine's psychoanalytic treatment confirms my experience with other postpartum patients and with the literature on this subject. She struggled with her femininity and was apprehensive of the combined roles of wife, lover, and mother. Her destructive feelings were for the most part not directed at the baby but at her partner and at herself. She became more dominating toward her partner as she felt herself to be a victim after the birth of her baby. Puerperium put a heavy burden on her habitual defences – denial, splitting, projective identification, and reaction formation. She temporarily lost her psychic equilibrium. Her former ego-strength was gone. Her increased masochism masked the fact that she felt a strong need to be in control, and she began to make use of obsessional mechanisms. She became simultaneously more dependent and more aggressive. Trying to be a perfect mother, she exhausted herself and was drawn in a downward spiral.

301

The analysis was effective in undoing the old balance and finding a new one. Among other things, it helped her to give up mothering her mother without a renewed psychic breakdown after her next pregnancy.

It seems that in women only a partial separation from the maternal object has to take place. There is a very fine line between healthy relatedness and pathological symbiosis, as becoming a mother involves the ability to internalize one's mother as a caregiver. Only if sufficient triangulation has taken place does the Oedipal constellation have a chance in the puerperium. Women who have not resolved their relationship to their primary object remain in a vulnerable state and risk becoming depressed in the process of becoming a mother.

To prevent the consequences for the next generation(s), treatment of postnatal depression is indispensable and can be very effective if provided promptly. The emotional upheaval of a woman in the postnatal period gives her a better chance to restructure her psyche than at other times of her life.

References

Anthony, E. J. (1983) 'An overview of the effects of maternal depression on the infant and child', in H. L. Morrison (ed.) *Children of Depressed Parents* (pp. 1–16). New York: Grune and Stratton.

Asch, S. S. (1966) 'Depression: three clinical variations'. *Psychoanal. Study Child*, 21: 150–171.

Asch, S. S. and Rubin, L. J. (1974) 'Postpartum reactions: some unrecognized variations'. *Am. J. Psychiatry*, 131: 870–874.

Benedek, T. (1973) 'The psychosomatic implications of the primary unit: mother–child', in T. Benedek *Psychoanalytic Investigations: Selected Papers* (pp. 255–276). New York: Quadrangle.

Bergler, E. (1959) 'Psychoprophylaxis of postpartum depression'. *Postgraduate Medicine*, 25, 164–168.

Bieber, I. and Bieber, T. B. (1978) 'Postpartum reactions in men and women'. *J. Am. Acad. Psychoanal. Dyn. Psychiatr.*, 6: 511–519.

Blum, H. P. (1978) 'Reconstruction in a case of postpartum depression'. *Psychoanal. Study Child*, 33: 335–362.

Bouchard Godard, A. (1979) 'Un étranger à demeure' [A stranger in the house]. *Nouvelle Revue de Psychanalyse*, 19: 161–175.

Brazelton, T. B. (1983) 'Le bébé partenaire dans l'interaction' [The baby as partner in the interaction], in M. Soulé (ed.) *La dynamique du nourisson, ou quoi de neuf bébé?* (pp. 11–27). Paris: Editions ESF.

Brody, S. (1982) 'Psychoanalytic theories of infant development and its disturbances: a critical evaluation'. *Psychoanal Q.* 51: 526–597.

Chasseguet-Smirgel, J. (1985) *Creativity and Perversion*. London: Free Association Books.

Cramer, B. (1983) 'La psychiatrie du bébé' [Infant psychiatry], in M. Soulé (ed.) *La dynamique du nourisson, ou quoi de neuf bébé?* (pp. 28–83). Paris: Editions ESF.

Deutsch, H. (1945) *The Psychology of Women*, Vol. 2. New York: Grune and Stratton.

Douglas, G. (1963) 'Puerperal depression and excessive compliance with the mother'. *Brit. J. Med. Psychol.*, 36: 271–278.

Field, T., Sandberg, D., Garcia, R., Vega-Lahr, N., Goldstein, S. and Guy, L. (1985) 'Pregnancy problems, postpartum depression, and early mother–infant interactions'. *Devel. Psychol.*, 21: 1152–1156.

Field, T., Healy, B., Goldstein, S., Perry, S. and Bendell, D. (1988) 'Infants of depressed mothers show "depressed" behaviour even with non-depressed adults'. *Child Dev.*, 59: 1569–1579.

Fraiberg, S. (ed.) (1980) *Clinical Studies in Infant Mental Health: The First Year of Life*. New York: Basic Books.

Freud, S. (1988) *My Three Mothers and Other Passions*. New York: New York University Press.

Gavin, N., Bradley, N., *et al.* (2005) 'Perinatal depression: a systematic review of prevalence and incidence'. *Obstetrics and Gynaecology*, 106: 1071–1083.

Halberstadt-Freud, H. C. (1980) 'Proust and perversion: some clinical and theoretical considerations'. *Int. J. Psycho-Anal.*, 61: 403–410.

Halberstadt-Freud, H. C. (1989) 'Electra in bondage: on symbiosis and the symbiotic illusion between mother and daughter and the consequences for the Oedipus Complex'. *Free Associations*, 17: 58–89.

Halberstadt-Freud, H. C. (1991) *Freud, Proust, Perversion and Love*. London: Harcourt Brace.

Halberstadt-Freud, H. C. (1993) 'Do girls change their object?', in H. Groen-Prakken and A. Laden (eds) *The Dutch Annual of Psychoanalysis* (pp. 169–190). Amsterdam: Swets and Zeitlinger.

Halberstadt-Freud, H. C. (2010) *Electra vs Oedipus: the drama of the mother–daughter relationship*. London and New York: Routledge.

Hayman, A. (1962) 'Some aspects of regression in non-psychotic puerperal depression'. *Brit. J. Med. Psychol.*, 35: 135–145.

Jones, E. (1942) 'Psychology and childbirth'. *Lancet*, 1: 695–696.

Ketai, R. M. and Brandwin, M. A. (1979) 'Childbirth-related psychosis and familial symbiotic conflict'. *Am. J. Psychiatry*, 136: 190–193.

Khan, M. M. (1979) 'The role of polymorph-perverse body experiences and object-relations in ego-integration', in C. Yorke (ed.) *Alienation in Perversions* (pp. 31–55). London: Hogarth Press. (Original work published 1962.)

Kogan, I. (1995) *The Cry of Mute Children. A Psychoanalytic Perspective of the Second Generation of the Holocaust.* London/New York: Free Association Books.

Lebovici, S. (1983) *Le nourisson, la mère et le psychanalyste: Les interactions précoces* [The infant, the mother and the psychoanalyst: early interactions]. Paris: Paidos/Centurion.

Lomas, P. (1960a) 'Defensive organization and puerperal breakdown'. *Brit. J. Med. Psychol.*, 33: 61–66.

Lomas, P. (1960b) 'Dread of envy as an aetiological factor in puerperal breakdown'. *Brit. J. Med. Psychol.*, 33: 105–112.

Mahler, M. S. (1968) *On Human Symbiosis and the Vicissitudes of Individuation: Vol. 7: Infantile Psychosis.* New York: International Universities Press.

Mahler, M. S., Pine, F. and Bergman, A. (1975) *The Psychological Birth of the Human Infant. Symbiosis and Individuation.* London: Hutchinson.

McDougall, J. (1970a) 'Feminine guilt and the Oedipus complex', in J. Chasseguet-Smirgel (ed.) *Female Sexuality. New Psychoanalytic Views* (pp. 94–135). London: Maresfield Library.

McDougall, J. (1970b) 'Homosexuality in women', in J. Chasseguet-Smirgel (ed.) *Female Sexuality. New Psychoanalytic Views* (pp. 171–212). London: Maresfield Library.

McDougall, J. (1986) 'Eve's reflection: on the homosexual components of female sexuality', in H. C. Meyers (ed.) *Between Analyst and Patient: New Dimensions in Countertransference and Transference* (pp. 213–228). Hillsdale, NJ: Analytic Press.

Molinski, H. (1972) *Die unbewusste Angst vor dem Kinde: Als Ursache von Schwangerschaftsbeschwerden und Depressionen nach der Geburt, mit 12 anschliessenden Falldarstellungen* [The unconscious fear for the child: As cause of problems during pregnancy and depression after birth, with 12 pertinent case studies]. München: Kindler.

Pines, D. (1972) 'Pregnancy and motherhood: interaction between fantasy and reality'. *Brit. J. Med. Psychol.*, 45: 333–343.

Pines, D. (1982) 'The relevance of early psychic development to pregnancy and abortion'. *Int. J. Psycho-Anal.*, 63: 311–319.

Proust, M. (1981) *In Search of Lost Time: Vol: 1: Swann's Way.* Trans. by C. K. Scott Moncrieff and T. Kilmartin. New York: Random House.

Roth, N. (1975) 'The mental content of puerperal psychosis'. *Am. J. Psychother.*, 29: 204–211.

Schwartz, A. (1986) 'Some notes on the development of female gender role identity', in J. L. Alpert (ed.) *Psychoanalysis and Women: Contemporary Reappraisals* (pp. 57–82). Hillsdale, NJ: Analytic Press.

Soulé, M. (1983) 'L'enfant dans la tête, l'enfant imaginaire' [The child in the mind, the imaginary child] in M. Soulé (ed.) *La dynamique du nourisson, ou quoi de neuf bébé?* Paris: Editions ESF.

Stern, D. (1985) *The Interpersonal World of the Infant: A View from Psychoanalysis and Developmental Psychology*. New York: Basic Books.

Welldon, E. V. (1989) *Mother, Madonna, Whore: The Idealization and Degradation of Motherhood*. London: Heinemann.

Winnicott, D. W. (1958) 'Primary maternal preoccupation', in D. W. Winnicott *Collected Papers* (pp. 300–306). Tavistock, London: Tavistock Publications. Original work published 1956.

Zachary, A. (1985) 'A new look at the vulnerability of puerperal mothers: a clinical study of two in-patient families at the Cassel Hospital? *Psychoanalytic Psychotherapy*, 1: 71–89.

Zilboorg, G. (1929) 'The dynamics of schizophrenic reactions related to pregnancy and childbirth'. *Am. J. Psychiatry*, 8: 733–766.

Zilboorg, G. (1931) 'Depressive reactions related to parenthood'. *Am. J. Psychiatry*, 10: 927–962.

Keeping envy in mind

The vicissitudes of envy in adolescent motherhood

Alessandra Lemma

What ties us to our objects? Is it love and gratitude – a sense that we have been given something freely, that we value it and can tolerate that we need the other person to provide this for us? Or is it envy and grievance – a sense that we are locked in dispute with the one whom we feel has deprived us of something good that *should* have been ours? Another way of looking at this is to ask whether the tie to our objects is one that supports our development and separateness or one that keeps us enslaved to the object by whom we feel deprived.

Klein's thoughts about love, gratitude and envy have always deeply moved me as they speak so directly to the struggles we all face when we try to make sense of how love and hate shape our relationship to the good things in our life. Her ideas have been especially helpful to me in my work with adolescent mothers and the children[1] born to young mothers, which is the focus of this chapter.

Envy and deprivation

In her seminal paper Klein (1957) focussed on a question we now all so take for granted it is hard to imagine it not being somewhere in our minds when we are with a patient: how did the baby experience the breast? Was it felt to be full or empty? Was it joyfully offered and received? Or was it felt to be selfish, "mean" and "grudging", as Klein put it, becoming the source of envy and grievance?

In this paper Klein introduces her notion of an innate, "primary envy" defined by the attack being on a "good" object *because* of its goodness. The idea of innate destructiveness has courted controversy. Klein has indeed been criticised for either dismissing altogether or for minimising the impact of the actual mother on the development of the baby. This paper, along with others, acknowledges that the "real" mother, not just the phantasy mother, plays an important part in helping the baby manage his envy. Klein refers to how the mother's state of mind at the time of feeding, for example, may well impact on the baby's experience of the breast. Moreover, she discusses the relationship between deprivation and envy:

> If we consider that deprivation increases greed and persecutory anxiety, and that there is in the infant's mind a phantasy of an inexhaustible breast which is his greatest desire, *it becomes understandable how envy arises even if the baby is inadequately fed* [my italics]. The infant's feelings seem to be that when the breast deprives him, it becomes bad because it keeps the milk, love and care associated with the good breast all to itself.
>
> (p. 183)

Although she refers to the unavailable breast as a source of deprivation and so as a trigger for envy, it is fair to say that Klein does not develop her ideas about this more reactive envy, lending primacy instead to envy deriving from an innate degree of death instinct. Yet, deprivation as an internal and actual experience figures in her thinking about envy and in her case material. Indeed, whatever assumptions we make about the origins of envy, the patient's experience as it appears in the transference is invariably one of feeling in some way deprived.

Although it is theoretically interesting to speculate about origins (and they can never be more than speculations), it is the patient's *experience* of envy and what she does with that experience that matters most in the consulting room. To this extent, although I remain unconvinced by the notion of innate envy, in my clinical work I have nevertheless found invaluable Klein's ideas on the destructive impact of envy on object relations, on how the self defends against awareness of envy and of how awareness of dependence on the good object can arouse a wish to spoil the goodness of the object. Whilst envy manifests in different ways, Klein helps us

307

to understand how the envious spoiling of the good object functions as a defence against psychic pain: the pain of separation, of loss, of longing and of awareness of envy itself.

In this chapter I am concerned with envy arising from an actual experience of deprivation. Just as Klein describes it in the case of primary envy, an experience of deprivation may also result in attacks on the good object (i.e. even when the object is not being depriving) as a way of defending against need and dependency on the object.

The source of envy

Motherhood during adolescence represents for most young girls a point of acute crisis. Internally, motherhood adds a layer of complexity to the psychic process of adolescence, which typically sets in motion an unsettling review of personal identity. The young person must now integrate into her sense of who she is the reality of the mature sexual body (Laufer and Laufer, 1984). This is inextricably tied with the resurgence of primitive anxieties about dependency and separation from parental figures and of Oedipal conflicts. These primitive anxieties are experienced all the more urgently in the minds of the adolescent girls who become pregnant largely because for many of them the earliest relationship with the mother was in some way disturbed (see, for example, Pines, 1988; Madigan *et al.*, 2006).

The mother who helps her baby to move away from envy towards gratitude is one who enjoys feeding her baby. Just as she freely offers her breast, she freely offers her mind too. She provides psychic nourishment – it is a breast with a mind (see Bion, 1962; Winnicott, 1954). A mother who does not enjoy "feeding" is therefore also experienced as withholding her mind. This may lead to the internalisation of an object felt to be unreceptive to the self's projections and therefore felt to be incapable of transforming psychic pain.

I would like to suggest that where the adolescent girl has internalised a maternal object that does not enjoy "feeding", the losses and anxieties associated with becoming a mother during adolescence are more likely to mobilise internally an experience of deprivation that cannot be reflected upon. As she turns to her internalised mother for understanding, this young mother meets an object that is not felt to be generous and capable of sustaining the self at a time of significant crisis. Her own experiences as a daughter, and now as a mother, become very confused in her own mind. She literally cannot "keep in mind" and bear either her own or the baby's experience of deprivation and the envy this may elicit in both of them. An internal climate of recrimination and grievance may then take root.

The troubled young mother's difficulties are indeed often manifest in her identification with the baby rather than with the wish to herself become a mother (Pines, 1988). The representation of her baby in her mind is thus typically distorted (see, for example, Slade *et al.*, 2005). In my experience the quality and perniciousness of the envy mobilised in the young mother towards her baby depends on whether the baby is represented in her mind as a rival robbing her of her adolescent freedom and opportunities *or* as a withholding, depriving mother who keeps all nourishment for herself.

If the baby is experienced more as a rival who deprives the young mother of her felt "adolescent" entitlement, I am suggesting that envy of the baby takes on a less pernicious course. This is largely because the young mother in this scenario has some sense of herself and of having a mind of her own, even if projective processes still hold sway, as is the case for most adolescents as they struggle to discover who they are. Becoming a mother, of course, impacts on the conflicts around separation and on the Oedipal anxieties that are inevitably revisited during adolescence, but this young girl is nevertheless approaching the challenges of early motherhood with a more integrated experience of herself. Crucially, she has some *desire* to separate from her primary objects, however ambivalent she may also feel about this.

As she feeds her baby, this young mother, I am therefore suggesting, relates to her breast as a "sexual breast". It is a symbol of her desire to develop her own emergent separate identity. Indeed, the typical "complaint" voiced by this young mother is that the baby "gets in the way of having a life". The baby is felt to deprive her of her entitlement to the developmentally appropriate need to experiment and "play" so as to find out who she is. Because she feels deprived of "opportunities", this can then interfere with her ability to take pleasure in her baby and in his pleasure and opportunities. Significant problems for both mother and baby can ensue. This is, nevertheless, quite different to experiencing the baby as getting in the way of the very psychic survival of the self, which is the internal experience I am primarily concerned with in this chapter.

Where the core anxiety in the young mother is about psychic survival and fragmentation of the self my impression is that the envy aroused in her by the baby takes on a more destructive course. Here, the envious attack is aimed at obliterating awareness in herself of longing, dependency and separation. She feels deprived of a nourishing, loving breast, but her own longing for the breast becomes converted into hatred. In this scenario, I am therefore suggesting that the young mother, whose experience of herself is as a deprived baby, envies the nourishing breast the baby depends on. In her mind, the baby is unashamedly "taking". She hates him because he is felt to be oblivious to what *she* needs. In other words, the baby is not a baby in this mother's mind; rather, the baby represents a depriving maternal object who has no awareness of her baby's needs. This young mother can therefore all too readily experience the baby as a hostile presence in her life. It is not just that the baby takes something away from her; rather, the baby torments her. In the transference, it becomes possible to discern how the aim of the envious attack on the good object is to eradicate *her* longing for the nourishing, loving breast.[2]

In two of the cases I worked with more extensively it became clearer in the transference that these young mothers envied a particular state of mind attributed to the baby/mother. Its main feature is an absence of any awareness of painful thoughts or feelings – a kind of psychic Nirvana where it is the "(m)other" who has to absorb all psychic pain leaving the baby, quite literally, *care-free*[3] to enjoy his feed. The "care-free" state of mind attributed to the baby/mother stands in total contrast to the young mother's experience of her own mind. Her mind now feels intruded upon by the baby's needs and by the disturbing feelings and thoughts that are stirred by the baby. Klein captures well the demand placed on the mother by the baby who feels: "it is up to her to prevent all pain and evil from internal and external sources" (1988: 185). The baby thus seeks relief from his own destructive impulses and his anxieties without any concern for the object. But the young mother's own deprived state of mind makes it less likely that she will be able to receive the baby's projections. This undermines the possibility for the baby's experience to be "kept in mind" by her.

The histories of these two young mothers suggested that their own mothers' difficulties had prematurely impinged on the earliest experience of dependency on an object who could digest disturbing states of mind. They powerfully conveyed through the transference an expectation that my mind would be unreceptive to their projections. I was often experienced as selfishly withholding my psychic space, which was felt to be unburdened by painful experiences. One of the patients often described me as "mean". She was convinced that I had "the answers" because my life seemed to her to be "cosy", but instead of relieving her of her pain I simply left her alone to work things out for herself. On one occasion, when I had to cancel at very short notice, this patient was convinced that I was going to have a last minute holiday. It proved impossible for her to even entertain the thought that I might be ill or have to attend to some serious matter. I was often therefore a depriving, narcissistic mother who was, moreover, experienced as provocatively flaunting her riches. This more provocative quality of the object was a striking feature in both cases: I was felt to be cruelly exposing what they lacked whilst I enjoyed privileged access to good things, in particular my unburdened mind. These young mothers were both at the mercy of an object felt to be narcissistically wrapped up in itself and in identification with it (as was evident in their own mothering).

The comforts of envy

The infant receives milk and other creature comforts from the breast. . . . Suppose his initiative is obstructed by fear of aggression, his own or another's. If the emotion is strong enough it inhibits the infant's impulse to obtain sustenance. Love in the infant or mother or both increases rather than decreases the obstruction partly because love is inseparable from envy of the object so loved. . . . The part played by love may escape notice because envy, rivalry and hate obscure it, although hate would not exist if love were not present.

(Bion, 1962: 10)

Bion's words were often in my mind as I worked with Ms A. whom I first met aged twenty-one. The needed, nourishing breast tormented her. Faced with the pain of longing for the object's psychic nourishment and love, hatred of the object provided a kind of comfort. Here the envious spoiling of the object was a defence against the pain of loving and the dependency this exposed. It killed two birds with one

311

stone, as it were: the envied object and the self who longed for the object (Segal, 1997). This process became the focus in my work with her.

Ms A. became pregnant aged sixteen. She was referred because of depression and difficulties in managing her son. From a clinical point of view, however, the most important feature of her presentation was her narcissistic personality. She was a bright and, in many respects, likeable young woman. By the end of the four years of treatment she had made some limited, but encouraging progress in her capacity to be more receptive to her son's needs.

Ms A. had been on drugs at a party when she had unprotected sex and became pregnant. Although not a heavy drug user she regularly smoked cannabis as a way of "not thinking", as she put it. Her parents were quite wealthy and had supported her financially, adopting a seemingly liberal attitude towards the pregnancy. Ms A. had nevertheless been suspicious of her mother's encouragement to proceed with the pregnancy at a time when it was clear that this would severely disrupt her studies and social life. She felt that her mother had envied her freedom and popularity with friends, especially since her mother had become quite ill around this time.

As our work unfolded it became clearer that Ms A. had always experienced her mother as exciting, provocative and unavailable. Ms A.'s mother had just turned nineteen when she was born. A picture of a narcissistic woman emerged whom Ms A. felt had resented getting pregnant. She had not had any more children, which had confirmed Ms A.'s belief that the mother had not really wanted her. The father had remained a hazy figure throughout her life: the provider of money but not much else as far as she was concerned. Ms A. shopped excessively, using material acquisition as a way of deflecting her need for the object's love. It was hard for her at first to even acknowledge that her parents had given her the money for shopping and for her analysis, if nothing else. Instead, Ms A. behaved as if this was "owed" to her, thereby bypassing an experience of being in any way dependent on them.

As a child, Ms A. felt she had always got in the way of her mother's work and her active and seemingly very exciting social life. She was left in the care of nannies for extended periods of time. This was the basis of her main accusation that her mother "wanted it all". It is, of course, impossible to know the actual quality of the mothering received by Ms A. I nevertheless gained the impression in the transference that she related primarily to an object felt to be wrapped up in itself and in some way denigrating towards her. I came to understand that Ms A. had not had an opportunity to internalise an experience of a maternal object freely offering her space in her own mind. This was at the root of her very entrenched grievance towards her mother.

Her son was experienced as spoiling the good things in her life. Ms A. ascribed malignant intentionality to his behaviour. For example, she once said to me that he had broken something in the flat "on purpose, to get at me because he knows I like it". She perceived him to be "without a care" or "always playing". She experienced this as if he were purposefully flaunting his freedom and this aroused her envy as she felt burdened by this thing she called "responsibility". Over time we came to understand that "responsibility" meant for her the burden of "thinking and feeling" for both of them. She envied therefore what she perceived to be his privileged psychic space unburdened by painful thinking or feeling. Of course, in reality, this little boy was very disturbed and burdened.

At some level Ms A.'s destructiveness towards her baby elicited profound guilt in her. But she could not turn to an internal object that could bear to know her and forgive her for what she had done to the baby. She had no choice, as it were, but to continue envying and hating her son who was felt to be the one draining her of all her resources. Grievance defended against the guilt about her own destructiveness.

Ms A. projected her view of her own depriving, narcissistic mother into her son and into me in the transference. She often ascribed a care-free, narcissistic, unthinking state of mind to me. She was then exposed internally to the presence of a "selfish", uncaring object who was felt to keep all good things for itself. This typically elicited a wish to rubbish or somehow spoil what I offered her or what she perceived to be good things in my life, as I hope to illustrate with a few sessions from the second and fourth year respectively of her analysis.

Year 2

In the Wednesday session Ms A. said that she felt very angry with her son because he asked too much of her when he had already taken all that she had. She accused him of being selfish and "always wanting more toys, more of everything", she said. She brought a dream in

313

which she answered a ring at her door and it was the porter handing her a parcel. She was then silent. I broke the silence and asked her if she could remember any more or had any thoughts about it and she replied emphatically that there was nothing more. She sounded irritated with me and I felt reprimanded for having asked for associations.

Ms A. added that she could not "afford the luxury of analysing dreams". She said that she had too much on her mind to "play around at being Freud" and anyway her life was still a mess thanks to me [she was referring here to her repeated accusation that I did not offer her enough practical help with her son]. I said that instead of helping her when she felt so besieged by her son's needs, she felt that I had handed back to her a parcel full of the feelings she wanted to get rid of whilst I kept a "luxury", fun parcel for myself.

On the Thursday session (the last session of the week for her), Ms A. sounded irritable. She told me that one of the schoolteachers had praised her son over a task Ms A. could never manage herself to get him to do (and with which this teacher had patiently helped this little boy over many months). She said that she had concerns about this particular teacher because she was often taking time off due to vague illness and her class then had to be run by an assistant teacher. She felt that they should not employ unreliable teachers. This was why she had decided to change schools because she did not have to put up with "their attitudes". She went on to say that she felt that as the school was a state school, the staff were probably envious of her more privileged background.

She then told me that she had been on the phone all day trying to get information about a breast enhancement. She said that one of her friends "had her breasts done" recently and she was now seriously considering this option for herself. She spoke to me about her hatred of her own breasts, which had been "sagging" since she stopped breastfeeding. [She had only breastfed her son for three weeks.] She had been thinking about breastfeeding on the way to the session after she had seen a woman on a bench in the park breastfeeding her baby: "There will be nothing left of them [the breasts] once he [the baby] has finished with them", she said. She then dismissively added: "My friends were having the time of their lives when my son was born and I was expressing milk. What fun! I gave up on this. Too much hassle . . . and the bottle anyway is good enough. He's such a little fatso [her term for overweight] so clearly it did him no harm." Her voice had a harshness to it that I had known on other occasions.

314

She went on to talk about how her friend's breast enhancement had not been such a success: "They look fake," she added somewhat disparagingly. [This was a friend who had been quite consistently supportive of her.] Her mood then flattened and she was silent for a while. I felt redundant in the session, a bit like the teacher and school who had been sacked by her.

She eventually resumed talking to tell me that her weekend was looking dreary because she had no help with her son as her parents would be away. She mocked her mother's tendency to "over-fill" her suitcase even when she was just going away for two days: "She always thinks she's going to see the Queen", she added. She said she had offered to pack her case because she wanted to spare her looking ridiculous.

Ms A. went on to say that she was fed up with everything and that despite her efforts to fit in analysis whilst she was also trying to resume her education *and* having to look after her son, she was still feeling stuck and unhappy. I was aware of feeling somewhat drained by her repeated accusations of being useless to her. Like her, I felt in need of some kind of breast enhancement. I said that she was surrounded by "chubby, over-full people", but that she felt drained of good things for herself. Ms A. said she hated analysis because it was "all talk" and she needed practical help. She thought that talking about feelings was overrated. She had recently read a review about a self-help book and she thought it was very good because it gave tips on how to manage. This is what she wanted and she said that maybe I should read it. She then angrily said that therapists should be more upfront about the fact that they never give actual help; instead they just talk about feelings. I said that she seemed to feel that my mind was full of useless ideas about feelings and that she now wanted to pack my mind with exactly what she thought should be in there about her for me to take away over the weekend. Ms A. laughed. She said that I had a way of putting things that made her laugh. I said that she hated the experience of actually feeling that what I offered her was of help; instead, it was more bearable to turn me into someone with "fake" breasts she could laugh at – not a real, helpful person she might actually miss.

Ms A. began to cry and then was silent for a long time. She eventually broke the silence and said she was upset because she felt that she was a bad mother and that she hated having to think about that, that she would rather be like her friend who was "without a care" and only had to think about where to go on holiday. Her tone then switched back into harshness and she called this friend "a stupid cow" because she had no idea about real life and anyway she just looked down on others. I said that she had managed to connect with an upset feeling inside when she saw herself as a "bad" mother and was able to tell me about it, but it quickly felt too painful. As soon as she connected with this feeling she hated me for making her think about these things, especially because I then went off for the weekend without any painful thoughts in my own mind. It was this unthinking, stupid cow of an analyst who was now looking down on her struggling with her feeling of being a bad mother.

Ms A. said: "Even the teacher is better than me at helping my son. I know she disapproves of me. They all do at the school. They all think: 'Rich kid gets pregnant . . . serves her right' ". She felt that everyone saw it as her mistake and that she had to pay for it. She said that her son had been a mistake she would have to live with for the rest of her life. "He's got it easy," she added. "Now he has me to do everything for him. He doesn't even have to think about brushing his teeth and then when he's older, because he's a boy, if he gets a girl pregnant he can just walk away just like his father did." She then shook her head and angrily repeated: "It's all crap, it's all crap anyway." She told me that she had been trying not to smoke [cannabis] but that she was going to get some because that was the only way she could feel at peace. She was planning to drop her son off at a friend's house and then she would just "get out of my mind".

I said that she feared that I disapproved of how difficult it had been for her to take pleasure in her son's recent achievement. It pained her that he could allow himself to be helped, but she could not. I said that she wanted to walk away from all this right now in the session and not have to think about anything. I added that this seemed like the only option open to her because she believed I also wanted to walk away now that I was faced with her feeling that what I offered her was "all crap". We were near the end of the session. Ms A. simply shrugged her shoulders and said that there was "a lot to be said for drugs". She was then silent until the end.

Discussion

In the Wednesday session Ms A. starts by telling me of her experience of feeling scooped out by her son's demands and then by me asking her to think about the dream. On reflection, I had intervened too quickly and unthinkingly, perhaps enacting the projective identification into me of this demanding, greedy child/mother who cannot think about *her* experience. She sees me only as interested in more good things for myself (her son, she tells me, always wants "more toys, more of everything"). She feels I ask *her* to provide me with analytic material for me to "play" with, but I give her nothing, leaving her to sort out the contents of her own mind whilst I have the "luxury" of playing at being Freud. By now in the work this was a familiar transference scenario whereby she experienced me as the one with no worries and no capacity to think about her. Like her mother, I was felt by her to always be in some other, more exciting, "luxurious" mental space where there was no space to think about her pain. Breaks were typically experienced by her as me cruelly forcing her to look at all the good things I had. By giving me her dream, she had wanted me to take away with me over the weekend a parcel full of her painful thoughts/feelings, but instead I became intrusive in her experience.

By the Thursday session Ms A. is feeling very besieged. She finds it impossible to enjoy her son's achievement and the fact that he was able to allow his teacher to help him. This helpful teacher becomes the target for the envious attack: she is unreliable and has to be sacked. Any envy is firmly located in the staff whom she feels envy her privileged background. The envious attack masks the pain of knowing that she actively spoils this good experience for her son. It is painful for her to acknowledge the teacher's help because this success horribly reflects back to Ms A. a sense of her own "badness".

Ms A.'s experience of feeling deprived is acute in this session, most probably because she is also facing the weekend break. I think she longs for me to feed her but this longing gets perverted: her envious undermining of me is her triumph over her desire. She tries to soothe herself through her thoughts about breast enhancement thereby letting me know that she can give herself something without needing to depend on me. I am anyway felt by her to be unreliable, like the teacher who goes off sick and all I offer is "fake" breasts anyway. Like her mother, I am narcissistically wrapped up in myself ("The Queen") and she has turned me into a useless object of ridicule that needs her help. The internal representation of the maternal object as "Queen" also conveyed Ms A.'s experience of her mother as cruelly parading the riches withheld from her. I think that it was

317

this more narcissistic quality of the object that fuelled the envious retaliation.

Ms A. is eventually able to respond to my interpretation about how she hates recognising any attachment or dependency on me and becomes distressed as she then sees herself as the bad mother. She manages to briefly stay with this feeling, which I think was genuine. But it then proves too much to bear and she quickly retreats into a denigrating stance: I become a stupid, unthinking cow "without a care". This is the state of mind she wants for herself (and that she lets me know she *will* get for herself later by smoking cannabis). In her experience I am like her son at this moment who, she says, "doesn't even have to think about brushing his teeth", while I leave her to think about being a bad mother. Crucially, at this point, I think it becomes clearer that her inability to allow space for a more feeling and thoughtful her is disrupted by the ascendance, again, of an experience of me not only as unable to feed her, but also as someone who would denigrate and shame her when at her most vulnerable. I think that Ms A. was in identification with this denigrating quality in her mother and she frequently experienced me in this way through projective identification.

Year 4

I would now like to present a brief excerpt from a session fifteen months later when she was coming only three times per week. By then Ms A. knew that I was pregnant. Before the announcement of my pregnancy she had in fact already decided to end the analysis because she was moving out of London. Although my pregnancy therefore was not the trigger for the ending, it did nevertheless mean that we would be ending three months before we had in fact agreed to end. This was the first session of the week for her three weeks after the announcement of my pregnancy. The week before I felt that we had made some meaningful contact.

Ms A. began by telling me that she had been listening to the radio whilst having breakfast and there had been a news item on child abuse. She was very critical of paedophiles and thought that there was no excuse for behaving in such a way towards children. As far as she was concerned such people should be locked up forever and, actually, the more she thought about it, she came to the conclusion that the death penalty should be brought in for those who committed the most serious offences. She went into quite a tirade about this. I eventually said that someone stood accused in her mind and had to be very severely punished.

Ms A. paused for a while, became tearful and then said that she had overstepped the mark the previous night with her son. She had shouted and sworn at him and then slammed the door behind her. He had been very upset. She regretted it but at the same time she was furious because he had torn up one of her photo albums. This was a particularly important one because it had photos of her days at secondary school and she liked to look back on this time. I said that there was perhaps a way in which my going off on maternity leave and cutting short the ending of our work felt like me perpetrating a henious crime against her – like me tearing up the album of our work together so that she was left with nothing good to hold on to. I said that she experienced this as spiteful, as me spoiling something important to her by effectively putting my needs before hers.

Ms A. said that she knew I had to stop. She felt ready to stop and in fact thought that she could have stopped much sooner as we were now "just covering old ground". She was silent for a while and then told me that she had a very bad dream two nights ago. She was not sure she should tell me about it "because it might come true".

Eventually she told me that in the dream I had given birth to a baby with Down's syndrome. She clearly felt uncomfortable elaborating. She became very restless on the couch and it took a long time for her to tell me that because of my age she thought it was more likely that I would give birth to a disabled baby. She imagined that I would find it hard working with someone like her at a time like this in my own life. It was nothing personal, but that's how life was – the older you got the greater the chances of disability. She imagined that I would not want such thoughts in my mind. She thought I had looked so happy since I became pregnant, "glowing and all that", she added. She said she could not bear to look after a disabled child. She hated herself for feeling this because she knew it was "wrong" but she felt repelled by disability: "I know people say babies with Down's syndrome are friendly, but I find them ugly." I said that she feared that I could not bear to look with her at her "ugly" feelings towards me. Instead, I would be repelled by the her who gives me a damaged baby. I said that she feared that I would neither understand her nor forgive her for this, but would sentence her to the death penalty instead.

Discussion

By the time this session took place Ms A. was more connected overall with destructive aspects of herself. She could think more about her grievance towards her mother and her son and by now she was more supportive of the therapeutic help he was also receiving.

Ms A. starts the session undermining the good work of the previous week by relegating it to a redundant "covering old ground". The dream is an envious attack on my ability to give life to a healthy baby. It also reflects her pain about losing me in the form of retaliation for the crime I perpetrate against her. My crime is not just that I leave her prematurely, but that I leave her so as to feed another baby when she is still so hungry. The experience of her own hunger for the breast and the fantasy of the baby inside me who will in reality have the breast triggers the wish to spoil and so she omnipotently gives me a disabled baby. Ms A. did feel envious of what she perceived to be my happiness about my baby and this gets projected into me when she voices how *I* will be envious of her youth.

I will not enter into further detail about the session. I simply want to draw attention to the heightened anxiety at the point at which she starts to tell me about the dream. One could understand this anxiety in different ways. I thought that it was connected to her experience of herself as spoiling something good for me and her fear about my response. Envy creates a fear of retaliation, which then reignites the destructive cycle. Ms A. anticipates an unreceptive mind that not only cannot bear to dwell on "ugly" feelings, but will actually punish her very brutally for having such feelings: I will execute her. The anticipated ejection from the other's mind is therefore experienced as brutal violence against the self and is terrifying.

Concluding thoughts

There are many possible readings of a paper as rich in ideas as *Envy and Gratitude*. For me, Klein's paper is fundamentally about the reality of the pain of loving and how envious spoiling is an attempt to obliterate any awareness of the anxieties that *will* arise when we can be vulnerable enough to love and accept our dependency on the other.

My work with young mothers and their children has helped me to appreciate that feeling "known" and forgiven by the object for one's destructiveness, as Klein evocatively draws out, fosters a capacity for loving. It promotes the most profound sense of gratitude towards our objects. It helps us to internalise a generous object that offers its mind freely and can therefore tolerate knowing about both the good and bad aspects of the self and other. Disturbances in the earliest relationship with the mother undermine the possibility for such an internalisation. In turn, as with Ms A., this can place the young mother and her baby at the mercy of a destructive cycle of envious retaliation.

Notes

1   I am referring here to work with adult patients who were born to adolescent mothers.
2   The mother's intolerance of the baby's access to good things may then be managed by establishing a relationship of ownership towards him. This thwarts the baby's attempts to separate from her. Instead, the baby is bound to her through obligation because she feels she has done so much for him. From the baby's perspective, I am suggesting that these are the foundations for an internal world dominated by an economy of ownership, debt and obligation.
3   I have chosen this expression because it has come up a few times in my work with young mothers where they have used it to refer to their perception of the baby's enviable state of mind.

References

Bion, W. (1962) *Learning from Experience.* London: Karnac.
Klein, M. (1957) Envy and Gratitude. In *Envy and Gratitude and other works.* London: Virago, 1988.
Laufer, M. and Laufer, E. (1984) *Adolescence and Developmental Breakdown.* London: Yale University Press.
Madigan, S., Moran, G. and Pederson, D. (2006) 'Unresolved states of mind, disorganised attachment relationships and disrupted interactions of adolescent mothers and their infants'. *Developmental Psychol.*, 42, 2: 293–304.

Pines, D. (1988) 'Adolescent pregnancy and motherhood: a psychoanalytic perspective'. *Psychoanal. Inq.*, 8: 234–251.

Segal, H. (1997) 'On the clinical usefulness of the concept of the death instinct', in J. Steiner (ed.) *Psychoanalysis, Literature and War.* London and New York: Routledge.

Slade, A., Sadler, L., Dios-Kenn, C., Webb, D., Currier-Ezepchick, J. and Mayes, L. (2005) 'Minding the baby: a reflective parenting program'. *Psychoanal. Study Child*, 60: 74–100.

Winnicott, D. (1954) 'The depressive potion in normal emotional development', in D. Winnicott *Through Paediatrics to Psychoanalysis.* London: Karnac.

"What is genuine maternal love?"

Clinical considerations and technique in psychoanalytic parent–infant psychotherapy

Tessa Baradon[1]

The question of what is genuine maternal love was posed by a mother struggling to understand and value the nature of her bond with her small baby. The question surfaced time and again in the context of this dyad's long-term parent–infant psychotherapy and has challenged me to examine my thinking and, indeed, has produced impassioned discussions within the Parent Infant Project team at the Anna Freud Centre. In this paper I will address this question through sessional material of this mother and baby and discuss issues of technique in response to it, including my counter-transference and conceptualization.

Asked about her position on the different heuristic models of the mind, Anna Freud replied: "I definitely belong to the people who feel free to fall back on the topographical aspects whenever convenient and to leave them aside and speak purely structurally when that is convenient" (Sandler with Anna Freud 1981). Parent–infant psychotherapy is a meeting point for the different disciplines addressing infant development: psychoanalysis, attachment, and neurobiological research. In facilitating our understanding of the ebb and flow of the therapeutic construction, Anna Freud's advocacy of conceptual flexibility in the aid of clinical expediency is often helpful.

The therapist working with young babies growing up in an environment of intergenerational deficits needs to understand the quality of mothering and the baby's predicament. Psychoanalytic concepts of "good enough parenting" and maternal failure, attachment paradigms of "security" and "disorganization," and neuropsychological discussion of relational trauma are useful frames of reference. Yet there is an additional ingredient to do with love, captured by the patient in her question: How can we integrate love into scientific and clinical discussion?

"Genuine maternal love" for the mother who asked the question was defined by selflessness. My clinical work has convinced me that the love of a mother for her infant and of a baby for his mother needs both measure and passion. It contains the temperate – that is, regulated kernels of love and responsivity, and passionate appetite, ownership of the other and capacity to be consumed by the other. These latter rest upon the mother's narcissistic love of herself in the baby, her adoration of "His Majesty the Baby" (Freud 1914), and her capacity to tolerate her hatred of her "bondage" to him (Winnicott 1949). Thus, her identification with her baby and yet her ability to differentiate between herself and her baby and allow individuation (Mahler *et al.* 1975) are required. Only then is the baby able to safely love his mother, in the sense of moving from relating to object–use (Winnicott 1969) and development of a sense of self as real. At the same time, "love" is not a static concept. In this paper I attempt to describe the development of this mother's love, matched by changes in her baby's expressed love for her, and the interventions that may have contributed to this process.

"Maternal failure" in psychoanalysis refers to intrapsychic processes in the mother which violate their infant's state of going–on–being, such as projection and attribution resulting in distortion of self (Silverman and Lieberman 1999), failure to protect the infant from impingements (Winnicott 1962), inability to contain the infant through "maternal reverie" (Bion 1962). "Disorganized" attachment describes a collapse of adaptive strategy when the infant is frightened, seen to develop in the context of mother's unresolved trauma and lack of reflective functioning thereof (Lyons–Ruth and Jacobvitz 1999; Fonagy 2001). "Relational trauma" depicts the neuropsychological disregulation of the infant in a situation in which danger emanates from the attachment relationship wherein the mother (a) disregulates the infant and (b) withdraws repair functions (Schore 2001; Perry *et al.* 1995; Tronick and Gianino 1986), leaving the baby in an "intensely disruptive psychobiological state" for extended periods of time (Schore 2001, p. 209). In this paper I consider those aspects of maternal "failure" and relational trauma that resulted from the mother's inability to meet her baby with passion and reverie. This included the negation of herself in him, dis–identification with his state of dependency, and projection into him with consequent distortion of self and object boundaries and impingements on individuation.

What is the experience of an infant within a primary relationship that fails to respond appropriately to his personal and intersubjective needs? From the observation of babies in this predicament, this maternal failure appears catastrophic. The infant patient, so danger-ously dependent on his mother's/caretaker's capacity to identify and understand, expresses extreme anxiety, fragmentation and, finally, retreat. Because the anxiety is embedded in their relationship – often underpinned and driven by intergenerational patterns of relating – it is enduring. Therefore the concept of cumulative trauma (Khan 1963), the repeated breaching of the adaptive and defensive struc-tures available to the immature ego, is pertinent.

Extreme maternal depression can constitute a situation of rela-tional trauma. Green (1986) discusses a situation where there is a mutative transformation of the mother from a live, vital presence to a dead detachment from her infant, and the trauma this inflicts on the baby. This is a particular situation where the infant has had an early period of resonance and lost it in the face of maternal loss and depression. But what of those infants who have been born into a relationship with a "dead mother", so to speak?

The psychotherapeutic work informs us about the experience and the developmental endeavors of babies in this predicament. Psychically they display the "dead baby complex" – a decathexis of the maternal object and apparent identification with the dead mother (Bollas 1999). These babies lie slumped and blank. They seem care-less of the maternal presence or non–presence beside them and appear non–present in their own bodies. Their precocious defenses of avoid-ance of emotional engagement with the mother, freezing and disas-sociation (Fraiberg 1982; Perry 1997; Schore 1994) put them in a state of unrailed/derailed development. I suggest that this was the predicament of the baby in the case to be discussed.

Parent–infant psychotherapy intervenes in the parent–infant system to achieve the best accommodations that can be made between a parent and baby for the baby's development. As an applied technique within the psychoanalytic framework it has its roots in the groundbreaking work of Selma Fraiberg and her colleagues (Fraiberg 1980; Lieberman and Pawl 1993). In recent years a model has been developed at the Anna Freud Centre (Baradon 2003; Baradon *et al.* 2005; James 2002; Woodhead 2004), the defining feature of which is the use of the analytic mind to scaffold the affective experiences and representations of parent and infant in relation to each other. Intervening at the procedural as well as declarative levels of self organization, the aim is to create meaning through validating and cohering the parent's experience and responding to the baby's requirement for an attentive, adult mind to meet his developmental and attachment needs.

In our model, the therapist straddles numerous roles in relation to her patients, both individually and collectively. She is a clinical "observer" (Rustin 1989), using observation as a mental stance and a technique to inform her understanding of the parent's and baby's (emergent) mental models of attachment relationships. She is, in parallel, an analytic therapist, employing psychoanalytic frames of reference and techniques in the work with what is manifest and conscious in the room and with the hypothesized unconscious fantasies and defenses underpinning these. Inevitably, she is a transference figure for the parent, sometimes benign but also at times perceived as hostile and/or persecutory. The therapist is a "new object" (Hurry 1998), offering a revitalizing attachment experience to parent and infant. As a new object for the baby, the therapist is also a "developmentalist," supporting the infant's development through providing contingent responses, stimulation, and regulation where the parent, at least temporarily, is unable to. In cases of severe maternal depression and withdrawal the therapist may also be the only "live company" (Alvarez 1992) for the child, providing the functions of "enlivening, alerting, claiming and reclaiming" (p. 197). Having the therapist to love, until the mother is able to receive and scaffold his love, may be pivotal for the baby's psychic survival. And finally, the therapist is an external affect regulator of the patient's disregulated states, particularly crucial in light of research suggesting that external regulation of the infant's immature developing emotional systems during critical periods may influence the experience-dependent structuralization of the brain (Panskepp 2001; Cirulli *et al.* 2003).

Parent–infant psychotherapy poses countertransference dilemmas particular to this method of intervention. Primitive emotions and projections are the fabric of infancy and parenting and invariably resonate with the therapist's past and present attachments. The actual presence of an infant in the room intensifies the sense of immediacy and clinical (and of course legal) responsibility toward the baby. With at least two, and often three, patients present – infant, mother, and father – the therapist's attention and receptivity are often pulled in different directions and her identifications may shift between the infant and parent, challenging the analytic stance. As always, the therapist's countertransference is used and must be watched – her own hopes and despair, riven identifications between mother and baby, and her rescue fantasies. Above all, the therapist needs to maintain sufficient emotional resonance with the mother, in the face of the acute emotional pain and helplessness of her infant. Without this there is no way for mother to empathically recognize the real infant as opposed to the infant within her whom she often treats with cruelty.

In the case under discussion, where the baby's early attachment needs were thwarted by his mother's failure to embrace him with "genuine" love, considerations of clinical process and technique were particularly charged. On the one hand, mother sought the ascetic and altruistic (A. Freud 1937) virtue of "genuine" love, devoid of all narcissistic investment and reward, and her severe depression was compounded by a sense of failing her own standards. On the other hand, her infant son was starved for the maternal appetite of ownership and adoration, and his experiences of going-on-being were distorted by her projections and hostility. These experiences of trauma for both baby and mother required ongoing scaffolding and regulation from me, the therapist, and I needed to be alert to the challenge to my capacities for "reverie" in my various roles and from within.

Thus the matrix of intersubjectivity, transference, and countertransference was extremely complex. It raised minute-by-minute questions of technique. Which patient/what material should be privileged at any given time, and in what domain of relational knowing (Stern *et al.* 1998) – procedural (psychological acts) or symbolic (psychological words) – would the communication be most effective?

Clinical material

Ms G was referred by her obstetrician just before her baby was due, with concerns about her depressive mood. A psychiatric report attached to the referral mentioned a long-standing history of eating disorders and self harm, and a number of attempted suicides requiring hospitalizations, the latest one year previously. Consequent upon the concern about this troubled young mother and her baby, a network of health and social service support was put in place.

Ms G was in a stable relationship with D, the baby's father. However, Ms G requested to attend without her partner, explaining that D reassured her that she is a good mother and that she needed her fears to be heard and not brushed aside. Although we ask to include fathers in the therapy where possible, I decided it was important to enable this mother to indeed be "heard" in her request and to explore the possibility of including the father after we had established a therapeutic alliance. In the course of the therapy father did become involved, but in this paper I will not discuss the work done with the triad. Mother, baby, and I met once a week for a period of two years. This paper focuses on the first year of therapy.

Tentative beginnings: mother, baby, and therapist

In the event, although I was in telephone contact with Ms G from the time of referral, we only met 3 weeks after baby Ethan was born. A vulnerable baby, he had required special care in the early postnatal weeks and Ms G stayed in hospital with him.

In the first session Ethan, still a fragile newborn, was asleep when they arrived. His painfully thin and pale mother sat sideways to me with her face averted. She spoke in a near whisper, her low voice and withdrawn facial expression camouflaging much of the terribleness of what she was saying.

Ms G explained that she had never thought she would have children as she was afraid that she would damage them. I wondered whether at the same time as being afraid to have a baby she had also perhaps hoped for one. Ms G thought not. She explained that the likelihood of conception was low as she has irregular periods because of her eating disorder. I asked how she had felt in her pregnancy and she said she had not wanted it, and had continued smoking and bingeing.

She had felt that the foetus was a parasite. She felt very guilty about this. I asked whether these kinds of thoughts were continuing. At this question Ms G became distressed, saying that she feels that she is "forced by him into an artificial position . . . of trying to be a good mother, who loves her child and takes care of him." Ms G said she does not feel like that much of the time. She added that she would not harm him physically.

Somewhere early in this conversation Ethan fretted a bit. Ms G immediately picked him up with extreme care and held him to her, his little body slumped against the palm of her hand. She checked with me whether she could feed him. She snuck him under her shirt, careful to keep her breast hidden. The "feed" was quickly over and Ethan went on sleeping. Ms G removed him from the breast and covered herself up.

We spoke about attending parent–infant psychotherapy. I wondered what she was hoping to get. She replied that she wanted a "filter" so that her feelings don't all come out on Ethan. I noted that I would not have been able to tell from her facial expressions and tone of voice when disturbing thoughts toward Ethan intruded during the session, and that from this I could tell that she was really trying to keep a tight grip on her feelings. Ms G reiterated her fear of damaging him through her depression as her mother, too, had been depressed and unavailable. I suggested that we would attend to both the good things that happen between her and Ethan, such as her gentle stroking of him that I had observed even when she was upset, and to her bad feelings and thoughts. Ms G hugged Ethan to her.

I felt that the central verbal and affective communication to me in this session was Ms G's sense of being damaged herself and, through her very being with her baby, of damaging him. Her state of primary maternal preoccupation had a particular quality to it: hypersensitive to the baby via herself, it seemed that projection did not aid her to "feel herself into her infant's place" (Winnicott 1956, p. 304) but that the infant was equated with her, as a disturbed extension of herself (King 1978). Moreover, his critical early hospitalization, in which her dread of damaging a child was actualized and exposed, seemed to have been a trauma which confirmed a psychic equation between her inner and external worlds (Fonagy and Target 1996; Target and Fonagy 1996).

In turn, I experienced Ms G and Ethan, separately and as a dyad, as extremely fragile and needing both to be reached out to and to be handled with care. On the one hand, I struggled with my own need to establish some contact with her averted face, as I strained to hear her whispers. I felt responsible for her very life, as I imagine rescue workers feel in response to the sounds of life after disaster. In this process of projective identification I assumed the omnipotence attributed to the "caregiver" in relation to the infantile self. At the same time I was acutely aware of the danger-in-contact ricocheting between us during the session, manifested in her whispers and cautious handling of Ethan. My association was to a sea of shards in which any movement could be calamitous. Only later did I realize how her history of self-cutting had penetrated my subconscious. Thus, from the beginning this was a dyad with whom I engaged in an intense and worried way, responding perhaps to her unconscious invitation to assume this mantle.

In the second session Ethan, now 4 weeks old, was a tiny little thing with big blue eyes and a peaky face. Initially he slept on his mother's lap, fists tightly clenched. Ms G stroked his hands but he did not relax his fists. A few times she pried them open and stroked his palms. Ethan's eyes flicked open when he heard a door slam and he started crying. He seemed to move quickly into a loud cry, with no fretting or building up toward the upset. He cried hard. Ms G put him to the breast and he sucked, then fell asleep. She put him on the mat and he opened his eyes. I spoke to him about his experience being in a big room and hearing my stranger voice and not knowing where it came from. Ethan stared fixedly toward the ceiling lights above him. After a while he turned his head slightly in his mother's direction, and confirmed that that was where his mummy was.

As I observed this tense baby, I wondered whether there was heightened sensitivity to invasive stimuli (lights, noise), carried over from the weeks in the special care baby unit. I also wondered whether he was already reacting to the conflicted and disregulated quality of maternal emotion, transmitted and received through the ministrations of care. His ordinary going-on-being seemed to be punctuated with periods of disassociation – as expressed in fixing on the lights, and "falling forever" – as expressed in his urgent cries. Again my own emotional responses were strong. This time the pull was toward Ethan, so desperately in need of enveloping in maternal love.

We had 6 more sessions over the following 6 weeks leading to the first break. The sessions acquired form and pace. Ms G sometimes looked my way and I found it less of a strain to hear her. Ethan moved between brief periods of wakefulness and prolonged periods of sleep. I found myself accommodating to their muted tone, characteristic of depressed mothers and their infants (Bettes 1988), by dampening my spontaneity, speaking slowly, riding the silences. But increasingly I also found my way to address the affects expressed verbally and in behaviors. Wary of the sadism of her superego and the masochism of her submission to it, I took care to acknowledge negative affect as conflictual, and positive interactions were noted without hollow reassurance that she was doing well. With Ethan I was relatively active, representing his mental states and communications, offering contingent responses, linking him up with his mother. I tried to balance offering myself to him for use as "live company" with awareness of Ms G's envy of what she perceived I had to give Ethan, and which she had never received. At times indeed I felt rich in resources, but at other times I felt dull and drained.

The meanings of dependency

When I collected Ms G and Ethan, now 12 weeks of age, from the waiting room after the 2 week break, Ms G gave me a very quick glance of tenuous pleasure and then turned away with an avoidance of my gaze and bodily withdrawal. I felt I had become dangerous again during the break – even more so as I believed, from her darting pleasure, that she had missed me. Ethan woke up as she put him on floor beside her. He looked bewildered. We settled on the carpet and Ms G placed Ethan against her feet, facing me. I thought she was in some way offering him as a "transitional object" for re-engagement. I adjusted my position so that Ethan could see my face directly. In so doing, I was also placing myself in Ms G's range of vision should she choose to raise her eyes.

I spoke to Ethan: "You're not quite sure where you are, are you? . . . you haven't been here for a while . . . have you?" He murmured. I asked him if it was all right to wake up in this room now, and Ms G reminded me that the last time he was quite upset. I acknowledged this. Ms G asked Ethan if he wanted to sit down and placed him on her lap. I said, "That way you are with mummy and can still see me . . . and still give these gorgeous little smiles." Ms G whispered, "Yeh." Ethan relaxed into her lap and looked back to me and made a gurgling noise. He gave a big smile and looked into my eyes for a few seconds, then looked away. Then he looked back, pursing

331

his lips, and eventually produced a rolling sound. In a lilting voice ("motherese") I to him, "It's a little conversation, isn't it?" His face opened and he smiled again, then looked away. I waited. After a few seconds he turned back to me. I said, "Are you ready to chat again? Hey . . . yes . . . yes . . . and when you've had enough you look away for a while, don't you?" Ethan gurgled again. Ms G looked down at Ethan and said, "He can be quite coquettish, sometimes he turns his head and looks from the corners of his eyes." I replied to Ethan, "mmm . . . hmm . . . I guess you're taking a breather then, aren't you, we adults do the same. Yah . . . Take a little break in a conversation, ah, otherwise it gets too much, doesn't it?"

Ms G's response to me in the waiting room suggested that the break had been experienced as an abandonment, in which I failed her as her primary figures had, and left her to struggle alone with disintegration. Yet, she allowed me access to Ethan (suggesting some goodness was retained) and through him, to herself. In talking to Ethan I was engaging in a process of emotional regulation through scaffolding his efforts at regulation (looking away) and placing them in the intersubjective domain. Using Ethan as a displacement, I could model for Ms G the process of ordinary, developmental self and interactive regulation (Beebe *et al.* 2003) in the pacing of an interaction. I was struck that the coquettishness she attributed to him in fact described her own conflict between engaging with me and withdrawing (e.g. when it "got too much").

Later in the session Ethan was sleeping, with Ms G stroking his head and hand. She related a visit by friends who played with Ethan. She asserted that he was happier when with them. I wondered whether she had felt the same when I was talking with Ethan earlier? Ms G prevaricated, "I couldn't see the expression on his face so I don't . . . he does smile at me, but he often spends a lot of time seemingly just staring at me with quite a pensive look on his face. . . ." I noted his looking to her earlier. She replied that she worried: "Should he be smiling at me more? Obviously he does smile at me and not something behind my shoulder that's taken his interest." I asked, "What are you like with people, do you carefully observe their expressions, maybe sensitive to what feelings they're communicating towards you?" Ms G said that she was trained from an early age to be aware of what somebody's going to need or want. I asked whether she was afraid sometimes of what he might see in her face. Ms G answered slowly, "I'm sure . . . that . . . that in my face there'll be the ambivalence that I often feel towards him . . . or my own difficult feelings that may have nothing to do with him."

In my experience, a mother questioning her baby's love for her is attributing her own conflicts to the baby. Ms G's fear that Ethan really preferred the company of others seemed multilayered, containing the fear of his rejection of her, a projection of her wish to get away from him, and the rivalry with him over me. At this point I was unsure whether words alleviated or intensified her conflict and I also felt that the urgency of Ethan's need for her was overriding. I therefore chose not to follow the route of interpretation and simply commented that he had been looking at her. Ms G was able to make use of my validation of Ethan's desire for her to express her conundrum – can she allow personalization: "Should he be smiling at me more?" This offered an opportunity to explore what Ethan might be avoiding. I learned that Ms G habitually scanned the object for their affective communications/demands and that, since Ethan's needs and wants evoked her hatred, it felt dangerous for him to look into her face/mind as he may see those emotions in it.

I was aware that she had not related to Ethan for some length of time and asked whether she was feeling ambivalent about Ethan there and then in the session? Ms G said she was not sure . . . perhaps her instinct was to touch him but she did not want him to feel smothered by her. She wondered if she is not perhaps too disengaged with him. I suggested that, on the contrary, I thought she was very engaged with him but that she is protecting him from the toxicity that she felt was passed to her by her mother and which she fears she may pass to Ethan. Ms G nodded. She said she wanted to make it clear that her mother did the best she could at the time and added that of course she feels that it wasn't good enough. I rushed in too quickly at this point, saying that perhaps in her attempts to protect Ethan she was keeping a distance between them that prevented them from spontaneous exchanges, such as laughing and playing together. Ms G replied that Ethan may in years to come experience her as in a state of severe depression or absent from him. Almost under her breath she murmured that if she were to leave through dying she would not come back. Ms G was quite tearful and picked Ethan up, caressing him. Then she said that she is not sure whether she's holding Ethan because he is a soft, comforting thing . . . and she put

333

him down on the floor, on his side facing away from her, and at a distance. He sucked hard on his hand and just lay there, looking into space.

The whole interaction was extremely painful as baby and mother seemed quite unable to come together. The essential elements of adoration and appetite for the baby were missing from Ms G's love. It seemed that his dependency, need, and desire for her resonated with the representation of him as parasitic during pregnancy – depleting her of self-hood. The transference to Ethan was thus of a consuming object like the mother of her childhood. This dilemma is likely to have been accentuated by her feelings of abandonment by me during the break. In an identification with the aggressor (myself), feelings of dependency and need in herself and in her baby were denied. At the same time, Ms G cared intensely that her child should not experience the maternal toxicity or disappointment in the object that she suffered. In this way, distancing him was an act of love as well as cruelty. Ethan, to my concern, veered between disintegration and precocious defense.

I felt caught in the middle and responsible for the devastation, as though during the break the therapy had replicated the hollow maternal stance – the offer of dependency withdrawn. Thus my maternal "best" was in fact toxic also for Ethan via the impact it had on his mother. Certainly my "too quick" response contained a veiled criticism (also reversing the attack on me): in protecting Ethan from damage you are in fact killing off a live relationship. Obviously, I may have responded from the countertransferential reserves of my own tetchy narcissism. We also know from clinical experience that past relational trauma can be reproduced in the present therapeutic situation, in the transference–countertransference transactions. Yet I think I was also "nudged" into the patient's unconscious wish-gratifying role (Sandler 1976), as Ms G went on to speak of Ethan's (and of course my) possible future loss of herself. The habitual solution to overwhelming dependency and inevitable disappointment was destruction of self and object.

With my therapeutic goods thus spoilt, resonating her emptied state, I was unable to protect Ethan, who was put down and away from us. As he lay rigidly on his side looking into space, I felt I was witnessing his emergent identification with the dead mother (Bollas 1999) – a kind of dying in situ.

Good enough loving and impingements

"I am trying to understand," said Ms G two months into treatment, "what is genuine maternal love?" She feared that when she did experience maternal feelings it was because of her "delight in his need (for her)" and that, therefore, her "motives are suspect." She weighed her gratification about his complete dependency on her against her wish to walk away. "I have to keep asking myself what is this about? Is it about me? About Ethan?" She dismissed my suggestion that it may be about both of them, and I commented on her fantasy that the ideal mother is selfless. Ms G confirmed this ascetic representation of the genuinely loving mother and said that the "ideal mother could understand all the baby's needs," thus rearing "emotionally, mentally and physically strong children." She said she was humbled now when she saw others managing to do this.

Ms G's repudiation of gratification as a constituent of the maternal bond could be traced to her grievance with her mother, past and present, in which she felt "used" by her mother for her own narcissistic needs. Moreover, she held her parents responsible for her damaged mental state and, even as an adult, had no real sense of volition to modify the childhood feelings of helplessness.

Yet, despite the relentless grip of the past, I observed her handling of Ethan extend to more animated exchanges. Ethan responded to these tentative "protoconversations" with widened eyes, excited kicking, and large smiles. He seemed to gain efficacy as a partner; for example when he lost her attention he would call her back by looking at her and cooing. When I pointed this out, Ms G said that friends visiting had commented that Ethan's eyes followed her wherever she is – tracking her voice when he could not see her.

As the months progressed the sessions felt safer, more predictable, encompassing a broader range of feelings, allowing Ms G to offer less ambivalent parenting and Ethan aspects of "good enough" relatedness, and thus also development. Indeed, during this period in the therapy, there were times in the sessions in which Ethan was a contented little baby.

However, these quiet periods of regulated positive affect were also the backdrop to rapid transition into states of inconsolable crying. I noted that sometimes Ms G reached out to Ethan, and he, in the process of being attended to, became distressed. His tiny body became rigid and he clawed at his mother's body. At such times Ms G moved through a repertoire of feeding, winding, rocking, walking – seeming to act promptly and contingently to effect "interactive repair" (Tronick and Weinberg 1997).

Four months into treatment, Ms G raised the question: Why is it so hard to soothe Ethan? Was he damaged at birth, would another mother get it right? I tried to explore with her what happens to her when he cries. Ms G confirmed that she gets very upset. I suggested that sometimes Ethan's cries feel like her own. Ms G became tearful and then reprimanded herself for not always acting the adult with him. I said that perhaps when they are both crying she no longer feels the mother. I also spoke about the rage that she feels when he triggers her pain. Ms G whispered that she feels so guilty and ashamed.

Thus, it was becoming clearer the extent to which Ethan was the barometer of her own emotional state. When his needs did not resonate with her own conflicts, Ms G was able to respond. Unpredictably, however, his ordinary infantile needs could trigger or link in with her own volatility. This is another aspect of relational trauma – where the quality of affective communication with the baby imparts trauma from the mother's internal world to that of the baby.

Through the most careful observation of their affective interaction and of my own countertransference, I came to understand a particular quality of interaction that was perilous to both. Ethan's cries retraumatized Ms G as her own unconsoled state as a small child came flooding back. At this point he became the frightening child to his mother, re-evoking her own disorganized attachments (Main and Hesse 1990). Unconscious conflict then permeated her ordinary maternal ministrations of feeding, changing, and soothing, and Ethan was disregulated by his mother's care. Balint (1992) describes this as "unconscious communication" – direct communication between the unconscious mind of a mother and her infant, in which the baby perceives and internalizes aspects of the mother's life of which she is herself unaware. And just as the meaning of her own affective state was unrecognizable to Ms G, so Ethan's communications could not be understood and contained. Their distress ricocheted between them, escalating to the point of collapse. What could I model in the sessions in terms of a holding response?

(Session continued) . . . When Ethan got restless I spoke to him. He responded with attentive pleasure. At one point he cooed extra loudly and drowned out Ms G's soft voice. I said playfully, "I couldn't hear your mummy there, do you mind!" Ethan kicked gleefully in response to my crooning voice and smiles at him. Ms G became very tearful. She said it was the ease with which I relate to Ethan and she has to try so hard.

I thought that addressing her envy would undermine her further, but perhaps she was ready to perceive his desire for her. I therefore asked what could help her recognize the cues from Ethan about good things he gets from her. Ms G's face became very tense. I felt I had suddenly frightened her. I wondered whether Ethan's love and dependency were difficult to recognize? Perhaps because she could not have these experiences as a child, as her mother was too depressed to be able to tolerate such feelings in her? Ms G whispered she did not want to repeat what had been her experience. I said that I thought she was struggling between her wish for Ethan to have a better experience and her fear of recognizing her importance in this and thus his dependency on her. Ms G said forcefully that other people's dependency on her was enormously difficult.

By this time Ethan was fretting and I wondered whether he needed his mummy again. Ms G sat Ethan between her legs and he looked at her. I said to him that he had called his mummy and she had gathered him up. Ethan sucked and chewed on his mother's fingers. This was the first time, I think, that he did not have a feed in the session.

Faced with a baby responding with joy to interactions with me (in the absence of such exchanges with his mother), and a mother who felt diminished by this, I was in a conundrum: to embrace the one seemed to be a rejection of the other. It was as though I had to experience the possibility that only one of the dyad could survive. If I was unconsciously being faced with the choice between them I, equally unconsciously, resisted it by re-placing Ms G as the object of her son's love. Perhaps I hoped that Ms G would allow herself the experience of Ethan's giving her pleasure and making her proud. Because she was more able to respond to cues of distress but not those of joy in relation to her, he was missing out on swathes of exchanges around emotional sharing, crucial for his development (Stern 1985; Trevarthen 2001). Indeed in this sense Ms G was not able to facilitate Ethan's development as an "emotionally, mentally, and physically strong child."

Yet, as the therapy progressed, it seemed that by my modeling more playful exchanges with Ethan while emphasizing my "notmother" status, Ms G was sometimes able to respond contingently and offer herself to be used by him.

337

Separation–individuation

In the course of a longer-term therapy the infant naturally moves from a state of total dependency on the mother toward the beginning of separation–individuation. This offers an opportunity to work with the mother's conflicts as they impact on her baby at each developmental phase.

In the treatment of Ethan and Ms G there were hints from the beginning that separation, like dependency, was an area of extreme difficulty. Ms G's history held no personal experience of moderated separation, only that of violent, mutually destructive rupture. The risk for this dyad was that separation–individuation would plunge mother into narcissistic despair and rage.

Sleeping and feeding were ubiquitous arenas for expression of conflicts over separation in Ms G's history and were, perhaps inevitably, the areas in which the conflicts were played out with Ethan.

In the early weeks Ms G reported that Ethan would fall asleep only when lying on her chest. This meant that any movement of his woke her up. She moved Ethan to his Moses basket at her side, but kept vigil through the night. She recalled childhood fears of the dark and of sleeping alone and felt unable to tolerate Ethan's cries when put into a cot. At the same she felt driven to madness and despair by lack of sleep. D, with his own difficulties in this area, was unable to offer support, and soon Ethan was restored to the parental bed. Ms G's chronic insomnia was thereafter channeled into night-times ruminations as she waited for dawn so as to escape from the bed to a strong coffee and cigarette.

With Ethan waking hourly, sleep disturbances became woven into the conflicts around feeding and weaning. Ms G repeatedly expressed her feelings that feeding was the sole good thing she could give him and admitted her gratification that only she could provide this. However, these feelings also came into conflict with her experience of his dependency as depleting. In the sessions I observed feeding encompass many regulatory functions, so that Ethan was put to the breast when he cried, when he was tired, when they were both at a loss as to play. With feeding used to meet such a variety of situations, it became difficult to tell when he was hungry.

At around 5 months of age, Ethan's weight began to drop and professional concerns about failure to thrive emerged. Medical opinion moved toward supplementary feeds, with a bottle also offering a possibility of respite from the hourly feeds at night. Ms G came under increasing pressure to achieve some measure of weaning. Her internal split was thus effectively externalized, with the medical network and her partner now carrying for her the thrust for forced separation, while she maintained the ubiquitous place of breast-feeding. It seemed important that at that point I did not 'know' what would be best, and held neither a wish for Ms G to wean nor for her to continue feeding.

During this period, Ethan 6–9 months, many threads in the therapy seemed to coalesce around the question of closeness versus distance and the losses implied in each. Week by week Ms G described her dread of the long days with Ethan while D was at work. She felt mired by his wish for her presence, for example crying when she left the room, and her inability to let him cry. She said that before Ethan was born she spent much of the time alone. I wondered if that was her way of keeping her emotions on an even keel and she confirmed this. I suggested that having Ethan with her all the time meant that she has no means of regaining her "emotional balance" (her words). Thus the closeness was experienced as loss of self, provoking rage. Getting away was a relief at that level, but it also brought with it the fear that she could disappear from their lives and it would not matter.

As Ethan became more mobile he could initiate movement toward and away from his mother.

Seven months into treatment. I noted how Ethan seemed to want to be close to her today. Ms G said she did not know if she wanted him close or not. She said her guilt at not really wanting his "relentless" closeness makes her try harder. I then witnessed this as Ms G finally allowed Ethan – who had been struggling for a while to get into her lap – to find a place there. He crowed and cooed and bounced. From the outside their little "reunion" seemed pleasurable and yet Ms G was talking about times when she feels she cannot go on. I asked whether those were times when she harmed herself. She was silent. Ethan seemed to get extremely boisterous in her embrace – sucking on her arm and blowing raspberries. He appeared to be both kissing and biting her and I said this to him. My thought was that they both moved between intimacy to destructiveness with confusing rapidity and that, despite being with them, I could not tell what felt good and what bad.

It is interesting that at age 8 months, when biting could be considered as a normal expression of desire (incorporation) and/or exploration, I attributed destructiveness to Ethan's biting of his mother. Was I taking on Ms G's attributions? In which case Ethan was subject to my projections as well as his mother's. Was I picking up on a particularly aggressive quality of relating in Ethan that could be a pointer to derailed development at this age? If so, why did I not follow this through with an explication of his aggression as reactive to his mother's unresolved ambivalence? Certainly, addressing his predicament would then need to have been privileged. In retrospect, I think that my shifting identifications with mother and with baby were enacted here through muddled, partial interpretations.

Just as imaging the baby's ordinary movement toward separateness was not available to Ms G, she was also not able to manage a normal loss through establishing the triad of mother, father and baby (Daws 1999). I noticed in the sessions that I felt increasingly forced to relate to Ethan, with Ms G watching and withdrawn, or to Ms G – with Ethan either observing or dis-engaged. Thus, the father/therapist was seen not as a gain but as a threat to the symbiotic tie. In the issue of weaning, the bottle symbolically represented the competent, third object, and there was a concrete idea that the bottle would deliver Ethan to his father. With this came powerful statements from Ms G that D and Ethan were doing so well together. There was affective undertone of not being needed any more, and I was left with a concern that intense pressure on her to wean could precipitate a crisis, primarily in terms of her desire to stay alive. My anxiety about a possible suicide attempt was high, and I checked that the network was in place. In retrospect, I believe I was also caught up in powerful projections around loss of myself, as we were approaching another break (9 months into treatment).

Anticipating this loss Ms G thought she and Ethan would miss their sessions with me, but she continued to insist that the solution was disengagement and self-sufficiency. Separation, as an intrapsychic process leading to growth, still felt beyond our reach.

Enacting rupture

On their return after the holiday, Ms G appeared terribly thin and wan, while Ethan seemed to have gained bulk and weight. My first thought was "he's feeding off her!" He also looked strikingly like his father, as though fulfilling her fears of losing him to D. They each responded to me with a measure of reserve.

Ethan took his time before he approached me: gazing at me from a distance and looking worried. After a while he gave me a smile and I smiled back and asked whether he was beginning to forgive me for the summer break. Ms G told me that on their holiday everyone had adored Ethan and that he had gone easily to the men but not to the women who wanted to pick him up. I wondered whether she was linking Ethan's reserve with me to this. She shrugged. I asked her what she made of her observation. She said, "It's like being run over by a red car and then not liking red cars afterwards." I said it seems to have reinforced her fear that she was not a good mother and as a result all women were like red cars to Ethan. Again she shrugged, this time seemingly in agreement. Ethan was crawling about – initially energetically but then looking lost. A number of times he headed toward his mother and then veered away. When he absolutely ran out of resources he crawled to her and tried to clamber onto her lap. Ms G held him loosely, pulling away a bit and getting her hair out of his clasp. She then abruptly stood up muttering that he needs a climbing frame, carried him over to one of the chairs and stood him there. Ethan looked tiny and forlorn across the room. I felt shocked. She came back to her place on the cushion. I said she was equating herself with the chair, as though it was not her – his mother specifically – that he needed. She replied that she does not want him to depend on her for his happiness. Feeling very anxious about what I was about to say, I asked whether she wanted him to be independent of her so that she could do away with herself if she felt she needed to. Ms G looked pale. She whispered that this was very selfish. I said perhaps she thought that in order to continue living she needed to feel that she could kill herself. Ms G said everybody had their escape routes.

Ethan had crawled back to our vicinity and was searching Ms G's bag. He pulled out a plastic container with food. We watched as he struggled to get an apple out. I accompanied him with words: is he wanting the apple, can he get to it? He managed to extract the apple and tried to bite into it. I asked him if he can eat it, is it too big? I said maybe Ms G thought I was fussing too much. She moved closer to him and asked him if he needed her to cut it for him, but Ethan had in the meantime made indentations with his teeth. He chewed on the apple for a while and then tried to get the bottle of baby food out. Ms G watched him closely and I found it agonizing that she did not capitalize on his interest. When she finally, tentatively offered him some food, he spat it out. She immediately put the bottle of food away. Shortly after this he began to cry.

Ms G told me that at D's insistence she had taken Ethan to a nursery that morning. I asked how they had felt about it. She said Ethan had choked on a brick during his visit. She conveyed immense sadness. I said she seemed torn between loving Ethan and wanting his love for her, and her fear that this dependency in both of them would take away her escape route. I suggested that the long break had probably also brought up these feelings in relation to me. Ethan was getting more upset and when picked up by Ms G he clung to her strongly. I said to him that he was showing his mummy how much he needed her and how frightened he gets when she thinks about leaving him. Ms G carried him over to the windowsill and sat him on it so he could look out. Ethan calmed, and soon after this it was time to end. Ms G fled the room clutching Ethan in her arms.

The story of the holiday could have been taken entirely as a transference communication: I had "run over" her dependence on me and left her, prematurely, to feed herself. Thus forsaken, she felt driven toward her habitual escape routes of self-denigration and self-harming, both to rid herself of her shaming infantile needs and as a retaliatory attack on me. Her rage with me was communicated in the narrative of the red car and enacted in substitution of climbing frame/chair for self, that is, in her refusal to embrace Ethan – again, an identification with the perceived aggressor.

A central dilemma in parent–infant psychotherapy is when to take up the transference to the therapist? Certainly the negative transference was in the forefront and needed addressing. However, my initial attempt to relate to my perceived dangerousness (via Ethan's avoidance of me) was shrugged off. I reckoned that to pursue the transference and/or her defenses could be experienced by Ms G as retaliation on my part (Steiner 1994). In retrospect, it is the displacements that perhaps could have been taken up, for it is there that the experience of cruelty lay. Addressing her rage with me may have relieved Ethan from the burden of carrying it.

With the rupture (break) with me unsufficiently reflected upon, what followed was Ethan's performing a transference enactment of failed self-feeding while the intergenerationally depriving mother stood by. By this point I was able to address the struggle to manage

alone, but although Ms G carefully watched Ethan, her active intervention came too late (like mine) and was rejected. I wondered
whether in fact Ms G experienced me as empathic toward Ethan
when I had been withholding toward her, and this perhaps contributed to her not helping him feed. I also thought she was possibly
punishing me through forcing me to witness her abandonment of
her child (which was painful to watch). In a similar vein, going to
nursery was experienced as forced upon them, with life-threatening
consequences. However, Ms G's sadness was here undefended and it
gave coherence to the preceding narratives. Acknowledging the
need and the pain allowed some movement – by the end of the
session Ethan was ensconced in Ms G's embrace.

The following session Ethan was unusually free and playful,
particularly in relation to the apple. He held it, bit into it, he lay on
the apple and rolled around. I noted Ethan's playfulness and Ms G
said she too had noticed it – it was so different from his clinging. I
suggested that he might be picking up that she and I were trying to
work something out and it was a relief to him. Ms G said, "Maybe
he is being trustful."

"Falling in love" as reparation

In one of her earliest sessions Ms G asked, "When does one know
that reparation has taken place?" "Reparation" was her choice of
word, denoting making up for her destructiveness. Toward the end
of the first year of treatment we came back to this theme. It was a
period of creativity following the enactment of rupture described
above. In the sessions there was a shift, with Ms G taking a slightly
more reflective stance (i.e. less rumination and self-reproach) than
hitherto. In the core relationship toward Ethan, so dominated previously by her ambivalence, there seemed to be a small flowering of
love. Between them there was a more robust link, which enabled
Ethan to move to and from his mother and to refuel from a distance
through gaze. Ethan also established his own little routine in the
sessions. He would start by checking out the toys and re-establishing
himself with me – little smiles, crawling over to me, gradually
climbing up to explore me. Then he would go over to Ms G's large
bag and get out his food parcel – an apple and berries in a plastic
bag. He had to work hard to get his hand into the bag, but Ms G

monitored his endeavors and encouraged him. Ethan then ate his fruit, swallowing some and spitting some out. Gradually eating and playing/exploring became somewhat more integrated, and he moved between the activities and us.

He approached his first birthday and this preoccupied Ms G. She said she still had not found the perfect present. She mentioned a cloth she'd had as a comforter which had worn away – she wished she still had it to give to Ethan. I said it sounded that she was wanting to protect and comfort him for the years to come. She replied that she had a lot to make up. I said this made me think of the perfect present as representing a wish to make good their very difficult early beginning. Ms G spoke of reparation and I thought she was also wondering about repairing something for herself. Her emphasis was on her wish to protect Ethan's trust and expectations that people will respond to him kindly. I suggested she may have felt unprotected and that cruelty hit her abruptly as a child. Ms G spoke about her mother doing her best, but that it was not good enough. She added that her mother does a lot of charitable work but she wishes she could have given the same to her children. I said that perhaps she feels that sometimes both her parents didn't really do their best and that some of the cruelty she experienced came from them – and this is what is so hard for her. Ms G struggled with this, though she did not deny it.

Ethan had finished eating and messing and was exploring under the table where he discovered the telephone wire and plug. Ms G initially asked him not to play with the cord and then went over and picked him up. Ethan gleefully crawled back to the table and Ms G became firmer in her tone of voice. I spoke about what was happening between them, reflecting that he really enjoyed being gathered up by his mother and had found a hide and seek game which he could play with her.

This session was characterized by a sense of calmness and reflection between Ms G and myself, the adults, and playful exploration on Ethan's part. It felt that I was allowed to hold a position of the benign "third," and this was perceived to be containing to both baby and mother.

The quest for the perfect present seemed to capture Ms G's regrets about the lacks of their beginning together, and her wish to celebrate their coming together through the love she had discovered within herself for her child. In wishing to extend the "comforter"

344

from her childhood to him, she also may have begun to mourn the lonely childhood she had, and to relinquish some of the envy of her child for the maternal comfort he could still have in his. Ethan's play with the telephone cord seemed to represent hope for more genuine, encompassing communication between them through which he could be gathered up and contained.

Discussion

Ethan's first birthday also heralded the end of our first year of work together – a good time to take stock. The wish, and failure as yet, to find a "perfect present" seemed symbolic of what had been achieved and of that which still needed to be addressed.

Ms G had approached parent–infant psychotherapy with the wish for a "filter" to protect her baby from the transmission of damage she felt had been done to her by the parenting she had received. In equal measure, although more hidden, was the fear of being damaged by her baby. This mutual threat was created through their very existences in relation to each other. As Ms G said, "Can one damage one's baby just by being available?" In the transference I was also often a source of danger, most spectacularly around breaks when my unavailability confronted Ms G with the extent of her dependency on me and my maternal failure to hold it. Ethan's postnatal vulnerability – his smallness, sensitivity to lights and noise, seemingly low threshold to "unpleasurable" experiences and the difficulties in comforting him – intensified the sense of fragility and risk. My countertransference fantasy that we were constructing the therapeutic space within a sea of shards highlighted the power of the emotions, projections and enactments.

In the course of the first year of the therapy there were some changes in the quality of the relationship between Ms G and Ethan. The most significant was the expanding sense of maternal love for Ethan. In the early months Ms G's fear of, and guilty hatred for, her baby's dependency overrode her ability to accept more benign feelings in herself. She defensively adopted an ideal of altruism that negated not only her passions but also his. Ethan was forced into precocious inhibition of attachment behaviors toward his mother. His turning from her, and her failure to meet her ascetic standards, compounded her depression. In the course of the first year of therapy there was a lessening of Ms G's preoccupation with the question of "genuine" maternal love and a move toward more ordinary, at times "good enough," mothering. She seemed more able to acknowledge and tolerate her wish to be central to Ethan and, albeit less consistently, her importance to him. Her gaze and facial expressions conveyed growing adoration of him. He in turn, could risk transferring his attachment from me to his mother. What facilitated these changes?

Perhaps "falling in love" could start to take root only after there was some measure of surviving the destruction and despair brought from her past primary relationships into her present ones. By the third quarter of the year Ethan, although delayed, was making up for the early impingements, and developmental tests confirmed he was on track. Thus Ms G's psychic reality of the inevitability of damage could, sometimes, be challenged by a different, external voice. Ethan, for his part, seemed to capitalize on the openings in their relationship and became more forward in expressing his desire for her. This, too, was a positive reinforcement which Ms G could at times perceive.

In the transference relationship with me I, too, was surviving her destructiveness and was not retaliating with narcissistic demands of my own. Thus Ms G was meeting with a different "motherhood constellation" (Stern 1995) from the persecutory internal one, one in which the intergenerational mother could be experienced as containing and repairing of the damaged child.

The clinical process, as the sessional material indicates, took place in the procedural and symbolic domains. Interpretations – using words as a means of giving meaning – were important to this mother, as were verbal (vocal, tonal) representations of his mind to Ethan. The procedural processes seemed to cohere more slowly. At first, the misattuned emotional "dance" between mother and baby was repeated in the interactions between the three of us. In time, I became better at matching and repair of the spontaneous gestures and affects that constitute "authentic person-to-person connection" (Stern *et al.* 1998, p. 904) and this then framed the developing relationships between mother and baby and myself.

Because so much in the earliest transactions between Ms G and Ethan was driven by her negative transference to him, offering myself as someone who could simply be with mother and baby and could reflect on them in relation to each other without fear of damage, seems to have been important. For quite some time it seemed that only in my mind could their survival as a dyad be contemplated. This raised the question of which patient should be privileged from moment to moment – Ethan, mother, father (present or absent), the relationships? At times I left a session feeling that more work should have been done with Ethan, for example to enhance his efficacy in engaging his mother. At other times I felt that the focus should stay with Ms G, to address her depression and the defenses and distortions that constituted her zone of safety but also derailed the relationship with Ethan. Despite the compelling nature of Ms G's narrative, it was crucial to keep Ethan in my mind at all times, so as not to slip into individual therapy in the presence of the baby. These issues were all the more urgent given Ethan's young age and the chronicity of Ms G's difficulties, spanning critical periods in his development.

Alongside the changes that marked the achievements of our first year together there remained areas of great vulnerability in their relationship. It seemed that the quality of love Ms G was able to offer Ethan was contingent on her emotional state at any given time and the extent of preoccupation with herself. Often Ethan had to make do with the crumbs of emotional availability that penetrated her depression and withdrawal. Not able to love herself in her baby, or to allow his appealingness to reflect on her, Ms G could not really entertain exuberant passion and appetite in her relationship with Ethan. Moreover, to be "consumed by the other" was only too real a threat and to be avoided at all costs. Thus Ethan was not able to safely experience himself as an object of hatred as well as of love. His own actions directed at separation–individuation were still, at times, subject to transferential attributions that frightened Ms G and evoked her rejection of him. In turn, Ms G's fluctuating emotional state, and particularly when she became extremely depressed, could be frightening for Ethan, betrayed initially in disintegrative crying, and later in occasional veering away in the midst of approach or a momentary freezing when mother seemed annoyed.

These thoughts about clinical process are relevant to the question of whether "genuine maternal love" exists. It seems to me that what Ms G captured in this term was the affective quality of her love for her baby. In presenting the question she was disclosing her knowledge that something was going very wrong for them. At the same time, bringing the question into the therapy also underlined Ms G's hope to do better by her baby: whatever her state of mind, however conflicted she was about the therapy, Ms G and Ethan attended their sessions without fail. In using the therapeutic space to risk intimacy, Ms G and Ethan were constructing their particular version of "genuine" love – somewhat more measured and a little more vibrant at the end of the year than at the beginning.

For myself – I was intrigued by this question in the context of my work with attachment disorders. It seems an important concept to hold in mind in the course of the therapy with mothers and babies. In the face of conscientious maternal care, it provides a framework for understanding a particular quality of "maternal failure" and ensuing relational trauma for the baby. It also suggests an outline of the clinical process that may be needed to free up object hunger and to encourage the risks of appetite and dependency, identification, and individuation in a dyad.

Note

1   The Anna Freud Centre Parent Infant Project team – Carol Broughton, Jessica James, Angela Joyce, and Judith Woodhead – have provided valued collegial consultation during the course of this work and on the paper. I also want to thank Dilys Daws for her interesting comments.

References

Alvarez, A. (1992) *Live Company*. London: Tavistock/Routledge.

Balint, E. (1992) *Before I Was I*. New York: Guilford Press.

Baradon, T. (2003) 'Psychotherapeutic work with parents and infants', in V. Green (ed.) *Emotional Development in Psychoanalysis, Attachment Theory and Neuroscience*. London: Brunner-Routledge.

Baradon, T. with Broughton, C., Gibbs, I., James, J., Joyce, A. and Woodhead, J. (2005) *The Practice of Psychoanalytic Parent-Infant Psychotherapy*. London and New York: Routledge.

Beebe, B., Rustin, J., Sorter, D. and Knoblauch, S. (2003) 'An expanded view on intersubjectivity in infancy and its application to psychoanalysis'. *Psychoanal. Dial.*, 13: 805–841.

Bettes, B. A. (1988) 'Maternal depression and motherese: temporal and intonational features'. *Child Dev.*, 59: 1089–1096.

Bion, W. (1962) 'A theory of thinking'. *Int. J. Psycho-Anal*, 43: 306–310.

Bollas, C. (1999) 'Dead mother, dead child', in C. Bollas *The Mystery of Things*. London and New York: Routledge.

Cirulli, F., Berry, A. and Alleva, E. (2003) 'Early disruption of the mother–infant relationship: effects on brain plasticity and implications for psychopathology'. *Neuroscience and Behavioural Reviews*, 27: 73–82.

Daws, D. (1999) 'Parent–infant psychotherapy: remembering the Oedipus complex'. *Psychoanal. Inq.*, 19: 267–278.

Fonagy, P. (2001) *Attachment Theory and Psychoanalysis*. New York: Other Press.

Fonagy, P. and Target, M. (1996) 'Playing with reality: I. Theory of mind and the normal development of psychic reality'. *Int. J. Psycho-Anal.*, 77: 217–233.

Fraiberg, S. (1980) *Clinical Studies in Infant Mental Health: The First Year of Life*. New York: Basic Books.

Fraiberg, S. (1982) 'Pathological defences in infancy'. *Psychoanal. Q.*, 1, 1: 612–635.

Freud, A. (1937, reprinted 1942) *The Ego and Mechanisms of Defence*. London: Hogarth Press and Institute of Psycho-Analysis.

Freud, A. (1981) See Sandler, J. with Freud, A.

Freud, S. (1914) 'On narcissism: an introduction'. *S.E.* 14: 69–102.

Green, A. (1986) 'The dead mother', in A. Green *On Private Madness*. London: Hogarth Press, pp 142–173.

Hurry, A. (1998) *Psychoanalysis and Developmental Therapy*. London: Karnac Books.

James, J. (2002) 'Developing a culture for change in group analytic psychotherapy for mothers and babies'. *Br. J. Psychother.*, 19, 1: 77–91.

Khan, M. M. R. (1963) 'The concept of cumulative trauma'. *Psychoanal. St. Child*, 18: 286–306.

King, P. (1978) 'Affective response of the analyst to the patient's communications'. *Int. J. Psycho-Anal.*, 59: 329–334.

Lieberman, A. and Pawl, J. H. (1993) 'Infant–parent psychotherapy', in C. Zeannah (ed.) *Handbook of Infant Mental Health*. New York: Guilford Press.

Lyons-Ruth, K. and Jacobvitz, D. (1999) 'Attachment disorganisation, unresolved loss, relational violence, and lapses in behavioural and attentional strategies', in J. Cassidy and P. Shaver (eds) *Handbook of Attachment: Theory, Research and Clinical Implications*. New York: Guilford Press, pp 520–554.

Mahler, M. S., Pine, F. and Bergman, A. (1975) *The Psychological Birth of the Human Infant*. London: Hutchinson.

Main, M. and Hesse, E. (1990) 'Parents' unresolved traumatic experiences are related to infant disorganised status: is frightened and/or frightening parental behaviour the linking mechanism?', in M. Greenberg, D. Cicchetti and M. Cummings (eds) *Attachment in the Preschool Years*. Chicago: University of Chicago Press, pp 161–182.

Panskepp, J. (2001) 'The long-term psychobiological consequences of infant emotions: prescriptions for the twenty-first century'. *Neuro-Psychoanalysis*, 3, 2: 149–178.

Perry, B. (1997) 'Incubated in terror: neurodevelopmental factors in the "cycle of violence", in J. Osofsky (ed.) *Children in a Violent Society*. New York: Guilford Press, pp 124–149.

Perry, B., Pollard, R. A., Blakely, T. L., Baker, W. L. and Vigilante, D. (1995) 'Childhood trauma, the neurobiology of adaptation, and "usedependent" development of the brain: How "states" become "traits".' *Infant Mental Health Journal*, 16, 4: 271–291.

Rustin, M. (1989) 'Observing infants: reflections on methods', in L. Miller, M. Rustin, M. Rustin and J. Shuttleworth (eds) *Closely Observed Infants*. London: Duckworth, pp 52–75.

Sandler, J. (1976) 'Countertransference and role-responsiveness'. *Int. Rev. Psycho-Anal.*, 3: 43–47.

Sandler, J. with Freud, A. (1981) 'Discussions in the Hampstead Index on "The Ego and Mechanisms of Defence": ll. The application of analytic technique to the study of the psychic institutions'. *Bulletin of the Hampstead Clinic*, 4, 5: 5–30.

Schore, A. N. (1994) *Affect Regulation and the Origin of the Self*. Mahwah, NJ: Lawrence Erlbaum Associates, Inc.

Schore, A. N. (2001) 'The effects of early relational trauma on right brain development, affect regulation, and infant mental health'. *Infant Mental Health Journal*, 22, 1–2: 201–269.

Silverman, R. C. and Lieberman, A. F. (1999) 'Negative maternal attributions, projective identification, and the intergenerational transmission of violent relational patterns'. *Psychoanal. Dial.*, 9, 2: 161–186.

Steiner, J. (1994) 'Patient-centred and analyst-centred interpretations: some implications of containment and counter-transference'. *Psychoanal. Inq.*, 14: 406–422.

Stern, D. N. (1985) *The Interpersonal World of the Infant*. New York: Basic Books.

Stern, D. N. (1995) *The Motherhood Constellation*. New York: Basic Books.

Stern, D. N., Sander, L. W., Nahum, J. P., Harrison, A. M., Lyons-Ruth, K., Morgan, A. C., Bruschweiler-Stern, N. and Tronick, E. Z. (1998) 'Non-interpretative mechanisms in psychoanalytic therapy'. *Int. J. Psycho-Anal.*, 79: 903–921.

Target, M. and Fonagy, P. (1996) 'Playing with reality II: The development of psychic reality from a theoretical perspective'. *Int. J. Psycho-Anal.* 77: 459–479.

Trevarthen, C. (2001) 'Intrinsic motives for companionship in understanding: their origin, development, and significance for infant mental health'. *Infant Mental Health Journal*, 22, 1–2: 95–131.

Tronick, E. Z. and Gianino, A. F. (1986) 'The transmission of maternal disturbance to the infant', in E. Z. Tronick and T. Field (eds) *Maternal Depression and Infant Disturbance*. San Francisco: Jossey-Bass.

Tronick, E. Z. and Weinberg, M. K. (1997) 'Depressed mothers and infants: failure to form dyadic states of consciousness', in L. Murray and P. J. Cooper (eds) *Postpartum Depression and Child Development*. New York: Guilford Press, pp 54–81.

Winnicott, D. W. (1949) 'Hate in the countertransference'. *Int. J. Psycho-Anal.*, 30: 69–74.

Winnicott, D. W. (1956) 'Primary maternal preoccupation', in D. W. Winnicott *Collected Papers: Through Paediatrics to Psycho-Analysis*. London: Tavistock Publications Ltd.

Winnicott, D. W. (1962) 'Ego integration in child development', in D. W. Winnicott *The Maturational Processes and the Facilitating Environment*. London: IPA Library, pp 56–63.

Winnicott, D. W. (1969) 'Use of an object and relating through identifications'. *Int. J. Psycho-Anal.*, 50: 711–716.

Woodhead, J. (2004) 'Shifting triangles: images of father in sequences from parent–infant psychotherapy'. *Int. J. Infant Observation*, 7, 2 and 3: 76–90.

13

Infant–parent psychotherapy on behalf of a child in a critical nutritional state

Selma Fraiberg and Edna Adelson[1]

In this paper we describe the treatment of an infant boy who was referred to our Infant Mental Health program at 5 months of age in a grave nutritional state. The baby was starving. His growth curve showed an ominous downward plunge which our pediatricians read as the profile of an infant who was moving toward the critical (and sometimes irreversible) state which is broadly covered by the term "failure to thrive." The term "failure to thrive" describes those infants who show growth failure in the absence of any organic cause. In strict usage it is employed for infants whose weight has fallen below the third percentile. It is almost universally associated with the impairment of the mother's capacity to nourish both in the concrete and in the psychological sense of the word.

The typical course of medical treatment for a failure-to-thrive infant is hospitalization with intensive one-to-one nursing care. With nurse-mothering and the introduction of a good nutritional regime, the baby begins to thrive. When his nutritional state is stabilized, he returns to his home. Typically, these gains are lost within a few weeks and the baby may return to the hospital again – and the cycle renews itself.

It is the mother who is the key. Whether or not the baby will thrive outside of the hospital depends upon the mother's capacity to follow the medically prescribed regime to insure adequacy in caloric intake for her baby and to provide the psychological nutriments for growth and development. But the dietary advice given by the hospital and the later guidance which focuses only on caloric intake and omits the developmental needs of infants are not successful (Whitten *et al.*, 1969). All reports agree that families of failure-to-thrive infants are difficult to reach and to engage in continuing contracts. However, a more favorable outcome is reported by Leonard *et al.* (1966) and Barbero and Shaheen (1967) when mothers were able to collaborate with the physician, social worker, or public health nurse in a satisfying relationship established during the child's hospitalization and continued into the posthospitalization period. Barbero and Shaheen describe their experience in which parents are encouraged to become active members of the hospital care team. They speak with feeling for the parents who see the child's improvement during hospitalization as a threat to their competence. "It is around this point that the art of the physician is required to avoid such injury to the parent" (p. 644). In evaluating their experience, Barbero and Shaheen conclude: "Early case-finding and diagnosis are vital links in the process of intervention" (p. 644).

In our own experience at the Child Development Project we have benefited in several cases from "early case finding." We are indebted to the pediatricians, nurses, and social workers at the University of Michigan's Mott Children's Hospital who read the ominous signs in a child's nutritional state and a mother's incapacities to nurture.

Our Infant Mental Health Program brings the skills of a psychiatric team into the home. Clinical assessment of the child and his family and close collaborative work among the clinical specialists on our staff are carried out within the framework of home visits. The treatment program which evolves is provided by one primary therapist who may be a social worker, a clinical psychologist, an educational specialist, a pediatric nurse, or a psychiatric resident. The therapy is conducted in the family living room (or the kitchen). The baby as patient is usually present with one or both of his parents. The sessions are, of course, focused upon the baby and his development, the parental concerns, and inevitably the conflicts which are impeding the parent in his or her relationship with the baby. Our concerns for the parent as well as the baby have made us welcome visitors to many "hard-to-reach" families.

"Back at the office" there is a supporting team for every therapist and every family. The therapist – even the expert with years of clinical experience – discusses his case with a consultant in regularly scheduled sessions. We have found this plan vital to the conduct of our program. The work with infants in jeopardy and their parents is painful, often emotionally depleting to the therapist. To sustain energy, hope, and objectivity; to insure that the best professional resources of our clinic are brought to the treatment program for each child; to examine the treatment process in fine detail – we need each other and use each other's support and expertness.

Our work is guided by psychoanalytic principles and two of our senior staff members are child psychoanalysts who participate in the case review and planning in all intensive treatment cases. However, the treatment program for each family is properly speaking a collaboration of disciplines in which social work, clinical psychology, developmental psychology, special education, pediatrics, medicine, and nursing are united with psychoanalysis in every phase of the work.

In the case of Billy and his teenage parents which we describe in this report, Vivian Shapiro was the primary therapist, Edna Adelson and Selma Fraiberg were the consultants.

Billy at 5 months

Billy Douglas was referred to our project by the Child Health Center at the University of Michigan Medical Center when he was 5 months old. Billy vomited after each feeding. He had not gained weight in 3 months. He was a full-term healthy baby, whose birth weight of 8 pounds put him in the 70th percentile. At 5 months he weighed only 14 pounds 5 ounces and was in the 25th percentile. He had become a tense, morose, somber baby who looked, in the doctor's words, "like a little old man." Dr. Robert Larson, then a pediatric resident at the Child Health Center, had worked intensively with Billy and his young mother for 2 months. Sensing the potential gravity of Billy's situation, he had begun to see Billy and his mother weekly at the outpatient clinic. He did extensive diagnostic studies and tried various medical interventions. He was puzzled, however, because there seemed to be no observable medical explanation for Billy's feeding difficulties. He also realized that the mother was becoming increasingly depressed.

Kathie Douglas was an anxious 17-year-old girl who had married Billy's 21-year-old father, John, only 2 months before Billy's birth. She was often unable to carry through with suggestions regarding food and medication. Dr. Larson called in a public health nurse to

354

see Billy and his mother weekly at home. Despite their best efforts, however, the doctor and the nurse observed that Kathie and Billy were not responding to their advice. At 5 months Billy's situation was critical. He was regressing and hospitalization was being considered. Further, Kathie seemed even more depressed, distant, and sometimes confused.

The medical team decided to make a referral to our Project. They requested both immediate clinical assessment and possible treatment for Billy and his mother. They were not certain there was a connection between the baby's health and the mother's deteriorating emotional status, but they felt that a better clinical understanding of Kathie and her baby might help explain why Billy was physically regressing and also indicate what psychological and medical interventions were needed.

Clinical evaluation

Our first task, then, during this medical emergency, was to make a psychological assessment of Billy and his family. The therapist began twice-weekly visits to the home for direct observation of the baby, his parents, and their modes of interaction.

Under all ordinary circumstances we devote approximately 5 weekly one-hour sessions to the clinical evaluation period. In Billy's case, the nutritional and psychological perils were so great that we knew, after the first three visits (1½ weeks), that intervention on a concrete educational basis must begin before the psychological complexities were fully understood. These earliest visits, however, gave us vital clues which we could pursue in the emergency period.

Initial observations of Billy and his parents

When the therapist first arrived at the Douglas's small apartment, she met a timid, sad-faced 17-year-old girl, who was Billy's mother, and a gaunt young man, the father, barely out of his teens, who was so uneasy that he did not acknowledge her presence until almost the end of this visit.

The therapist's first impression of Billy brought the doctor's words to mind. "Billy looked like a little old man." Billy was in his crib.

355

He was up on his hands and knees, staring at the door, when she entered the room with his mother. His eyes met the therapist's with an intense stare and a fixed smile. His stare never wavered.

Billy was motorically very precocious and was able at 5 months to turn over quickly, to creep, to grasp and manipulate objects. On the whole, however, he was a very tense baby. All of his movements and efforts at communication had an urgency that was unusual in a baby of this age. When the therapist held him for a moment, she could feel the strain and tension in his body.

Billy seemed unusually aware of sounds. In particular, his mother commented that Billy responded quickly to any sounds related to feeding. She illustrated this by opening the refrigerator door while Mr. Douglas held the baby. Billy almost jumped out of his father's arms, his mouth opened, anticipating food, and his whole body strained toward the refrigerator. As his mother approached him with an eyedropper with vitamins, Billy, still in his father's arms, leaned back, opened his mouth, his hands became inert, and he looked like a starving baby bird awaiting food from his mother. Mother and father seemed uncomfortable with Billy. They treated him like a newly arrived stranger whom they had to approach cautiously and from a distance.

In early home visits the therapist saw that Billy spent his day either amusing himself on the floor or in bed. He was capable of spending a lot of time in solitary play with toys. There were few signs of human attachment. Even though he could creep, Billy rarely approached his mother. He rarely made eye contact with her. He rarely smiled unless his mother used gross tactile play. When he fussed his mother put him to bed with a pacifier and honey.

Billy's mother said sadly that Billy did not enjoy cuddling. She said that when she held him in her arms, he seemed to turn away from her. In fact, neither mother nor father held Billy in a close ventral position. They held him so that he was constantly facing away from them.

Already, it was obvious to us that this baby and his parents were out of synchrony with each other. There was none of the normal spontaneity or joy in mutual gazing one would expect between parents and baby at this age. Billy was a somber, tense baby who seemed to be starving. His mother was also morose and somber and, as we shall see, both parents were hungry and starving in their own way.

We soon learned that this new family was in a state of great stress and deprivation. They were living in poverty, supported only by Mr. Douglas's small earnings and food stamps. In addition to the financial stress, Mr. and Mrs. Douglas had lost the support system of their extended families by their move to a strange city. They felt abandoned and overburdened. There simply were not enough financial or emotional resources in this new family unit to satisfy the needs of mother, baby, and father.

Billy's mother, at 17, seemed pathologically young and childlike. Her schoolgirl face, her T-shirt bearing a high-school insignia, gave her the appearance of a girl surprised by the events that had brought her to motherhood.

In response to the therapist's comment that this year must seem different from last year when she was still at school, Kathie spoke of her feelings of loss. She missed her hometown, her high-school friends. She missed going to school. So much was unfinished and now everything had come to an end. In her mind Kathie was not Mrs. Douglas; she was a misplaced teenager keeping house. All this emerged in a sad and distant voice. The therapist was struck by the depth of Kathie's depression, which was evident in her posture as well as in her words. Her range of affect was constricted. Her movements were slow. Her speech was halting, and she seemed distant and sometimes confused. She rarely made eye contact with the therapist.

The full weight of Kathie's depression soon became evident. She said that most of the time she was holding back feelings of rage that were so strong that "if I let go, I would kick the walls out of the house." She was having many somatic complaints, headaches, backaches, gynecological problems, and was also overweight. She sadly spoke of herself as feeling and looking like a fat old lady. She felt guilty about imposing on her husband for his time and attention.

John Douglas was also very young. At 21, he was haggard, thin, frightened, and embarrassed by difficulties he could no longer cope with by himself. He was much more hesitant than Kathie to engage in any interaction with the therapist. He literally turned away from her during her first few meetings with him. When he did talk to her, it was through a teasing question to Billy. "Billy, do you want to go home with her?" We believe he was simultaneously expressing his ambivalence about Billy and questioning the therapist's attitude toward his own worth as a parent. The first time he directly looked

357

at her and smiled was about a month after she started visiting when he told her that Billy seemed happier, that he liked to play more.

Billy's state and his feeding problem made intervention imperative, yet, after two sessions in the home, we had not yet observed a feeding which would provide tangible clues. Although the therapist had arranged to come at mealtimes, Kathie avoided feeding Billy in her presence. Kathie was, perhaps, not yet sure of her, not yet ready to reveal herself in the situation in which she was most inadequate. It was in the third session that Kathie volunteered to let the therapist see how Billy was fed.

How is Billy fed?

As part of our assessment a video play session was arranged at our office playroom.[2] This session was primarily planned so as to permit the baby's own play as well as spontaneous mother–baby interaction. What occurred gave us a sobering picture of the isolation and the estrangement of baby and mother. As if he were alone in the room, the baby engaged in solitary exploration of toys and furniture. He never once sought his mother with his eyes. He was mobile, but never crept toward his mother. His mother looked distant and self-absorbed.

Then Billy uttered sounds of complaint. His mother said that it was time for his bottle and volunteered to feed Billy. She said, "Watch what he does when I show him the bottle." She placed the bottle on the floor, several feet away from Billy, who was on hands and knees. Billy's face registered alertness and urgency – no smile, but urgency. And the 5-month-old baby began to creep the long distance toward the bottle. He reached for it unsteadily, but could not quite grasp it. Finally he did grasp it, mouth open hungrily, but it was bottom up. He could not quite orient it. At last he got the nipple into his mouth. He sucked solemnly, greedily.

While the therapist watched this scene, masking her inner pain and horror, the schoolgirl mother explained that this was the way Billy took his bottle. "He likes it that way. He likes to have his bottle alone, on the floor." After a while the therapist suggested that Mrs. Douglas sit with Billy in our rocking chair and feed him. The second observation gave us another piece of the puzzle. Kathie now held Billy loosely in her arms. Billy was still supporting his own bottle. The mother, looking tired and apathetic, said that Billy usually finished his bottle in 4 minutes. "Sometimes, however, if the bottle is slow, it takes an hour." She talked as though it were his feeding, not something that she had anything to do with. She herself looked distant and empty. Our impression was that although Billy was in his mother's arms, he was still feeding himself. There was no mutual gaze, and little tactile contact. The mother was right: the baby turned away from her. She looked uneasy and sad and sometimes irritated.

Later in this visit Kathie started to rock herself in the rocking chair while holding Billy loosely in her arms. She looked like a little girl rocking herself, almost a parallel play situation, the hungry adolescent mother rocking and nurturing herself, allowing her baby to drink his bottle in her arms. Yet, as cold as the scene appeared to us, Kathie seemed to get some pleasure from this unusual closeness between herself and Billy. While watching this videotape later she commented that this was in fact a good feeding, a better feeding than usual.

Why can't Kathie feed her baby?

As a treatment team we reexamined the videotape and the detailed notes of the home visits. We asked ourselves, "Where shall we begin? This is a schoolgirl mother who cannot feed her baby and who avoids physical contact with him." To encourage intimacy in feeding leads at best to mechanical compliance, as we saw on tape. There were few rewards for mother or baby.

Yet, we must promote this intimacy and proper feeding and we must, at the same time, seek the answers to the crucial diagnostic questions that will lead to help. What lies behind the avoidance of physical contact? Is it the destructive rage which Kathie had expressed in her first session? "I could kick the walls out of this house." Is it the mother's own unsatisfied hungers, body hungers as well as psychological hungers, which have led her unconsciously to withhold love and nourishment from her child? Was there something else on the mother's face and in her voice and manner as we watched the video story. An aversion to feeding? Disgust?

We would have to find out much more. But a teenage girl, even under more favorable circumstances, does not give her trust so readily to a helping person. We would need time to explore the dimensions of this conflict. But this teenage girl was a mother, her baby was our patient, too – and the baby was in great peril.

No case report can ever do justice to the feelings of the therapist who works with infants and their parents. There is an urge to rescue the baby who is in danger, to mother him oneself. There are deep reproaches, even anger toward the schoolgirl who is starving her baby, which must be expressed and which must be dealt with by the therapist lest it intrude in the work. In this situation we were helped by the fact that all of us are child therapists. We saw the mother herself as a child, an unfinished adolescent who still needed a mother herself. She was frightened, helpless, hungry, depleted. This did not imply that the therapist must become a mother or a mother substitute, but if we understood the child who was the mother and responded to her feelings of anguish and deprivation, we might earn her trust. Only on this basis was there hope for treatment.

In the home visits that followed the illuminating feeding session, Kathie began to respond to the therapist's deep concern for her as well as the baby. She began to speak of deep revulsion in the feeding of Billy. She was repelled by Billy's vomiting, she confessed, and had been since his birth. She was sickened by the sight, the messiness. The therapist saw for herself the horror and panic which came over Kathie when she anticipated – or only imagined – that the baby was going to spit up or vomit.

At the end of a bottle feeding (Billy was taking his bottle on the floor), Kathie hurriedly picked up Billy to burp him. We would expect, of course, that she would hold Billy upright against her shoulder. Instead, she rushed to the bathroom with the baby, faced him over her arm so that he was hanging over the bathroom sink – and Billy vomited his meal into the sink. In this way Kathie avoided her worst fears that the baby would throw up in her arms. And the strategy that she employed virtually guaranteed that the upside-down baby would throw up his dinner!

Until the therapist discussed her observations with Kathie, it had not occurred to the mother that she was precipitating the baby's vomiting. In her mind the only alternative was dreadful: to have the baby vomit in her arms. Thereafter Kathie could tell us more. She had noticed that when Billy was 3 months old and had begun taking solids in his diet, the hue and texture of the vomit had changed. She was so repelled that she reduced Billy's solids to a minimum as a way of avoiding the revolting mess. We now had another vital clue: the decline in Billy's weight curve had started at 3 months.

What, in fact, constituted Billy's daily food intake? Kathie was not sure. During the first visits the therapist often heard Billy's piteous cries of hunger. When she said to both parents that Billy seemed very, very hungry, they were astonished. The father said, "Do you think he is still hungry? I think he is just like me. I could never be satisfied. I could eat everything that was given to me right now." The mother said resentfully that Billy never seemed satisfied; he was always begging for food. "If we gave him everything he wanted, he'd eat us out of house and home."

It soon became clear that neither of these young parents had any real sense of how much food Billy needed. Actual hunger was part of their daily experience and they had to limit severely their own appetites in many ways. At some level both Kathie and John seemed to feel that Billy would simply have to share in their hunger. Apparently, they did not fully understand that his life was at risk.

Assessment and intervention plan for the emergency period

Our initial assessment gave us many of the vital clues to Billy's feeding problem. Billy was starving. But he was not "refusing" food, he was being deprived of food. The vomiting, according to our observations, was induced by his mother's unique procedures for burping, which were in turn related to her dread of being defiled by vomit.

The psychological picture was beginning to emerge: a teenage mother who avoided contact with her baby; a baby who crept toward his bottle on the floor and fed himself; a mother who had a deep inner revulsion against messiness and possibly toward the baby himself; a mother who was afraid of her own destructive rage; a mother who was an adolescent with unsatisfied bodily and psychological hungers.

The baby was in nutritional peril and in great psychological peril, for in none of our observations did he show signs of attachment to either of his parents. At an age where preferential smiling and vocalization should emerge toward the baby's partners, we saw none. At an age where the baby normally seeks eye contact with his partners, we saw gaze avoidance. At an age when a mobile baby seeks his partners through his own mobility, Billy sought no one. He did not enjoy closeness in his mother's arms, and was stiff and resistant in the arms of any human partner. His mental abilities seemed well within the Bayley ranges (Bayley 1969), which testified for some adequacy in stimulation and experience.[3] But what could not be measured through any existing scale was the effect of emotional impoverishment and unsatisfied body hungers in this baby, now almost 6 months old.

At this point we faced a therapeutic dilemma. As clinicians we knew that the psychopathology of these young parents, and particularly the mother, would not be accessible to us within a few weeks, but the baby could not wait for the resolution of his mother's neurosis. In this medical and psychological emergency we formulated our plans for the first phase of treatment. We would concentrate on the feeding problem, giving direct advice and guidance. We would do everything possible to promote the attachment of baby and mother. We would use our clinical insights to guide us during this emergency period, but we would not expect to gain full understanding of the parental psychopathology at this time.

The transference to the therapist would be fully utilized in this emergency period. This was an adolescent girl with her own developmental needs. The therapist's professional caring could be a form of nurturance for the mother. The adolescent need for identification models could be employed in a sensitive offering of this professional help.

The emergency period of treatment

The period that we speak of as "emergency treatment" lasted for 2 months. It was really synchronous in time with the assessment period. During this period Billy began to eat normally, the vomiting virtually ceased, and he began to gain weight in a stable and satisfactory manner.

The therapeutic relationship

The therapeutic sessions with Billy and his mother took on a pattern that was set by Kathie. She had chosen a meeting time at home

362

shortly before Billy napped. At the beginning of each visit, the focus was on Billy. Either the therapist and Kathie would observe Billy playing or Kathie would feed him or have some questions or – more often – complaints about Billy. Usually, midway through the visit, Kathie would put Billy to bed and the remainder of the time would be hers.

The therapist found out very quickly that if she responded to Kathie's own needs and feelings, either covertly or overtly expressed by her, Kathie would soon, and often in the same session did, attend to some of Billy's needs. For example, as the therapist acknowledged that she understood how hard it was for Kathie to try and hold a baby who turned away, Kathie was able to hold Billy with tears in her eyes instead of putting him down.

Many aspects of the positive transference became available to the therapist in helping Kathie on behalf of Billy. Kathie was initially very dependent and related to the therapist as a child to mother. (For example, when the therapist visited, she had to let herself in, hang up her coat, find a place to sit down while Kathie often continued to sit slumped in a chair in the living room.) The therapist responded to Kathie's need for a mother, while taking care, of course, to offer her another kind of "caring for Kathie" which was part of a therapeutic relationship.

The therapist sympathized with Kathie's sense of loss in leaving her own family and in leaving childhood as an unfinished adolescent. She responded to Kathie's feelings that no one cared for her and that she was physically deteriorating. She helped to arrange free medical service for Kathie at a health clinic which had been available but which she had not been able to seek out. She encouraged Kathie in her efforts to finish high school, and praised her for any accomplishments regarding her own efforts to continue her artwork.

We knew that Kathie felt inadequate, had been told she was by her mother, and in a sense by Billy himself as he repeatedly seemed to reject her food. The therapist was very careful not to compete with Kathie in any way for Billy's attention, nor did she actually intervene and do things for Billy, even though at times she could hardly restrain herself. It was important for Kathie to feel that the therapist, as a child consultant, identified with her as a mother facing problems in caring for her baby and that she had confidence that Kathie, with her help, could give Billy what he needed to be a healthy baby. Together they observed Billy, his preferences and his dislikes and took joy in any of his accomplishments. Billy's accomplishments were always related back to Kathie's efforts. The therapist especially shared her observations with Kathie of any special feeling that Billy expressed toward her, as his mother, such as a preferential smile or a reaching out to her. Kathie's feeling of failure was so strong that she was amazed when Billy preferred to go to her rather than to the therapist. She clung to any bit of evidence that Billy liked her. When she saw the scene of herself in the rocking chair with Billy, she said, "That looks so peaceful. Billy looks so contented."

Guidance: infant nurture and mother nurture

Within this framework, and relying very largely upon the positive transference, the therapist introduced suggestions for feeding and burping Billy that were effective in a very short time. While these issues are treated topically in the pages that follow, they were actually concurrent and interwoven in every session.

The first concrete changes came in Kathie's willingness to try to hold Billy for a feeding. Kathie had said that Billy did not like to be held; she knew this because he turned away. The therapist commented that even though Billy turned away, his body seemed to be more relaxed and she thought this indicated that he did like his mother to hold him. It was obvious that Kathie's bland, sad face could not hold Billy's attention when she was trying to feed him in her arms. One time, as the therapist watched Kathie try to feed Billy in her arms, Billy repeatedly turned away. Seeking a tactful way to guide Kathie to a livelier exchange with her baby, the therapist asked her if she ever told Billy stories. She said, "No." The therapist asked if she could tell Billy a story while Kathie held him and she agreed. The therapist began her story, "Once upon a time there were three bears," using what Stern (1973) describes as "normal baby talk expression" – elongation of smile, rise and fall of voice, exaggerated nuances. All of these are typical exchange behaviors between baby and mother. All were missing from Kathie's conversation with Billy.

Billy and his mother both loved the story. Billy began to smile and make eye contact with the therapist and his mother, as together they watched him. Kathie so enjoyed this herself, as both child and mother, that she herself began to tell Billy stories and, of course, Billy quickly began to respond. However, this took so much effort on Kathie's part that she was often fatigued and once again lapsed into her silent behavior.

A major concern was the burping process. The therapist had made many suggestions to Kathie about burping Billy, and had tried to help Kathie understand how her method would precipitate vomiting. It was only when the therapist actually stood beside Kathie, however, and shared with her the tension she was feeling, as she put Billy gently over her shoulder with the diaper underneath him, that she was gradually able to begin burping Billy in a normal fashion.

Kathie began to feed Billy the bottle in her arms on a regular basis, but did not yet give him solids. During a number of interviews it became clear that this was part of more complicated feelings about feeding Billy. At this point we identified two fears: Kathie's fear that "Billy would eat the family out of house and home" and that he would throw up endlessly. While we recognized that these fears were deeply rooted in Kathie's personality, we knew that we could not uncover the origins of these fears in the emergency period. And Billy's needs were paramount. We would have to help Kathie in a concrete, educational way to provide caloric adequacy for Billy.

The therapist could use the positive transference in supporting Kathie step by step in a feeding program for Billy. It was futile, of course, to challenge Kathie's irrational belief that Billy would "eat the family out of house and home" or that he would "throw up endlessly." The therapist only sympathized with Kathie's fears and led her gently into a collaboration on Billy's behalf. With pencil and paper and measuring cups the therapist and Kathie worked out quantities and sample feedings. We soon saw that Kathie could follow this regime. Long afterward we are still wondering how this was possible in view of the fact that quantities of food were still bound to profound conflicts in Kathie. Our best guess is that the objective, "on paper" feeding plan relieved Kathie of the responsibility for dealing with her own unconscious and dangerous impulses toward her baby. The therapist, "siding with the ego," was lending her own quiet authority to support Kathie's positive strivings to mother and her defenses against the destructive wishes.

In many discussions with the therapist, Kathie expressed her fear and revulsion of Billy's throwing up. The therapist acknowledged that she could understand how especially difficult it was for Kathie to hold and feed Billy. She told Kathie that together they would pay special attention to ensure that Billy would not throw up through overeating and that she wanted Kathie to observe carefully how much he ate and whether or not he threw up. With much relief that the therapist understood her difficulty, Kathie agreed to place Billy on a solid feeding schedule, which she and the therapist monitored carefully.

Billy began to gain weight steadily. Vomiting virtually disappeared. By 7 months Billy had gained 2½ pounds and reached the 50th percentile in weight; Dr. Larson was satisfied that Billy was no longer in nutritional peril (see Figure 13.1).

The family's progress

During the time this work was progressing, we were, of course, concerned with the well-being of the whole family, Mr. and Mrs. Douglas and Billy. An important part of the work was the help that was given Mr. Douglas. He came from a large, impoverished

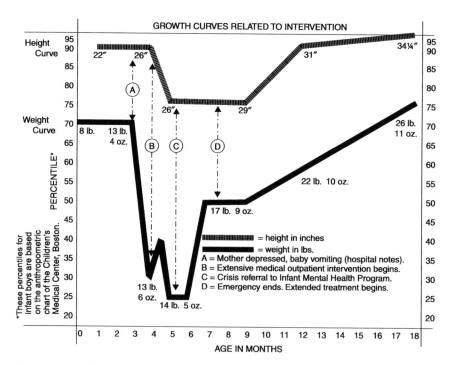

Figure 13.1 Billy's progress.

family and had suffered physical and emotional privations in his own childhood. As a young husband and father he was again struggling with poverty and hunger, and his depressed young wife drained his emotional resources. Each member of the family was hungry for physical and emotional sustenance. When John was home, he, too, shared his worries with the therapist, who responded with sympathetic understanding and with attention to his problems. She helped John and Kathie find ways to work out their present financial difficulties. She let them know that their hunger was her concern as well.

In summary, the work during the emergency period brought Billy to nutritional adequacy and his parents had formed a strong alliance with the therapist on behalf of their baby. Kathie, however, was still depressed, and we remained concerned about her and Billy.

The extended treatment phase

Reassessment

The period that we speak of as the extended treatment phase carried the work with Billy and his parents for a full year beyond the emergency period. While Billy had made progress, we still regarded him as a baby "at risk" in the psychological sense. In the area of human object relations we saw much we considered ominous. Billy did not respond to his parents in ways that were appropriate for a child of his age. Billy still avoided eye contact with his mother, by turning away. He preferred play with toys rather than human partners. When he was hungry or in need, he still cried helplessly and piteously.

It seemed to us that Kathie was now able to follow much of the therapist's advice, but her responses were always mechanical. She was still unable to mother Billy in a harmonious and spontaneous manner; she still seemed estranged from her baby. She appeared to hold back food and only slowly responded to Billy's hunger cries. She was not empathic with Billy's attempts to communicate distress or hunger. The interaction between mother and baby was still erratic, and Billy could never really count on a pleasurable response from his mother. Very often Kathie teased Billy with food and seemed to be competing with him.

As part of our continuing assessment, when Billy was 7½ months old, we videotaped another playroom visit which included a Bayley developmental assessment and a spontaneous feeding.[4] This tape spoke eloquently for the mother's ambivalence toward her baby and for pathological tendencies in both.

In one scene Kathie was holding Billy in her arms in a close and tender way while she was feeding him his bottle. Suddenly, Kathie pulled the bottle away, tossed back her head, dropped some milk in her own mouth, and then engaged Billy in a teasing game, in which she was competing with him for his bottle. It was painful to watch, but more painful was our witness to the baby's reactions: he was laughing. He had become a partner in this sadomasochistic game, a game that was repeated several times.

We have learned to give such "baby games" serious clinical attention. Some of our most important clinical insights have been derived from observing parents at play with their babies. The parent in conflict frequently reveals the essence of the conflict in play, in the "harmless games" (Fraiberg, 1974).

What we saw on tape, then, was a young mother competing with her own baby for his bottle. The moments of tender mothering were interrupted by an intruding thought, and feeding the baby became "teasing the baby," "taking food out of his mouth," "jealousy," "competition." As we watched this tape as a staff, we were struck by the thought that the mother behaved as if her baby were a sibling – and at that point the story began to come together for us.

The ghost in Billy's nursery

By this time we had come to know a fair amount about Kathie and her own childhood. In the emergency phase of treatment, this was information which we could register and store, but could not put to use for Kathie's treatment. Kathie had regarded herself as the unwanted middle child of her family, the no-good child who could "never do anything right." While Kathie had spoken with some acidity about her mother and her older sister, she could barely control her rage when she spoke about Essie, her sister younger by 5 years. "Essie got everything," she said bitterly. Her memories of Essie, which may have been distorted, linked Essie to food in many ways. One of the bitterest memories, possibly a screen memory, was of a

368

time when Kathie's parents took Essie out for an ice-cream cone and left Kathie home to do the dishes. Essie was the good child, the child that Kathie's mother favored.

We knew that Billy had been the "intruder" in Kathie's current life, the unwanted baby, the baby who "spoiled everything" for her, the baby who was taking food out of her mouth. There was a ghost in Billy's nursery, we thought, and the name of the ghost was Essie. Essie was the first intruder, the first baby in Kathie's life, who deprived her of the good things in life, of mother, and, in symbolic terms, of food. If we were right, the therapeutic problem for us was to get the ghost out of the baby's nursery. We would need to help Kathie deal with the repetition of the conflicted past in the present, to disengage Billy from the figures of the past.

The infantile conflicts and repetitions in the present

Our treatment during this period united guidance on behalf of Billy and a therapy which explicitly focused on Kathie's conflicts in mothering and their origins in her own childhood conflicts. The setting remained the same: home visits, scheduled twice weekly. Kathie was a willing and eager collaborator in her own treatment, to find out "why" she felt herself the victim of her own past.

Typically, the sessions would begin with Billy in the living room or the kitchen, and the therapist and Kathie would speak about his progress, or discuss any of Kathie's questions. The therapist continued, of course, to offer her observations and to help Kathie observe Billy, to interpret his needs and his signals, to praise his accomplishments and her own growth as a mother. Kathie's own needs for the therapist's time sometimes brought her into competition with Billy. Billy always had "his" time, during part of each session, and sometimes when Kathie felt most urgently in need of time with the therapist, she would say, "Shh, Billy, it's my turn now." Usually, the visits were timed so that Billy's nap would divide the time and give Kathie some time for privacy.

In nearly every session childhood grievances appeared with more and more intensity. But vitriolic hatred toward Essie, the first intruder, dominated many of these hours.

The transference was employed both to open up the past and to offer Kathie, the "unfinished adolescent," a new figure for identification and for undoing the powerful effects of her own mother, remembered as rejecting, critical, suspicious, and harsh, the "witch–mother" of early girlhood and adolescence.

The flow of memories converged again and again on the time following the birth of Essie, a period which marked a profound shift in Kathie's relationship to her own mother. Allowing for much distortion in adolescent memory, the figure of Essie, the baby who robbed Kathie of her mother, and the figure of the mother who "rejected" Kathie for the new baby were persistent ghosts. Along with these memories came overwhelming feelings of grief, depression, mourning for herself as a neglected, unwanted child. These were the feelings which had been revived with the birth of Billy. In Kathie's living room, with her own baby, the therapist often had the eerie feeling that she was witnessing another time, that Kathie was again the bereaved 5-year-old robbed for the second time by a baby. Motherhood had brought regression, and Kathie was locked once again in the infantile conflict.

The relationship with the therapist opened up many pathways for "undoing." "My mother never listened to me," was Kathie's reproach, a recurrent theme in these hours, but the therapist listened and responded to Kathie's feelings of grief and rage. "My mother said I was bad. It was bad to hate my sister." The therapist acknowledged and accepted the feelings of jealousy and anger toward the sister "who got everything." "My mother never understood me." The therapist explicitly told Kathie that she wanted to understand her. "My mother said I couldn't do anything right." The therapist, siding with Kathie who wanted to "do things right," could give honest support to the many aspects of Kathie's growth as wife and mother in which she showed her good capacities. Since Kathie believed that her own mother did not find satisfaction in motherhood and did not provide a model for mothering that Kathie felt she could use, the therapist shared many moments with Kathie when she received great satisfaction with Billy. Moreover, she offered an alternative model for mothering, which Kathie could use if she wished.

When muted or sullen anger appeared in the transference, the therapist helped Kathie put her anger into words and to discover that the anger would not destroy the therapist, or the positive relationship to the therapist, and could, indeed, open pathways to the conflicted past and ways to find meaning in that anger.

We now select themes from the work of this period. In the process of treatment these themes were, of course, interwoven.

Kathie, Essie, and Billy

The story of Essie, the first intruder, emerged as a central theme in Kathie's sessions when Billy was 8 months old. Kathie was still a reluctant mother to her baby, mechanically following the advice on feeding, now holding Billy for feedings and providing adequacy in caloric intake, but with little spontaneity or joy in her exchanges with the baby.

As memories of Essie emerged with rage toward that first baby "who spoiled everything," and as grief for herself as a small girl was revived, we began to see, for the first time, a spontaneous reaching out to Billy. The therapist described this in an excerpt from a visit with Kathie when Billy was 8 months old:

I had asked Kathie if she could tell me what it was like for her when her own baby sister was born. She said, "I've told you I hated my sister, how she always came between me and my mother. I don't remember much. When my sister was little, I remember being outside of the house much of the time. I do remember a couple of things. I didn't want to play with her. I hated to be told to play with her and I told my father that I hated her."

At this time, Kathie had her hand raised and was shaking it in the air. (I think she was nonverbally imitating her father talking to her and speaking for her father.) She said, in a deep voice, "No child of mine can hate another sister, you play with her."

After a while Kathie continued: "The first time I really got angry with my sister was when my parents took my sister out for ice-cream and left me to do the dishes. I was so mad, I decided to run away. My mother found me and dragged me back to the house. She was angry at me for leaving." I asked if she had told her mother how she felt. Kathie said she had told her mother that she had run away because she didn't want to be left at home when they went out. I asked if her mother had understood. Kathie said sadly, "She said she did, but," and she shook her head helplessly, "nothing changed."

At this moment a dramatic shift occurred: Kathie got up, went to Billy who was playing on the floor, swept him up in her arms, brought him back to her lap, hugged him, and started to play pat-a-cake with him, in a warm,

371

thoughtful manner. She looked over at me, I was facing Billy's back, and she invited me to come and see Billy's face. Billy was ecstatic. This play was quite exciting for me to see. On previous visits I had suggested traditional baby games which Kathie could play with Billy. Kathie had never before picked up on this.

In this excerpt, then, we see that as Kathie reexperienced the rage toward Essie, she could turn toward her own baby and spontaneously show her affection for him. She played a game with him with full enjoyment, and we recall the words she had used in the early part of this session when she spoke of Essie, "I didn't want to play with her. I hated to be told to play with her." As the affective pathways led back to Essie, Kathie was able to disengage Billy from the first intruder and, as if some preconscious association had taken place around "play," she gave the "no" to Essie and the "yes" to Billy. Where Kathie's mother "didn't understand" and both parents sternly prohibited the expression of anger toward Essie, the therapist understood and accepted the words, "I hated her." The play with Billy was also, then, a gift to the therapist.

This was the first time that we saw this pattern. We were to see it many times in the sessions that followed. When Kathie expressed strong feelings of anger toward her sister or sadness in remembering the rejection by her own mother, she was able to reach out to Billy and to hold him close to her. The therapist could now become more active in interpreting to Kathie the displacement of feelings from Essie to Billy.

The ghost of Essie appeared in many disguises. For weeks the therapist was puzzled by a complaint from Kathie: Billy, Kathie said, drove her to distraction when he followed her around the house. From the therapist's point of view, Billy's following of mother and touching base with her were most welcome signs of the growing attachment between Billy and his mother. Kathie found it nearly intolerable and took a dim view of the therapist's ideas on the subject.

Then, in an interview, when Billy was 8½ months old, Kathie quite unconsciously provided the vital clue. The therapist again described the session when Kathie was expressing a tirade against Essie:

"The worst thing that I hated – I was about 9 or 10 – was when my sister followed me all around the house. She used to stare at me and whisper like me and repeat what I said. I used to tell my mother, but my mother said I was crazy and she could not understand what I was talking about. I couldn't stand it. I spent more and more time away from home. I wanted my mother to stop her, but my mother wouldn't." I asked her what it was that had bothered her so much. Kathie said that she didn't know, didn't care, she only hated it. She just didn't want to have anything to do with her sister at that time.

After a few moments I asked her what it was like for her when Billy followed her around the house. Kathie said, "It's entirely different." Then she laughed. She understood. Kathie went to Billy and picked him up. She cuddled him, and put him on her lap so that he was lying on her knee, and tickled his back until Billy was laughing and giggling. He seemed delighted.

With this new insight, Kathie could now use more of the developmental and guidance information that the therapist offered. For example, regarding Billy's following her, the therapist explained that he wanted to keep her in sight at home because he was attached to her. At 8 months mother's presence was reassuring. As Billy grew, he would be able to remember her presence even if she was in another room. He would not have to follow her all the time.

Kathie's relationship to Billy was beginning to have moments of tenderness, spontaneity, and joy. She was making obvious progress in becoming a mother to Billy. She was manifestly enjoying Billy, proud of his achievements, gratified by his steady weight gain, and eager for his response to her.

However, although the teasing games with Billy receded during this period, the therapist still caught glimpses of "teasing" which concerned us. On an educational level the therapist had dealt directly with the teasing games during feeding. She pointed out that these were games which might lead to problems which Kathie would not really want to see in Billy. She spoke of the meaning that food and love had for babies as well as adults. What did these games mean to Billy? Kathie consciously made an effort to give up the teasing games, an effort which was partially successful, yet the urge to tease Billy broke through in a game, and more explicitly in withholding food from Billy when he was manifestly hungry, Kathie responding only to his most urgent cries.

Billy meanwhile was responding to his mother's efforts by sometimes showing preferential responses to his mother in significant ways, but one aberrant tendency remained. At 9 months of age he still avoided eye contact with his mother. Even in baby games with Kathie when she smiled and encouraged him, he turned his head away from her. In one sequence on tape we saw Kathie playing pat-a-cake with Billy on her lap, facing her, and the baby, though participating in the game, averted his head to avoid eye contact with his mother. Kathie, encouraged by the therapist, repeated the game until finally Billy rewarded his mother by smiling and cooing, but still turned away from her. The therapist interpreted the smiling and vocalizing as his way of telling mother he enjoyed the game. Perhaps soon he would also give her the reciprocal gaze she so wanted as affirmation of his affection toward her. Kathie, we saw with sadness for her plight, had to work very hard to woo her baby after the many months of avoidance and neglect.

Then, when Billy was 11 months old, the meaning of the teasing games and a facet of Kathie's uncontrollable urge to inflict pain broke through in a session. The therapist summarized the critical material:

> Kathie had recently returned from a visit to her own family, and was angrily recounting what had happened. Once again Kathie did the dishes while Essie disappeared from the kitchen, and once again Essie got all of mother's attention.
>
> Kathie said, "I hate my sister. She doesn't do anything. Just like now when my mother needs her. I have hated her ever since the time I was asked to take care of her and my little cousin together. I could have been with my friends, I really didn't want to do it, but I did. After a few days my sister said to me, 'Bug off, we all hate you, we don't want you here.' "
>
> In response to my question, "What did you do?" Kathie said, "I told my mother. She just shrugged it off." I asked, "How did you feel?" "I hated her." I said, "It really hurt, didn't it?" She replied, "Yes." Her face was red and she was very tense. I said, "It seems as though you are still angry." She said, "Yes."
>
> Kathie continued, "I told you how I would try to get her into trouble, how I would make up stories, how I would tease her. I would tell my mother things that she would do. When she got me really mad I would shake her."
>
> At this moment she turned to Billy who was playing on the floor, and took his arm and showed me how she would shake her sister, saying, "I would shake her like this and like this." Billy started to cry, obviously scared. I was scared for him. Kathie stopped abruptly. She was shocked and said, "Sorry Billy, I didn't mean to hurt you."

I said, "I can see how angry you feel at your sister and now I understand how you felt before." Kathie nodded. I asked her whether she sometimes got mad at Billy as she got mad at her sister, as though he were like her sister.

Kathie had an immediate response. She said, "No," in an emphatic voice and moved away from me. "I never get mad at Billy that way." Soon Kathie went over to Billy, started to play with him, got down on the floor, and for a long time held him and cuddled him.

Thus the teasing and sadistic rage toward Essie emerged from memory and could also be observed in a direct displacement toward Billy. After many interpretations, in this visit and others, of the repetition of feelings from the past in the present, Kathie's quick denial finally gave way to affirmation and insight.

The insight was very meaningful to Kathie and further freed Billy from being the target of her feelings of anger toward her sister. During the next visits we began to see a new depth in the relationship between Kathie and Billy. Teasing of Billy was significantly reduced and began to disappear. Kathie began spontaneously to reach out to Billy and, on her own, began to interact with him in such a way that both of them received great pleasure. Our observations also began to show some incidents of mutual gaze and approaches between Billy and Kathie.

Kathie and her mother

The competitiveness with Billy was only one of the many themes that appeared throughout the work with Kathie. There was another important theme. We had often observed her seeming indifference to Billy's cries. Many times it seemed as if she and Billy were crying together. There was no mother present in the room. With great sadness and anger Kathie would say that her mother had not understood her. Once again the therapist acknowledged that Kathie too had many needs to be heard, to be loved, and to be understood and nurtured.

The therapist asked many times what it was that Kathie most wanted her mother and perhaps the therapist to understand. Gradually her true feelings emerged. She did not want to be a mother, she had never wanted to be a mother, and she was not ready to give up her role as a child. She had in fact not really separated from her own family.

With great sadness Kathie told the therapist of the very painful relationship she had had with her own mother. She felt that her mother was never satisfied with her, especially as a daughter. Kathie said that she had always been the family boy, loved by her father and ridiculed by her mother. As a little girl she had never played with dolls, but had always preferred to play with the neighborhood boys. As she approached puberty, she was accused by her mother of being too seductive. Nothing she did was right. With great hurt she described how her mother had said that she could never be as pretty as her older sister or as good as the younger sister. She began to go out with John, whom her mother had liked. During this time Kathie's mother had begun to enter menopause and was wishing explicitly for a grandchild. Kathie's older sister did not have any children. Kathie got pregnant and had Billy. Kathie, with hurt and anger, said that now her mother had a grandchild, but for her Billy's birth was not all that it was supposed to have been. The fantasy of renewed babyhood for Kathie never materialized. Now that Billy was born, he was the grandparents' pride, not Kathie. She was only 17 and faced with an entirely new role, that of motherhood, which she did not want.

In work with Kathie, her ambivalence toward Billy now became overt. Even as she expressed her ambivalence, we began to see progress in her relationship with Billy. As Kathie spoke of these feelings, she began to be able to respond to Billy.

Nearly every session was related to Billy's needs in one way or another. Billy was approaching 12 months of age, a time when he did not yet have words for needs. As Kathie would weep for herself and berate the mother who never heard her cries and needs, Billy oftentimes needed her.

At first she was unable to interpret Billy's cries and the therapist would talk for him. For example, many times Billy was in his playpen and wanted to get out. Kathie was unable to respond. The therapist would talk for Billy and say, "Mom, I'm trying to tell you that I want out of the playpen, but I don't have any words yet." Kathie would respond. They had many discussions about the ways in which Billy tried to communicate with her without words. When Kathie did respond, the therapist always rewarded her efforts, speaking for Billy, who was not yet able to show her that he appreciated her efforts. The therapist might say, "Isn't it good to have a mommy who hears you and understands you? Even mommy has to be understood."

The first sign that Kathie was beginning to hear Billy and to be empathic with him was her ability to comfort him when he cried. She would pick him up in her arms, hold him closely, and pat his head. Eventually she anticipated his needs for both food and play. She took pride in his attempt to communicate and in her attempt to understand him, which the therapist encouraged and reinforced. She began to identify more strongly as Billy's mother. In fact, she started to let the therapist know that she knew Billy better, and the therapist, of course, stepped back from the role of active interpreter.

As we traced the content of these sessions "on being a mother" and the therapeutic work in this area, we could see the effects of reexperiencing, "undoing," and insight in Kathie's own ability to be a mother.

When Kathie's own cries were heard by the therapist, she began to respond to her baby's cries. When Kathie's needs were "understood" by her therapist, she began to interpret the signs of needs in her baby. When hostile feelings toward Billy could be put into words, they no longer exerted their influence in distancing Kathie from Billy; she was free to enjoy him. When the powerful ambivalence toward her own mother came into the therapeutic work, Kathie "completed" her own adolescence and became free of the "witch–mother" who impeded her own development as wife and mother.

Termination of treatment and follow-up

The major part of our therapeutic work was achieved by the time Billy reached his first birthday. Our work continued until Billy was 18 months old, when the family moved to another community. John found new work, which brought financial security to the family.

Billy, at 1 year of age, already reflected both the changes in Kathie which were brought about in her treatment and the developmental guidance which Kathie could now use on his behalf with spontaneity and self-assuredness.

There were no residual feeding problems; Billy at 12 months and at the follow-up (25 months) was a child who enjoyed food. He had no food idiosyncrasies or conflicts with his mother around feeding.

There were no symptoms or disorders in the areas of orality or beginning autonomy. We watched carefully for signs of affective disturbances and saw none. We worried about possible residues from the sadomasochistic feeding games, which had so concerned us when Billy was 8 months old, but we could identify no sequelae in the second year behavior picture. We did observe that John still occasionally teased Billy in words or games (Kathie did not) and that Billy at these times did not participate in these games, but turned away from his father, typically moving toward other games or toys. (We wish that we could have provided more help to John in this area, but we are satisfied that Billy did not offer himself as a partner in such games.)

In his second year, Billy was a cheerful, exuberant, busy little boy, curious, eager to learn, pleased with himself. Language development was excellent. Most important of all, Billy's attachment to his mother was secure, mutually satisfying, and demonstrably joyous. In direct observations and in a number of vignettes on videotape we saw special smiles for mother, good eye contact, seeking of mother for comfort and protection, enjoyment of games and play with mother and father, and, equally important, a steady growth in self-confidence and independence. Billy had become an endearing child to both his parents and their pride and pleasure in him came through in nearly every visit. (He was also, objectively, an endearing child as others saw him.)

The therapeutic work with Kathie succeeded in freeing her and Billy from those aspects of a conflicted childhood which were being reenacted between her and her baby. To some measure, we believe, the work also resulted in the completion of Kathie's own adolescence. The resolution of infantile conflicts between Kathie and her mother freed her to become a mother and a wife in her own rights. For not only did Kathie become a mother who enjoyed her child, but we saw many positive changes in her relationship to her husband, and the marriage gained stability.

When Billy and his parents were seen in follow-up at 25 months, we were satisfied that he and his parents had sustained the gains of treatment. With only minimal support and guidance from the therapist during the period that followed their move from our community, both parents showed growth as young adults and had brought wisdom and good judgment to their rearing of Billy. They were justifiably proud of Billy and his achievements and spoke tenderly of his affectionate nature and his endearing ways of greeting his parents when he woke each morning.

Toilet training was proceeding smoothly. There was no sense of pressure in either Kathie or John. In Billy's play we discerned no anxieties in connection with the toilet or with cleanliness.

Recalling Kathie's earlier revulsion toward vomiting and messiness, we were interested to see that none of this had carried over to the toilet training of Billy. Since our work had not dealt with the deeper layers of this revulsion in Kathie, we wondered why the area of toilet training had not been contaminated. Then the therapist remembered that throughout the early critical period of the treatment, she had observed many diaperings of Billy, but at no time had Kathie shown revulsion toward the baby's feces or cleaning the anal region. It was, then, specifically an oral revulsion on Kathie's part, in which food and vomit may have had anal determinants, but were curiously not manifest in connection with anal functions.

One vignette from our last records of Billy and his family is cherished by all of us. The therapist had made a visit to the new home of the Douglas's when Billy was 20 months old. Billy remembered her well and was very much a delighted child seeing an old friend. At one point he left the room and returned with a handful of Chinese noodles which he pressed in the therapist's hand. Kathie said, "He likes you. He always does this. He likes to share his favorite foods with people he likes."

Notes

1 Vivian Shapiro is a senior social worker at the Child Development Project, Department of Psychiatry, University of Michigan; Selma Fraiberg is Professor of Child Psychoanalysis and Director of the Child Development Project; Edna Adelson is a senior psychologist on the staff of the Child Development Project. The Infant Mental Health Program described in these pages is supported by the Grant Foundation of New York.

2 We customarily videotape a play session and Bayley testing at this point in an assessment. This is done only with the consent of parents, of course, and we do everything possible to make the taping nonintrusive. We never invite intimate discussions at these times. We do not use video for treatment sessions, but we find that the taping of play sessions and testing is almost always of great interest to parents, and the

playback of the tapes for the parents is valued by them and by us as an opportunity to observe the baby and themselves. In Billy's case because of the urgency of the feeding problem, a formal Bayley testing was postponed until nutritional adequacy was achieved at 7½ months.

3   We did not observe Billy engage in age-related social personal behavior, such as frolic play and early vocalizations.

4   The Bayley showed that Billy was slightly above the median, in both mental and motor scores overall, but differentially lagged in beginning language items.

References

Barbero, G. J. and Shaheen, E. (1967) 'Environmental failure to thrive'. *J. Pediat.*, 71: 639–644.

Bayley, N. (1969) *Bayley Scales of Infant Development*. New York: Psychological Corporation.

Fraiberg, S. (1974) 'The clinical dimensions of baby games'. *J. Amer. Acad. Child Psychiat.*, 13: 202–220.

Leonard, M. F., Phymes, J. P. and Solnit, A. J. (1966) 'Failure to thrive in infants'. *Amer. J. Dis. Child.*, 111: 600–612.

Stern, D. N. (1973) 'Mother and infant at play', in M. Lewis and L. Rosenblum (eds) *The Effect of the Infant on the Caregiver*. New York: Wiley, pp. 187–213.

Whitten, C. F., Pettit, M. G. and Fischoff, J. (1969) 'Evidence that growth failure from maternal deprivation is secondary to undereating', in S. Chess and A. Thomas (eds) *Annual Progress in Child Psychiatry and Child Development*. New York: Brunner/Mazel.

14

Bodies across generations and
cycles of abuse

Estela Welldon

This chapter will explore the specific struggles of women attempting to fulfil the function of mothering, when they have been themselves the object of early abuse, at times repeated through several generations. While some women from an emotionally disadvantaged background manage to be very good mothers, others do not. I will argue that repetition is a key factor in understanding their difficulties. Much against their conscious intention, as adults they repeat the early traumatic situation again as victims, and sometimes also as abusers, and they repeat their pregnancies which to them represent a concrete solution; with their babies they repeat their mother's behaviour and they induce in their children a repetition of their own feelings. I will also discuss that in some of these cases there is a strong sadomasochistic tone in their relationships, which leads them to co-create a sadomasochistic parental couple which has a powerful hold on them and which generates further perverse behaviour – the 'malignant bonding' (Welldon 2007, 2010). I intend to show that these abusive mother–child situations are very difficult to handle for the professionals involved and that a psychoanalytic understanding is essential in helping them to provide realistic and clear-sighted interventions. I shall illustrate this with the case of Ms B, a young woman whose expectations of motherhood were profoundly dissociated from the reality of becoming a mother.

The long-term consequences of childhood abuse and neglect for a girl can result in further abuse and neglect of her own body, and can lead to acts of self-harm such as eating disorders, substance abuse, self-cutting and self-burning. These usually appear during adolescence when these young women become aware of the similarities between their bodies and their mother's. These self-attacks also represent their often unconscious wishes of revenge against their mothers linked to a conscious wish to have a different destiny. Later these acts of self-harm can be superseded by sadomasochistic relationships with violent men, whose attacks might come to represent the women's own self-hatred (towards their female bodies). This perpetuates and reiterates the early abuse. Some of these women fall pregnant and have babies leading to a process of identification with the aggressor in which the victims may become victimizers of their own children.

Having a baby provides a unique reassurance to some women that their bodies and their reproductive functions are still intact. This reassurance also represents their unconscious wish to be like their mothers, toward whom they are highly ambivalent. Also, having babies may be the only way for some to communicate and express their own emotional needs, which have never been properly addressed nor recognized.

The complexities of the body–mind relationship become clear in observing that a woman's *body* responds adequately to the physical demands of the pregnancy, but she may feel unable to respond *emotionally* to the newly born or growing baby's demands. This discrepancy happens regardless of their conscious commitment to take proper care of their babies. Their determination and wish to fulfil a maternal role in a rewarding and adequate way suddenly and unexpectedly fails, and they end up inflicting harm either on themselves or on their babies.

The repetition of trauma

Some young women, who encounter great difficulties in mothering their babies, repeat the process by having several children. What is the object of the repetition compulsion by which some emotionally severely damaged young women have more and more babies? Perhaps to create an illusion linked to the pleasure principle which then becomes in itself a self-destructive quest. McDougall tells us in *Theatres of the Body* (1989) that: 'The body, like the mind, is subject to the repetition compulsion' (p. 28), and she also reminds us that Freud (1920) in 'Beyond the Pleasure Principle' linked repetition compulsion to the destructive impulses.

In her attempts to deal with her intense ambivalence towards her mother, the young woman may either identify with a fertile mother whom she loves, and the pregnancy is very much welcome and idealized as the evidence of her wholeness, or her hatred towards her mother can result in the unconscious hatred for the object – the baby. I have observed these phenomena in my assessment and treatment with psychologically damaged women.

One of the few ways for these young women to ensure they are still able to produce something beautiful from inside themselves is by producing a new baby, who will also represent basic and primitive nurturing needs they have experienced all through their lives. In other words, the babies are unconsciously being used as the evidence of their inner goodness. However, this emotional reassurance is short-lived and at times, breaks down, especially when confronted with external pressures first created by the new baby's demands and, later on, by social agencies concerned about the baby's safety. At these times, deep and primitive anxieties regarding their own functioning as 'good enough mothers' emerge powerfully. They are evoked by their experiences with their own mothers, who were felt to be inadequate or absent and sometimes neglectful and abusive. This creates a sense of loss: what appears initially to be an inability to mourn for the important loss or absence of maternal care, proves to be an unconscious 'chronic mourning' for a good enough parental figure. If detection of the real problem is recognized and professional help is offered to the young mother, she will react defensively as if attacked, even though internally she may feel relieved that her difficulties have been recognized and that assistance will be available to her, in contrast to what happened to her own mother. However, at this point her baby has become the focus of concern and not herself, in other words, the attention is transient, short-lived and exclusively geared to her pregnancies or babies, not to her own needs. A new pregnancy is experienced by the mother as the only way to obtain any help. As we shall see later, there are also other internal unconscious pressures and symbolizations in operation.

In some cases, if the children are at risk and are removed from the mother, her quest for a new pregnancy becomes an almost compulsive need. This repetition becomes, in her mind *and* body, a triumph over the temporality of previous pregnancies, namely an omnipotent wish to overcome or actually deny the loss of a previous child with a renewed pregnancy. The mourning is intermittently forgotten, and multiple identifications take place: that is, the mother becomes, not only both the lost baby and the new baby but also the maternal body, which simultaneously provides an illusory and concrete reality of being able to produce new pregnancies. The idea of the *forever* mother remains alive.

Women can perceive their children as extensions of their own bodies, at times, like 'part–objects' with a fetishistic quality. They oscillate between seeing their children either as their healthy part or as needy and vulnerable, or as demanding and 'bad' aspects of themselves. Motherhood then becomes a substitute for the mother's own emotional growth. This is often associated with 'compulsive caregiving' (Bowlby 1980: 157) The young mother attributes to the cared-for baby all the sadness and neediness she is unable to acknowledge in herself; and the baby stands vicariously for the mother who gives the care. This process where the parental role is 'swapped' between parents and child develops during childhood when children feel responsible for the welfare of their unhappy or damaged parents. According to Bowlby, these individuals seem to display in the first instance a *prolonged absence of conscious grieving*, but they are actually suffering from unconscious *chronic mourning* (p. 138). This is inextricably linked to extreme traumas associated with loss of maternal care during early childhood, which are responsible for producing insecure attachment.

Obviously relationships between mothers and daughters are of fundamental importance in the function of motherhood since identification with the same gender and possible repetition patterns in motherhood are bound to happen. Bowlby adds that 'should such a person become a parent there is danger of her becoming excessively possessive and protective, especially as a child grows older, and also of inverting the relationship' (p. 206). In my clinical experience I have observed that these traits could also extend to intense ambivalence, resulting in periods of over-protectiveness followed by neglect and abuse. Hence, the cycle of abuse across generations through women's bodies continues in perpetual motion regardless of social class or social and academic achievements.

In 1923 Freud spoke of repetition as underlying the first great anxiety – the state of birth and the infantile anxiety of longing: 'the anxiety due to separation from the protecting mother'. Bronfen (1992) argues that 'while the reality principle injures narcissism, it is also through repetition that narcissism asserts itself, tries to antidote the incision of the real by substituting it with images, with narrative, with objects' (p. 31). This becomes especially poignant when associated with repeated pregnancies in women with very low self-esteem. Bronfen in using Freud's 'fort-da' episode posits a powerful argument by showing that the maternal body becomes the site of death because it is so uniquely connected to the stage prior to life. According to her, any attempt at mastering the maternal body could symbolize being in control of both the forbidden and the impossible since the maternal body is inscribed by the death drive, the beginning of life and the essence of loss and division. This theoretical approach might partly help to understand the clinical findings of the repeated and constant attacks that some women inflict onto their own bodies and their own babies. Babies become fetishes that the mother uses as a denial of separation and death. Hence the repetition of pregnancies may be seen as an attempt to preserve the lost object, but this aim is doomed to fail since the lost object is the image of her own abandoning and neglecting mother and more internal and external sufferings are inevitable.

Perverse transference

There is a growing general consensus regarding the crucial importance of the interpretation of transference and countertransference in the understanding and treatment of patients with perverse characteristics. It was Etchegoyen (1978) who first introduced the concept of 'transference perversion' characterized by the eroticization of the therapeutic relationship with a peculiar type of narcissistic object-relation. The patient permanently tries to create a delusional subject–object unity provoking excitement and impatience in the analyst. Etchegoyen also made us aware that these processes must be uncovered in order to solve potential problems relating to dissociation of the ego, subject–object confusion and transformation of desire into ideology.

Ogden (1996) has provided another dimension to this hypothesis, asserting that the patient uses sexualization as a way of protecting himself or herself against the experience of psychological deadness.

Hence the compulsive eroticization is used to create an illusory sense of vitality. In my view there is an escalation of the perversion which is 'acted in' in the transferential process with the psychoanalyst. In my work with perverse patients I have found helpful Etchegoyen's and Ogden's conceptualizations. The interpretation of the negative transference when working with these patients is crucial as it gives them a sense of being understood, and it is equally important for the clinicians. They may otherwise become involved in 'rescue' fantasies with their patients, who are in some cases very adept in eliciting such feelings in those around them and in sensing the therapists' emotional response. Therapists may feel ashamed of their impatience and frustration and try to conceal it with an even more 'benign' response which will be not only useless but also utterly despised by the patients. These women have a deeply engrained 'training' from conception and birth at feeling, and actually being in reality, rejected, abandoned and humiliated by their carers, and they may develop an identification with the rejecting and contemptuous image.

I very much agree with Ogden's concept of compulsive eroticization being used to create an illusory sense of vitality. I have noticed that this is often accompanied by manic defences in an attempt not to succumb to a sense of dread, depression, and deadness. Green (1972) talks of the identification with the dead mother as the only means to establish a reunion with the mother, and observes that, instead of real reparation, mimicry is created which represents melancholic reparation. In other words, the longed for reunion with the mother never happens.

Sadomasochism

I have written elsewhere (2002) of the difference between the patterns operating in domestic violence and sadomasochism in couples. It seems to me that according to clinical findings repeated ill treatment of women is unconsciously accepted by women with the hope of breaking up their own cycle of self-destructiveness. The man perpetuates an early behaviour of self-inflicted harm. According to Motz (2001), clinicians are reluctant to explore the role of the victim or her participation for fear of appearing as if they were blaming her for the abuse, but in fact both perpetrator and adult victim are active participants in this pattern. Motz states that the abuser tries to create an illusion of omnipotence to compensate for his own feelings of inadequacy and helplessness which are unconsciously projected onto his victim. The victim then introjects or absorbs his feelings of inadequacy and contempt becoming increasingly depressed. The abuser is totally dependent on his victim's devotion and dependency on him for the boosting and stability of his own self-esteem. The victim on her part identifies with the aggressor by projecting on him her aggressive impulses, punishing herself and getting rid of guilty feelings at the same time. To the abuser, the victim represents unconsciously other figures from his early history, such as a powerful, dominating and contemptuous mother. Motz affirms that the abuser projects his blueprint of uncaring and rejecting women onto his partner and is oversensitive to any issues of separation. She also suggests that often a man who abuses his partner or children has had an early experience of witnessing parental violence and has learnt that fathers beat mothers, and that concern and emotional involvement are all expressed through violence. Hence, the unconscious role taken by both partners which frequently goes back to early witnessing of parental violence facilitates a repeated pattern of being involved in an abusive relationship where mutual projections make it very difficult if not impossible, without professional help, to part from one another.

The malignant bonding

A violent and self-destructive relationship is strengthened by sadistic sexual acts perpetrated against dependent persons, such as the couple's children or other immature individuals who fall under their control and dominancy. Not only are there notorious cases from the media but I have also been able to corroborate this process in my own clinical findings, and I have termed it 'malignant bonding'.

'Malignant bonding' is a different condition from either the erotic sadomasochism or the 'relational perversion' (Pandolfi 1999; Filippini 2005). I am concerned here with the couple's destructive and sadistic activities, which in virtue of being shared by the two partners can add an extremely exciting and erotic quality to their perverse bonding. Furthermore, this can be initiated equally by the man or by the woman. They have become partners with equal participation in the designing and the execution of their actions as a defence against their severe very early traumatic experiences. I have observed that the difference of male and female perverse actions lies in the object or target. Whereas in men it is usually directed towards the outside, in women it is either against themselves – their bodies in self-destructive patterns – or against objects which are regarded as their own creations, that is, their babies.

Many cases I am familiar with share a disturbing aspect represented by the recording of the victims' responses while the crime was being perpetrated, either through tape recorders or more recently filmed on home videos and similar devices. This suggests a compulsive need in the perpetrators to repeat again and again to themselves the tortures inflicted on the innocent victims. I find this feature most distressing. Freud in 'Beyond the Pleasure Principle' linked the destructive impulses to the need to repeat, to re-present, to double, which leads to a blurring of the distinction between oneself and the other. When the perpetrators make a recording of the confused, terrorized, painful reactions of their victims are they using this as an object of identification with their own childhood? Do they do it to make themselves feel powerful and in complete control of the torture inflicted because they need this 'reassurance'? Is the listening 'addiction' associated with early sexual abuse and the need to form sadomasochistic relationships in which they have the monopoly of power?

Ethel Person (1999) has coined both terms 'the body silenced' (when there is lack of sexual desire) and 'the body as the enemy' (when the patient is afflicted by hypochondriac symptoms) in a rich and comprehensive study of the beating and sadomasochistic fantasies in women. I believe that a fitting term for my female patients' specific predicament in relation to their bodies and babies could be 'the body as torturer', as it is through the body that they inflict torturing experiences on themselves. This would reflect the compulsive urges these women experience towards their bodies, unconsciously making them function as an effective torture tool in their becoming victimizers to themselves and to their babies. Also present are different degrees of disassociation, the most severe corresponding to Munchausen's syndrome by proxy. At other times, a partner is unconsciously designated as the torturer.

Countertransference issues in the treatment of abusive mothering

The cycle of abuse becomes even more painfully apparent when court reports are requested as evidence for life-changing decisions regarding the future of a family, especially of a mother and her baby. In my long professional career and despite my writings on clinical findings about perverted motherhood (Welldon 1988), I had been rather skilful in avoiding writing court reports or appearing in court as an expert witness. This state of affairs ended a few years ago when I was giving a lecture on female abusers and was confronted by a colleague about my 'cowardice' in refusing to lend the weight of my clinical experience in assessing parenting abilities. At that point I felt forced to 'grow up' before retirement, so I reluctantly agreed to be more co-operative and active in preparing court reports and giving evidence. I found it to be a painful and excruciatingly difficult process in view of the complexity of the decisions concerning the future of parents and babies.

As clinicians working with patients who suffer in the predicaments we have been discussing, we are aware of the extreme importance of using the psychoanalytical model, and, as I mentioned earlier, specifically the interpretation of the transferential and countertransferential processes. This fosters in the patients a degree of emotional growth and capacity to reflect on their problems rather than enacting them.

The dynamic process is quite different when we are functioning from our professional work as expert witness in family or criminal courts with the purpose of assessing maternal abilities, which is a rather static and judgemental process. It is obvious that we have a great deal of reluctance in so doing since the psychological and the legal worlds are still miles apart. There are often conflicts between legal requirements and psychodynamic evaluations. For example, a frequent disagreement concerns the question placed by the legal system to these young women and to their assessors, as to whether they are able to place the baby's needs before their own.

However, I believe that our expertise is of great value when applied to the legal world and furthermore I consider that it is our duty to inform and educate those who are unaware of the conflicts emanating from the complexities attached to women in their maternal role. It is with this intention that I am writing about this subject in this book.

★   ★   ★

I have felt powerfully immersed in an internal world of agony and overwhelmed by a sense of responsibility, when confronted with a mother who loves her baby and believes she is the one who should be the carer but simultaneously *knows* she is incapable of doing so.

On one occasion I felt so emotionally trapped in this situation that I decided to attend an art exhibition in an attempt to liberate myself from the emotional disturbance which was pervading my personal life. The court report I was preparing concerned a mother who was deeply bonded to her child, but due to difficult circumstances preceding and surrounding her baby's birth, adoption would be the likely recommendation. Social services had already taken away two children due to neglect and abandonment because of mother's inability to take proper care of them.

I went to the Giacometti exhibition in London and quickly and unexpectedly became distressed when closely observing a sculpture of a woman with hands out ready to hold a baby who has become the 'invisible object' not only metaphorically but in reality, like all those mothers we see whose babies have been or are about to be taken away. The woman's face in the sculpture appears superficially to be devoid of feelings although when observed closely it appears like a frozen mask reflecting an unbearable psychic pain that has to be blocked off.

The sculpture is framed in a rigid chair that may symbolize her having to be held or contained for her own safety or that of others because her child has been taken away from her. The piece is entitled: *Hands Holding the Void (Invisible Object)*. I wondered why on earth, when so many sculptures were on show at the exhibition, my eyes, heart and senses took me to this particular piece which was so relevant to my work. I realized the impossibility of escaping from the experience of breaking up the most profound bonding – that of mother and baby. I was just too emotionally involved to allow myself to have a break. Such is the nature of this type of work which holds you permanently in its grip.

I suggest that being professionally involved in these cases evokes distressing feelings which may contribute to reluctance, on the part of professionals working on child abuse cases, to consider the part played by the mother – as if it is unbearable to think that a mother, who is clearly suffering, can inflict tremendous suffering on her child. We observe this phenomenon again and again but still it goes unrecognized and unacknowledged.

Evaluation of maternal abilities is further complicated by the fact that during the process much attention, monitoring and care is provided to the mother and her 'satellite' baby. At last she experiences the attention and care she needs and wants which perhaps she has never received before in her life. This strengthens her and enables her to care for her baby. She is also trying of course to positively impress the professionals in order to be able to keep the baby. The consequence is often that she produces the 'best mothering' and the baby represents the good part located both inside and outside mother's body. However, when the involvement of helpful professionals is over, the pressure of the process disappears and the mother is left to her own devices. The support and incentive to demonstrate the 'best mothering' fades away. The cycle of abuse is reinstated and an old and familiar sense of being neglected reproduces the unbearable pain which is once again projected on the baby.

I shall try to demonstrate with a clinical example the pervasiveness of the cycle of abuse through the maternal body which derives from and results in painfully inappropriate and abusive mothering.

Ms B

I was asked to assess Ms B's maternal abilities because of the impending birth of her fourth child. She had a most dramatic, deprived and horrendous early life history. She was a 28-year-old woman, the second child in a family of four by the same mother and father. Her own mother was only 16 when she married. She has a 29-year-old sister and two brothers aged 25 and 27. She also has two younger half sisters aged seven and eight by her mother's remarriage.

Ms B had been previously assessed and her older three children had been taken into care by social services at an early age due to domestic violence. (I have referred to this earlier under the heading sadomasochism.) This new baby was the product of a relationship with a 14-year-old boy whose parents had taken Ms B to court because of 'indecent assault on a minor'. He later denied being the father. The new baby, Cindy, was removed from birth and placed with foster parents. Ms B was allowed three times weekly supervised contact for three hours.

And now let me tell you some of Ms B's history. Her father began to sexually abuse her from the age of 12, involving masturbation, oral sex and full sexual intercourse. She described it as being raped by her father, who was often drunk. She was extremely scared of him and frequently wished she was dead. Ms B always felt different from the rest of the family.

Her father secured a small flat from where he began to operate as a pimp advertising her services as a prostitute. Her father used to get her drunk, and she had to perform 'all sorts of kinky sex'. While she was having sex with other men her father would be a witness. Ms B believes her father made her have sex with other men, not just because of money, but also because it gave him sexual gratification to see her suffering by being used and abused sexually. Her mother, although aware of these events, did not intervene, either because she was unconcerned or because she feared her husband's violence. In fact, when she insisted on talking to her mother, her mother's first reaction was to beat her and later to join her husband in acts of sexual abuse. He advertised in the local newspapers the services of his wife and his daughter for pornographic and prostitution purposes. Later these cuttings were used as evidence during his criminal trial. We can see here the evidence that both parents were engaged in a sort of 'malignant bonding' becoming united 'parents' in a cruel and sadistic attack on their daughter.

The abusive sexualization of the relationship to their daughter appears in both parents, and may have been used as a manic defence against the severe emotional deprivation that they themselves may have experienced in their early childhood. A process of denial is being created to avoid 'the black hole', the dread of emptiness which is represented by the generational absence of 'good enough parenting', and becomes a chronic, but masked, depression which is linked to experiences of deprivation, neglect and abuse. This 'solution' becomes an intergenerational legacy bound to be transmitted on to future generations if not properly understood. Ms B had to struggle against deep wishes to be dead or to kill herself. She also experienced murderous feelings towards her father.

Freud (1923) writes: 'The emergence of life would thus be the cause of the continuation of life and also at the same time of the striving towards death; and life itself would be a conflict and compromise between these two trends.' I have noticed that our patients experience the death instinct as destructive narcissism that is eroticized. It is extreme and enacted sadomasochism where the individual feels pushed from within to take risks, which involve life-threatening situations to fight death itself in order to secure survival. The survival, despite and because of all risks involved, reassures and offers a guarantee to them that they are still alive.

★   ★   ★   ★   ★

Ms B told me that for most of her childhood she was 'opening [her] legs for different men to make them and [her] father happy. Where I was fighting it for years, in the end I just gave up fighting. Then I looked on rape as an everyday thing like housework.' While all this was taking place she turned to alcohol, because the more she drank, the less pain she felt. She added that she had 'always been good at just blocking off the worst bits'. This became a long-established pattern. For example, at school she pretended that everything at home was all right: 'I learnt to live in a world where nothing is as it seems. All I have around me is silent fear. I lived with more self-hate as the years of being raped went on. I felt there was something wrong with me.' These events were obviously interfering with her progress in school, manifesting in her behaviour being out of control and difficult to handle.

As a teenager she was involved in acts of violence, including attacks on herself, which expressed the hatred she felt against herself and her body. She used to cut herself on her arms and her face, sometimes requiring many stitches which left visible scars. I would suggest that the hatred was mixed with the eroticization of pain which she had absorbed from her parents' perverse activities, which made self-harm particularly compulsive since it provided her with sexual excitement despite her conscious efforts to fight against these repetitive sadomasochistic traits. Such is the quest for a nurturing and good enough breast that despite her mother's collusive behaviour with her father she decided at 17 to leave home together with her mother hoping for a new nurturing relationship. This failed bitterly, and after a few months and many quarrels her mother left her. This disappointment led her to call her father in a compulsive need to continue the abuse. He told her how remorseful he felt about all he had done to her and was able to convince her that she should return home. But as soon as she did so her father began to rape and beat her again. He was worse than ever before because he was very angry, not only because she had dared to leave home, but also because he blamed her for her mother's leaving him.

She felt like a prisoner because he wouldn't let her walk outside the front door on her own or with any of her siblings. She still remembers vividly the last time her father raped her because he became more violent than usual and began to attack her with a knife. She 'saw everything red' and decided to leave home and report him to the police.

She described bringing the case against her father in court as a nightmare: 'I didn't know what I was going to be put through; it was like a knife going through your heart. My Dad looked at me and told me: "I will kill you". My Dad's solicitor was very nasty to me and said I was making it all up and that he had never done anything against me. I started shouting at him, telling him he was sick in the head.' As a result of the court appearance and on the strength of the evidence put forward by the prosecution of the old adverts in the local newspapers which she had carefully kept, her father was sent to prison and sentenced for rape, prostitution and incest. Meantime, her mother had remarried.

After a period of promiscuous behaviour, Ms B started a relationship with Jason, a drug addict with a criminal record, with whom she had her first three children, around the same time as her mother had two more children in her new marriage. Jason and Ms B used to indulge in much drinking and drug abuse. At the beginning he was considerate but quickly he became very nasty and violent towards her. He began to hit her, beat her up and break things in the flat they shared. Soon after she fell pregnant with their first baby he was sent to prison. After his release the fights continued and the violence at home escalated further and further. She began to experience him as being like her father, but still felt very much in love with him. Revealingly she said: 'Things have not changed a lot really because Jason hits me in front of the kids and does the things my dad used to do to my mum. When Jason starts beating me up I feel as if it is my dad beating me up again and that I am the child again. I get very scared because he behaves then like a madman. Every time I tell Jason that we are finished he starts acting like a child about to lose his mum, then I feel sorry for him and stay with him.' Although she was aware of the repetition, she was unable to disengage herself from this pattern. In other words, awareness does not equate to insight.

394

Every attempt she made to terminate this relationship was doomed to fail since she tried very hard to convince herself that he was a caring, loving person and consistently facilitated their being together. De Zulueta (1993) vividly describes this pattern when she discusses the aftermath of violence which brings victim and abuser together in a state of calmness in which the victim forgives and becomes reconciled with the brutal partner in the yearning for the fantasy of many sexually abused victims of 'being one again' (1993: 186). This happens because they become mirror images of each other with an unconscious resonance of the early sexual abuse and the compulsive need for revenge. This achieved 'calmness' is only transient because it responds to unconscious projections of their own cruelty and sadism onto the other. Person and Klar (1994: 1075–6) note that the significance of trauma seems to be cut off from awareness in the person who has suffered the trauma.

Ms B's relationship with Jason became more violent when she fell pregnant for the second time. She was against pursuing this pregnancy but she acquiesced to Jason's determination for her to have his second baby. In the meanwhile she tried several times to separate from Jason without success because of her own inconsistency and ambivalence. By this time she had become 'addicted' (her own word) to more violence and accepted a situation which repeated the abuse she had suffered previously.

Jason was delighted at the birth of their second child, a boy called Jason after his father. However, the domestic violence continued, and the two young children were neglected and put at risk. Eventually they were removed and placed with foster parents. Ms B felt very upset about social services taking away the children because, in her opinion, they had never been hurt. This response revealed her degree of dissociation, namely her lack of awareness of her children's needs and of the long-term consequences they would suffer from being the constant witnesses to their parents' ferocious fights and of her own battering at the hands of their father.

She felt completely isolated and unable to rely on anybody including her brothers and sister who were very angry with her because of her 'sending' their father to prison. Ms B had been left on her own without any family resources, and had further perpetuated herself in the victim role. However, as a result of her father going to prison, she felt that she had inadvertently liberated her mother from her marriage to her father and had 'allowed' her to find a 'good' relationship leading to 'good' parenting of new babies, her own half-siblings, around the same age as her own children. After the court appearance Ms B received some counselling, but she interrupted it because she could not tolerate examining old areas of intense pain. She resorted to drinking in excess and taking overdoses. In discussing her drinking she said that 'without the drink I would most likely have gone mad. Drinking did save my life in a funny sort of way.' Dissociation was progressing as a desperate means of survival. Joseph (1981) describes the silencing of psychic pain that patients attempt as the only concrete way of dealing with it.

Unexpectedly Ms B learnt that her son Jason, by then aged 18 months, had died in an accident while living with foster parents. Surprisingly enough she never expressed any angry feelings against the authorities on this account. Quite the contrary, she expressed feelings of guilt for not having her little boy living with her at that time. Instead, she felt in urgent need of an immediate replacement for Jason junior – a pathological mourning process was in full operation. I was amazed when she told me that on reflection her 'serious' problems began when Lenny, the youngest baby boy, was born. She was bitterly disappointed because he did not resemble little Jason at all. She felt completely detached from him and unable to create any bonding. She was unable to mourn Jason and the bereavement had brought alive all her old and apparently dormant episodes of unacknowledged grief associated with the absence of good enough parenting and the losses of her parents and of her first two children. The mothering disturbance of a replacement child following the unmourned loss of a previous child has been well described by Lewis (1978, 1979) and by Etchegoyen (1997).

I think this sense of estrangement from her new baby enabled her to give him up for adoption and also to terminate her relationship with his father. She began to live on her own. A few months later her estranged partner Jason was found dead from an overdose. She told me: 'My first reaction was a great sense of relief in knowing that I couldn't any longer be addicted to him or to be brutalized by him.'

A brief period of promiscuity was followed by her openly seducing Alan, a 14-year-old boy, for whom she used to babysit. She enticed him with the idea of becoming a proud father and soon after she became pregnant. According to her, despite his youth, Alan was very supportive, mature and kind to her and both were very happy about the pregnancy which was a 'planned' one.

What appears to be a new scenario is actually the old one turned upside down. She was now cast as the abuser. She may have anticipated that for once she would be in complete control of a relationship by being involved with a youngster who would feel very proud of the achievement of becoming a father at such an early age, and she believed herself to be in command of the situation. Instead, as soon as the pregnancy was announced she became again a victim, with Alan's parents taking her to court charged with indecent assault on a minor. She was sentenced to two years probation. Subsequently she breached the probation order by approaching Alan with letters. During the court case Alan denied being the father of the baby and she was much mocked by him and his parents. However, she kept insisting that he was a very nice person who treated her very kindly and never admitted feeling exposed and humiliated. She felt unable to acknowledge the degree of cruelty and sadistic behaviour from Alan and his family towards her. She used denial and defensive self-deception when claiming she was able to have a good and equal relationship with Alan, whose views about becoming a father could not have been taken seriously in any realistic sense.

Ms B was unaware of the links between the early abuse and her 'addiction' to forming sadomasochistic relationships. In effect, the sadomasochistic relationship *is* the abuse – the abuse lives on encrypted in the present sadomasochistic relationship. This is what repetition compulsion means – the past *is* the present (Abraham and Torok 1987). The most striking feature of Ms B's sessions with me was her fixed smile, by which she tried hard to convey the picture of a person who has resolved all her previous problems and is ready to lead a different kind of life. It seemed to me that her fixed smile and her ready laugh at any comment being made contained an intense denial of the pain and deeply ingrained hurt feelings. I am reminded of Joseph's (1981) conceptualization of the 'growing pains', making the important point that only when people can take in the capacity for suffering are they able to experience the capacity for enjoyment.

The problem about this complete split and denial of her feelings of frustration, anger, hurt and pain is that they could emerge unexpectedly and suddenly, either in acts of self-destruction or acts against the outside world. I felt it was impossible to predict if these could be directed against her new baby girl. Mrs B took unnecessary risks at the time, for example, ending up in jail for eight days while pregnant because of breaching the terms of her bail condition by approaching Alan. This suggests an incapacity to take into account the needs of her unborn baby, putting his care at risk. Once more her self-deception, lack of emotional maturity and inability to learn from past experiences were in evidence when she was taken by surprise that her new baby girl Cindy was eventually taken away from her. She had never imagined that this could happen.

Despite the fact that she had been able to disentangle herself courageously from the incest, her self-destructiveness had continued mercilessly. This included repeated episodes of severe self-harm, overdoses and suicide attempts; acts directed against one's body, which are in some cases precursors of acts directed against one's baby. The attacks on herself were provoked by feelings of anger, despair, isolation and an extreme inability to trust anybody with her feelings. She was acting out her sadomasochistic needs against her own body, protecting everyone else around her from her rage, this being her only way of making herself feel better and at peace by acquiescing to her excitedly sadistic superego demands. Later, in her relationship with Jason, she repeated the abusive situation. In this case, the effect of the abuse was also extended to their children, in a way of which Ms B was utterly unaware. When she was a victim of Jason's brutal attacks, she had became severely dissociated, in other words, completely unavailable or unable to take proper care of herself or her children, so the children became the object of neglect as a continuation and expansion of her own abuse. After all and sadly she could not escape following her mother's engagement in a malignant bonding.

Exploring this young woman's ideas about what she would like to do in life, she expressed a wish to be either a nurse or to work in an old people's home. Sometimes young women in similar circumstances claim that they want to keep on having more children or to have a job taking care of other women's children. They also often express a desire to be with handicapped people. It is very difficult for them to see any link between their own areas of need, deprivation and neglect as children and adults and their wish to take care of children in a way in which they would themselves have liked to have been treated. This wish suggests a degree of reparation for their own feelings of being so undeserving, damaged and ruined forever that, because of guilt and shame, the only way they are able to provide some care for themselves is by proxy, by projecting into others, considered to be 'blameless vulnerable people', their own unacknowledged internal needs. They find it difficult, if not impossible, to establish any significant relationships of mutuality and care, often protesting an emotional 'self-sufficiency' (Bowlby 1980) which is very precariously based.

The problem is that, as Garland (1998) argues, the nearer the re-enactment is to the original trauma, the more it represents an inability to make use of thought processes and symbolism. This will lead to a compulsion to repeat, which again brings us back to the original trauma. I suggest that we are capable of looking at this cycle of victim–perpetrator more easily in other victims of abuse than in those who repeatedly fall pregnant. Maternity, or the capacity to be fecund, is viewed in a different light because the mother's body is actively involved in the delivery of both a perpetrator in action and a victim in the future. The newborn baby may well be in a process of identification with her self-abusive mother and as such when grown up, if a girl, could be involved in acts of self-harm and later of harm to her babies. That is why I called it 'the body as a torturer'.

I do not believe that we can break the cycle by offering her a baby, however seductive the picture is of a young mother and her baby together. Instead, we should be offering this young woman who is so badly emotionally and mentally damaged professional help for herself. It was painful to watch how all Ms B's efforts to fight against her terrible fate were doomed to fail due to the fixed belief she holds of not being able to contain any good bits, or being deserving of some peace of mind. Perpetuating her role as the abused child in her sadomasochistic relationship with Jason, she was unconsciously prepared to put her own children in a traumatizing situation of violence and neglect, and finally she herself became an abuser, albeit a more benign one, with the 14-year-old boy. Is the cycle of abuse completed? I do not believe so, since a new baby has been born whose father denies being her father and whose mother is left once more on her own with a highly self-denigratory image, since her expectations of her self-esteem being increased by becoming a mother have once more been bitterly disappointed.

References

Abraham, N. and Torok, M. (1987) *The Shell and the Kernel: Renewals of Psychoanalysis*. Chicago: University of Chicago Press, 1994.

Bowlby, J. (1980) *Attachment and Loss: Vol. III: Loss, Sadness and Depression.* London: Hogarth Press and Institute of Psychoanalysis.

Bronfen, E. (1992) *Over Her Dead Body: Death, Feminity and the Aesthetic.* Manchester: Manchester University Press.

De Zulueta, F. (1993) *From Pain to Violence: The Traumatic Roots of Destructiveness.* London: Whurr, p. 186

Etchegoyen, A. (1997) 'Inhibition of mourning and the replacement child syndrome', in J. Raphael-Leff and R. J. Perelberg *Female Experience: Three Generations of British Women Psychoanalysts on Work with Women.* London and New York: Routledge, pp. 195–218.

Etchegoyen, R. H. (1978) 'Some thoughts on transference perversion'. *Int. J. Psycho-Anal.*, 59: 45–53.

Filippini, S. (2005) 'Perverse relationships: the perspective of the perpetrator'. *Int. J. Psycho-Anal.*, 86: 755–773.

Freud, S. (1920) 'Beyond the pleasure principle'. *S.E.* 18: 1–64.

Freud, S. (1923) 'The ego and the id'. *S.E.* 19: 1–66.

Garland, C. (1998) *Understanding Trauma: A Psychoanalytic Approach.* London: Duckworth.

Green, A. (1972) *On Private Madness.* London: Rebus Press, pp. 142–173.

Joseph, B. (1981). 'Towards the experiencing of psychic pain', in B. Joseph, *Psychic Equilibrium and Psychic Change: Selected Papers of Betty Joseph.* London and New York: Tavistock/Routledge, 1989.

Lewis, E. (1979) 'Inhibition of mourning by pregnancy: psychopathology and management'. *BMJ* 2: 27–28.

Lewis, E. and Page, A. (1978) 'Failure to mourn a stillbirth: an overlooked catastrophe'. *Br. J. Med. Psychol*, 51: 237–241.

McDougall, J. (1989) *Theatres of the Body: A Psychoanalytic Approach to Psychosomatic Illness.* New York: Norton.

Motz, A. (2001) *The Psychology of Female Violence: Crimes Against the Body.* Hove, UK: Brunner-Routledge.

Ogden, T. H. (1996) 'The perverse subject of analysis.' *J. Amer. Psychoanal. Assn.*, 44: 1121–1146.

Pandolfi, A. M. (1999) 'Le perversioni relazioni nella coppia e nella famiglia'. Paper presented at Convegno Internazionale CeRP 'Lo psicoanalista con e senza divano. Individui, famiglie, i situzioni tra psicosi e perversioni'. Verona, 12–13 November.

Person, E. (1999) 'Corpo riddotto al silenzio, corpo nemico: una fantasia di percosse nella genesi del sadomasochismo e dell'ipocondria', in F. Molbino and C. Zanardi (eds) *Sintomi Corpo Femminilita: Dall'isteria alla bulimia Clueb.* Bologna: Cooperativa Libraria Universitaria Editrice, pp. 305–325

Person, E. and Klar, H. (1994) 'Establishing trauma: the difficulty in distinguishing between memories and fantasies'. *J. Amer. Psychoanal. Ass.*, 42: 1055–1081.

Welldon, E. V. (1988) *Mother, Madonna, Whore: The Idealization and Denigration of Motherhood*. London: Free Association Books.

Welldon, E. V. (1999) 'La ripetizione dell'abuso e dei maltrattamenti da una generazione all'altra', in F. Molfino and C. Zanardi (eds) *Sintomi Corpo Femminilita: Dall'isteria alla bulimia Clueb*. Bologna: Cooperativa Libraria Universitaria Editrice.

Welldon, E. V. (2001) 'Babies as transitional objects', in B. Kahr (ed.) *Forensic Psychotherapy and Psychopathology: Winnicottian Perspectives*. London: Karnac.

Welldon, E. V. (2002) *Sadomasochism: Ideas in Psychoanalysis*. New York: Totem Books; London: Icon Books.

Welldon, E. V. (2007) 'The malignant bonding'. Unpublished lecture at APRAGI School of Psychotherapy, Torino.

Welldon, E. V. (2010) *Playing with Dynamite: A Personal Approach to the Psychoanalytic Understanding of Perversions, Violence, and Criminality*. London: Karnac.

Index

abandonment, fear of 143
Abarbanel, J. 21, 39, 55
Ablon, S. L. 84
abortion(s) 2, 72, 207, 255, 256, 280;
  intentional (clinical example)
  274–6; planned 267, 269, 274, 275,
  277; spontaneous 267, 268, 269,
  277
abuse: child 318, 390; cycle(s) of,
  across generations 381–99; early/
  childhood, and addiction to
  sadomasochistic relationships 397;
  sexual 260, 388, 392, 395
abusers, female 389
abusive mothering,
  countertransference issues in
  treatment of (clinical example)
  389–99
abusive parenting 255
acupuncture 242
Adelson, E. 26, 257, 259, 261, 262,
  352–77, 379
adolescence 35–8; and experience
  of shame 98 [and hatred, mother's
  capacity to bear 105, 109]; and
  feminine identity 274; and
  mother–daughter bond 28;
  motherhood during 308–11;
  mothering/motherhood in 54,

261–4, 359 [vicissitudes of envy in
  306–21]; and myth of Medea 179,
  187; narcissistic abuse by mother
  during 195; psychic breakdown
  during 194, 198; and
  reconfiguration of psychic life 74;
  and repression 125; resolution of
  sexual identity 268; search for
  autonomy during 52, 296;
  self-abuse during 382;
  "unfinished" 369–70 [completion
  of 377, 378]
adoption 165, 198, 206, 225, 226,
  228, 245, 390, 396
adoptive mothers 141
aggressor, identification with 21, 334,
  342, 382, 387
AID 206
AIH 206
Allison, G. H. 160
alternative medicine 242
ambivalence (*passim*): concept of 17;
  decrease in (Klein) 88; manageable
  88, 98, 108; maternal 48, 256, 270
  [clinical example 89–95; towards
  foetus 277; manageable 85; and
  shame 85–110; towards baby
  52–4]; towards mother 383;
  parental 53; pre-conceptive 53;

402

Down's syndrome 185, 189, 319
dreams during pregnancy 72

eating disorders 184, 257, 328, 382
ectopic pregnancy 69, 75, 210, 213,
    214, 215, 220, 223, 225
ego: boundaries, loss of 154;
    immaturity 65; maturity 65
ego ideal 98, 99, 102, 105, 237
Ehrensaft, D. 164
Electra: complex 259, 290–3; myth
    291, 297
embodied simulation 5
Emde, R. N. 4, 5
enactments 245, 294, 345
endocrinology, reproductive 164
'enigmatic message' 7
envy: comforts of (clinical example)
    311–20; and deprivation 306–8;
    maternal 15; pathological, of
    mother's creative ability 234;
    primary 307, 308; unbearable 182;
    vicissitudes of, in adolescent
    motherhood 306–21
Erikson, E. 8, 9
erotic sadomasochism 387
erotic side of maternality 5–7
erotic transference, male analysand's
    116
eroticization, compulsive 386; *see also*
    sexualization
erotism, maternal 6
erotogenic zone, skin as 5
estrodial 246
Etchegoyen, A. 385, 386, 396
ethnic groups, migrations of 169
Euripides 70, 172, 173, 177, 182, 195,
    200, 291
Evans, D. 116
expert witness, role of 389

failure to thrive 338; clinical example
    352–79

Faimberg, H. 258, 259
Fain, M. 11, 15
family planning 207
'fantasy child' 13
father: body ego of 154–5; daughter's
    identification with 8; 'Law of' 29,
    31; Oedipal 26, 30, 160 [mother's
    28]; pregenital 198; pre-oedipal
    198; and problems in motherhood
    30; and space of third 26–31;
    weak/ineffectual 'Law of' 29, 31
Faure-Pragier, S. 20, 160, 161
Feder, L. 53
feeding, baby's oral pleasure in 6
female abusers 389
female body ego 139
female destructiveness 70, 170, 195
female development 45, 46, 116, 133,
    287, 290, 291, 297
female gender identification 50
female gender studies, literature on
    117
female identity, development of 199
female life cycle 298
female pathology 291, 297
female violence, transgenerational
    transmission of 173
'feminine complex' (Klein) 30
femininity, primary 114, 137
feminism 46
feminist movement 46
fertility 9, 34, 160–3, 192, 233–9, 241;
    diagnostic assessment of,
    psychotherapy during (clinical
    example) 210–28; problematic
    207; procedures 242; symbol of 18;
    transgenerational 180; treatment
    162
fetish, baby as 385
fibroid tumours 248
foetus, maternal ambivalence towards
    277
Fonagy, P. 102, 108, 196

30570786R00243

Printed in Great Britain
by Amazon

Unconditional Love and Respect

How Positive Parenting Can Elevate the Relationship Between You and Your Child

Laurena Charley M.D.

Unconditional Love and Respect

Unconditional Love and Respect

CONTENTS

Unconditional Love and Respect

INTRODUCTION

Parenting is the hardest job that you will ever have. If you have a child, then you know that this is true. Your child will do things that push your buttons and even infuriate you, yet at the end of the day, you want to be able to go to bed knowing that you showed him or her in every way possible how much you love him or her. You want to have a positive and meaningful relationship with your child but imposing discipline and consequences always stand in the way.

Positive parenting is a parenting style that helps do away with these paradoxes by placing the child's need for a relationship at the center of everything you do. When the connection comes before correction and relationship comes before rules, you put yourself and your child in a situation in which he or she wants to learn from and have a relationship with you. Positive parenting reduces the stress of the parent-child relationship, thereby eliminating many negative behaviors that are caused by stress. It also empowers parents to approach their children in ways that are meaningful to the child's developmental level so that lessons imparted are not lost.

This book will guide you through some of the principles of positive parenting so that you can begin to use them with your own child and reap the rewards of a happy and healthy home.

CHAPTER 1: THE POSITIVE APPROACH

Karen was at her wit's end. Her son, Josh, was getting into trouble at school; she got a call or an email from his teacher at least once a week. She had tried everything she knew to do: taking away his video games, prohibiting him from watching television, sending him to his room, not letting him go out with his friends, forcing him to do his homework before he could do anything else. She had even gotten him into counseling, but he smart-mouthed her every time he went. Karen had no desire to continue paying money every week for him to verbally abuse someone. Despite her best efforts, his behavior and grades continued to deteriorate. In fact, the harder that she tried to discipline him, the more he acted out at home, too. Her house was becoming an increasingly difficult place to be because her relationship with her son was so unpleasant.

Karen sat down at her desk at work, trying to focus on the project that she needed to finish by the end of the week. She got started on it, but after only half an hour, her phone was buzzing. She looked down at it and saw, with at least a small amount of apprehension, that the school was calling her. She ignored the call, hoping that maybe the school could handle this one. After all, they were the trained professionals, right? And nothing that she was trying at home was working. She put her phone on silent and got back to work.

Not five minutes later, her desk phone rang; the receptionist was calling her. "Hello?" she said.

"Hi, Karen? There's a call for you on line 3. Can you take it?"

"Do you know who the caller is?"

"The principal of your son's school."

A knot of dread and anxiety filled Karen's stomach as she accepted the call. "Hello?" she said, trepidation filling her voice.

"Ms. Jones," the principal said. "Josh is in the office with me. He just cursed out his teacher."

"I'm so sorry," she stammered. "I don't know what's gotten into him lately."

"I'm afraid that your son's behavior has gotten out of control. He is going to be suspended for the next five days. Please come over now to pick him up. I trust that when he comes back, he will have learned how to show respect."

Karen's heart sank. What was she going to do with Josh at home for the next week? She wouldn't be able to work, and this big project was due in just a couple of days! Maybe his dad could take him until he was allowed to go back to school. She leaned back in her desk and groaned before picking up the phone to call her manager. "Hello, David?" she said when he answered. "I have to go pick up my son at school. I'll be back in a couple of hours."

While driving to Josh's school, a horrifying thought hit Karen. She wasn't just lost and confused about how to handle Josh. She didn't even like being a parent anymore. She felt like she was just trying to survive until he finished high school and moved out of the house. Something had to change.

Can you relate at all to Karen's story? Do you ever feel like no matter how hard you try to discipline your child, he or she just becomes more rebellious? Do you feel like your relationship with your child is fraught with negativity and stress? You are not alone.

Oftentimes when we think of discipline, we think of the negative consequences that we must impose on our children in response to misbehavior. More often than not, we end up frustrated and the children don't "learn their lesson," leading to more and more misbehavior. The problem with this approach is that it doesn't take into account what discipline really is. The word discipline comes from the word disciple. A disciple is someone who follows a leader or a teacher. Rather than negative consequences, discipline is actually the process of teaching your child. It extends far beyond outward behaviors because first and foremost, it deals with what is going on inside the child, causing the misbehavior. When those root causes are addressed in such a way that the child's basic needs are met, the misbehavior begins to go away on its own.

This is not to say that correction is not necessary. Correction is absolutely necessary, as children do not have the neurological development necessary to make good and meaningful choices for themselves, not the way that adults can. They can be much more impulsive and selfish, and unable to regulate some of their own emotions and behaviors. Correction should be viewed as part of discipline: teaching the child how to behave appropriately, in such a way that the child knows that he or she is loved.

Correction is a far cry from punishment. Punishment includes things like spanking and yelling. It negatively affects the child and does not address the behavior or cause of the behavior. While correction has a negative impact on the misbehavior (for example, the misbehavior of slamming doors is negatively impacted when the child no longer slams doors), punishment has a negative impact on the child. Punishment makes children feel that they are worthless, incapable of doing anything right, and undeserving of love. Not only does it not correct the misbehavior, but it also leaves marks that do not easily go away.

The positive approach to parenting advocates discipline and correction and rejects all forms of punishment. Sometimes yelling may be necessary, especially if the child is in danger (yelling at a five-year-old who is about to step out in front of a car is protecting, not punishing); however, for those inculcated with a mindset of punishment and imposing negative consequences, a complete paradigm shift may be necessary.

Positive parenting begins with changing the way that you see your child and your role as a parent. Take, for example, the word authority. When people think about the word authority, they may envision someone over them who must be obeyed, at all costs. The person to be obeyed may be a boss, a political leader, or a child's parent. However, the word authority actually comes from the word augment, which means to increase something. It is the same root as the word author or someone who is telling a story. In other words, your position of authority over your child is not one of demanding obedience but rather one of helping your child author his or her story. While obedience is an important part of the parent-child relationship, it should never be considered the goal. Your job as a parent is not to make your child obey you. Rather, obedience is a means to the end of raising a healthy, happy, and confident child.

Our actions always begin as beliefs. Beliefs about ourselves and the world around us — whether it is a safe place or a dangerous one, whether we are worthy of love or deserving of neglect and abuse — from the way that we think. Those thoughts, in turn, are displayed as behaviors. If I believe that I am worthless, I will act as if I am worthless by doing negative things such as hurting other people. If I believe that I am loved and valued, I will act as if I am loved and valued by being kind and treating others with respect. This applies both to you and your child. If your child forgot something and in turn, you call your child a liar, you are actually creating a self-fulfilling prophecy; the child who believes that he or she is a liar will become one, and you will have one lie after another to deal with. However, if you are understanding of your child and accept that a seven-year-old is liable to forget things (aren't we all liable to forget things?), and instead of calling him or her a liar you help your child recall the truth, you have set him or her up, to tell the truth without fear. If you believe that your primary role as a parent is to make your child behave, then you will pursue that goal at the expense of meeting your child's basic needs, especially those of knowing that he or she is loved and valued. However, if you believe that your primary role as a parent is to prepare your child for the world in such a way that he or she is aimed for a successful life, then you will make choices that will gear your child towards a positive self-identity and the ability to succeed.

At its core, positive parenting is a belief system. It is believing that encouragement and love promote far more goodness than any kind of punitive action. It is believing that children should be able to live their lives free from crippling fear, doubt, guilt, and shame and should grow up with love and respect. You believe that your child deserves respect, even when he or she misbehaves. Most of all, positive parenting is believing in your child, believing that even when your child messes up, he or she has what it takes. Your child is enough, and both of you know this. He or she has no need to strive for your love and attention because they are unconditional.

CHAPTER 2: BASIC CONCEPTS OF THE POSITIVE APPROACH

When Karen got out of the car and made her way through the parking lot and to the school's main doors, her cheeks burned with shame. She knew that the teachers and administration blamed her for Josh's poor behavior. Even before entering the principal's office, she could feel the penetrating glare that she knew would speak volumes about her own inadequacies as a mother.

Josh was sitting in a chair across from the main reception desk in the office. He barely even glanced up when he saw her; he picked up his backpack and stood up to leave. Without saying a word or making eye contact with anyone, not even Josh, she signed him out of school. Josh followed her out of the office, through the parking lot, and into the car.

They didn't say a word until they arrived home. Karen parked in the driveway and didn't make a move to get out. Josh just sat there. "What am I supposed to say?" she asked him quietly. "I'm supposed to be at work right now. I have a big project that is due. And instead, I have to figure out where you will go for the next week because you can't seem to behave. I'm trying, Josh. I'm really trying. But I am so ashamed of how you acted."

Josh mumbled something under his breath, but Karen didn't hear it. "What was that?" she said.

"I'm sorry," he mumbled again, only slightly louder this time.

"Sorry doesn't fix this. If you can't get your act together, I could lose my job."

Wordlessly, Josh got out of the car and made his way inside. Karen followed him and went straight to her bedroom. She closed the door behind her and sat down on her bed, too overwhelmed to cry. A few minutes later, she picked up the phone and dialed the number of the therapist that Josh had verbally abused in all of his sessions.

"Hello?" the therapist said on the second ring.

"Hi, Justine," Karen said. "This is Karen Jones. You saw my son, Josh, a few times earlier this year."

"Oh, yes. I remember him."

"I'm sure you do. He had some rather colorful things to say to you. Look, I'm at my wit's end. He just got suspended from school, and I don't know what to do. I'm just wondering if, maybe..." She paused for several moments before continuing. "Maybe the problem isn't Josh. Maybe it's me."

"Why do you say that?" Justine asked.

"Because I no longer even like being his mother. I don't like how that feels."

"Why don't you come in this afternoon? I can see you at 4:30."

"I'm not sure that therapy will help Josh."

"This session isn't for Josh. It's for you."

Karen paused again. She looked at the clock; it was already 11. Feeling that she had no energy left, she knew that there was no point in returning to work. She would have to call David and let him know that she wouldn't be back for the rest of the day. "OK," she said to Justine. "I'll be there."

After hanging up, Karen sat on her bed. She was going to be home with Josh for the next five hours. What on earth was she going to do with him for the next five hours? For the next week? Surprised by her own actions, she went to Josh's room and knocked on the door. She could hear the music blaring from inside his room.

A minute later, he opened the door. When she looked at him, she realized that what he needed wasn't more groundings, more things are taken away, fewer privileges. What he needed was her. "Are you hungry?" she asked.

Josh shrugged his shoulders.

"Come with me to the kitchen. Let's cook something for lunch."

At those words, the expression on Josh's face perked up and looked almost surprised. "Okay," he muttered. "Can we have macaroni and cheese?"

"Sure," she said.

Karen is on the process of realizing that her attitude towards her son and lack of belief in his own abilities and character is ultimately what is holding him back. If she doesn't like her son and no longer enjoys being his mother, then him coming to like himself and develop a healthy self-esteem is virtually impossible. He will continue to rebel and act out as a primal way to try to gain the affirmation that he isn't getting at home. But if her attitude towards him changes, if she can see him for all the potential that he holds despite the poor choices that he is making in the moment, then he will have a better chance of developing into an emotionally mature young man and succeeding in life.

Communicate with Your Child

Communication is at the heart of all successful relationships. Lack of communication in any relationship setting leads to unfulfilled expectations, lack of trust, disrespect, and ultimately a dissolution of the relationship. Your child is not as mature as you are, but the parent-child relationship must be built on strong and effective communication.

What does your child enjoy doing for fun? What does your child need to know or hear from you? What are his or her favorite foods? Who are his or her friends, and what makes a good friend? What does he or she enjoy about school, and what would make school more enjoyable? Why does he or she feel angry, sad, happy, nervous, guilty, or ashamed? Why did he or she feel the need to tell a lie instead of the truth? These are just a few very important things that you should know about your child. If you want to know them, talk to your child about them!

Good communication is always built on mutual trust and respect. If someone in a relationship is afraid of retribution for any reason, communication will be shut down. Open and honest communication with your child means that he or she cannot have any reason to feel afraid of what you may do or say when you hear what he or she really thinks. Assure your child that you are more interested in getting to know him or her as a person than you are about providing negative consequences for thoughts or choices that may be inappropriate. Help your child feel free to open up to you about important things.

Make sure that you communicate in a way that is age appropriate. A rebellious teenager who doesn't seem to be interested in a relationship with you should not be treated like a preschooler. Rather, he or she should be treated like a young adult who is capable of making good decisions, whether or not those good decisions are currently being made. A kindergartener is not capable of processing abstract, higher thought about things like morals and ethics. Make sure that you are connecting with your child on a level that he or she can understand.

After learning to successfully communicate with you, your child will be much more well-equipped to communicate well with others.

Follow Your Child's Lead

If you are like most parents, you probably entered into

parenthood with a set of expectations of what you would do with your child: vacations you would take, pleasures that you would share, foods you would cook together, books you would read, sports you would play, etcetera. Now that you are in the throes of parenting, some of those expectations are probably being disrupted on a routine basis. No matter how much you loved reading *The Boxcar Children* as a kid, your child may just not be interested. Even though you always dreamed of teaching your child to play soccer, he or she may not even be interested in sports at all.

Instead of trying to force your child to do things that he or she isn't even interested in, follow the child's lead. Look at what he or she is interested in, whether it be rock climbing or playing with cats or reading. Some things that your child is interested in may either be inappropriate (such as books with sexual themes) or need clear limitations (such as video games). As much as is responsible, encourage your child to follow those pursuits.

Maybe discipline that was effective on you is entirely ineffective on your child; furthermore, maybe discipline methods that work for one of your children are completely lost on another. That does not mean that there is a problem with your child! Far from it. All children are different. They have different personalities and experience the world differently. Again, follow your child's lead. If your preschooler thinks that timeout is a game, then instead of letting him or her press your buttons, maybe you should find an alternative to time out. If grounding only makes your older child more secretive and determined to keep things from you, then you may want to reconsider that method of discipline. Do what works for your child, not what you think should work.

Genuinely Praise and Compliment Your Child

Children are in the process of developing their personalities, and they need encouragement from the adults in their lives to help them along. Providing them with genuine praise and compliments helps them to discover what they excel at and what they enjoy.

Flattery is not genuine. Most people, including children, can spot flattery a mile away. Many either ignore it or draw back from it. Few people like a flatterer and the last thing that you want to do is to set your child up to be manipulated by flattery. Don't lavish in praise indiscriminately.

Make your compliments and praise specific to the child and what he or she is doing. If your preschooler wants to color all of his or her pictures yellow, say that he or she likes yellow, and yellow is a wonderful color. This will affirm your child as well as his or her interests. If your older child is showing a penchant for social justice, point that out. Let him or her know that wanting to help people have equal rights and be treated fairly is a noble goal that more people should pursue. Your child may be even more determined to pursue those ambitions!

Make Time for Your Child

Children spell love t-i-m-e. Few things are more discouraging or disheartening to a child than for the adults in his or her life to not make time. Make a habit of having family dinners in the evening. Instead of insisting that your child read a book instead of playing video games, either read a book together or join in on the video games! Go to the park. Watch movies together. Instead of just trying to survive the week, spend quality time with your child.

In summary, positive parenting is not a prescribed set of rules to follow with a promise of certain results. Rather, it is an emphasis on building a healthy relationship with your child so that positive interactions can occur naturally on a regular basis. That positivity is the basis of your relationship, and it sets your child up for a healthy sense of self in the face of a difficult world.

CHAPTER 3: UNDERSTANDING DEVELOPMEN-
TAL APPROPRIATENESS

Your three-year-old son wants a car for Christmas. Obviously, there is no way that you are going to go to the car lot to buy your
preschooler a new vehicle. So, what do you do? Do you ignore the
request for a car, or do you try to figure out what your child is really
asking for? Using the positive parenting concept of communicating
respectfully with your child, you ask him why he wants a car and
what kind of car he wants. When he answers you by saying that he
wants it for his race track, you realize that what he actually wants is a
toy race car, not a brand-new Prius! That is a much more developmentally appropriate gift.

Humans are born with the most undeveloped brain of almost
any mammal. The brain takes about 21 to 25 years to fully develop;
during that time of development, children and adolescents are capable of processing some tasks but not others. For example, the survival center of the brain is almost fully developed at birth, so even very
young children are capable of going into "survival mode," which may
manifest itself as a temper tantrum. However, they are not capable of
higher levels of thought, such as moral reasoning. Developmental

appropriateness is about understanding that there are some things that children can do at different stages of their development, and there are some things that they are incapable of. This is not because of unwillingness to learn but because their brains are not yet able to do certain things; furthermore, they need someone to teach them how to do things when they are ready to move on to that next level.

Developmentally appropriate practices are those that take into consideration the child's developmental level (regardless if that is the same as the child's chronological age) and individual personality. This chapter will look at developmental appropriateness at each stage of maturity; while the stages of maturity will correspond to a particular age for purposes of organization, your child's chronological age may not be directly correlated to his or her stage of maturity.

Infant (Birth to One Year)

Babies are incredibly selfish. Their worlds begin and end at their own selves, and for this stage in their lives, that's OK. They need someone else to meet their needs of food, drink, staying clean, and love and affection. They need someone to regulate their schedules by making sure that they eat and sleep at regular intervals. They aren't concerned about anyone else's needs because they are so preoccupied with getting their own met. While that level of maturity is not appropriate for an older child and certainly not for an adult, it is entirely in keeping with the developmental level of an infant.

In order to reach their potential so that they can progress to the next stage of development, babies need for their caregivers to respond to their needs. When your infant daughter cries because she is hungry and you immediately feed her, she learns that she is safe and can trust you. When your infant son is fussy because he has an ear infection and you comfort him by holding and rocking him, he learns that he is secure and loved. The development of trust is the most crucial thing during this stage of life, and it is learned by you, as the parent, responding to every single one of your baby's needs.

Your infant is unable to experience any world outside of his or her own self. Expecting an infant to share toys with another infant or give you a break because you are feeling tired is far beyond his or her capabilities. Babies are selfish, and that's OK. What's important is that they don't remain selfish as they grow but rather learn, as they are developmentally able to, to care for other people. This is learned by them seeing you care for them and meeting their needs.

Toddler (One to Two Years Old)

At this stage of development, your child is developing some independence and is learning to do some things for himself or herself. Your toddler is developing autonomy and learning to see that he or she is a distinct person, separate from you. One of the greatest temptations at this stage is to insist on doing everything for your toddler still because you can do it faster and more effectively. Dressing your daughter instead of letting her dress herself, at least partially, or feeding your son because he makes too big of a mess when he feeds himself is certainly easier. However, positive parenting is about following your child's lead, encouraging, and praising him or her for accomplishments. When your child sees himself or herself as capable of doing things independently, he or she develops self-confidence.

Preschool (3 to 5 Years Old)

At this stage of development, children begin to take initiative to do things on their own. Instead of you telling your son to get dressed, he may decide to change clothes multiple times throughout the day. Instead of you trying to get your daughter to play, she may initiate play on her own. At this stage, it is important that you allow your child to take initiative, whenever you can safely do so, and follow what your child is doing. For example, if your daughter wants to play house, play house with her. Instead of dictating which of her toys is "mommy," "daddy," "baby," etcetera, let her decide. This ability to take initiative in positive ways helps to develop leadership abilities so that when your child is older, he or she won't just follow the crowd. It also lets your child know that you are supportive of the things that he or she enjoys; in turn, you help his or her personality develop in positive and meaningful ways.

Elementary School (6 to 12 Years Old)

As a school-aged child, your child is probably interacting much more with his or her peers than with family members; in fact, friends may have more influence over your child than you do. That's OK and perfectly normal! Encourage him or her to spend time with friends, and when appropriate, spend time with your child and his or her friends.

At this stage, your child needs to feel that he or she is competent and able to perform well in an area that is valued. Your encouragement in areas that your child feels are important is very significant. This is not the same as teaching your child to follow the crowd or that he or she must derive identity from having what everybody else has. Rather, it is about teaching your child that he or she is a valuable and capable human being who is learning to find a place in the world outside of the home.

Remember that open, honest, and respectful communication is one of the primary concepts of positive parenting. If your son comes to you wanting to join a baseball team but has never expressed interest in baseball before, ask him why he wants to join a team. Maybe he wants to use it as an opportunity to spend more time with his friends or to get exercise. Maybe he has always enjoyed watching baseball but never felt comfortable asking you about playing it himself. If his interest seems to be genuine, then encourage him to join the baseball team.

Adolescence (13 to 21 Years Old)

Many parents dread the teenage years. They are stereotyped as being fraught with rebelliousness and lack of any concern for your authority as a parent. However, positive parenting says that with the right attitude, adolescence doesn't have to be that way. You can continue to be highly influential in your child's life by continuing to nurture a positive relationship in which he or she feels respected, loved, and valued.

At this stage, children (now young adults) are looking for their own identity outside of you. They are learning to see the world and think for themselves, and consequently, may not agree with everything that they have been taught. That's OK. Cherish the fact that your child is turning into a competent and capable young adult who is able to think for himself or herself rather than just doing what everybody else says. However, that is easier said than done when your teenage son is questioning the religion that you brought him up in or your teenage daughter is insisting that you are intruding on her personal space by refusing to let her have a boyfriend.

At this point, try to maintain open and honest communication in which you talk with your child about values and morals. What values are most important to him or her? Social justice? Animal rights? Free speech? Affirm the values that are important to your child and help him or her learn positive ways of expressing those values. While using foul language at school is not an appropriate use of free speech, writing a letter to the school administration about a contentious policy is. Encourage your child to express those values positively.

In summary, developmental appropriateness acknowledges your child's level of maturity and personality and tailors the activities that you do with him or her as such. It affirms your child at every level of development so that he or she is able to become a competent and confident adult.

CHAPTER 4: ACCEPTING YOUR CHILD

In the book *The Kite Runner*, the character Rahim Khan tells the main character's father that children are not like coloring books. You don't get to just color in the spaces with any color that you see fit. Rather, children come with their own personalities, needs, and aptitudes that should be nurtured rather than bent to fit what you expect them to be. Accepting your child for the wonderful person that he or she is, without asking him or her to be anything more, is the heartbeat of positive parenting.

Temperament and Personality

All children are born with their own temperaments and per-

sonalities. While you may have wanted a child whose personality mir-

rors your own, what is important is to celebrate the personality that

your child does have and encourage him or her to develop and use it

to its full potential. Your child may be particularly impulsive (even

more so than other children at that age) or enjoy doing things that his

or her peers don't find interesting. That's OK! Your child is a unique

individual who has so much to offer the world.

Even though your child's personality is still developing, there

are many personality profile systems that can help you understand

what his or her distinct needs and goals are. Some parents are con-

cerned that using a personality profile will put their children in a box

and subconsciously cause them to conform to what a particular per-

sonality type says. However, personality profiles can actually be very

affirming and let both you and your child know that he or she is both

unique and shares characteristics with other people

Why Does My Child Do That?

At a nice restaurant, your school-aged daughter is banging on the table and talking so loudly that people on the other side of the room can hear everything being said. To make matters worse, she is talking about something rather embarrassing. You tell her to be quiet and act respectfully, at which point she bursts into tears and yells that you just don't understand. What on earth is going on with her?

In sensitive situations like this, the temptation is often to try to deal with the negative behavior so that your daughter understands that she is acting inappropriately. However, there is clearly something going on below the surface that is motivating this behavior. It could be as simple as your daughter trying to get attention or copying something that she saw a friend or TV actor do, or it could be that she is trying to process events and emotions that she does not yet have the capacity for. Whatever is going on, you need to talk to her to find out what is actually going on and deal with the root cause rather than the symptom (the negative behavior).

When Your Child Needs Special Help

All children are special and need special help throughout their lives. However, some children have special needs that require a higher level of intervention. These needs can include processing disorders, intellectual delays, developmental delays, emotional dissonance, physical disabilities, and mental illness. Helping your child to understand his or her special need and accept it as a part of the amazing person that he or she is, is a positive way of not only you accepting your child, but helping your child accept himself or herself.

Jordan and David both have dyslexia and are now in high school. Jordan's parents got help from a special education coordinator as soon as she received the diagnosis and worked with her extensively at home to help her succeed academically despite her learning disorder. By the end of junior high, she was comfortable talking openly with her peers about her experiences with a learning disorder and even felt that it was something that set her apart as a unique individual. David's parents, however, waited for him to accept that he had dyslexia and decide to get help on his own. In truth, they didn't want to deal with the fact that he needed extra help. He went through junior high and high school feeling that he was stupid and incompetent; as a result, he made very poor choices that led to him failing many of his classes.

The difference in these two scenarios is that in Jordan's, open communication between her and her parents led to her accepting her learning disorder and succeeding in spite of it. In David's, lack of communication led to him feeling that his learning disorder made him stupid. Open communication that helps your child see a special need as something that makes him or her special is crucial to developing self-acceptance.

In summary, your child's self-acceptance begins with your acceptance of him or her without asking anything more. You appreciate and celebrate his or her personality and special needs, even if they weren't what you anticipated. Furthermore, you look at negative behaviors as symptoms of a problem and try to understand what is actually going on with your child.

CHAPTER 5: MISTAKEN GOALS

Ever since the divorce, Josh had been so angry, but neither of his parents seemed to care. He had tried to talk to them about it, but they seemed to be too busy or preoccupied to make time for him. The truth was that he blamed himself for what happened. He wished he wasn't so angry all the time, but he couldn't help how he felt. And today, when his teacher gave him detention for being late to class, that was the last straw. He never meant to say what he said to her. Those words just came out. And now, his mother was angry at him. No, not angry. She was ashamed of him. In his bedroom on his first day of suspension, he turned on music so loud that it could drown out the world that was falling apart.

When his mother knocked on his door, he didn't know what to expect. Undoubtedly, she would give another long and tired angry tirade about his inexcusable behavior and demand to know what had gotten into him. And she wouldn't be interested at all in talking about the divorce. She wouldn't even acknowledge that he, too, had the right to be hurt by it.

When she told him to come down to the kitchen so they could

make lunch together, he was shocked. Maybe his mom wanted to spend time with him, after all. Maybe, just maybe he could finally talk to her about the divorce.

All along, Karen was worried about the symptoms rather than the problem. As a result, her son's behavior grew worse because the problem festered and contaminated many areas of his life. This scenario is an example of a mistaken goal: Karen was concerned about correcting her son's behavior instead of dealing with the real issues that were causing the negative behavior in the first place. This chapter will look at some frequently mistaken goals and what the heart of the problem is, i.e., what the child is actually looking for.

Undue Attention

When was the last time your child did something seemingly because he or she just wanted attention? Maybe your daughter screamed at the top of her lungs while you were on an important phone call, or your son kept changing the television channel while you were trying to watch the news. The temptation in these types of scenarios is to ignore the negative, attention-seeking behavior. However, what the child is actually seeking is not just attention; rather, he or she does not have maturity or vocabulary to tell you that he or she believes that he or she is only special when you are paying attention or your child is doing something important. You need to remind your child that you love him or her no matter what and redirect to a more useful and positive activity.

Trying to Be the Boss

Children are, in many ways, quite powerless. They rely on adults for everything; because they are unable to work to support themselves with an income, they need adults to provide them with food, clothing, and shelter. Because their brains haven't yet matured, they rely on others to help them with complex situations that they are not yet able to handle. Left completely on their own, they can't do much at all.

But sometimes, they want to believe that they are in charge. They may make demands or try to order you or others around, and sometimes may act in ways that feel quite threatening. Oftentimes, this is a means of communicating that they feel angry or powerless and need to feel that they are in control of their own lives. This kind of behavior is particularly common, to a very large extent, in children who have suffered some kind of trauma because they have learned that they really are not in control of their lives. If you respond negatively, with anger or demands, you reinforce the belief that the child is not in control of his or her own life.

Instead, take the opportunity to teach your child about boundaries. You cannot force him or her to do anything because he or she is in control of his or her own actions. Work together to set reasonable limits on this kind of unacceptable behavior, and talk together respectfully about what is going on and what your child needs from you. Remember that the best way to teach is by example, so if you need to teach your child about boundaries, the best way is for you to model clear boundaries.

In addition, look for ways to give your child a choice as often as possible. Let him or her decide on whether to eat oatmeal or eggs for breakfast. Doing so reinforces the idea that he or she is able to make meaningful choices and therefore actually does have some control over his or her own life.

Seeking Revenge

Children have a very powerful innate sense of justice. If you doubt this for a minute, try giving one child a larger slice of cake than the other. Oftentimes, they will go to great lengths to try to get revenge on someone that they perceive has been treated better or who has hurt them. A preschooler may kick over a tower of blocks that someone else made because that other child pushed him over on the playground. Revenge-seeking behavior is closely related to the pursuit of justice, especially in children who are not yet able to grasp the abstract concept of justice as something distinct from getting even.

Oftentimes, the reaction from adults is to retaliate by punishing the child rather than trying to understand where the negative behavior came from. This retaliation can actually be perceived as you seeking revenge on the child, thereby reinforcing the behavior rather than regulating it. Children are still developing emotionally and need consistent validation of their own feelings. Instead of punishing your child for revenge-seeking behavior, try to understand where that behavior came from. Oftentimes the child is hurt and angry, and those feelings are coming out negatively and even destructively. Acknowledge his or her right to be angry, and take this opportunity to teach him or her about how to deal with anger and make amends in interpersonal relationships.

In summary, children often act negatively because they are unable to communicate very real problems that they are experiencing. Positive parenting looks at behavior as symptoms of these problems and, rather than trying to force the child to act better, helps the child deal with the bigger issues so that the negative behavior can resolve itself.

CHAPTER 6: COMMUNICATION

Karen set a pot of noodles on the stove to boil while Josh grated the cheese. She wasn't sure of how to approach Josh, but she knew that if she didn't find out now what was going on, she might lose him forever. "So, what's really bothering you?" she asked.

Josh just shook his head, not looking up from the cheese that he was grating.

"I'm supposed to think that you just felt like cursing out your teacher without any kind of provocation?"

Josh shrugged his shoulders. "Sure, think whatever you want to," he mumbled.

Karen put the lid on the noodles and turned around to face him. She knew what she needed to say, no matter how uncomfortable it made her feel. "You used to be a lot happier and never got into any trouble. I know that the divorce was hard on you, and I wasn't exactly there for you. I'm sorry about that. I take full responsibility for not being there for you."

Josh stopped grating the cheese but didn't look up. A closer look revealed that his eyes were red and watery; he was on the verge of tears. The room was silent for a minute except for the sound of the water boiling.

Finally, Karen broke the silence. "You're going to be home for the next week, without school or homework or football practice. I think that this would be a good opportunity for us to talk about the divorce and see if we can come to some kind of understanding. I, um, I want to make amends with you for how much I ignored you and your feelings."

Now, Josh did cry. Silently at first, then deep, wracking sobs. "I miss the way things used to be," he whispered between tears. "I miss having Dad around. He left because he didn't want to have to deal with me."

At this, Karen's heart sank. "Oh, no, sweetie. That's not what happened at all. Your dad and I agreed to divorce because we weren't happy with each other. We kept hurting each other and didn't know how to stop. It had nothing to do with you. Your dad loves you and was so happy being with you. The problem was between your dad and me. It was not about you, not at all." She wrapped Josh in a hug, and they both cried together.

Beyond removing negative punishments and enforcing positive discipline and redirection, positive parenting seeks to establish a strong, healthy, and vibrant relationship between you and your child. All relationships are built on communication, and the one with your child is no different. Communication with your child may feel like a daunting task. After all, getting your child to listen without you having to yell or when he or she has already tuned you out (does he or she put fingers in the ears and yell when you try to say something?) is like climbing Mt. Everest.

Communicating with your child involves making your child a part of decisions, treating him or her respectfully, and understanding his or her developmental level in such a way that you are able to connect with him or her on it. However, any true relationship with your child begins and ends with clear, respectful, and honest communication. Furthermore, your child having good communication with you as the parent opens the door for having good communication with other people in his or her life. This chapter will look at some key concepts of good communication, particularly with a child.

Show Genuine Interest

When was the last time someone asked you a casual question,

such as how your weekend was, but clearly was not interested in the answer? After enough experiences with a person only feigning interest but not really caring about what you have to say, you will begin to tune that person out and ignore his or her questions. Why should your child respond any differently when you don't seem to be genuinely interested in what he or she has to say?

When your child tries to tell you something, stop and listen. No matter how trite or mundane the conversation may seem, your child needs to know that you care about what he or she has to say in order for good communication to be established. Put down your phone. Turn off the television. Listen to your child. Respond to what he or she tells you. Ask questions. Engage him or her in a conversation in which he or she feels that you really are interested and care about what he or she has to say.

Respect Confidentiality

When your child needs to discuss something important with you and others are around, ask if the conversation should be in private. If so, move into a quiet space that will be free from interruptions from other people. If your child says something that he or she does not want for you to repeat, respect that confidentiality. Your child needs to trust you. Don't ever embarrass your child; don't bring up sensitive topics in front of other people or use something that he or she told you in confidence against him or her.

Cool Down

Your child just said some very inappropriate and rather embarrassing things in front of your friend. You feel angry and embarrassed, and want to let your child know immediately that such behavior is not OK. However, before you confront your child, you need to confront your own emotions. Not dealing with your own emotions in a positive and healthy way teaches your child to do the same. Furthermore, communicating emotionally is never effective communication. It ends in yelling and tears, and the message gets entirely lost.

Level Down

Unless you have an older teenager, you are probably taller than your child. Trying to talk on equal ground with someone who towers over you can be intimidating, to say the least. You don't want your child to feel intimidated when he or she talks to you, so do everything you can to get down to his or her level. Sit down so that you are on the same level as your child and maintain eye contact.

You probably have a vocabulary that is much larger than your child's and can communicate thoughts that are much more complex and abstract. When you are communicating with your child, though, you need to adjust your language so that he or she can easily understand what you are trying to say. Use words that your child already knows. While helping your child build a strong vocabulary is a worthy goal, using unfamiliar words will detract from the message that you are trying to send. Don't use overly complex sentences. Try to not use abstract concepts but rather concrete examples. For example, instead of talking about kindness as an ethical imperative, give an example of a time when you noticed your child being kind or when someone else showed kindness to him or her. Try to drive your points home in as few words as possible rather than spending several minutes explicating your opinion and defending it. If your child is unable to understand what you are trying to say, the message will be lost and he or she will be less willing to try to communicate with you in the future.

Be Polite

"I had a great weekend. Thanks for asking. My friend and I went skiing "

"You went skiing? I love skiing! Did you do the bunny trail, or were you more geared towards the diamond trail?"

"We did the diamond trail, and you won't believe who – "

"Last time, I just did the bunny trail. We went up to Colorado for a family vacation."

"Anyway, like I was saying, we went skiing and you won't believe who showed up."

"Really? I had a surprise visitor just last night. My mom flew in to surprise the kids and me."

"Will you please listen to what I am trying to tell you?!"

Have you ever been in a conversation like that? You are trying to say something that you believe is important, and the other person is genuinely interested in what you have to say. In fact, he or she may be too interested because you keep getting interrupted with side questions and comments. In the end, you feel like the message that you are trying to communicate is lost.

Have you ever done that with your child? In the effort to get him or her to talk more, you ask so many questions and keep interrupting that the story he or she is trying to tell gets lost. Maybe he or she stormed out, angry and frustrated, and you had absolutely no idea why.

When you're listening, just listen. Your turn to talk will come. For now, your child wants to tell you something important and needs to know that you care. Use nonverbal gestures, such as facial expressions, to show your concern at different points of the story. Make mental notes of questions that you want to ask or points that you need more details on. After your child is finished talking, then it is your turn. Interruptions, even well-intentioned interruptions, teach the child that interrupting other people is OK and he or she does not need to listen to them attentively.

Do not ever use demoralizing or degrading language with your child. Don't even insinuate that he or she doesn't know something because "You're just a child." You want your child to feel competent and valued, and degrading language quickly destroys everything that you have worked so hard to build up. Reminders that he or she is a child and needs help with certain things is not the same as putting him or her down for being a child.

In summary, good communication with your child is built on the same principles as good communication with any other person. Be polite and listen respectfully. Make yourself a safe and trustworthy person for others to confide in. Avoid communicating when you are too emotional. In the end, by communicating respectfully with your child, you are teaching that he or she is worthy of respect and clear communication. That primes your child for success in any area of life.

CHAPTER 7: BOUNDARIES

Josh set out bowls of the macaroni and cheese while his mother stirred the cheese into the noodles. They sat down at the table together and began to eat in silence. Finally, his mother spoke.

"Our actions have consequences. Not just your actions, but my actions, too."

Josh didn't say anything. He continued eating, not sure of where his mother was going with this.

"When I was five, I took my best friend's toy pony home with me. She got angry and yelled at me for stealing it from her. I didn't think of it as stealing; I had borrowed it so that I could keep playing with it after I had to go home. It was stealing, but in my five-year-old mind, it was a perfectly innocent and acceptable thing to do. Well, when she yelled at me, I got angry at her and called her some pretty ugly names and threw the pony at her. You can probably imagine that we weren't friends anymore after that. I couldn't understand why she didn't want to be my friend anymore, but we had both hurt each other a lot. I mean, I stole her toy, called her names, and then threw the toy at her!"

Josh let out a small chuckle. "Yeah, that was pretty bad."

"The real problem there was that I didn't take responsibility for my own actions. I *had* stolen her toy and should have apologized for it. I had called her mean names, but I felt that my actions were entirely justified because she had yelled at me. Do you see where I'm going with this?"

"That I'm not the only person who has ever cursed out the teacher?"

Karen shook her head. "That's not quite it. When your father and I got divorced, it was because of our own actions. We have to take responsibility for our actions. Unfortunately, while what we did was not your fault in any way, you were probably the one hurt the most. But the divorce was because of our actions, not yours. You did nothing to deserve what happened, and I'm sorry that you have to live with the consequences. You don't have your dad around, and that's hard."

Josh tried to swallow back tears, but the dam inside of him broke. "I always thought that you blamed me for it. A lot of times, I heard you fighting over me, like who was supposed to pick me up and who was supposed to take me to buy new clothes. If it wasn't for me, you wouldn't have had all those fights."

Karen shook her head, now in tears, too. "No, Josh. We fought about those things because we didn't know how to communicate with each other, not because you had done something wrong."

Boundaries are about understanding that you are responsible for your own self and nobody else. While you certainly can and should have concern for others, you can only control your actions and your choices. Nobody, not even you, can control your child's behavior except for your child. Teaching your child about boundaries is crucial for him or her to learn to regulate his or her own behavior.

Before you can help your child learn about boundaries, you need to have healthy boundaries yourself. You need to show your child that you are in charge of your own behavior and that, while you want him or her to act appropriately, you are not in control of his or her behavior. Your child needs to see you taking responsibility for your own actions so that he or she can learn to do the same.

Helping children set boundaries is an important aspect of positive parenting. Rather than imposing negative discipline, they learn that their actions have natural consequences, be they positive or negative. This chapter will explore the importance of setting boundaries with your child.

Natural Consequences

Too often, children grow up believing that the only consequences for their actions are the ones that their parents impose. If their parents catch them lying, they might get grounded. If they get a bad grade, their parents might take away some privileges until their grades go up. The solution, in many children's minds, is to keep their parents from knowing what is actually going on in their lives. They learn to be sneaky and do things behind their parents' backs to avoid facing the negative discipline that their parents impose. The end result is that they don't learn that their actions have real consequences beyond their parents. They may not realize that lying isn't just breaking a house rule but it damages trust and relationships; if their primary goal is to not get caught, then they may try to continue lying as an adult and not realize how destructive that behavior is.

Positive parenting advocates allowing children to bear the natural consequences of their actions. For example, if despite your encouragement, your child decides to go outside in freezing weather without a coat, he or she must face the natural consequence of being cold. You did not force him or her to wear a coat because your child is responsible for his or her actions. This is teaching good boundaries. If your child lies to you about having folded his or her laundry, instead of immediately imposing negative discipline, talk to him or her about lying and try to uncover what is actually going on and try to help him or her understand that lying has very real consequences of its own.

The conversation may go like this one.

Parent: You are a very hard worker and an encouraging person. But I can't help notice that lately, there have been a lot of fibs, half-truths, and lies. I know that honesty is important to you, and your honesty is important to me. So, I can't help but notice these lies and wonder where they are coming from.

Child: (says nothing but looks down)

Parent: When I was your age, I would tell my parents that I ate toast for breakfast when I actually had cereal. I was worried that if they found out that I had used the last of the milk for cereal, that they would be angry. Do you ever feel like that?

Child: (looks up at you with a sheepish grin) You lied to your parents?

Parent: Yes, I did. I didn't think of it as a lie, but I wasn't being honest with them.

Child: I really wanted to watch television because I worked hard at school all day and needed a break. That's why I didn't fold the laundry. I'm sorry that I lied to you about it.

Parent: Thank you for being honest with me. Next time, please tell me that you need a break and will fold the laundry afterward.

In that scenario, the child was empowered to take full responsibility for his or her actions because he or she did not feel threatened by the parent's response.

Boundaries and Homework

Whose responsibility is it to make sure that homework gets done? To an extent, it is your responsibility as the parent. You need to make sure that your child has a quiet study area and can study uninterrupted for as long as necessary. You need to provide encouragement and motivation and make sure that your child has the necessary resources, such as supplies for school projects and books from the local library. He or she needs to know that you are available to help. You need to take as much stress off of homework as possible by not pressuring your child to be perfect. Most importantly, you need to let him or her know that your love is unconditional and is not tied to performance at school.

However, the actual completion of the homework is your child's responsibility. Too often, children think that their success in school is the responsibility of their teachers and parents. They need to be taught from an early age that while parents and teachers provide them with the opportunity to learn, their education is in their own hands. They must do the hard work of learning and applying themselves so that they can eventually reap the benefits of a good education. They are responsible for their actions at school and they alone bear the consequences of those actions.

When your child is struggling in school and/or having difficulty completing homework, a very easy temptation to fall into is for you to do the homework instead. However, this teaches that you are the one who is responsible for his or her education and success. Bad grades become your fault, not your child's responsibility. Instead of doing the homework, talk to the teacher about what your child is struggling with. Many teachers are happy to work with parents and children by providing extra help or extensions on assignments so that the children are able to complete them and learn the necessary material. You can also find a tutor to help your child in those problem areas. Older children who have already learned that material and college students make great tutors and can be much cheaper than going to a professional company.

Boundary-Oriented Solutions to Discipline

As previously stated, discipline is not about imposing punishments to teach your child a lesson. If he or she yells at you and you yell back and then ground him or her, you are actually reacting to your child's misbehavior and letting it guide your decisions; in effect, you are retaliating against your child. This view of discipline actually reinforces a mentality of revenge so that your he or she will be more apt to grow up thinking that retaliation is more important and valuable than love and compassion.

Discipline actually means the process of teaching. What do you want to ultimately teach your child? Would you rather him or her walk away with the message that yelling is bad or that he or she is valuable and has the right to be heard without needing to resort to yelling? Positive parenting looks at boundary-oriented solutions to discipline that respect the child's ability to make choices for himself or herself. This section will look at different strategies for positive

56

discipline that teach good boundaries.

Understand Your Child's Limits

Your two-year-old daughter just bit another child. You firmly tell her that biting is not OK, but a minute later, she does it again. It's important for you to understand that biting is actually normal two-year-old behavior; however, being normal at a certain level of development does not mean that that behavior is not harmful or should be tolerated. Developmentally, a toddler cannot understand that biting is wrong. The best solution is to remove her from the situation so that she is no longer prone to biting that child.

Your twelve-year-old son just made some inappropriate comments to his aunt, and you feel embarrassed about the things that he said. Instead of you apologizing for his actions, talk to him about what is going on. Has he been seeing a lot of relatives this weekend and been told one too many times how much he has grown? He may have reached his limits and really can't handle one more person squeezing his cheeks. Let him know that you respect his limits and remove him from the situation until he has calmed down and can apologize for what he said to his aunt.

Redirect

Redirection is a powerful tool in helping children find alternatives to their inappropriate behaviors. If your preschool son is throwing a fit in the middle of the grocery store, it can be very tempting to yell at him to stop. However, this kind of retaliation reinforces the idea that yelling is an appropriate way to get what you want. Instead, ask him to help you pick out oranges or find the biggest grapefruit. He now has an alternative to his negative behavior of throwing a fit, with the added bonus of being part of helping choose the family's food for the week.

Don't Use Bribes

Your school-aged daughter just acted exceptionally well on a family outing. At the restaurant you went to, she used her manners and thanked the waiter for bringing out their food. At the park, she played with her younger brother and helped him go down the slide for the first time. You want to reward this behavior by giving her a sweet treat before supper. However, this kind of a reward teaches that that kind of behavior is not what is expected of her on a regular basis. It uses an external motivator to modify her behavior, making sweets a reason to act rightly, rather than teaching her internal motivation to regulate her own behavior. She may go on to behave in a certain way when you are looking so that she can be rewarded rather than behaving with integrity when you are not looking.

The best reward for your child, what he or she really wants, is quality time with you. Instead of rewarding good behavior with a bribe, reward it with positive affirmations. Spend extra time together, during which you let her know that you are proud of her for having integrity in all aspects of life.

In summary, boundaries begin with you as a parent knowing what you can and can't control. In turn, you teach your child what he or she can and can't control, and that no one else is able to control his or her actions. The result of having good boundaries instilled is a healthy, happy, confident, and respectful child.

CHAPTER 8: UNDERSTANDING YOURSELF AS A PARENT

Our children serve as mirrors in which we can see both the best and worst of our own selves. Because they imitate us in everything, we need to make sure that we understand our own selves and what we are actually teaching them. As a parent, you need to understand your own personality — including your strengths and weaknesses — and your own leadership style.

Understanding Your Own Personality

What makes you sick? What do you like? What turns you off? What makes you feel guilty and what makes you feel ashamed? These are important questions for you to be able to answer. Sometimes your child may do something that isn't particularly bad, but still rubs you the wrong way and makes you want to lash out in anger. Understanding these triggers is important for you to enforce positive discipline at all times.

Taking a personality test can be a powerful way of understanding your own personality. The Enneagram is an in-depth personality profile system that shows you what your base personality is, what you resort to when you are unhealthy, what you look like when you are very healthy, and what your greatest needs, desires, and fears are. Understanding who you are outside of your role as a parent will make you more self-aware and a more effective parent.

Understanding Your Own Leadership Style

Different people have different leadership styles, and understanding what your own leadership style is important because as a parent, you are leading your child. Autocratic leaders make decisions without any input from others and expect those decisions to be followed without question. Democratic leaders allow for input from other people as part of the decision-making process. Visionary leaders recognize the people who are involved as part of the process and seek to integrate their strengths and abilities at every level. Your leadership style impacts very much how you interact with your child.

If you realize that you have on particular leadership style but would like to be a different type of leader, great. This is an area that you can grow in. Seeing you grow is a great opportunity for your child to learn the importance of a growth mindset.

In summary, understanding your own self is crucial to understanding how you see yourself as a parent and what your role is. Your own personality and leadership style have a huge impact on how you interact with your child.

CHAPTER 9: LOVE AND JOY IN THE HOME

Significance of Birth Order

While the birth order has nothing to do with the genetic material inherited from parents, it can have a huge influence on a child's behavior and personality. The firstborn child is a bit of an experiment for many parents, as they don't have any experience yet with parenting. They may be overly strict, concerned about all of the minutiae of the child's life, and constantly giving the child attention. As a result, the firstborn may become a bit of a perfectionist and people-pleaser. In contrast, if a couple goes on to have a second child, they may be more lenient and lax in some of their rules but aren't able to give as much attention as they were able to give to the firstborn. As a result, the second child may feel more entitled but also be jealous of the older sibling and have to vie for attention. He or she may feel the need to strive to succeed so that his or her accomplishments can shine in the light of the perfectionist older sibling. The youngest sibling is usually more coddled than any older ones because the parents have learned to pick their battles and want to take some time to indulge the baby. As a result, the youngest may not feel the need to strive hard and be more extroverted and social.

The significance of birth order is not necessarily that a child came in that particular order but that the parents treat him or her in a certain way *because* of the birth order. Being aware of this can help you understand why you are interacting with your child in a certain way and why he or she may have certain tendencies. The fact that your firstborn came first does not mean that you need to demand perfection from him or her; rather, through positive parenting, you can let that child know that he or she is already enough and does not need to be anything more. The fact that your youngest child came last does not mean that you need to indulge him or her; that child still needs positive discipline and encouragement in order to succeed.

Getting to Know Your Child

In today's ultra-competitive culture, it can be very tempting to focus on getting your child to do well in certain areas that are considered to be important, such as school or athletics. As important as helping your child succeed is, it should come second to believing in him or her. The difference between pushing for success and believing in your child is how well you get to know him or her.

Your child is not a little version of you. He or she is not in your life to make it easier or to fix any problems that you may have. He or she is a unique individual with his or her own gifting, likes, dislikes, aptitudes, and aversions. You may have loved sports and have a child who couldn't care less about them. And that's perfectly OK.

When you are trying to get to know someone, say, a friend, you don't do so by applying your own preconceived expectations of what you believe this person should be like. Rather, you spend time together, enjoy each other's company, and talk about things that you or the other feel are important. Getting to know your child is no different. Don't begin by expecting your son to be something that he's not or requiring your daughter to excel in something that she isn't even interested in. Spend time with them to find out what they want to do, what's important to them, and what makes them tick. You will find that both you and your child will be happier and have a better relationship for the effort.

Encouraging

Children thrive on praise and encouragement, and they need to hear constant affirmation from their parents. This is how they develop their self-esteem, develop a positive self-image, and come to appreciate their own personalities. Encouragement and praise are more than flattering your child for everything that he or she does. Rather, it is a lifestyle of providing your child with ample opportunities to explore the world in a positive way.

Remember that actions always speak louder than words. If your son is on a baseball time, whether or not he is any good at it, go to every single game and cheer for him until you are hoarse. If he stunk it up by dropping every ball and striking out, comment on other things that he did well, such as sportsmanship and being a team player. Those qualities are more important than winning a baseball game, and if your son loses every game but came out knowing that he is a good sport, then that season was a success.

Culture of Honor and Respect

Imagine a home where nobody likes each other. They tolerate living under the same roof but much prefer to keep to themselves. Whenever they do have to interact, it is usually short, curt, and disrespectful. Family life is such a chore and a burden that it isn't even worth the effort. Maybe you don't have to imagine that home. Maybe it's your home now or was the home you grew up in, and you want a change.

The true key to having a happy home life is developing a culture of honor and respect. Insisting that your children honor and respect you will actually create an atmosphere of hostility. Developing a culture of honor begins with you honoring your child consistently. You acting in a way that is honorable will teach your child through an example to act honorably.

Children live up to the expectations that you set for them. If you expect them to put up a fight when doing homework or chores, they will fight you. If you expect them to be disrespectful, they will far exceed any standard you could impose. If you expect them to treat each other and you with respect and honor, and you consistently model that behavior and provide positive discipline when they do not live up to that standard, they will learn to do the same.

CHAPTER 10: POSITIVE PARENTING FOR TOD-
DLERS AND PRESCHOOLERS

Toileting

Potty training can be a stressful experience for both parent and child. Accidents can occur anywhere and on anything. Constantly getting your child to sit on the potty and then him or her having an accident two minutes later can be frustrating and disheartening. Positive parenting has some advice to help both of you get through potty training intact.

Avoid using rewards. Positive parenting is about teaching the child to regulate his or her own self rather than being motivated by external factors. While handing out M&Ms or putting a sticker on a reward chart every time your child uses the potty can be a short-term way to get him or her to use the potty, once those incentives are gone, he or she may regress and stop using the potty. The fact is that most of the time when parents say that their children are potty trained, they actually mean that the parents are potty trained. The parents are equipped with M&Ms and know how to nag the child into using the potty. You want your child to want to use the potty on his or her own, without an external motivation.

Wait until the child is ready. Get your child a potty when he or she is about 18 or 20 months old and let him or her sit on it whenever he or she wants to. This gets the child used to the idea of the potty, whether or not he or she is ready. A stack of picture books next to the potty can make sitting on it more fun. However, most children are not ready to begin potty training until they are closer to two-and-a-half. Toddlers may ask to start using the potty like Mommy and Daddy or may want to stop wearing diapers to be like a friend who doesn't wear diapers. Those are sure signs that the child is ready.

Don't shame your child. Toddlers and preschoolers will have accidents, even after they are fully potty trained. That's OK! Don't make them feel ashamed or punish them for having an accident. When an accident does happen, guide them through the natural consequences of having to change their clothes; older preschoolers can pour soap into the washing machine and press the start button to clean their soiled clothes. Guide your child to his or her room to pick out a change of clothes. Your child needs to change his or her own clothes; doing this for him or her will communicate helplessness rather than self-empowerment. Afterwards, ask how being in soiled clothes feels and what he or she can do to prevent accidents from occurring in the future.

Eating

Getting a toddler or preschooler to try new foods can feel impossible than climbing Mount Everest. Positive parenting has some strategies to make mealtime less of a hassle.

Get your child involved. Let your child help prepare the meal in whatever way he or she is capable. Maybe your three-year-old daughter can pick out what bananas or oranges to get at the grocery store, or your four-year-old son can mix ingredients together. When your child is a part of the meal-preparation process, he or she will be proud to show off those accomplishments to others in the family and be more likely to dig in.

Make not eating your child's problem, not yours. Remember that setting boundaries are about teaching your child to take responsibility for his or her actions. It's never too early to begin teaching about boundaries and letting your son or daughter face natural consequences. Don't put up a fight trying to get him or her to eat something. Rather, let your child deal with the natural consequence of refusing to eat: being hungry. When he or she comes to you asking for something to eat, offer the food that was refused at mealtime.

Stop forcing vegetables. Toddlers and preschoolers have very high nutritional needs, so it makes perfect sense to try to get them to eat a lot of vegetables. However, their palates can be very sensitive to the bitter compounds in many vegetables; this sensitivity decreases over time. Forcing them to eat vegetables actually makes them even more averse to them and usually ends in an unproductive power struggle between parent and child. Offer your child plenty of fruit at meal and snack times, which will meet his or her nutritional needs. Make vegetables available, and let him or her see you eating them frequently. Your child may want to try some out of curiosity or to be more like you.

Sleeping

When was the last time you had a battle with your child over bedtime or taking a nap? Toddlers and preschoolers can be very temperamental about going to bed. Imagine the following scenario between a parent and a two-year-old:

Parent: Mary, it's time to go to bed.

Mary: NOOOOO!!!

Parent: Come on, Mary. I'll tuck you in.

Mary: No! I'm not going to bed!

The struggle escalates until both the parent and child are exhausted and frustrated with each other. Dealing with this situation on a daily basis can be a particularly taxing aspect of parenting a preschooler. But try to imagine it from a two-year-old's perspective. Imagine that you are in the middle of reading a great book, and someone comes and tells you that it is time for bed. You insist that you aren't ready yet, but that person puts you into pajamas, carries you to your room, and makes you lie down and go to sleep. You would probably feel like you are being controlled and even dominated by the other person. Odds are that your child feels the same way.

At the toddler and preschool age, children are beginning to develop independence and see themselves as autonomous people. As such, they are particularly resistant to any kind of controlling influence. While they do need to obey and respect you if they feel as if you are controlling them, you will end up in an unproductive power struggle. Here are some positive parenting tips to make bedtime less of a hassle.

Take care of yourself during the day. At the end of a long and stressful day, wanting to get your child into bed without any struggle so that you can have some rest and relaxation of your own is certainly understandable. However, if you make a point to take care of yourself during the day and not only after your child has gone to bed, you will feel less stressed about getting him or her into bed. When you are less stressed, your child will be less stressed.

Begin the bedtime routine an hour before bedtime. Giving yourself and your child plenty of time to prepare for bed can prevent the need to rush. You can relax and enjoy your time together. After all, before you go to sleep, you want to feel relaxed. Feeling tense and stressed will make sleep more difficult. Give your child plenty of time to enjoy a bath, pick out a toy to sleep with, and read a book together. Feeling relaxed will help him or her sleep better.

Let your child know what is coming next. Your child may feel that your insistence on him or her going to bed is interrupting an important activity. If your son is building a tower out of blocks when you tell him that it is time for bed, he may feel that bedtime is an intrusion on something important. Instead, let him know that he has 15 more minutes to play with his blocks before he needs to get into the bath.

Give your child choices. While bedtime itself is not negotiable, you can still give your child choices so that he or she does not feel like you are exerting control. Asking your daughter if she wants to wear the pink pajamas or the red pajamas or asking your son what book he wants to read before bed can make them feel empowered and less stressed. They will be more likely to comply with bedtime.

Be consistent. Consistency is key with children. Toddlers and pre-schoolers, in particular, need a steady routine so that they know what to expect in a world that can be very confusing. Don't change your child's bedtime and be firm about going to bed. At the same time, provide a clear and consistent routine.

None of these bits of advice or quick fixes for the challenges that come with the toddler and preschool years. Rather, they are tips on how to make these processes smoother while imparting the messages of positive parenting: self-control, self-regulation, and empowerment.

In summary, making your child a part of things like mealtime, bedtime, and potty training can make these transitions less stressful. By being able to help prepare the meal or choosing what book to read before bed, children feel empowered and more willing to comply with their routines.

CONCLUSION

In conclusion, positive parenting imparts to kids not only the lessons of right and wrong but also the ability to act with integrity, even when nobody is watching. It fills them with self-esteem and confidence so that they don't feel the need to act inappropriately to get people to pay attention to them. When they know that they are loved unconditionally by their parents and have secure relationships with them, they are equipped to engage in healthy relationships with their peers and others outside of the family.

A relationship with your child is fostered in the same way as a relationship with any other individual: with open, honest, and clear communication; by spending quality time together; and by appreciating the other person for who he or she is. These are all things that your child needs from you, and positive parenting provides a way to meet these needs while still administering guidance and discipline.

With an understanding of clear boundaries, in which the child understands what he or she is responsible for and has to face the natural consequences of his or her actions, parenting becomes less of a power struggle and more of an enjoyable relationship in which both parties get to know and appreciate each other. Without power struggles and all of the tension and stress that they create, family life becomes more satisfying and pleasurable.

In the end, discipline becomes more effective because it is actually teaching the child rather than trying to coerce a certain behavior. The child is prepared to face the world as a confident and competent individual.